A VOLUME IN THE SERIES

Culture, Politics, and the Cold War

edited by

Christian G. Appy

OTHER TITLES IN THE SERIES

James T. Fisher, *Dr. America: The Lives of Thomas A. Dooley, 1927–1961*

Daniel Horowitz, *Betty Friedan and the Making of "The Feminine Mystique": The American Left, the Cold War, and Modern Feminism*

Tom Engelhardt, *The End of Victory Culture: Cold War America and the Disillusioning of a Generation*

Christian G. Appy, ed., *Cold War Constructions: The Political Culture of United States Imperialism, 1945–1966*

H. Bruce Franklin, *Vietnam and Other American Fantasies*

Robert D. Dean, *Imperial Brotherhood: Gender and the Making of Cold War Foreign Policy*

Lee Bernstein, *The Greatest Menace: Organized Crime in Cold War America*

David C. Engerman, Nils Gilman, Mark H. Haefele, and Michael E. Latham, eds., *Staging Growth: Modernization, Development, and the Global Cold War*

Jonathan Nashel, *Edward Lansdale's Cold War*

James Peck, *Washington's China: The National Security World, the Cold War, and the Origins of Globalism*

Edwin A. Martini, *Invisible Enemies: The American War on Vietnam, 1975–2000*

Tony Shaw, *Hollywood's Cold War*

Maureen Ryan, *The Other Side of Grief: The Home Front and the Aftermath in American Narratives of the Vietnam War*

David Hunt, *Vietnam's Southern Revolution: From Peasant Insurrection to Total War*

Patrick Hagopian, *The Vietnam War in American Memory: Veterans, Memorials, and the Politics of Healing*

Jeremy Kuzmarov, *The Myth of the Addicted Army: Vietnam and the Modern War on Drugs*

Robert Surbrug Jr., *Beyond Vietnam: The Politics of Protest in Massachusetts, 1974–1990*

Larry Grubbs, *Secular Missionaries: Americans and African Development in the 1960s*

Robert A. Jacobs, *The Dragon's Tail: Americans Face the Atomic Age*

Andrew J. Falk, *Upstaging the Cold War: American Dissent and Cultural Diplomacy, 1940–1960*

Jerry Lembcke, *Hanoi Jane: War, Sex, and Fantasies of Betrayal*

Anna G. Creadick, *Perfectly Average: The Pursuit of Normality in Postwar America*

Kathleen Donohue, ed., *Liberty and Justice for All? Rethinking Politics in Cold War America*

Jeremy Kuzmarov, *Modernizing Repression: Police Training and Nation Building in the American Century*

Roger Peace, *A Call to Conscience: The Anti-Contra War Campaign*

Edwin A. Martini, *Agent Orange: History, Science, and the Politics of Uncertainty*

Sandra Scanlon, *The Pro-War Movement: Domestic Support for the Vietnam War and the Making of Modern American Conservatism*

Matthew W. Dunne, *A Cold War State of Mind: Brainwashing and Postwar American Society*

American Immunity

AMERICAN IMMUNITY

War Crimes and the Limits of International Law

Patrick Hagopian

University of Massachusetts Press
Amherst & Boston

Printed in the United States of America

ISBN 978-1-62534-047-4 (paper); 046-7 (hardcover)

Designed by Jack Harrison
Set in Adobe Minion Pro
Printed and bound by the Maple-Vail Book Manufacturing Group

Library of Congress Cataloging-in-Publication Data
Hagopian, Patrick.
American immunity : war crimes and the limits of international law /
Patrick Hagopian, University of Massachusetts Press, Amherst and Boston.
pages cm. — (Culture, politics, and the cold war)
Includes bibliographical references and index.
ISBN 978-1-62534-047-4 (pbk. : alk. paper) —
ISBN 978-1-62534-046-7 (hardcover : alk. paper)
1. Veterans—Legal status, laws, etc.—United States.
2. Retired military personnel—Legal status, laws, etc.—United States.
3. Military privileges and immunities—United States. 4. War crimes—History.
5. My Lai Massacre, Vietnam, 1968. 6. Vietnam War, 1961–1975—Atrocities. I. Title.
KF7745.H34 2013
341.6'90973—dc23
2013035123

British Library Cataloguing-in-Publication Data
A catalogue record for this book is available from the British Library.

CONTENTS

ACKNOWLEDGMENTS

I acknowledge the financial support of the British Academy, the Lancaster University History Department Research Support Fund, and the Lancaster University Faculty of Arts and Social Sciences for the research in this book.

I acknowledge with gratitude the assistance of Luis M. Acosta, Emily Carr, Frank Alan Herch, Debbie G. Keysor, Megan Lulofs, and Christine Sellers, Law Library of Congress; Jeffrey M. Flannery and Lewis Wyman, Manuscript Division, Library of Congress; William H. Davis, Archivist, National Archives and Records Administration, Center for Legislative Archives; Robert Ellis, Archivist, National Archives and Records Administration, Federal Judicial Records; Mary Kay Schmidt, Archivist, Special Access and FOIA Staff, National Archives and Records Administration at College Park; Paul B. Brown, Archives II Reference Section, National Archives and Records Administration at College Park; Terrance Rucker and Matt Wasniewski, House of Representatives Office of History and Preservation; Betty Koed and Katherine Scott, Senate Historical Office; Zoe Davis, Head of Reference and Information Services, Senate Library; Fred L. Borch III, Regimental Historian and Archivist, the Judge Advocate General's Legal Center and School, Charlottesville, Virginia; Glen R. Asner, Senior Historian, Historical Office, Office of the Secretary of Defense; Carolyn Thorne, Office of the Secretary of Defense; Records and Declassification Division, Office of the Secretary of Defense; Kimberly Harper, Debbie G. Keysor, and Belinda Vogel, the State Historical Society of Missouri, Columbia; John Nemmers, Descriptive and Technical Services Archivist, Department of Special and Area Studies Collections, Smathers Library, University of Florida, Gainesville; Laura Clark Brown, Research Archivist, and Matthew Turi, Manuscripts Research Librarian, Southern Historical Collection, Wilson Library, University of North Carolina, Chapel Hill; Hilary Dorsch Wong, Senior Manuscripts Processor, Division of Rare and Manuscript Collections, Kroch Library, Cornell University; Mary Nelson, Special Collections and University Archives, Wichita State University Libraries, Wichita, Kansas; Edwin Moloy, Curator of Modern Manuscripts, Harvard Law School Library Historical and Special Collections; Abigail Malangone, Archivist, Richard Nixon Presidential Library and Museum, Yorba Linda, California; Diana Manipud, Patricia J. Methven, Lianne Smith, and the staff and trustees of the Liddell Hart Centre for Military Archives, King's College, London; Jenny Brine, Helen Clish, and Lorna

Pimperton, Librarians, University of Lancaster Library; Interlending and Documents Service, University of Lancaster Library; Hugo L. Black Jr., the executor of the Hugo L. Black Papers, Library of Congress; and Edward W. Brooke, the donor of the Edward William Brooke Papers, Library of Congress.

While one can easily agree on the necessity for justice, sometimes the possibility of justice is more in doubt. Members of the Judge Advocate General's Corps of the U.S. armed services have at times been called on to act as their nation's conscience, as when Capt. Aubrey M. Daniel reminded President Richard Nixon of the need to respect the legal process and when judge advocates acted unstintingly in the defense of the rights of detainees at Guantánamo. I rest my hope for the world in the example of their respect for the law. I have never encountered in any professional community such intellectual generosity and conscientiousness as in the current and former military lawyers and legal scholars who responded to queries from a newcomer in their field. One of them even wrote from a war zone to offer his detailed advice. I am grateful to Brian J. Bill, William G. Eckhardt, Melissa Epstein, Glenn R. Schmitt, and J. T. Parker; and to Terry Chapman, Eugene Fidell, Louis Fisher, William Schabas, and Gary D. Solis. Michal Belknap gave me a lead that helped me track down the Jordan memorandum. R. Kenly Webster kindly responded to an e-mail inquiry.

Colleagues in a number of fields provided me with advice, encouragement, and support. They include Chris Appy, Beerd Beukenhorst, Ronika Chakrabarti, Nicola Clarke, Charlotte Dickenson, Paul Gilroy, Ruud Janssens, Rhodri Jeffreys-Jones, Dan Larsen, Corinna Peniston-Bird, Paul Quigley, Doug Rossinow, Derek Sayer, Kirsten Smith, and David Sugarman. I am grateful for the attention and questions of audiences at the conference "Whose Vietnam?" at the University of Amsterdam in October 2010; the American History Workshop at Edinburgh University in March 2012; the Transatlantic Studies Conference at the University of Cork in July 2012; and the conference "Confronting U.S. Power after the Vietnam War" at the University of Sheffield in October 2012; as well as of successive groups of students in the Law 311 course at Lancaster University.

Thanks are due to Kendrick Oliver and J. T. Parker for reading and commenting on drafts of the manuscript as well as offering other advice, and to the reviewer for the University of Massachusetts Press who retained his or her anonymity. As ever, I appreciate the support of all at University of Massachusetts Press, particularly Clark Dougan, a wonderfully encouraging editor, and the always efficient Carol Betsch. I appreciate the diligence and care with which Lawrence Kenney edited the work and with which Mary Bellino further prepared it for publication.

Any mistakes are, of course, mine alone.

AMERICAN IMMUNITY

INTRODUCTION

The American Exemption

The history of international humanitarian law in the post–Second World War period is marked by two inconsistent—indeed, diametrically opposed—tendencies: first, the promulgation of universal standards of justice, the creation of institutions where they can be enforced, the advancing application of the principle of universal jurisdiction, and the global reach of the forces on which the enforcement of the law must rely; second, the capacity of the greatest of the great powers to achieve immunity from the application of those standards to itself and to its citizens.[1] These two tendencies rest on the same set of conditions: the preponderance of U.S. military power, allowing it to serve in the role of the world's policeman and hence to choose when and whether to subject its own citizens and troops to international law.

For forty years in the second half of the twentieth century there was no U.S. jurisdiction in which veterans of the U.S. armed forces could be prosecuted for crimes they committed while in military service beyond the nation's borders. During this period American troops could literally get away with murder as long as their crimes were not detected or were covered up until after they had separated from military service. This was not merely a theoretical possibility: some twenty former soldiers did, indeed, get away with murder.

The jurisdictional problem was well known to the politicians who might have solved it: legislators were aware of the jurisdictional gap or jurisdictional void from the moment it opened up in 1955, when the U.S. Supreme Court struck down as unconstitutional Article 3(a) of the Uniform Code of Military Justice.[2] This measure provided for the prosecution by court-martial of military veterans for crimes they committed outside the United States while in the armed forces. When the Supreme Court struck down that provision, Justice Hugo Black's opinion for the court drew attention to a proposal that, because the judgment precluded military courts thereafter from trying veteran suspects for crimes committed while in uniform overseas, jurisdiction over such suspects should be vested instead in federal district courts. Accordingly, concerned members of Congress began to try to pass a law to achieve this purpose, and they and their successors continued to propose such bills periodically for the next forty years. Yet time after time these efforts came to nothing. Instead, the jurisdictional gap widened because of later court decisions that immunized civilians accompanying the armed forces overseas from court-martial prosecution except in time of war; this lacuna became more significant when a military court determined that "time of war" referred only to wars declared by Congress and when the burden of American military deployments was carried in increasing proportion by civilian employees of the government and by private security contractors. The court decisions and the lack of congressional action to close the widened jurisdictional gap created a "legal Bermuda triangle" confounding the U.S. government's "moral obligation to punish criminals."[3]

The possibility that American troops might commit murder while in uniform and then might subsequently escape detection appeared at first a distant possibility to legislators and commentators.[4] However, the uncovering of the My Lai massacre in Vietnam in 1969 revealed to the nation and the world that U.S. troops were not only capable of the mass murder of civilians but had actually committed such a crime and had escaped detection because of a year-long cover-up. Some 90 percent of the army unit whose members perpetrated most of the killings were by then out of uniform and consequently could not be prosecuted in any court.[5] At this point the leading protagonist in the efforts to fill the jurisdictional void, Sen. Sam Ervin of North Carolina, predicted that the legislative efforts that had been "bogged down by congressional and administrative apathy" for the past dozen years might finally succeed because of the impetus the My Lai case provided. "Unfortunately," a congressional aide observed, "it may have taken a massacre" to win executive and congressional backing for a legislative remedy.[6] That prediction was not realized. Even though the My Lai massacre and its cover-up had drawn attention to the legal defect that was conferring impunity on suspected murderers, Ervin was unable to win sufficient political support to close the jurisdictional gap through which the suspects had escaped justice.

After the revelation of the mass killings at My Lai, the legislators' behavior could no longer be explained as the result of apathy: in the quarter century from 1969 to 1995 the legislative inaction and governmental indifference to America's international lawlessness were knowing and willful. Why, in the aftermath of the revelations about My Lai, did the legislation fail?

First, and most important, public knowledge of the massacre and its aftermath had an effect opposite to the one Ervin anticipated: much of the public reacted negatively to the conviction of 1st Lt. William Calley, the sole serviceman found guilty of participation in the atrocity. Many citizens believed he was a scapegoat, that higher commanders were ultimately responsible for the crimes of which he was convicted, that Calley was merely doing his duty, and that similar crimes were widespread in Vietnam. They wrote to their elected representatives in huge numbers appealing for leniency or a presidential pardon. In these circumstances legislators had no popular encouragement to seek any new measures for trying veterans who had taken part in the atrocity or for devising legislative means to prosecute former members of the armed forces who might be accused of similar crimes in the future. Legislators rightly perceived that there were no votes to be gained by closing the jurisdictional gap and no motive—other than decency, a respect for human life, and a regard for international law—to take up a jurisdictional issue that appeared marginal to the concerns of their constituents.

Second, the executive branch, particularly the department that would have taken the lead in the prosecution of veterans, the Justice Department, lacked the will to pursue a legislative remedy. By a historical accident, the incumbent president and attorney general in the period after the disclosure of the My Lai massacre, when the legislation had the greatest prospect of winning approval, were deficient in the moral qualities that might have equipped the executive to defy the trend in public opinion and provide Congress with political leadership. Despite the early support among army judge advocates for remedial legislation, the Defense Department too had dragged its feet in drafting laws to plug the jurisdictional gap, and until 1968 it worked with the House Armed Services Committee to block proposals for such legislation. In 1970 an important report by a House Armed Services subcommittee prompted the Pentagon to declare its backing for such a law, but the moment passed: when this effort failed, the setback blighted the cause Ervin had advocated for the previous decade.

Third, although Ervin was in some ways the best-suited advocate of remedial legislation, in other ways he was the worst. He had a reputation for independence of thought and for taking a variety of policy positions, some of which aligned him with conservatives and some with liberals. In 1972, at the end of the decade in which he had repeatedly proposed legislation to close the jurisdictional gap, the *Congressional Quarterly* reported that his voting record made him the most independent member of the Senate.[7] His contrarian disposition and his intellectual and political independence as well as his particular committee responsibilities made him the obvious legislator to take the lead in proposing bills to close the jurisdictional gap; although his eloquence could occasionally sway his Senate colleagues, however, these same qualities prevented him from being a leader of a voting bloc.[8] Ervin's bills to close the jurisdictional gap were never reported out of the subcommittee he chaired.

To list these factors as though they were separate phenomena is perhaps to overcomplicate the matter. Let us put them together in the common picture to which they belong: by 1971 the nation's political leaders knew there was no U.S. jurisdiction in which military veterans could be tried after they had committed war crimes such as massacring civilians, yet they did not muster the political will to support the legislative remedy that had been known from the moment the jurisdictional void opened. Thomas Jefferson once observed, when contemplating the institution of slavery, "I tremble for my country when I reflect that God is just."[9] If a just God had searched the United States in the late twentieth century, he would have found plenty of citizens and even some legislators worthy of salvation from the fire, but never a sufficient number to form a legislative majority in the U.S. Congress.

There is a wealth of scholarship on the subject of the My Lai massacre and the subsequent courts-martial, including some extremely fine works. Michal Belknap's *The Vietnam War on Trial* focuses on the courts-martial of Calley and the commanding officer of Charlie Company, Capt. Ernest Medina; Michael Bilton's and Kevin Sim's *Four Hours in My Lai* offers a comprehensive narrative of Charlie Company's actions at My Lai and the post-massacre investigations; Kendrick Oliver's *The My Lai Massacre in American History and Memory* offers a thorough assessment of the political and cultural responses to the incident.[10] Much of the scholarship, however, leaves lacunae by understandably tending to ignore the trials that did not take place, those of the veterans who escaped justice because there was no jurisdiction in which they could be tried. This book focuses instead on the things that did not happen and on the reasons they did not happen: the jurisdictional gap that remained unfilled because of the repeated failure of the remedial legislation; the prosecutions that did not occur; the issue of command responsibility that was evaded; the international standards with which the United States consequently did not comply. Only by seeing the pattern of the nonevent can one carve out more clearly in relief the shape of what transpired and the character of the world we inhabit as a result.

When legislators advocated the passage of remedial laws, they did not invoke the nation's responsibility to uphold international legal standards by punishing Americans who committed war crimes. Instead, their principal arguments revolved around the need to protect the interests of American suspects and defendants by affording them the procedural protections and constitutional rights they would enjoy in American courts. Proponents of the remedial legislation said that the only alternatives to closing the jurisdictional gap were either to forego prosecution altogether or to countenance the possibility that American citizens would be tried in foreign courts, where they might not enjoy these protections and rights. The jurisdictional gaps were ultimately closed only when the prospect of an international criminal court began to loom on the horizon and when state parties to treaties began to initiate legal proceedings against foreign suspects based on the claim of universal jurisdiction. In other words, only when there was a realistic prospect that American veterans and civilians accompanying the armed forces might be called on to surrender to the jurisdiction of a foreign or international court did legislators muster the will to enact a means of prosecuting them in U.S. courts.

The failure because of legislative inaction to prosecute the My Lai veterans is a sufficiently noteworthy subject in itself to need no other justification for its study than the enormity of the crimes that were involved and the corresponding enormity of the injustice when many of the guilty escaped punishment. It is also a topic with a larger meaning. The pattern of nonevents investigated in this book, the unconcern with which the U.S. government allowed the impunity of its veterans to persist for year after year, and the passivity with which its allies looked on are telling signs of a contemporary problem: the problem of the American exemption in a world of advancing universal juridical standards.[11]

In the post–Second World War international order, American military power contributed equally to two countervailing tendencies: first, the spread of universal juridical standards regarding the conduct of war; and, second, the practical immunity from prosecution in international forums of American citizens and troops. As Costas Douzinas argues, these two tendencies were products of the human rights revolution in the period after the war. Human rights "provided a high moral ground for the new order and the United Nations, its prime institutional expression." But, as he maintains, the commitment to morality and rights was "accompanied by the principle of non-intervention in the internal affairs of states. The promotion of morality and the defence of sovereignty, two allegedly antagonistic principles, served two separate agendas of the great powers: the need to legitimise the new world order through its commitment to rights, without exposing the victorious states to scrutiny and criticism about their own flagrant violations."[12] The United Nations was "the main arena for the jealous protection" of state sovereignty.[13]

In the context of intrastate relations, sovereignty refers to the monopoly of legal and political authority of a state over its citizens and subjects.[14] The formal equality of sovereigns as they meet in the international arena is constituted as a correlative of this domestic authority. As all state sovereigns are the supreme political authority and arbiter of the law in their own national sphere, they mutually recognize one another's dignity as sovereigns and the supremacy of one another's systems of legal authority within the sphere of their jurisdiction. Yet it is incorrect to consider these two aspects of sovereignty—the inner facing, toward citizens and subjects, and the outer facing, toward other sovereigns and the arena of international relations—as though they are related in a temporal or logical sequence. The primordial authority of the sovereign state is constitutively Janus-faced. The sovereign state's monopoly of political and legal authority within a polity entails at once the establishment of the boundaries around that polity, that is, the formation of a political entity and national–territorial legal jurisdiction, and the protective bounding of that jurisdiction over against all others, both internal and external, who might otherwise make claims of authority challenging the sovereign's.[15]

The constitutive feature of sovereignty relevant here is the supremacy of the Constitution, as the basic and highest law of the United States, against any other law, foreign or international. The judges and legislators with whom I am concerned believed they upheld U.S. sovereignty by resisting the application of international standards to its citizens and by protecting them from the reach of foreign and international courts. A half century of Americans' exemption from prosecution is not, as it may seem, merely a historical oddity and an aberration but is an expression of the authority of a national sovereign unimpeded by any rival force.

American veterans' immunity from prosecution did not begin with the abrogation of constitutional rights by the executive branch and the suspension of the rule of law as theorized in Carl Schmitt's concept of "the exception"; it started with a court decision asserting the inviolability of constitutional rights.[16] The jurisdictional gap that immunized veterans from prosecution for overseas breaches of the law arose from the rigorous adherence of the government to the procedures of judicial review. Following the Supreme Court's judgment, all three branches of government perpetuated the inconsistency between the conduct of the United States and international standards through their actions and inactions. If there is an American exception, it lies in the capacity of the United States, in the post–Second World War system of international relations, to stand outside the norms of international law in ordinary times as well as during emergencies. To put this another way, the United States has, since the Second World War, authorized itself routinely to police a system of law universally binding on others from which it reserves the right at any moment to exempt itself. This is not solely an American phenomenon. Because of the preponderance of U.S. military power, however, this propensity is most likely to be realized and to reach its highest pitch in actions taken by the United States that are at variance with international legal standards.[17]

The standards governing warfare that have been codified in international law since the Second World War, enunciated in the Geneva Conventions, the Charter of the International Military Tribunal for the Prosecution and Punishment of the Major War Criminals of the European Axis (the Nuremberg Tribunal), and the Charter of the International Military Tribunal for the Far East (the Tokyo Tribunal), are universal and binding on all nations. There are no longer distinct pockets of territory in which diverse legal standards apply, as was commonplace in centuries past.[18] Nor do imperial powers declare the existence of disparate categories of human groups who, lying outside the community of so-called civilized nations, are not expected to adhere to practices of just war and who do not enjoy the protection of the law.[19] Yet, as Michael Ignatieff has pointed out, ever since the U.S. government played a leading role in setting up the Nuremberg trials, "the U.S. has promoted universal legal norms and the institutions to enforce them, while seeking by hook or by crook, to exempt American citizens, especially soldiers, from their application. From Nuremberg onward, no country has invested more in the development of international justice for atrocity crimes and no other country has worked harder to make sure the law it seeks for others does not apply to itself."[20] If one recognized the twin principles of universal standards and equality before the law (or accepted the supposition that "we live in a world that is, or should be, without exception") U.S. citizens and nationals would in theory be subject to the same standards as those of every other nation.[21] This book concerns how that principle was abrogated in practice through the superpower exemption that conferred immunity from prosecution on American perpetrators.

In the mid–twentieth century, when the United States was supplanting its Western European allies as the leader of an alliance of liberal democracies, it did not seek to replace them by taking over their colonial empires. Instead, it superseded them by overseeing a process of decolonization. It would dominate the world not through the administrative control of territories but by less direct means: through the projection of its military power; a system of military bases around the world; an alliance with proxies, political, economic, and military, who would be its agents and junior partners in formally independent countries; direct and indirect military intervention when these proxy arrangements were threatened by independence movements or excessively independent governments; the extension of its economic and commercial interests and those of the corporations to which its interests were tied; access to markets and raw materials; diplomatic influence; and the dissemination of cultural products and ideological values.

The fact that the United States did not generally seek direct administrative and political control of an overseas empire made it distinct from the European powers it supplanted. A former assistant secretary of defense has recently commented, "Lacking a stomach for empire or colonial occupation is one of the important ways in which American political culture differs from that of imperial Britain. Americans like to promote universal values."[22] America is exceptional, according to this account, in that it seeks no territorial aggrandizement. Presidents Lyndon Johnson and Richard Nixon said as much about the nation's war effort in Vietnam. Johnson said, "Our objective is the independence of South Viet-Nam, and its freedom from attack. We want nothing for ourselves—only that the people of South Viet-Nam be allowed to guide their own country in their own way." Nixon said, "Never in history have men fought for less selfish motives—not for conquest, not for glory, but only for the right of a people far away to choose the kind of government they want."[23] President Barack Obama echoed those claims when U.S. troops withdrew from Iraq. As he said, "Unlike the old empires, we don't make these sacrifices for territory or for resources. We do it because it's right. There can be no fuller expression of America's support for self-determination than our leaving Iraq to its people. That says something about who we are."[24] In this enduring account, whose rote repetition appears to be a requirement of high office in the United States, America is exceptional because it renounces territorial expansion as an object of its policies.[25]

The notion of universal values opens the door to an alternative concept of the American exception: the drive to exempt the United States from the norms to which others are subject. If values are truly universal, and if they are enshrined in a system of international justice applied equally to all, then Americans would prove their status as the paramount believers in the universality of those values by subjecting themselves to the enforcement of legal norms as stringently as they enforce them on others. In observing those standards the United States would not claim the extreme degree of virtue that some conservatives believe entitle it to absolve itself from the application of every rule but would attain a more modest threshold of virtuous conduct: ordinary compliance with the law.

The United States has fiercely protected its prerogative to try its nationals and troops for offenses committed during armed conflict. Because of its power, there was—and is—no force on earth that could compel the United States to submit its nationals and troops to foreign or international legal forums. This situation places the onus of responsibility on the United States for ensuring that its own legal institutions and courts respect and observe the same standards it has promulgated through its adherence to international agreements and its participation in international tribunals. The American exemption demonstrated in this book rests in the fact that the United States has routinely promoted certain values and the correlative legal standards while routinely failing to observe them.

The blind spot in Americans' perception of their international lawlessness discloses itself in numerous statements made by U.S. officials, many with the same unremarked silences and exclusions. When the U.N. ambassador Madeleine Albright spoke to the United Nations to recommend activation of a tribunal to prosecute atrocities in the former Yugoslavia, she remarked, "The Nuremberg principles have been reaffirmed. . . . This will be no victor's tribunal. The only victor that will prevail in this endeavor is the truth. Unlike the world of the 1940s, international humanitarian law today is impressively codified, well understood, agreed upon and enforceable."[26]

Despite the codification of and agreement about the law, the United States had still, at that stage, failed to pass the legislation required to punish "grave breaches" of the Geneva Conventions that the signatories of the conventions committed themselves to passing. As Albright spoke there was still no U.S. jurisdiction in which one could try American veterans who had committed crimes in military service overseas, placing the United States at odds with the principles she cited. Listing twentieth-century failures to enforce international justice, David Scheffer, who served under Albright as ambassador-at-large for war crimes issues, catalogues a roll of dishonor from the atrocities against the Armenians to the genocidal assault against the Kurds, but missing from this list are the unpunished crimes committed by U.S. servicemen in Vietnam.[27] Narratives like these from figures like Albright and Scheffer claim a place for the United States at the forefront of efforts to create institutions that enforce international law, without regard to the crimes that the decades-long tolerance of the jurisdictional gap permitted to go unpunished. To call these accounts hypocritical is to do an injustice to hypocrites. According to the proverb, hypocrisy is the tribute vice pays to virtue, but to aspire to the station of a hypocrite one must at least acknowledge one's viciousness, of which these American leaders seem unaware.[28] If the claim to American virtue is a pretense, it is a pretense that has become so practiced that one can catch no glimpse of a covert truth behind the liberal mask. These diplomats appear truly to believe what they profess.

Conservative assertions of the moral quality of American power are no less self-satisfied and self-serving. Convinced that the United States is a righteous nation with an international mission to promote universal values of which it is the quintessential embodiment and exponent, conservatives have recently "rallied around exceptionalism." In foreign affairs, they "hold the idea of the nation in high esteem and bristle at the notion of America['s] being governed by diktats of the international community."[29] In discussing the National Security Strategy of 2002, Francis Fukuyama noted its "implicit recognition of American exceptionalism": the United States claimed a right to launch preemptive or preventive warfare as a means of preventing terrorism, although it would object to other nations' announcing a similar general strategy. Fukuyama wrote, "The fact that the United States granted itself a right that it would deny to other countries is based . . . on an implicit judgment that the United States is different from other countries and can be trusted to use its military power justly and wisely in ways that other powers could not."[30]

Opponents of the extension of the International Criminal Court's (ICC) jurisdiction over American citizens and troops have justified standing apart from the court on the basis of America's unique combination of goodness and strength. As one of them said, the U.S. military, not the ICC, is "the greatest force for peace on this Earth." Any institutions or measures that inhibit that force—such as the prospect of accountability to an international forum—are therefore bad for the world's interests, not just for those of the United States. In the words of the U.S. senator Rod Grams, "Ironically, the very nations that have created a court which inhibits our ability to project force have repeatedly called on the United States to be the global enforcer."[31] In this account, the proper order of the world is for the "global enforcer" to fulfill its appointed role by policing international law and for the rest of the world to be grateful. As the sole remaining superpower, the United States on this theory has greater responsibilities than others for enforcing the international political order, responsibilities that require "greater flexibility" in addressing them.[32]

Critics of American foreign policy have taken the United States to task for remaining aloof from international treaty obligations that would constrain its conduct of foreign and military policy, resisting the norms of international law, and being prone to acting unilaterally rather than seeking approval from international organizations.[33] They have complained that in the field of international agreements the United States "has not signed conventions, unsigned them later, or been a grudging member in technical violation of their norms."[34] Some conservatives have bullishly justified this behavior and, being opposed to America's acceptance of the strictures of international law, have impugned the concept itself. John Bolton, a member of the Project for a New American Century and President George W. Bush's ambassador to the United Nations, said, "It is a big mistake for us to grant any validity to international law even when it may seem to be in our short-term interest to do so—because, over the long term, the goal of those who think that international law really means anything are those who want to constrict the United States."[35]

Bolton draws attention to the questionability of international law as law, pointing, for example, to the circularity in the logic of customary international law: one of its bases is state practice, or the practices of states that are presumed to have met international approval or acquiescence by dint of the absence of challenges mounted by other actors. Accordingly, customary law is modified through its violation, so long as states avoid sanction for their transgressions and can therefore claim that custom condones their actions.[36] Bolton's argument itself has a circular logic, though: one reason he doubts the validity of the concept of international law is that it lacks an overarching enforcement mechanism, but such a mechanism is likely to remain absent the better he succeeds in undermining the legality of international law.[37]

Bolton's argument crystallizes the issue. As an America-first defender of U.S. sovereignty, he sees international law as an imposition on and a usurpation of that sovereignty. As Bolton says, "We should be unashamed, unapologetic, uncompromising American constitutional hegemonists."[38] The repudiation of the legitimacy of international law, however, leaves the United States in the international arena with no obvious alternative to accepting either international anomie or the principle of might makes right; it also undermines the entitlement of the United States to participate in any action predicated on the requirements or prohibitions of international law. Such a position might appeal to some in the nation commanding the most powerful military force and to its most submissive acolytes, but only at a cost to the legitimacy of the edifice of international law which the United States helped elaborate in the post–Second World War period and whose preservation may reasonably be regarded as an American national interest. With the loss of legitimacy comes a pull away from the tendency to compliance; and if the United States, according to Bolton's preference, should repudiate and delegitimize the concept of international law, other nations will no doubt ask themselves why they should comply with it. Charles Simic argues that the United States "regards itself as a country whose exceptional moral standing exempts it from accountability for the war crimes it commits. The trouble with that is that everybody else feels the same way. The belief that one ought to be able to kill one's enemies and live happily ever after is nearly universal."[39] If the United States allows itself license to interpret international legal standards flexibly and to set them aside when they interfere with its supposed superpower–enforcer prerogatives, others will justifiably feel inclined to follow suit.

Advocates of accession to international standards must, however, reckon with the lack of democratic accountability of international organizations. To this there is no obvious solution on the horizon, and only the distant prospect of some form of "international democratization" that must be years in the distance, if it is realizable at all.[40] As Richard Falk and Andrew Strauss argue, the existence of a global people's assembly would "challenge the traditional claim of states that each has a sovereign right to act autonomously, regardless of adverse external consequences."[41] The question this prompts, though, is whether the advocates of democratization unwittingly reinforce Bolton's position. If democratic global government (which might be seen as dystopian by some and impractical by others) is what it would take legitimately to challenge the sovereign autonomy of states, does this leave the United States in the meantime to assert a constitutionalist hegemony untrammeled by the requirements of international law? The larger issue that the jurisdictional gap opens up is a conundrum characteristic of the era of post–Second World War international law and globalization. So long as sovereignty and democratic accountability remain lodged at the national level, self-interested, self-deluded, or hypocritical inconsistencies in the enforcement of international legal standards can clothe themselves in the respectable appearance of a defense of sovereignty—in the case of the United States, of constitutionally protected citizens' rights.

In the vexed history of double standards in the postwar period, the United States has failed to apply to its own citizens and troops the legal standards it has applied to the leaders and troops of defeated enemies and of so-called rogue nations. In claiming the prerogative unilaterally to define rogue status and determine which regimes deserve to be so designated, America asserts its superiority over international standards, processes, and institutions. As Jacques Derrida states, accordingly, "The most perverse, most violent, most destructive of rogue states would thus be, first and foremost, the United States." And, he adds, in a remark that implicates those who act as enablers of the United States, "sometimes its allies."[42]

Justified though it may be by repeated instances of hypocrisy, double standards, and the transgression of international norms, does the epithet *rogue* suffice to analyze the position of the United States in the current international order?[43] How can one understand the exemptionalist position the United States frequently takes with respect to the legal norms that other nations are expected to observe?

Let us note the structural resemblance between the sovereign's position in Schmitt's state of exception—standing outside the normally valid legal system and at the same time belonging to it; suspending the rule of law the better to enforce it—and the position the United States has claimed in the international legal order. Here, the United States, as the strongest military power, is the principal enforcer of international law, and yet it seeks to protect its troops and citizens from subjection to international and foreign courts and has licensed itself to define international juridical standards such as the provisions of the Geneva Conventions however it pleases.[44] The extraordinary posture the United States assumes, as the principal enforcer of the law whose agents are immune to the law's application, is a position of unaccountable power.

The jurisdictional gap is a reminder that such asymmetry is not characteristic solely of wartime states of emergency. The American exemption, or the presumption of "special status" allowing the United States a freedom of action and an immunity from sanction that other nations do not enjoy, is not solely an artifact of the country's stance in the "war on terror" or the result of post–Cold War unipolarity.[45] In its constitutionalist variant, American immunity and the American exemption have been a product not of a state of exception but of ordinary times[46]—although ordinary times in the United States during the Cold War included the repression of domestic dissent and the use of military means to oppose Communism on a world scale.[47] These purposes were accomplished, however, within a constitutional system in which the rule of law remained in force, not during a state of emergency that suspended the applicability of the Constitution and the normal operation of the courts.

The jurisdictional gap emerged from the Supreme Court's scrupulous adherence to constitutional rights and thereafter from the concerted actions and inactions of all three branches of government. Once set in place, it was a determinate feature of the asserted supremacy of the U.S. Constitution over other laws, foreign and international. Both an anomalous rupture in the legal order that offends against the most basic concepts of justice and fairness and an integral component of the irregularity of the international system in which we live, the jurisdictional gap discloses the open secret of our times: the asymmetry in an international legal order at once distorted and protected by U.S. power.

CHAPTER ONE

"A Very Simple Provision"

The Uniform Code of Military Justice and the Jurisdictional Gap

In 1950 President Harry Truman signed into law the Uniform Code of Military Justice (UCMJ), which took effect the following year.[1] Four years later the Supreme Court struck down the provision in the UCMJ that allowed courts-martial to prosecute veterans for crimes they committed while in military service outside the United States. This decision opened up a jurisdictional gap that persisted for the next forty years. During that period there was no U.S. jurisdiction in which former American service personnel could be tried for crimes they committed overseas, so long as their crimes were not detected or were covered up until they had left military service.

The UCMJ replaced the Articles of War, the Articles for the Government of the Navy, and the Disciplinary Laws of the Coast Guard.[2] The term *uniform* conveyed the scope of the law as applying equally to all the armed services. The new system would answer some of the criticisms of the administration of military justice made during the Second World War, when critics pointed to its inconsistency and to excessive command authority over courts-martial, both of which undermined the rights of the accused.[3] An enormous number of courts-martial had taken place during the war, the vast majority of which led to convictions. The army alone convicted ninety thousand soldiers in general courts-martial, and there had been over one hundred executions of personnel.[4] Returning veterans complained that military justice was a fraud, intended to legitimize the system of military discipline, and when they returned home they demanded reform.[5]

In line with the unification and reorganization of the defense establishment carried out after the war, the UCMJ diminished the danger of inconsistency by providing that the same structure of offenses, punishments, and procedures would now extend across all the armed services; it also afforded new protections to the accused, such as automatic review of verdicts and sentences and the prohibition of command interference with judicial processes.[6] The code made available free legal counsel for the accused in general courts-martial, required warnings of rights before a suspect could be questioned, and granted free transcripts and counsel for appeals. It also created the Court of Military Appeals, a civilian court to hear court-martial appeals. The secretary of defense predicted that the new code would increase public confidence in military justice while protecting the rights of the military personnel subject to the law.[7]

During the hearings leading to passage of the UCMJ, members of both houses of Congress discussed whether military courts should have jurisdiction over former servicemen. In the House subcommittee hearings, legislators were concerned that the bill, as originally drafted, made no provision for the prosecution of former servicemen who had committed crimes while in military service overseas, other than those who continued in their attachment to the armed forces through membership in the Reserves.[8] Rep. Reese De Graffenreid, a Democrat from Texas, and Rep. Charles Elston, a Republican from Ohio, raised this issue during their questioning on March 18, 1949, of Felix Larkin, assistant general counsel of the Department of Defense, who had played a major role in drafting the legislation. Elston put the matter dramatically: "A man might commit murder the day before his term of enlistment was up and step out of the service and could not be prosecuted."[9]

Recent events had demonstrated that such a scenario was not merely a hypothetical possibility. As a historian of military justice wrote, "In World War II a cluster of sensational and widely publicized cases gave Congressmen a graphic demonstration that American servicemen could commit serious crimes in foreign parts, conceal them until their discharge from the service, and thereafter thumb their noses at the law."[10] In his congressional testimony Larkin recalled the often-cited case in which Capt. Kathleen Durant stole the crown jewels of the royal House of Hesse and became subject to prosecution only because investigators worked overtime so that charges against her could be preferred just before her enlistment expired. Larkin said that if she had not still been in the service "there would have been no way of trying her at all because the offense was committed overseas."[11]

Also fresh in Larkin's mind and those of the legislators was the case of Chief Petty Officer Harold Hirshberg, in which a suspect had escaped punishment because he had briefly separated from the armed forces before reenlisting. The Supreme Court decided he could not be tried for an offense committed beyond U.S. borders during his prior period of enlistment. Shortly before Larkin appeared before the subcommittee, its members heard from Frederick Bernays Wiener, a former army judge advocate who had successfully argued the Hirshberg case for the government at the U.S. circuit court before the conviction was nullified by the Supreme Court. He said that it might be well for the committee to "plug up that little loophole" the Hirshberg case left, which, "in effect, made an honorable discharge a pardon for undetected crime."[12] Larkin acknowledged that if that sort of case recurred, under the code as drafted the "Federal Courts would have no jurisdiction. And the military would not have had any either."[13]

This gap arose because the jurisdiction of state and federal courts did not extend to most crimes committed outside the United States. In general, the jurisdiction of the states is restricted to the territories of those states; federal criminal jurisdiction is limited in both its reliance on statutory grants of authority and its territorial reach. In 1812 the Supreme Court ruled that the jurisdiction of the inferior federal courts relies exclusively on statutes defining the offense and the penalty for it.[14] The courts accordingly have no right to define common law crimes. Criminal jurisdiction "is subject to rigorous scrutiny" when applied extraterritorially.[15] The main exception in which the courts accepted the extraterritorial jurisdiction of federal courts involved crimes against the U.S. government. In 1922 the Supreme Court held that an offense injurious to the government for which Congress provided no territorial limitation could be tried by a federal district court no matter where the offense was committed.[16] The definition of an offense injurious to the government included such acts as fraud and embezzlement, counterfeiting, illegal immigration, smuggling, and crimes which endanger national security, such as treason, espionage, and attacks on high-ranking U.S. government officials. With respect to such offenses, though, the courts often decided they would apply a statute to extraterritorial conduct only when Congress made clear that the statute should have that effect.[17]

In contrast to the geographical restrictions on the jurisdiction of state and federal law, the UCMJ applied wherever the armed forces operated. De Graffenreid therefore proposed, "I believe we can put a provision in here, that would be perfectly constitutional, that . . . the mere fact that [the perpetrator of a crime] is discharged at a later date and returns to civilian life ought not to free him from being prosecuted in a military court for an offense that he committed while he was in the service." De Graffenreid overlooked the doubts—justifiable, as they turned out—that Larkin had expressed about the constitutionality of such an extension of the jurisdiction of military courts. Larkin had described it as a "difficult legal problem."[18] The legislators were undeterred. Elston observed that "where [a perpetrator] has committed a serious offense, he should not be permitted to escape by reason of the fact that he is out of the Army." He proposed a "very simple provision to the effect that any person who commits any offense and is subject to prosecution under this code may be prosecuted even though he may no longer be in the service." The only exceptions and restrictions he accepted were that the statute of limitations should not have expired, that the prosecutions should be for major offenses, and that the cases should not come under the jurisdiction of one of the states. Setting aside his constitutional doubts, Larkin dutifully responded, "I think we certainly would not object to that." He agreed to draft an amendment to extend the scope of Article 3(a) from members of the Reserves to any veteran.[19]

The House subcommittee considering the bill adopted a revised Article 3(a) which explicitly vested jurisdiction in courts-martial for offenses against the UCMJ committed outside the United States, even if the suspect had subsequently left the armed forces. The revision allowed trial by court-martial of anyone who had committed a serious offense against the UCMJ (one punishable by five years or more of confinement) and who could not be tried by a federal or state court. Restricting the law to serious offenses was intended to guard against "capricious action" on the part of the military authorities.[20]

Two weeks after the subcommittee chairman announced the amendment to the UCMJ, Maj. Gen. Thomas H. Green, the judge advocate general of the army, presciently drew Congress's attention to the risk that the Supreme Court might strike down the revised Article 3(a). Green referred to the U.S. courts' traditional reluctance to extend military jurisdiction over civilians, which he predicted would cause "public revulsion." As he explained, "It has been my experience that no matter how just and fair the system of military justice may be, if it reaches out to the civilian community, every conceivable emotional attack is concentrated on the system." Green recognized that nonmilitary personnel who travel and serve with the army must be subject to military discipline, but he pointed out that when there was no such exigent need for the exercise of military jurisdiction over civilians, "Congress has been very zealous to preserve civilian jurisdiction."[21] Green was not alone in this view. Wiener said Green's Senate testimony was an "honest expression of a reasonable military man who is opposed to the extension of military power over the civilian population."[22] Larkin and the Defense Department had, however, shown little willingness to accommodate the army's earlier objections to various provisions of the draft law, and Green proved no more capable of persuading Congress than of winning Larkin over to his views.[23]

Green proposed a legislative alternative to extending court-martial jurisdiction over veterans. He asked Congress to "confer jurisdiction upon Federal courts to try any person for an offense denounced by the code if he is no longer subject thereto."[24] He told Congress, "If you expressly confer jurisdiction on the Federal courts to try such cases, you preserve the constitutional separation of military and civil courts, you save the military from a lot of unmerited grief, and you provide for a clean, constitutional method for disposing of such cases."[25] Congress ignored his warning.

The Article 3(a) of the UCMJ signed into law in 1950 stipulated that veterans could be tried by court-martial for serious offenses against the code after they had separated from the armed forces.[26] No sinister intent should be attached to the passage of a provision that in retrospect can be seen as always at risk of being struck down by the courts. The legislators were trying to solve two problems: first, to satisfy the Reserve components that they would not be recalled to active duty to be tried for trivial or minor offenses (hence the requirement that the crime be punishable by at least five years' confinement)[27]; and, second, to close the jurisdictional gap that conferred immunity on veterans from prosecution for major offenses. As the committee chairman, Rep. Overton Brooks, said, the law would "correct the absurd situation of permitting an honorable discharge to operate as a bar to a prosecution for murder or other serious offenses."[28]

Barely a month after the UCMJ was signed into law in May 1950, the Korean War broke out. The Supreme Court's ruling that struck down as unconstitutional Article 3(a) of the code arose from an incident in the war. Sgt. Robert Toth, a sergeant of the guard at an air force installation, took part in the killing of a Korean civilian who Toth alleged had been trespassing and had attempted to grab Toth's pistol from its holster when taken into custody.[29] (Through the decades considered in this book, the unarmed victims of U.S. military personnel seem to have had a propensity to lunge for the Americans' weapons or make other threatening moves that provoked the Americans to kill them.) In 1953, five months after he had been honorably discharged from the armed forces, Toth was arrested by air police in Pittsburgh and returned to Korea for trial by court-martial.[30] The two other air force personnel who had committed the crime and who were still in military service when they were prosecuted were convicted at court-martial, and Toth was named as a co-conspirator. After his arrest, Toth's sister filed a writ of habeas corpus, which was granted. The government appealed, and the appeals court upheld the right of the armed services to try former servicemen for crimes they committed while in service.[31] When the Supreme Court reviewed the lower court's decision, its judgment held that the Constitution would not allow Toth, once released from the armed forces, to be tried by court-martial. The government had already taken the position that because of territorial limitations on the jurisdiction of federal and state courts, no civilian court could try Toth. Thus, there was no U.S. jurisdiction in which his offense could be tried. The case had immediate repercussions for five other cases of former army personnel in which court-martial jurisdiction had been asserted.[32]

In his draft opinion in *Toth v. Quarles,* Justice Black referred to constitutional protections of due process and the right to trial by jury under the Fifth and Sixth Amendments. Black's opinion had not at first seemed destined to prevail. When the court began to consider the case after hearing arguments in March 1955, Justice Stanley Reed's opinion upholding the constitutionality of Article 3(a) commanded the majority. In the summer of 1955, though, the force of Black's argument began to win over sufficient justices to persuade the court to restore the case to the docket for reargument. After the reargument in October 1955, Black's opinion became the opinion of the court.[33]

Justice Black was the first of Franklin D. Roosevelt's appointees to the Supreme Court bench. An Alabamian, he was a lawyer and a seasoned politician who had served as a U.S. senator, and in both of those capacities he pursued the creed of the southern populist, representing the interests of the downtrodden and the poor, including a number of black clients.[34] His pursuit of political support in his state had, however, led him to join the Ku Klux Klan, and he was not above appealing to juries' prejudices when doing so would help him win a verdict. These prejudices may, indeed, have been close to his own views: he spoke often of the superior virtues of Anglo-Saxons, and as a politician he argued for closing the door to immigrants. Black left the Klan only a short time before declaring his candidacy for the Senate, and his former Klan membership made his nomination to the Supreme Court enormously controversial. He salvaged the nomination by explaining his actions in a radio broadcast heard by millions, the majority of whom decided that he had exonerated himself.[35]

Black had won a reputation as a sharp, fiercely competitive, and invariably well-prepared trial lawyer, but he lacked impressive academic credentials and had no experience as a judge. His approach to judging at first upset other members of the Supreme Court bench. From the start he placed little value on being a team player. Unusually for a new associate justice, he wrote many dissents in his first term, including twelve in which he was the lone dissenter.[36] His very first dissent challenged the probusiness precept that corporations counted as persons who enjoyed the due process protections of the Fourteenth Amendment, an issue that had not even been raised on appeal. Never mind that he was contesting an idea that had held sway since the late nineteenth century: "A constitutional interpretation that is wrong," Black asserted, "should not stand." Some of his colleagues saw his lack of experience as leading him pointlessly to challenge settled constitutional law. One arranged for Felix Frankfurter, then a law professor regarded as having a brilliant legal mind, to give Black some remedial instruction, suggesting, "He needs guidance from someone who is more familiar with the working of the judicial process than he is." Frankfurter's assistance came in the form of a letter setting out the limits on judges' lawmaking power.[37] The condescension did nothing to endear the professor to the jurist.[38]

Frankfurter saw himself as the heir to Justices Oliver Wendell Holmes and Louis Brandeis, and he became known as "the nation's foremost citizen-academic, a professor with a limitless public-interest portfolio."[39] Before his appointment to the Supreme Court in 1939, two years after Black's, Frankfurter had exerted influence at the highest echelons of government, recommending his protégés and allies for positions in the Roosevelt administration and various judicial posts. Many, including Frankfurter himself, assumed that after his appointment to the bench he would be the natural leader of the liberal justices whom Roosevelt nominated to the Supreme Court. In an effort to secure such a role Frankfurter not only wrote closely reasoned memoranda and made painstaking conference arguments but also, fueled by an inexhaustible energy, personally cultivated several newly appointed justices. Frankfurter tended, though, to speak to them as though they were his law students, and some found his efforts at tutelage patronizing and overbearing: "The more Frankfurter lectured, the less influential he became with his liberal colleagues."[40] When others disagreed with him, he tended to entrench their differences by indulging in personal denigration and backbiting. Frankfurter dismissively regarded Black as a results-oriented politician rather than a judicial authority, but Black's stature increased because of both the force of his arguments and his ability to persuade "without lecturing like a Harvard professor."[41] As adherents gravitated to his views, Black's influence grew, and he, not Frankfurter, became the leader of the court's liberal bloc, a position in which he was securely ensconced by the early 1950s.[42]

Black was considered an absolutist when it came to the constitutional protections of the rights of the individual[43]—although this supposed absolutism had its limits, as when Black deferred to the military authorities and the political branches in allowing the exclusion of Japanese Americans from the West Coast during the Second World War in a judgment that, despite his denials, was shaped by racial prejudice.[44] While Frankfurter too had strong libertarian beliefs, he believed the courts should exercise restraint in reviewing the acts of the popularly elected branches of government.[45] Black believed that the judicial restraint Frankfurter advocated smacked of the notion of parliamentary supremacy, which the United States had repudiated when it threw off the imperial yoke. When legislators exceeded their constitutionally defined powers, Black did not hesitate to strike down the laws they passed.

Among Black's strong convictions was the constitutional guarantee of jury trials, a position he vigorously championed in a series of cases.[46] Prior to *Toth,* Black, whether in the minority or the majority, consistently asserted the primacy of Article III courts, the superiority of the duly constituted civilian courts to military courts, and the necessity for trial before a court rather than the imposition of legislatively determined punishments.[47] (Article III courts were created under Article III of the Constitution, which establishes the "judicial power of the United States" and vests it in federal courts.)[48] In an opinion of

1946 Black affirmed the long-established doctrine that military tribunals could not supplant civilian courts when the latter were in operation. Anticipating arguments Black made in *Toth,* his opinion for the court stated, "Legislatures and courts are not merely cherished American institutions; they are indispensable to our government. Military tribunals have no such standing."[49]

In 1953 Black joined Justice William O. Douglas, his closest ally on the court, in a dissent in the Supreme Court's review of the court-martial of defendants convicted and sentenced to death after making confessions that the convicts said were coerced.[50] Chief Justice Fred Vinson's opinion for the court had reaffirmed that "the decisions of the appellate military tribunals should be 'final,' and should be 'binding' upon the courts," meaning that the Supreme Court had only a limited right to review the proceedings of military tribunals and courts-martial. So long as the military appellate system had examined the petitioners' arguments about the coerced confessions and so on, the Supreme Court had no role in reconsidering the same issues.[51] One of the death sentences was commuted, but two of the convicted airmen were executed in 1954. The case left a bad taste in the mouths of anyone who was worried about whether the much-lamented failings in the military justice system had been resolved by the UCMJ.[52]

In 1953, on Vinson's death, Earl Warren succeeded him as chief justice, and his appointment helped solidify the liberal majority on the Supreme Court bench. When the court first heard arguments in *Toth* in March 1955, Warren and Douglas concurred with Black's draft opinion. After the case was reargued, Frankfurter and Justices Tom Clark and John Harlan joined them. *Toth* was the first of a number of decisions in which the Supreme Court struck down jurisdictional provisions of the UCMJ.

Black's *per curiam* opinion in *Toth* stated,

> We find nothing in the history or constitutional treatment of military tribunals which entitles them to rank along with Article III courts as adjudicators of the guilt or innocence of people charged with offenses for which they can be deprived of their life, liberty or property. Unlike courts, it is the primary business of armies and navies to fight or be ready to fight wars should the occasion arise. But trial of soldiers to maintain discipline is merely incidental to an army's primary fighting function. To the extent that those responsible for performance of this primary function are diverted from it by the necessity of trying cases, the basic fighting purpose of armies is not served. And conceding to military personnel that high degree of honesty and sense of justice which nearly all of them undoubtedly have, it still remains true that military tribunals have not been, and probably never can be, constituted in such way that they can have the same kind of qualifications that the Constitution has deemed essential to fair trials of civilians in federal courts.[53]

The court found that Congress's power to authorize trial by court-martial was limited to the "least possible power adequate to the end proposed," which, following William Winthrop's *Military Law and Precedents,* it held to be maintaining discipline among troops in active service.[54] This principle determined that, while Congress had the authority to establish a court-martial system as a "prompt, ready-at-hand means of compelling obedience and order" in the armed forces, the needs of military discipline could not override the right to jury trial of a former serviceman who had been separated from the armed forces for months, years, or even decades.[55]

The concept that the principal function of armies is to fight wars, not administer justice, and that the military justice system was at least in part a disciplinary function of the military machine, had long been recognized.[56] Indeed, it was enunciated by the chairman of the House Armed Services Committee in the floor debate leading to the passage of the UCMJ. As Rep. Carl Vinson said, "The objective of the civilian society is to make people live together in peace and in reasonable happiness. The object of the armed forces is to win wars." The civilian and military justice systems were bound to differ, to a degree, in their purposes, and the problem deriving from this disparity was that of creating a military justice system which "not only preserves and protects the rights of the members of our armed forces, but also recognizes the sole reason for the existence of a military establishment—the winning of wars."[57] The distinct purposes of military and civilian courts underpinned the Supreme Court's concern about extending the jurisdiction of courts-martial over anyone but serving military personnel. Moreover, although the lower courts had long differed on the issue of the constitutionality of laws conferring military jurisdiction over civilians, leading authorities on military law had also expressed long-standing doubts as to their constitutionality.[58]

Black argued that although Article I, § 8 of the Constitution granted Congress the power "to make rules for the government and regulation of the land and naval forces," the natural meaning of this power was restricted to "persons who are actually members or part of the armed forces." Actually, this natural meaning was not quite as self-evident as Black made it appear. As Robinson Everett, a former commissioner for the U.S. Court of Military Appeals (C.M.A.), later counsel to the Senate Subcommittee on Constitutional Rights, and then chief judge of the C.M.A., remarked, "The existence of this 'natural meaning' is rather surprising, since it does not seem to have been clearly glimpsed by many of the persons most concerned with military jurisprudence."[59] The Fifth Amendment contains an exception to the guarantee of a trial after indictment by a grand jury: the amendment says that it does not apply to "cases arising in the land and naval forces . . . when in actual service in time of War or public danger." As Justice Reed argued in his dissent in *Toth,* if by "case" one understands the series of events that constituted an offense, rather than litigation, Toth's actions could certainly have been construed as having arisen during his service in the land and naval forces in time of war.[60]

In the discussion of the case in February 1955, Black and Frankfurter strained to find grounds to take exception with that view and proposed a tenuous distinction between the words *arising* and *arose*.[61] Reed cut through the sophistry by straightforwardly stating, "This is within the exception to the Fifth Amendment. Toth was in the army. This case '*arose*' while he was in the service. I affirm."[62] Given this view, the constitutional provision to "make rules" to regulate the land and naval forces, combined with the Fifth Amendment exception, provided grounds for the extension of military jurisdiction to a civilian whose alleged crime had taken place during his military service in a war zone. In oral arguments before the Supreme Court, the government's advocate returned several times to the view that interpreting the Constitution in that way neither conflicted with settled ideas of justice nor established a dangerous power. He bolstered his argument by referring to America's allies who conferred jurisdiction over civilians on courts-martial and cited narrower precedents in the United States dating back to 1863 that did the same.[63] Moreover, in a separate dissent Justices Minton and Burton, who had joined Reed in his dissent, took the view that because Toth had only a "conditional discharge" at the time of his arrest he was not a "full-fledged civilian."[64]

Their reasoning ran up against the traditional reluctance of the court to countenance military courts' jurisdiction over civilians. Black's opinion states that the UCMJ "sweeps under military jurisdiction over 3,000,000 persons who have become veterans since the act became effective." The act brought not just this enormous number of people but a "vast number and variety of offenses" under military jurisdiction, and the court ruled that this was an unconstitutional encroachment on the domain of the civilian courts. So long as one ignored the Fifth Amendment exception regarding cases "arising in" the land and naval forces and overlooked the practical considerations about the efficacy of civilian courts in the case of offenses committed overseas, Black's opinion had a solid foundation: after all, the Constitution specifies not once, but twice, that all criminal prosecutions shall be tried by jury, in Article III, § 2, clause 3, and in the Sixth Amendment.

The court found that Congress could not ignore safeguards in the Bill of Rights in making rules to govern the land and naval forces, and it declined to infer from the "necessary and proper" clause that Congress could circumvent those safeguards. Quoting General Green's congressional testimony, Black made it clear that others in Toth's position need not escape prosecution from that point on. He said that "it was wholly within the constitutional power of Congress to follow [Green's] suggestion and provide for federal district court trials of discharged soldiers accused of offenses committed while in the armed services." "There can be no valid argument, therefore," Black continued, "that civilian ex-servicemen must be tried by court-martial or not tried at all. If that is so, it is only because Congress has not seen fit to subject them to trial in federal district courts."[65]

The dissenters argued that if a federal court tried a suspect like Toth, the ex-serviceman "must face a jury far removed from the scene of the alleged crime and before jurors without the understanding of the quality and character of a military crime possessed by those accustomed to administer the Uniform Code of Military Justice. Or perhaps those accused will be extradited and tried by foreign law."[66] They noted that, despite objections on constitutional and on policy grounds, Congress had chosen to vest jurisdiction in courts-martial rather than in federal district courts, and they held that it was not for courts to question the wisdom of Congress's judgment.[67]

Everett, who was an air force judge advocate during the Korean War, challenged the *Toth* judgment and pointed out some practical difficulties arising from the legislative remedy Black proposed: if federal courts' jurisdiction expanded to cover offenses committed overseas, "how and from whom will the grand and petty jury be selected? Certainly it will be impossible to fulfill the goal of the sixth amendment that the accused be tried 'by an impartial jury of the state and district wherein the crime shall have been committed.' "[68] Moreover, a federal district court would probably not have the authority to hold sessions overseas, "where the witnesses would generally be more available and where local conditions could be observed by the trier of fact." It might be difficult or impossible to get witnesses, especially foreign witnesses, to come to the United States to testify at a trial, and bringing members of the armed forces back from overseas to testify might disrupt military operations.[69] These pragmatic considerations favored the use of a military court because, unlike a civilian court, a court-martial could be readily convened anywhere in the world that the armed forces had a presence.

As Everett pointed out, the court's ruling might have a pernicious effect: "If the proceedings were to be held overseas, near the scene of the crime, they simply could not be accomplished in American civil courts. In practice, then, the choice as to many offenses committed overseas by former servicemen must be between trial by court-martial and no trial at all; and consequently the Supreme Court's decision in the Toth case will signify that some alleged vicious crimes will go unpunished."[70] (Everett continued to make the same arguments over the years, both in his published writings and, as we shall see below, in testifying to urge passage of the War Crimes Act.)[71] Thus, there were strong practical reasons for preserving court-martial jurisdiction over military veterans—and there was also, in the Fifth Amendment exception, a plausible constitutional argument for doing so. These considerations were swept aside, however, by the constitutional scruples of the court's majority and by their assertion that the exception applied only to current, not former, servicemen. In light of the court's decision, and in line with his predecessor Green's recommendation, Maj. Gen. Eugene Caffey, the judge advocate general of the army, suggested, "Amendatory legislation should be enacted which will vest in the United States district courts the jurisdiction lost to the services by virtue of that decision [*Toth v. Quarles*]."[72]

If the jurisdictional gap that the court decision opened up was not reason enough for Congress to enact a legislative remedy, that motive was redoubled (in legal, although not political terms) by the need to fulfill the commitment of the United States to enforce international law. Just as the UCMJ had been an effort to take on board the lessons of the Second World War in a national law governing U.S. armed forces, the Geneva Conventions of 1949 attempted to codify existing customs and treaties in light of the experience of the world war. As the general counsel for the Department of Defense explained in the Senate ratification hearings, "The widespread and deliberate evasion of the principles of civilized warfare which was displayed by a number of states during World War II pointed forcibly to the need of a thorough overhauling of the existing treaties in order to make them responsive to the techniques and problems of modern warfare." Practically every new provision of the conventions "is a consequence of problems encountered . . . during that conflict."[73]

The conventions were transmitted to the Senate in April 1951, but the State Department recommended that ratification be delayed during the Korean War. By 1955 several dozen nations had acceded to or ratified the conventions. Once the State Department saw that the Soviet Union was attempting to gain a "propaganda advantage" from the fact that the United States had still not ratified them, the secretary of state told the Senate that there was no longer any need to delay action.[74]

In June 1955 the Senate ratified the Geneva Conventions.[75] This action came at almost the exact moment the Supreme Court decided to renew its attention to the Toth case, which was restored to the docket for reargument on June 6, 1955. It is tempting to seek a connection between these events, and it is even possible to construct a hypothetical relationship between them: Black's opinion, which had been drafted as a dissent, recognized that it lay within the legislature's means to plug the jurisdictional gap that would open up if Article 3(a) of the UCMJ were declared unconstitutional;[76] now, by ratifying the Geneva Conventions, the legislature had committed the United States to enact whatever laws were required to punish "grave breaches" of the conventions, and this step might conceivably have prompted the legislative remedy Black advocated.[77] However, Justice Black's and Chief Justice Warren's papers offer no documentary support for any supposition that the court took into account the ratification of the conventions—besides which, the jurisdictional problem *Toth* raised affected a broader range of crimes than grave breaches under the conventions.

In the hearings preceding Senate ratification of the Geneva Conventions, the executive branch responded to legislators' queries by asserting that present legislation was sufficient for that purpose. Assistant Attorney General J. Lee Rankin said, "We have laws that cover all these subjects," and a "review of existing legislation reveals no need to enact further legislation in order to provide effective penal sanctions for those violations of the Geneva conventions which are designated as grave breaches."[78] There seemed to be no need for new legislation because "the treaties are very largely a restatement of how we act in war anyway."[79] Although in signing the Geneva Conventions nations committed themselves to pass legislation to allow their provisions to be enforced, after the *Toth* decision, if any veterans were discovered to have committed grave breaches of the conventions while serving their nation overseas, Rankin's statement that there were laws to cover such crimes was no longer true in every conceivable circumstance. Far from invoking the Geneva Conventions as an added reason for closing the jurisdictional gap, though, many elected officials in Congress, revealing their general concern that Americans should remain exempt from the alien legal standards enshrined in foreign and international law, were more concerned with ensuring that no treaty should impose any new requirements on American domestic law. The facts underlying Toth's case showed that an American serviceman might well commit a crime that was not detected until after he had left the forces. The Supreme Court had opened up a jurisdictional gap that rendered discharge from military service a grant of immunity from prosecution for crimes committed while in uniform abroad, and the obvious legislative remedy was surrounded by practical difficulties. Congress would contemplate this conundrum, without solving it, for the next four decades.

CHAPTER TWO

"Treaty Law" and "Murdering Wives"

The Widening of the Jurisdictional Gap

Given that the ratification of the Geneva Conventions underlined the need to close the jurisdictional gap, it is striking that legislators did not raise the issue in their subsequent proposals for laws to fulfill this purpose. Their reticence is explicable by the political controversies surrounding international agreements that impinged on U.S. legal and constitutional matters. In the 1950s an important body of opinion in the United States considered international agreements to be vehicles for perceived "communistic" schemes to curtail Americans' liberties and to restrict the sovereignty of the nation. These attitudes are evident in the debate about "treaty law" and the Bricker amendment.

Sen. John Bricker, a Republican from Ohio and the author of the Bricker amendment, was a leading member of the school of thinking that regarded international organizations such as the United Nations as sources of potentially dangerous encroachments on American sovereignty. A former governor of Ohio and the Republican vice presidential candidate in 1944, Bricker was said to be "no savant": "His mind had been compared to stellar space, a huge void filled with a few wandering clichés," chief among which were anti-Communism and a suspicion of international organizations.[1] A poll of Washington correspondents in 1949 voted him the worst senator, despite strong competition in the category.[2] Bricker's views on the threat posed by the U.N. and international agreements were influenced by Frank E. Holman, elected president of the American Bar Association in 1948. Holman, an archconservative and devoted supporter of the anti-Communist senator Joe McCarthy, was exercised about a host of international agreements emanating from the U.N. and, reviving constitutional issues that had arisen thirty years earlier, he warned that America's entry into these agreements might override states' prerogatives and abrogate constitutional protections of individual liberties.[3] In September 1951 Bricker introduced the first of several proposals for a constitutional amendment aimed at protecting the "sacred rights" that U.S. citizens enjoy "under the Bill of Rights and the Constitution."[4]

Bricker's and Holman's agitation arose from their interpretation of the dangers posed by Article VI, § 2 of the Constitution (the Supremacy Clause). Under this clause, treaties constitute the supreme law of the land. Whereas statutes are made "in pursuance" of the Constitution, Article VI, § 2 specifies that treaties are made "under the Authority of the United States," while Article II, § 2 states that treaties are made by the president, with the advice and consent of the Senate, so long as two-thirds of the senators concur. Critics of "treaty law" feared that the provisions of international agreements could therefore become U.S. law, enforceable on citizens and overriding state and federal laws with which they conflicted, without being approved by the lower house of Congress.[5] The critics' anxieties were exaggerated: the Supremacy Clause does not state that treaties are superior to the Constitution (and hence to the Bill of Rights) or to statutes. Bricker and his cohorts were nevertheless beset by fears about the damage that treaties might inflict on the checks and balances in the Constitution. They insisted that "no agreement with a foreign nation could deny Americans their constitutional rights nor enlarge the powers of either the executive branch or the federal government generally." Anxious about foreign-inspired, undemocratic impositions on the nation, Holman perceived threats to U.S. sovereignty and American liberties in the proposed Genocide Convention and the Universal Declaration of Human Rights as well as in many proposals of the International Labor Organization.[6] Bricker named the Covenant on Human Rights, which codified the principles of the Universal Declaration of Human Rights, as one of the reasons for his introduction of a constitutional amendment, because it would have set economic and social rights on the same plane as the civil and political rights enshrined in the U.S. Bill of Rights.[7]

To conservatives the human rights treaties "represented instruments for legitimizing international review of U.S. domestic affairs, including the treatment of blacks; internationalization of a human rights standard that included Communist ideas; and federal action at the state and local level to remedy racial injustice."[8] As Natalie Kaufman argues, these worries emerged from a parochial and ethnocentric worldview, "a perspective suspicious or disdainful of things foreign," and a strong belief in the superiority of the United States. As one Senate opponent of "treaty law" put it, "I don't think the peoples of the earth are in any position where they can tell this great people on morals, politics and religion, how they should live. I still feel that we are ahead of them in that respect."[9]

The debate about "treaty law" meshed with two of the principal political issues of the 1950s: the conflict over racial segregation and civil rights and domestic and international anti-Communism. Diplomats who were preoccupied about America's international reputation believed that the pursuit of racial equality in the United States would assist in a propaganda war against the Soviet Union and improve America's standing before neutral and friendly nations;[10] in a symmetrically opposed argument, opponents of "treaty law" played on segregationists' fears that America's alignment with international organizations and agreements might usher in racial equality at home. As L. A. Scot Powe has argued, although the opponents of "treaty law" couched their arguments in constitutionalist terms, their real fears were that "communists would be choosing American governing rules and that international organizations, with so many third-world votes, would eradicate local customs and institutions (like segregation)."[11]

The adoption of the Genocide Convention by the United Nations and its transmittal to the Senate for ratification in June 1949 underpinned Bricker's determination to achieve passage of his amendment. The language of the Genocide Convention prohibited the infliction of "mental harm" on members of a group of people. Opponents of the convention were afraid that, by enforcing the prohibition of mental harm with respect to the treatment of African Americans, the federal government would use the treaty to invalidate state laws and dismantle the system of legalized racial segregation in the South. The Genocide Convention also proposed the creation of an International Criminal Court. Segregationists raised the possibility that U.S. citizens might be tried in an international penal tribunal for acts of racial discrimination that could be construed as genocide under the terms of the convention.[12] As we shall see, this complex of attitudes—a belief in the superiority of American laws and institutions and a suspicion of foreign entities, particularly foreign or international courts—cuts across the half century this book considers, from the debates about "treaty law" in the 1950s to the opposition to the International Criminal Court in recent years. The arguments that germinated during the hearings on the Genocide Convention "blossomed into full-fledged opposition to all human rights treaties during the hearings on the Bricker Amendment."[13]

The motives underlying the proposal of the Bricker amendment are pertinent to my argument here because they demonstrate the nationalistic self-satisfaction, colored by a belief in the superiority of U.S. law and the inviolability of American customs, that made resistance to the imposition of international standards and the jurisdiction of foreign and international courts a point of pride among America's political leaders. This attitude placed a double-edged rhetorical weapon in the hands of those on both sides of the legislative debates about the jurisdictional gap: advocates of legislation to plug the jurisdictional gap pointed out that, in the absence of such a law, the only judicial forums in which the relevant crimes could be prosecuted would be foreign or international courts, in which American defendants would not enjoy the procedural safeguards and constitutional protections they would have in an American court; opponents of the enforcement of international standards on the United States remained indifferent to the nation's nonconformity to those standards in the case of breaches of the law immunized from prosecution by *Toth*.

For the purposes of my argument here, the Bricker amendment controversy makes vivid the tensions besetting a nation struggling to accustom itself to its role as a leader of an international coalition of nations tied together not just by military alliances but also by a network of mutually binding international agreements. Opposed by President Dwight Eisenhower, whose robust argument managed to win over six senators, the amendment failed to achieve the required two-thirds majority in the Senate, falling short by a single vote when a version of it was put to a vote in 1954.[14] When Senate support for the amendment was at its highest, the Eisenhower administration committed itself to not ratifying the human rights treaties under debate, and for decades the U.S. government failed to pass the Civil and Political Rights Covenant, the Genocide Convention, the Convention against Racial Discrimination, the Economic and Social Rights Convention, the Convention Banning Discrimination against the Rights of Women, and the Convention on the Rights of Children.[15]

The controversy about the Bricker amendment and treaty power explains why advocates of remedial legislation to close the jurisdictional gap did not highlight the need to conform with the Geneva Conventions. Years later, Monroe Leigh, the former assistant general counsel for international affairs at the Department of Defense, who had testified for the Eisenhower administration in the Geneva Conventions ratification debate, revealed that concern about the Bricker amendment had persuaded the administration to soft-pedal the issue of legislation to implement the conventions. As he told Congress forty years later, "The position of the Government as to implementing legislation was influenced by the Bricker Amendment controversy." The Eisenhower administration "did not wish to draw any kind of controversy about the Bricker amendment" because it had just survived the near-passage of a version of the amendment; consequently, it "took the minimalist approach" and "wanted as little legislation as possible in implementation of the 1949 treaties."[16]

Confirming Leigh's recollections, Sen. Bourke B. Hickenlooper, a Republican from Iowa and a party leader in foreign affairs, asked during the Geneva Conventions ratification debate whether the obligation to enact legislation necessary to punish "grave breaches" enlarged the powers of Congress beyond those it already possessed under the Constitution.[17] His query comports with the misgivings of opponents of "treaty law" about the expansion of the powers of the federal government beyond their current limits as a result of obligations imposed by treaties. To have brought up the requirement for a new law to enforce the Geneva Conventions would have complicated the argument by reminding legislators of the fraught issue of "treaty law." Underpinning the relationship between the Geneva Conventions and the jurisdictional gap was the reality that for some legislators, resisting the imposition of international standards on the national laws of the United States was a principled defense of sovereignty.

The same body of opinion that was suspicious of "treaty law" was also fiercely protective of American sovereignty when considering the subjection of American military personnel to any legal forum in which procedures and standards foreign to the United States might prevail. Bricker was one of those who argued for legislation conferring exclusive legal jurisdiction on the United States over its forces in all circumstances, even when the troops were stationed in allied countries.[18] In 1957 some of Bricker's Senate colleagues proposed that the Senate adopt a resolution favoring the retention of primary jurisdiction by the United States over troops stationed overseas.[19] H.R. 8658, introduced a few days earlier, would also have ensured U.S. courts' exclusive jurisdiction over military personnel overseas;[20] another House bill, H.R. 8704, would have prohibited the delivery of members of the armed services to the jurisdiction of any foreign nation.[21]

These bills were prompted by the Girard affair, a dispute about whether a Japanese or American court should exercise jurisdiction over Spec. William S. Girard, a member of the U.S. armed forces whose reckless conduct resulted in the accidental killing of a Japanese civilian. Girard played a cruel game in which he threw brass bullet casings from his post in order to tempt Japanese civilians who were salvaging casings nearby to approach him; he then fired a bullet casing at them by using blank cartridges to propel it from his grenade launcher. One of the civilians was fatally wounded, although the killing does not appear to have been deliberate. (The incident is similar to ones that Vietnam veterans described in which they threw cans of food in the path of heavy truck traffic, tempting Vietnamese onlookers to risk injury and death by dodging the vehicles to retrieve the cans.)[22] Although in the vast majority of cases the Japanese authorities ceded jurisdiction to the United States to try American troops stationed in Japan, in this instance there was an outcry in the Japanese press. The United States enjoyed the right to exercise primary jurisdiction over its troops in any offenses "done in the performance of official duty." Girard's commander asserted that he had killed the woman in the performance of official duty, but the Japanese disagreed.[23] The executive branch's decision to cede jurisdiction to Japanese courts produced an uproar in the United States, and "Congressmen, from left to right" began "hammering at" that decision.[24]

The legislative proposals prompted by the Girard case touched on the jurisdictional conflicts about the forum in which U.S. troops stationed in allied nations and who were suspected of committing crimes might be tried. Following the Second World War, the United States assumed unprecedented international military responsibilities by stationing troops in friendly nations around the world in time of peace. The United States and the host nations negotiated status of forces agreements (SOFAs) that conferred concurrent jurisdiction over U.S. forces on United States and host nation courts. In practice, SOFAs generally allowed the United States a good deal of influence over whether to allow troops stationed overseas to be tried by foreign courts. (Concurrent jurisdiction prevailed except in cases where one or the other party, the host nation or the United States, had exclusive jurisdiction because an act was defined as an offense only under the laws of one or the other.)[25] The United States negotiated over forty such agreements with its allies between 1951, when the first one was signed by the United States and Britain, and 1957.[26] By that time the United States had seven hundred thousand troops stationed in forty-nine countries.[27]

The argument in favor of SOFAs was that the host nations were inconsistent in their legal standards, sometimes showed excessive leniency toward U.S. troops, did not always feel an imperative to try them, and did not observe the same judicial processes as American courts. The judge advocates general were worried that congressional attempts to override SOFAs might give some North Atlantic Treaty Organization (NATO) allies an excuse to reopen SOFA negotiations, and that any attempt to undo or abrogate the agreements would undermine the international position of the United States. They said, "The solution to the furor over trials of servicemen abroad lies with an 'education' of the American people as to their benefits, rather than any changes in the treaty."[28]

The recognition of foreign jurisdiction over U.S. troops caused some Americans disquiet, though. Bricker argued that accepting the criminal jurisdiction provisions of SOFA treaties would "amount to penalizing the American soldier in an effort to please our NATO allies."[29] In addition to certain legislators, many influential citizens were sharply opposed to such agreements. The president of the National Economic Council, for example, said they were one of the "Communistic schemes" cooked up by a State Department more concerned with other nations' attitudes than with vital American interests.[30] At a pro–Bricker amendment dinner it was charged that status of forces legislation deprived American soldiers of their constitutional rights by subjecting them to foreign courts.[31]

The debates about the Bricker amendment and the argument about the desirability of SOFAs disclose one of the two countervailing tendencies in the post–Second World War period: as we have seen, that period witnessed the promulgation of universal standards of justice in treaties and in the actions of international entities such as the Nuremberg and Tokyo tribunals, the Geneva

Conventions, and the Universal Declaration of Human Rights; but national sovereignty and nonintervention in the domestic affairs of states were also among the central principles enshrined in the U.N. Charter and important treaties.[32] The debates of the midfifties I have described reveal the reaction of Americans who wished above all to protect U.S. sovereignty and to promote the exclusive jurisdiction of U.S. courts over American troops. The bills conferring exclusive jurisdiction on U.S. courts were unsupported by the executive branch, yet they nevertheless demonstrate the degree to which a substantial body of legislative opinion recoiled from allowing foreigners to exercise jurisdiction over American service personnel.

No legislation denying the jurisdiction of foreign nations over U.S. forces stationed on their territory had any likelihood of passing, and there was certainly no possibility of its being signed into law. As the State Department pointed out in relation to H.R. 8658, any statute denying jurisdiction to foreign governments would be a legal nullity as far as those governments were concerned, in view of the fact that every nation is supreme within its own borders and has exclusive jurisdiction over offenses committed on its territory unless it surrenders such jurisdiction—a view in which the Supreme Court concurred.[33] Such a law would also contradict bilateral agreements that the United States had entered into with its allies with regard to jurisdiction over U.S. troops stationed on their territory, would undermine the reputation the United States had for entering such agreements in good faith, and would encourage host nations to abrogate their commitments under such agreements.[34] The agreements themselves seemed perfectly reasonable measures to the deputy judge advocate general of the army, who suggested that one should view matters from the perspective of the host countries. Those nations merely wanted to exert some local control over the "killings, assaults, sexual crimes and highway offenses which, even in the best-regulated armies, inevitably take place."[35] They resented the sort of regime that prevailed under conditions of military occupation, when local authorities exercised no control over the occupying forces. Some legislators agreed with this view and reminded their constituents that the United States had justified its right to independence, among other reasons, because of the abuses of imperial troops quartered among the populace.[36]

Time magazine saw SOFAs as a sign of America's watchfulness over its troops worldwide: "By watching vigilantly over the lot of its men in foreign courts, the U.S. is extending around the world its concern for and its principles of justice and law. And under the status-of-forces agreements now operative, the U.S. conveys to the world that it is not in the empire-building business, that its concern for legal right is couched in its own example."[37] This claim was eroded, though, by the continuing failure throughout the remainder of the 1950s to close the jurisdictional gap opened up by *Toth v. Quarles.*

The first legislative proposal to create a forum other than a military court in which to try veterans for crimes they committed while in military service overseas was made before *Toth* produced the jurisdictional gap. It addressed a similar jurisdictional lacuna that had arisen under different circumstances. Former members of an American military intelligence team were held to be responsible for the disappearance and presumed murder of an American intelligence officer in Italy in 1944.[38] Because the crime had taken place before passage of the UCMJ, it was prosecutable as an offense against the Articles of War, which the UCMJ had superseded, and the Department of Defense ruled that it was covered by the old Manual for Courts-Martial of the United States Army, which provides that court-martial jurisdiction over army personnel ceases when they are discharged or otherwise separated from the service.[39] A special House of Representatives subcommittee determined that although there was probable cause to prosecute the two former team members accused of the crime, they could not be tried in any American court.[40] After the suspects were convicted in absentia in an Italian court, the subcommittee chairman, Rep. W. Sterling Cole, proposed a law that would give federal district courts jurisdiction in such cases. His proposal was referred to a subcommittee of the House Judiciary Committee and died there without any further action.[41]

After the *Toth* decision opened up what he called a "huge gap in the law," Cole reintroduced the law as H.R. 81 and asked the chairman of the Judiciary Committee to hold hearings in the near future. The chairman, Rep. Emanuel Celler of New York, recognized the new urgency of the bill by commenting, "This bill is too important to sit on."[42] Celler's remark reflected the vastly expanded import of the legislation: initially intended to plug a jurisdictional gap affecting the limited number of veterans who had committed as-yet-undetected crimes overseas before passage of the UCMJ (which, as enacted, provided for the court-martial prosecution of veterans for crimes they committed while in military service), it now potentially affected the increased number of veterans who were immunized from prosecution as a result of *Toth.* And although the Supreme Court had not yet cast its judgment in *Reid v. Covert,* a case involving a woman who had killed her soldier husband in military quarters in England—and which might, depending on how the court ruled, further widen the jurisdictional gap—the chief counsel for the House Judiciary Committee noted that H.R. 81 would also make civilian defendants accused of crimes similar to hers subject to the jurisdiction of the federal district courts.[43] Reports were requested from the Department of Defense, the Department of the Interior, and the State Department, but despite the importance the House Judiciary Committee attached to the proposal, no reports were received, and the bill was not voted out of committee.[44]

Exactly a year after Cole introduced H.R. 81, and taking account, as Cole had, of the added impetus supplied by *Toth,* Sen. Thomas Hennings of Missouri proposed his own legislation to fill the jurisdictional gap. Hennings chaired the Senate Judiciary Committee's recently established Subcommittee on Constitutional Rights. He explained the background of the bill to his Senate colleagues, summarizing the effect of *Toth v. Quarles,* praising the wisdom of the court's decision in asserting the supremacy of civilian courts, and making clear that his bill would carry out Justice Black's implied legislative recommendation. Justifying the bill in the rhetoric of patriotism, he said it would allow a federal district court to try such crimes as "treason and collaboration with enemies of the United States."[45] Reports were requested from the executive branch, which evidently did not support the bill because none was received.[46] The Department of Defense supported the principle involved in H.R. 81 and in Hennings's bill, S. 2791, but concluded that the proposed legislation presented "certain practical and legal difficulties."[47] Because of the absence of a formal report, it is not clear what the Department of Defense considered those difficulties to be, but the Civil Liberties Committee of the National Lawyers Guild drew attention to one: although it, too, approved of the bill in principle, it said it would be expensive for a soldier who had allegedly committed a crime while serving in a distant continent to prepare a defense once he had returned to the United States. It suggested that the accused should be granted funds to depose witnesses and that there should be a brief statute of limitations within which an indictment should be brought for any alleged crime.[48] As the issue of geographical distance, the ability to prepare a defense, and the difficulty of obtaining witnesses continued thereafter to be the problems to which critics of similar legislation drew attention—and indeed had already been remarked upon by Everett—it is reasonable to infer that these were among the Pentagon's concerns. Because the bill involved jurisdiction over civilians, the Department of Defense suggested that the Department of Justice might take the lead in devising solutions to these problems, but neither executive department put forward any legislative proposals. The bill was not voted out of the Senate's Constitutional Rights Subcommittee and died on the adjournment of the 84th Congress.[49]

On the other side of the world, a train of events advanced that would draw the United States into a military involvement that eventually converged with the history of legislative failure that began with the Cole and Hennings bills. In December 1950 the United States had entered into a mutual defense treaty with France and the nominally independent states of Cambodia, Laos, and Vietnam.[50] It then assumed the vast majority of the burden of funding and supplying the French in their anti-Communist campaign in Vietnam. In September 1954, after the French defeat at Dien Bien Phu and the signing of the Geneva Agreements that brought about a cessation of hostilities and the withdrawal of the French from Indochina, the United States negotiated the formation of the Southeast Asia Treaty Organization (SEATO), which established the principle of collective self-defense for the countries of Southeast Asia.[51] While the National Lawyers Guild was composing its response to Hennings's bill S. 2791, the first national assembly was elected in the newly created South Vietnam in defiance of the Geneva Agreements of 1954 that ended the First Indochina War and despite a boycott by opposition political parties.[52] The Geneva Agreements called for North and South Vietnam to be reunified by 1956, with elections to be held north and south of the dividing line across which the belligerents had been required to regroup. Instead, Ngo Dinh Diem, whom Secretary of State John Foster Dulles saw as the "only means" to "save South Vietnam and counteract revolution," consolidated his power in the south and declined to hold the reunification elections, which Diem would undoubtedly have lost to the Communists.[53] Just as the deadline for the election was about to expire, Sen. John F. Kennedy declared on June 1, 1956, that South Vietnam was "the cornerstone of the Free World in Southeast Asia, the keystone to the arch, the finger in the dike."[54] A week later the first uniformed Americans fell as casualties amid the campaign to support the fledgling nation Kennedy called "our offspring."[55] By the time bill S. 2791 died, the United States had determinedly thrown its weight behind South Vietnam. The United States began a process of nation building, giving the Diem regime economic, diplomatic, and military assistance to transform South Vietnam into an anti-Communist bulwark. In May 1957 President Eisenhower and Diem issued a joint communiqué reaffirming that South Vietnam was covered by the Southeast Asia Collective Defense Treaty.[56] At the same time legislators were beginning to wrestle with the consequences of the jurisdictional gap, the United States was becoming embroiled in another military engagement in Asia that carried the same potential the Korean War had for criminal actions by members of U.S. forces.[57]

In the late 1950s the jurisdictional gap widened as a result of several Supreme Court decisions, beginning with *Reid v. Covert* in 1957, that further limited the scope of the UCMJ by declaring the superiority of Article III courts over military courts.[58] The *Toth* decision encouraged Clarice Covert and Dorothy Krueger Smith, who had been imprisoned after being convicted of murdering their American soldier husbands in Great Britain and Japan, respectively, to petition for writs of habeas corpus in the federal courts. (Smith's father, Walter Krueger, had submitted the petition and was the respondent in the case, which is why it is called *Kinsella v. Krueger.*) Covert and Smith came within the jurisdiction of the UCMJ because of Article 2(a)(11), which stated that, subject to treaty provisions, "persons serving with, employed by, or accompanying the armed forces" outside the United States were subject to the code. Initially, the Supreme Court had upheld Covert's and Smith's convictions and approved court-martial jurisdiction over them and their crimes.[59] At that stage Justice Tom Clark, for the court, regarded court-martial jurisdiction as preferable to the "widely varying standards of justice unfamiliar to our people" that might pertain if their cases were heard in foreign courts. He said that, as matters stood, the "essential choice involved here is between an American and foreign trial."[60] As Black had suggested in his *Toth* opinion, if the choice was as Clark described it, that is, between a U.S. court-martial and a foreign trial, Congress had the power to alter the situation in such cases by providing for federal court jurisdiction over such crimes. However, Clark's opinion raised the same practical objections to bringing the suspects to the United States for trial that Everett had contemplated:

> Both the Government and the accused would face serious problems in the production of witnesses. Depositions for the Government are not permitted in criminal cases. . . . Attendance of foreign witnesses could be only on a voluntary basis, and the testimony of no foreign witness could be compelled if the witness or his government refused. The expense of transporting witnesses would be considerable for the Government, and probably impossible for a defendant, whose successful defense may depend on the demeanor of one witness. In fairness, the Government would have to bear the expense of transporting the defendant's witnesses as well as its own, and the possibilities of abuse are obvious.[61]

Clark's opinion made a glancing reference to the debate about "treaty law" in Congress by stating that, because foreign nations had voluntarily relinquished jurisdiction to the United States by means of carefully framed agreements, the issue centered on Congress's determination of the appropriate forum in which the U.S. trial should take place. Thus, "no question of the legal relation between treaties and the Constitution is presented."[62]

Clark distinguished *Covert* from *Toth* by arguing that Toth had been discharged from the armed services and returned to the United States before charges were filed against him for a crime committed in Korea. In contrast, Covert was (at least initially) charged, tried, and convicted while "within the provisions of Article 2(11) of the UCMJ," that is, while accompanying the armed forces in the country where her husband was based. As Clark stated for the court, "We are not deciding here when, in other circumstances, Article 2(11) jurisdiction may terminate. In this case we hold only that military jurisdiction, once validly attached, continues until final disposition of the case."[63] Through this reasoning Clark dealt with the fact that Covert was retried in the United States.

In his opinion for the court in *Krueger,* Clark upheld the court-martial conviction on different grounds. Smith's crime and the subsequent court-martial prosecution had both occurred in Japan, and Clark pointed out that in the past the Supreme Court had upheld trials by Article I courts when the crimes had occurred in a foreign country, particularly an Asian, "non-Christian" country. The Constitution therefore did not guarantee a right to trial in an Article III court. In framing this argument, Clark relied on *In re Ross,* in which an American seaman was convicted by a consular court in Japan, and the conviction was upheld by the Supreme Court.[64]

The original judgments in the *Covert* and *Krueger* cases were unsatisfactory for a number of reasons. There was considerable doubt from the start about the validity of vesting jurisdiction over civilians in courts-martial, and these doubts were magnified by the court's ruling in *Toth.*[65] In the conference regarding *Toth,* Black had foreseen that the case had implications for trying civilians "who happened to be attached to the army" and contemplated how far the Supreme Court should allow court-martial jurisdiction to be extended.[66] The decision to allow a court-martial to prosecute military dependants seemed to be at odds with the striking down of the conviction of a former serviceman.[67] Clark's attempt to sidestep the jurisdictional question in *Covert* was unconvincing. In the conference regarding *Covert,* Chief Justice Warren had expressed strong doubts: "It is hard to believe that a housewife and youngsters living in Tokyo or London are members of the armed forces for military purposes."[68] Black said plainly, "The military has no authority here."[69] Frankfurter said the real problem was that "we can't say that these women are members of the armed services." Nevertheless, he and several justices were initially willing to affirm Covert's conviction and reverse Smith's. Justice Sherman Minton came to the opposite judgment, being willing to affirm Smith's conviction, with *In re Ross* as the controlling precedent, but not Covert's. Justice Harlan entertained the same view as Minton, although in his case it was "tentative."[70] The bench's opinions were thus less than coherent, and some justices changed their minds after the conference. The court was rushed in its deliberations in the first hearing of the cases, and the justices were rushed again to file their opinions a short time after the arguments were heard.[71] The court voted 5–3 in favor of upholding both convictions, Frankfurter filing a reservation.

These circumstances help explain how Covert's and Smith's formidable lawyer, Frederick Bernays Wiener, managed the rare feat of getting the Supreme Court to rehear the cases of the "murdering wives," as Justice Frankfurter referred to them. Although the composition of the court had altered after two retirements from the bench, this is not what brought about the court's reversal of its previous ruling.[72] More significant, Frankfurter, whose reservation strongly disagreed with the majority's reasoning, had come to believe there was a compelling interest to reconsider the case. He filed a petition for a rehearing. Frankfurter gave voice to a number of justices' doubts about the reliance in

Krueger on *In re Ross,* a case, Frankfurter said, that "represents, historically and juridically, an episode of the dead past about as unrelated to the world of today as the one-hoss shay is to the latest jet airplane."[73] He also doubted the relevance of another basis for the court's decision, provisions made by Congress for dealing with "unorganized" territories acquired by the United States.[74] Frankfurter referred to *Toth* and cited Winthrop's view that the Fifth Amendment clearly distinguishes civilians from the military: "It recognizes no third class which is part civil and part military—military for a particular purpose or in a particular situation, and civil for all other purposes and in all other situations."[75] He thought the court had rushed to judgment and should have taken more time to reach its decision.

However forcefully Frankfurter criticized the court's action, procedurally a petition for a rehearing required that one of the justices who had sided with the original majority change his mind. Justice Harlan did.[76] Harlan stated in his petition for rehearing that, although he might regard overseas service dependants as part of the military establishment, without further argument he was not ready to sustain their being tried by court-martial.[77] If upholding the court-martial conviction rested, as the majority in the initial hearing held, on the inapplicability of Article III abroad, Harlan doubted whether the military ought to have been allowed to retry Covert at court-martial once it had returned her to the United States, where the Constitution unmistakably did apply. In his eventual concurrent opinion with the court's judgment after the rehearing, Harlan raised another doubt: he wondered whether "there are provisions in the Constitution which do not necessarily apply in all circumstances in every foreign place," a line of thought that required a judgment about the circumstances of the case and thereby potentially left the door open for a court-martial to try a citizen despite her civilian status.[78]

Harlan's uncertainties about the original decision upholding the convictions differed from Black's reasoning. In his concurrent opinion after the case was reheard, Harlan believed it came down to which constitutional guarantees should apply overseas: in other words, it was a matter of judgment whether Covert and Smith should have enjoyed the right to a jury trial.[79] For Black, seeing the case in that way reflected the sort of judicial determination of reasonableness which, in his view, lay outside the province of the courts.[80] Black's judicial activism did not seek to supplant the political branches' deliberations on matters of policy with those of a court; it was a black-and-white matter requiring the literal application of constitutional protections. For Black, the issue turned on whether Covert and Smith were in the armed forces or not. That question alone was sufficient to dispose of the matter cleanly on constitutional grounds because it determined whether they were entitled to trial before a jury or could be prosecuted by a court-martial.[81]

Harlan, in his petition for a rehearing, had referred to the "Bricker Amendment controversy" in his discussion of difficult constitutional issues that "we should avoid if at all possible."[82] Early memoranda by Black, which might have been destined to evolve into the majority or a minority opinion, depending on how many justices joined him, unabashedly referred to the superiority of the Constitution over the treaty-making power of the United States.[83] Frankfurter tried to persuade Black to write an opinion on narrow grounds so that it might win the support of a large majority, even, as he suggested, of a unanimous bench.[84] Frankfurter, like Harlan, thought that injecting the Bricker amendment problem into the court's reasoning was unwise. He considered it unnecessary to declare the superiority of the Constitution to treaty provisions in order to arrive at a judgment of the cases.[85] He pressed Black to remove the "treaty discussion" from the draft opinion Black had circulated, on the grounds that it was superfluous to the judgment. Frankfurter believed it risked "needlessly fanning the flames of the Bricker amendment controversy" in light of the "active agitation, of which my Brethren cannot be unmindful," provoked by the Girard case.[86] His fellow justices might well have been mindful of the controversy because on the very day Frankfurter signed his message to them, a special Senate committee was meeting to discuss the Girard case. At that meeting Sen. Sam Ervin expressed considerable disquiet at the terms of the agreement that allowed a Japanese court to assert its jurisdiction over Girard's crime.[87] "It is not my wont," Frankfurter claimed, "to renew discussion after a matter has gone against my view." Yet he felt so deeply about the "stirring of inevitably mischievous controversy" that he was conscience-bound to do so.[88]

Whereas Frankfurter urged caution and restraint with respect to this politically sensitive subject, Black grasped the nettle to resolve one of the main points of contention raised by the opponents of "treaty law." Black's published opinion was more emphatic than his earliest drafts had been about the superiority of the Constitution to any treaty. Frankfurter declined to join in Black's opinion, filing a concurrent opinion instead.

In arguing that the court should confirm the convictions, the government had contended that the prosecutions by court-martial fulfilled the obligation of the United States under SOFAs with Great Britain and Japan.[89] Black acknowledged that there were agreements between the United States and Great Britain and between the United States and Japan which provided for the jurisdiction of U.S. courts over crimes committed by U.S. servicemen and military dependants in those foreign countries. The government contended therefore that the provision of the UCMJ that allowed court-martial prosecution of the defendants was "necessary and proper" in order to fulfill the obligation of the United States under the international agreements.[90] The court's ruling in

Covert affirmed, however, that no treaty can be in direct violation of the Constitution or abrogate the protections that the Bill of Rights confers on citizens.[91]

Black's opinion stated that the two defendants were entitled to the protections of the Constitution even though their crimes took place overseas. "At the beginning," Black argued,

> we reject the idea that, when the United States acts against citizens abroad, it can do so free of the Bill of Rights. The United States is entirely a creature of the Constitution. Its power and authority have no other source. It can only act in accordance with all the limitations imposed by the Constitution. When the Government reaches out to punish a citizen who is abroad, the shield which the Bill of Rights and other parts of the Constitution provide to protect his life and liberty should not be stripped away just because he happens to be in another land.[92]

In this case, Article III, § 2 of the Constitution and the Fifth and Sixth Amendments guaranteed the right to jury trial after indictment by a grand jury. Courts-martial therefore could not try civilian dependants of service personnel for capital cases during peacetime.

The court's judgment in *Reid v. Covert* followed the judgment in *Toth.* As Wiener had argued, the Supreme Court's original judgment upholding the conviction in *Covert* was "completely irreconcilable with Toth v. Quarles." Black agreed and found "no supportable grounds upon which to distinguish the Toth case from the present cases. Toth, Mrs. Covert, and Mrs. Smith were all civilians. All three were American citizens. All three were tried for murder."[93] As the Constitution granted them protections no matter where they were, all three were entitled to the constitutional right to indictment by a grand jury and jury trial: "The fact that Toth was arrested here while the wives were arrested in foreign countries is material only if constitutional safeguards do not shield a citizen abroad when the Government exercises its power over him. As we have said before, such a view of the Constitution is erroneous. The mere fact that these women had gone overseas with their husbands should not reduce the protection the Constitution gives them."[94] The court agreed with Winthrop that "a statute cannot be framed by which a civilian can lawfully be made amenable to the military jurisdiction in time of peace."[95]

Black's opinion implicitly addressed the Bricker amendment controversy by stating,

> There is nothing in this language [Article VI, § 2, the Supremacy Clause] which intimates that treaties and laws enacted pursuant to them do not have to comply with the provisions of the Constitution. . . . It would be manifestly contrary to the objectives of those who created the Constitution, as well as those who were responsible for the Bill of Rights—let alone alien to our

> entire constitutional history and tradition—to construe Article VI as permitting the United States to exercise power under an international agreement without observing constitutional prohibitions. . . . The prohibitions of the Constitution were designed to apply to all branches of the National Government, and they cannot be nullified by the Executive or by the Executive and the Senate combined.[96]

This directly attacked the issues surrounding the Bricker amendment, as Bricker himself recognized soon afterward. "Right down our alley," he said, referring to the court's judgment. "That's exactly what we are driving at."[97]

Black's opinion also repudiated the use of overseas American "consular courts" in which the United States had once claimed the right to prosecute its citizens and others who were subject to its laws in "Far Eastern," "other than Christian" countries. Black stated that the blending of executive, legislative, and judicial power in one person, as in the consular courts, is "ordinarily regarded as the very acme of absolutism." Although the Supreme Court held in *Ross* that the "Constitution can have no operation in another country," Black found that holding to be "obviously erroneous" and founded "on a fundamental misconception." Subsequent court rulings had repudiated the *Ross* approach; moreover, as Black argued, "Congress has recently buried the consular system of trying Americans. We are not willing to jeopardize the lives and liberties of Americans by disinterring it. At best, the Ross case should be left as a relic from a different era."[98] Black distinguished the recent courts-martial from the Insular Cases, in which the Supreme Court had found it inexpedient to require jury trials in the island possessions of the United States, on less emphatic constitutional grounds, saying that those territories had different traditions and institutions and the relevant cases did not involve military trials. He ended that passage of argument in high dudgeon: "The concept that the Bill of Rights and other constitutional protections against arbitrary government are inoperative when they become inconvenient or when expediency dictates otherwise is a very dangerous doctrine and, if allowed to flourish, would destroy the benefit of a written Constitution and undermine the basis of our Government." If the government could not meet its foreign obligations within the bounds of the Constitution, Black suggested it could follow the prescribed mechanism in proposing a constitutional amendment.[99]

Black's plurality opinion had the support of only four justices, including himself. Frankfurter and Harlan concurred in striking down the conviction, but on narrower grounds. Frankfurter specified that the matter before the court involved both capital crimes and military dependants, not any other category of civilians.[100] As he argued, the court had traditionally adhered to a doctrine of never anticipating a question of constitutional law in advance of the necessity of deciding it; and of never formulating a rule of constitutional law broader than is required by the precise facts of the case to which it is to be applied.[101] Black's opinion recognized that the cases involved capital crimes, but the terms of his opinion were not restricted to such cases alone, as he made references throughout to civilians' unqualified right to jury trial after indictment by a grand jury. Although Frankfurter thought civilian dependants should have the right to civilian court trial for offenses committed during peacetime, his concurrent opinion omitted any reference to the conflict between treaties and a defendant's constitutional rights; Harlan was similarly agnostic on that matter and argued that the right to jury trial should be confined to capital crimes committed during peacetime.

As a plurality decision, the holding of the court was the general result of the case. It pertained only to capital cases involving civilian dependants such as Covert and Smith, leaving it unclear whether the court would uphold prosecutions under the UCMJ of civilian employees and contractors of the armed forces, and of any civilians in noncapital cases.[102] At this stage it was Frankfurter's narrower view that determined the court's holding. Nevertheless, the *Ross* doctrine that the Constitution does not protect U.S. citizens outside the country suffered a fatal blow with the *Covert* and *Krueger* decisions.

Frankfurter's and Harlan's concurrence left only two justices opposed to overturning the convictions.[103] One of those, the conservative Harold Burton, retired in October 1958 and was replaced by the more moderate Potter Stewart, further changing the complexion of the court.[104] In his dissent in *Covert,* the other, Justice Clark, pointed out the practical difficulties that would arise if Congress authorized the trial in an Article III court of a military dependant for overseas crimes:

> Aside from the tremendous waste of the time of military personnel and the resultant disruptions, as well as the large expenditure of money necessary to bring witnesses and evidence to the United States, the deterrent effect of the prosecution would be nil because of the delay and distance at which it would be held. Furthermore, compulsory process is an essential to any system of justice. The attendance of foreign nationals as witnesses at a judicial proceeding in this country could rest only on a voluntary basis, and depositions could not be required. As a matter of international law, such attendance could never be compelled, and the court in such a proceeding would be powerless to control this vital element in its procedure. In short, this solution could only result in the practical abdication of American judicial authority over most of the offenses committed by American civilians in foreign countries.[105]

Even Justice Harlan referred to the "ridiculous burden" that trial in the United States would impose on the government.[106] The court was unmoved by Clark's reasoning. *Covert* marked the direction of the court's thinking and was cited favorably in subsequent decisions, including ones that Clark wrote.[107]

The *Covert* opinion was important not only in itself in broadening the category of defendants who could not be tried by court-martial, but also in reaffirming the court's support of the concepts on which the *Toth* judgment had been grounded. The decision was the first bulwark protecting the *Toth* judgment from possible backtracking by the court. While *Covert* had noteworthy political implications in its references to the relationship between treaties and the Constitution, another subtext ran through it. It was rumored among military lawyers that, after the failure of the first legislative effort to close the jurisdictional gap opened up by *Toth,* the Supreme Court was using these cases to draw Congress's attention to the need for remedial legislation to close a now-widening jurisdictional gap.[108] Yet Congress still did not take the hint by passing the requisite law. Worse still, no new legislative proposals appeared on the horizon.

The press noticed the expanding jurisdictional problem to which *Reid v. Covert* gave rise: "The baffling question raised by the decision," one newspaper said, "is how trials of offenses by the dependents of servicemen abroad will now be handled." The editorial stated that there were practical difficulties in setting up civilian courts in all the countries where American troops were stationed—not to mention diplomatic problems in trespassing on the sovereignty of an ally by establishing civilian courts on its territory. The newspaper followed the dissenting judges' conclusion that the most logical solution was to allow the host nation to try the civilian suspects in its courts, but that would work only in countries that had judicial standards "comparable to our own," not in those which were "virtually bereft of judicial standards."[109] Of course there was another alternative: the passage of legislation that would fill the now-broadened jurisdictional gap.

Events moved in the other direction, though. Far from closing the gap by passing a remedial law, Congress failed to act, and the gap grew wider still. In a string of cases that all tended in the same direction, the Supreme Court struck down several further provisions of Article 2 of the UCMJ that provided for court-martial jurisdiction over civilians, until most of the article became void. In one of those cases the court's opinion referenced *Toth* as a landmark ruling but also drew lessons from *Covert.*[110] Just as *Covert* seemed logically to follow *Toth,* so the later cases were logical extrapolations from *Covert.* Their effect was to bar court-martial jurisdiction for both civilian dependants and civilian employees of the armed forces, in both capital and noncapital cases, in time of peace.[111] Thus, the narrow holding determined by Frankfurter's concurrence gave way to the more expansive view pronounced by Black's opinion in *Covert;* consistent with their earlier view of the matter, Harlan and Frankfurter dissented in the judgments that collapsed the distinction they had made between capital and noncapital cases.[112] After the cases decided in 1960, Article 2 of the

UCMJ continued to apply only to civilians who were employed by, serving with, or accompanying the armed forces in the field in time of war.[113] Now, the *Toth* judgment was shielded from review and possible reversal by a phalanx of cases involving jurisdiction over nonveteran civilians. The issue of what constituted "in time of war" became central in cases that arose during the conflict in Vietnam; the jurisdictional question accrued new meaning in recent times with the increase in the number of contractors and other civilians serving in wars and so-called contingency operations. Courts-martial continued to exercise jurisdiction over retired members of the armed forces.[114]

Whether or not the Supreme Court intended to exert pressure on the legislature through the series of decisions that began with *Reid v. Covert* and continued in the 1960 cases affecting jurisdiction over civilians, those decisions certainly caused consternation among the judge advocates general of the army, navy and air force. The army was keen to plug the widened jurisdictional gap with a law vesting in federal district courts jurisdiction over any offenses civilians committed; in the absence of such a statute, they could not activate the provisions of SOFAs that allowed the United States to exercise jurisdiction over its citizens. The army's approach might best be described as pragmatic. Its judge advocates said, "While a statute *would not be aimed at actual trials,* it would permit the services to request waivers of jurisdiction in capital and other important cases from foreign governments [under the terms of SOFAs]. Without such a statute, they feel they would be hard pressed to justify requests for waivers in such cases and without making such requests, there would be political repercussions at home."[115] This line of reasoning figures in the motivation leading to the passage of the Military Extraterritorial Jurisdiction Act (see chapter 7).

The navy judge advocates were the most exercised about the loss of court-martial jurisdiction over civilians. In contrast, the air force was content to allow foreign courts to try U.S. civilians.[116] From this point on, the discussion of remedial legislation for the widened jurisdictional gap frequently intertwined the topics of SOFAs, the position of civilians accompanying the armed forces, and the venue in which to try veterans who were suspected of having committed crimes beyond the jurisdiction of U.S. civilian courts. The problem can be summarized as one of whether to allow American citizens and nationals to be tried in foreign or in U.S. courts, and, if in U.S. courts, whether in military or civilian ones.[117]

The Supreme Court decisions captured the attention of Senator Hennings, the legislator who had been most bothered by the jurisdictional problem. Soon after the decision in *Covert* in 1957 a recently appointed investigator for the Constitutional Rights Subcommittee received a staff memorandum referring to the Toth case and saying that the suspect "went unpunished for lack of forum [in which to try him]." After *Covert,* "the question of lack of forum is, as a result of the decision, more alive and more important than it was a year ago." The memorandum suggested that Hennings's bill S. 2791 be redrafted and a new bill introduced, one that would cover civilian dependants as well as veterans. If the Supreme Court was trying to get the attention of Congress, it had succeeded, at least in the case of the chairman of the Constitutional Rights Subcommittee—although not in the way it would have wished. A cover note attached to the memorandum referred to the Supreme Court's "disgraceful opinion or, rather, group of opinions" in *Covert* and *Krueger.*[118]

In April 1958, as the other cases having to do with civilian dependants and employees of the armed forces began to be accepted for review by the Supreme Court, the assistant counsel of the Constitutional Rights Subcommittee prepared a number of memoranda on the relevant cases, and in December 1959 the subcommittee's chief counsel commissioned a report beginning with the *Toth* judgment, running through the *Reid v. Covert* decision of 1957, and describing the remainder of the cases pending in the Supreme Court. Perhaps in an effort to bring pressure to bear on Congress to enact a legislative solution, Hennings intended to draw public attention to the jurisdictional issue by writing an article for a popular magazine.[119] In the event, his death in 1960 prevented him from pursuing the matter.

Meanwhile, on the other side of the Pacific a storm gathered, one that would blow through the yawning gap that still existed in U.S. law a decade after Hennings's death. In 1959 the South Vietnamese government, with which the United States had allied itself, passed a repressive law, no. 10/59, leading to the arrest of tens of thousands of people considered to be Communists and to many executions.[120] Soon after, the Vietnamese Communists began to fight back, launching a guerrilla war in South Vietnam to liberate the country from the Diem regime. They attacked a residential compound in Bien Hoa and killed two American soldiers, part of the U.S. Military Assistance Advisory Group. They were the first of the fifty-eight thousand American uniformed personnel listed on the Vietnam Veterans Memorial killed by enemy action in the conflict.[121]

After *Toth,* whenever an American veteran was accused of a crime committed while he was in military service overseas, the only way to guarantee his prosecution according to U.S. standards and procedures was to pass either a law plugging the jurisdictional gap or a constitutional amendment restoring court-martial jurisdiction over such offenses. In the absence of such a measure, the only alternatives were for the accused veteran to be prosecuted in a foreign court in the country where the alleged crime took place or not to be prosecuted at all. Proponents of bills intended to close the jurisdictional gap repeatedly made this sort of argument in favor of the legislation, but their colleagues were largely unmoved.

The legislators' "hammering at" the exercise of foreign courts' jurisdiction over Girard's crime contrasted with their silence, after the Hennings bill died, over the jurisdictional gap that allowed veterans immunity from prosecution for crimes they committed in host nations or war zones. These contrasting postures show where the legislators' attention, in matters of military justice, was directed. The Supreme Court had ruled against court-martial jurisdiction over cases like Toth's; a substantial body of congressional opinion was against prosecution of active-duty service personnel by foreign courts; the executive branch raised all manner of difficulties in the bills that provided for civilian courts' jurisdiction over veterans' offenses against the UCMJ, if the crimes were committed overseas; and legislators were unable to muster sufficient enthusiasm for a bill closing the jurisdictional gap to vote it out of committee. The warnings voiced during the UCMJ hearings in 1949 about how veterans might get away with murder appeared to have been forgotten.

CHAPTER THREE

"A Very Undesirable Situation"

Sam Ervin and the Constitutional Rights Subcommittee

In January 1961 Sen. Sam Ervin assumed the chairmanship of the Subcommittee on Constitutional Rights of the Senate Judiciary Committee. Although critics of his reasoning and his politics, particularly his defense of racial segregation, have doubted whether his reputation as a defender of the Constitution was entirely deserved, Ervin was known as a leading congressional expert on constitutional matters.[1] From the early days of his senatorial career he had been a ferocious and effective advocate of civil liberties, a critic of governmental abuses of power such as the assertion of executive privilege—stances that allied him with congressional liberals—while also being a leading proponent of a "soft Southern strategy" opposed to civil rights legislation, a position that accorded with that of conservatives, particularly southern Democrats. A hawk regarding Vietnam War policies, he nevertheless defended the right of antiwar protesters to distribute literature on military bases and opposed government surveillance of peace marchers. A law-and-order conservative, he opposed a crime control package that gave the government preventive detention powers and permitted no-knock drug raids. His various positions "defie[d] all the easy generalizations of political journalism."[2] While a member of the Judiciary Committee, Ervin simultaneously sat on the Senate Armed Services Committee and was one of the two members of the Armed Forces Subcommittee that annually reviewed SOFAs.[3] He was a cosponsor of the resolution favoring primary jurisdiction by the United States for overseas offenses committed by its troops.[4] Ervin's convergent committee responsibilities made him the leading advocate in Congress of efforts to revise the UCMJ.

The Constitutional Rights Subcommittee was established to examine the "extent to which the Constitutional rights of the people of the United States were being respected and enforced."[5] Under Hennings's leadership the subcommittee had investigated the legal rights of service personnel.[6] It had sent an observer to the Girard trial in Japan, and, years later, Ervin continued to express the subcommittee's concern about the principles raised in that case. Demonstrating his overriding interest in securing the rights of accused personnel, Ervin worried that servicemen's rights might be "abridged" when they found themselves under the jurisdiction of a foreign government.[7] Ervin had been outraged by instances of command influence over disciplinary hearings, the denial of legal representation to court-martial defendants, and soldiers' receiving less-than-honorable discharges without due process, which he suspected resulted from the military authorities' attempt to circumvent the requirements of the UCMJ.

Ervin had special reason to sympathize with the predicament of accused servicemen. During the First World War, Ervin himself had been relieved of his command and faced the possibility of a court-martial after he lost his nerve during an incident in the trenches of the Western Front. He resigned his commission and reenlisted as a private, later redeeming himself by winning the Distinguished Service Cross for heroism in combat.[8] Ervin continued to champion the cause of servicemen's rights when he assumed the chairmanship of the subcommittee.[9] Over the course of the first dozen years he acted in that role, Ervin's campaign to plug the jurisdictional gap was part of a larger program of reform of the UCMJ.[10]

Ervin proposed measures to ensure that all troops were guaranteed legally trained counsel whenever they were involved in courts-martial or in administrative proceedings that might lead to less-than-honorable discharges. He wished to reduce commanding officers' authority over the choice of court-martial personnel; to establish that an experienced, impartial law officer would preside over major disciplinary actions; and to protect the rights of the accused to confront and cross-examine witnesses.[11]

Ervin called hearings of the Constitutional Rights Subcommittee in 1962 to examine these matters, and while the bulk of the hearings addressed issues of fairness and due process, they also discussed the legislation required to close the jurisdictional gap. The army, navy, and air force all recognized the need for remedial legislation.[12] Soon after the enactment of the UCMJ in 1951, the leading lawyers and jurists charged with administering military justice formed a code committee for the purpose of overseeing the operation of and proposing amendments to the UCMJ. The committee had become convinced during the ten years of operation of the UCMJ that some revision of the code was necessary to bring about the "proper and orderly administration of military justice," without which administration of the code might not withstand the strains of another major war.[13]

The code committee undertook to draft an omnibus bill revising the UCMJ to address these matters all together.[14] In June 1961, soon after Ervin began his chairmanship of the subcommittee, the army drafted legislation that would have closed the jurisdictional gap, sending it to the Department of Justice and the Department of Defense for comment.[15] The navy, whose judge advocates had been more disturbed than the other services about the loss of jurisdiction over civilians after *Covert,* raised the possibility of a constitutional amendment to address that problem—the result of which would presumably have been to reinstate court-martial jurisdiction over nonveteran civilians. The air force, through the Department of Defense, actually drafted a constitutional amendment to fulfill that purpose. None of the services made a similar proposal for a constitutional amendment regarding veteran offenders, and the army, navy, and air force all backed the idea of legislation to vest jurisdiction over veteran offenders in civilian courts for offenses against the UCMJ committed overseas.[16] However, when the code committee broke down the omnibus bill into alphabetically designated components, it was notable that none of them contained language to close the jurisdictional gap.[17] This was an early indication of the political problems obstructing efforts to fix the gap: for the remainder of the sixties the executive branch opposed any specific legislative remedy.

Ervin drafted eighteen bills related to military justice, all intended to address the issues that the hearings in 1962 had deliberated over. He introduced them in the Senate in August 1963, and the following month identical bills were introduced in the House of Representatives.[18] The armed services' code committee, however, preferred its own "G" and "H" bills, and they were subsequently introduced in the House. This began a process in which Ervin consistently proposed his own bills and the armed services, via the code committee, consistently sidestepped them by working with legislators in the House.[19]

Ervin explained the purposes of his bills by referring to shortcomings in the operation of the UCMJ and in the system of administrative discharges and to the improved rights that citizens enjoyed in the civilian justice system, with which, he suggested, military justice should come into line. Now that in its famous *Gideon* ruling the Supreme Court had established the right to counsel as a fundamental right in federal and state courts, Ervin had an additional argument why servicemen should enjoy the same right.[20] His proposals included two bills that would have closed the jurisdictional gap, one covering veteran offenders, the other civilians accompanying the armed forces. Counterpart bills were introduced in the House.[21] Ervin articulated a constitutionalist motive for plugging the jurisdictional loophole by explaining that if a veteran defendant committed a crime overseas, he or she could be extradited to the country where it occurred in order to be tried there—but that the trial would not be subject to the U.S. Constitution and might not furnish some of the procedural safeguards familiar in the U.S. court system. Trying the defendant in a U.S. court would guarantee such protections while also preempting the need to deliver or extradite the defendant to a jurisdiction overseas. Ervin noted that the armed services had studied the problem of how to close the jurisdictional gap but that "somewhere along the line action apparently has bogged down."[22]

Well might Ervin have felt frustrated, as his reference to the action's being "bogged down" implied, and worse was to follow. The code committee said it shared the same "general objective" as Ervin, namely, to improve the administration of justice in the armed forces. However, it continued to recommend the enactment of its own draft legislation, including its "G" and "H" bills, and declined to make any new legislative proposals to fill the jurisdictional void.[23] In their reports on the legislation, only one executive department approved Ervin's bill, and the two that really counted opposed it. The Treasury Department had no objection to one of Ervin's bills, S. 2014, but thought that because crimes like fraud and embezzlement, which might most plausibly go undetected for a period, could be prosecuted under existing law, "the bill's added jurisdiction would be limited in its impact to the rare crime of violence which goes unreported or undetected when it occurs."[24] In contrast, although it recognized the necessity of filling the "jurisdictional loophole" opened up by *Toth*, the Department of Defense and the secretary of the army opposed the bill, explaining that there was insufficient justification for the "difficult and burdensome administrative problems" it would entail.[25] They did not explain why those problems would outweigh the obligation to try veterans for serious crimes for which they had escaped punishment while in the armed forces. The Pentagon recommended that Congress enact the code committee's "G" and "H" bills, which contained no provisions related to the jurisdictional gap.[26] The Department of Justice was opposed to S. 2014 for the same reason as the Pentagon and averred that any necessary prosecutions might be conducted by the countries in which the suspects had been stationed. The department questioned "whether the need for the legislation is of sufficient importance to justify the administrative and financial burden which would result from its enactment."[27] Neither executive department opposed to the bill specified what the burdensome administrative problems were, although Treasury had mentioned the difficulty of conducting investigations in foreign countries in preparation for trials that would be conducted in the United States, and others had pointed out practical problems. For example, in the Senate hearing in 1962 leading up to the drafting of S. 2014, the law professor Kenneth Pye had begun from the premise that the Supreme Court decisions in *Toth* and the later cases having to do with civilians created a "grave hiatus in our pattern of criminal jurisdiction." However, even if remedial legislation was passed, he said, "I do not think there would be many prosecutions, because of the problems of obtaining witnesses, because of the practical logistical problems, and because of the fact that usually we just let these matters rest after a while."[28]

Such problems had been grappled with ever since *Toth* and, as we have seen, had been raised by Justice Reed's dissenting opinion in that case. Nevertheless, Pye came down in favor of the legislation. After all, no matter how great the imaginable problems that might arise in particular cases, it was difficult to see why legislators would wish to rule out the possibility of any prosecutions by declining to pass the remedial legislation. And the "limited impact" and "burdensome problems" arguments tended to contradict one another: if it was thought unlikely there would be a frequent need to prosecute crimes that were undetected until the perpetrator had left military service, the burdensome requirements would accordingly have to be endured equally rarely.

Of all the Judge Advocate General's Corps, the army's early on favored a statute to close the jurisdictional gap. Thomas H. Green, the army judge advocate general, had proposed such a bill in his testimony in 1949, his successor Eugene Caffey had endorsed the proposal in 1955, and the army drafted a bill in 1961. Thereafter, however, all the armed services hesitated to commit to a legislative solution. Once the code committee had heard from the executive branch departments, it put forth no provisions to close the jurisdictional gap among its raft of alphabetically designated draft bills. While the armed services' responses to questionnaires circulated before the subcommittee hearing recognized the need for remedial *legislation* in the abstract, the services' civilian masters evidently drew the line at approving any particular *law*. Nor did they propose an alternative solution to the problem of the jurisdictional gap, as the dissenting Supreme Court justices had contemplated when they said that only a reversal of *Toth* or a constitutional amendment could reinstate court-martial jurisdiction over overseas offenses perpetrated by suspects who had left the armed services. As we have seen, the air force and navy had both, for a time, supported such a constitutional amendment to cover civilians accompanying the armed forces.[29]

Years later the Department of Defense blamed others for opposing the legislation to close the jurisdictional gap since 1960, saying that it had backed the required legislation ever since the relevant Supreme Court decisions but that its first task was to win over the Department of State and the Department of Justice, above all Justice, because there would be an "added burden" on it. Perhaps by then the Pentagon had forgotten its own complaints about the "burdensome administrative problems"; or perhaps its spokesman was hoping everyone else had. While the spokesman may not have assigned the responsibility for opposing the bills with perfect accuracy, his department's institutional memory may yield an insight into the nature of the perceived burden: "They would have the responsibility of doing the prosecution. It is not a burden to be sneered at, because of the problems . . . of obtaining foreign witnesses and so forth." He said these responsibilities would impose on the Justice Department's workload and budget.[30]

In the 1960s the executive departments apparently found it difficult to conceive that American troops would commit offenses in sufficient numbers to make a new law necessary—or at least they professed to believe that. They saw the obligation to conduct investigations in one place and prosecutions in another as an overwhelming burden. Less easy to explain, assuming prosecutions presented this difficulty, is why it would have been administratively inconvenient to pass a law allowing the exercise of political and legal judgment whether any particular prosecution was necessary and in the national interest. Here, one sees evidence of the administration "apathy" about which Ervin complained a few years later; and not just apathy but willful negligence in failing to pass legislation that would have met the obligation to punish violations of the laws and customs of war.

Undeterred, Ervin reintroduced another set of eighteen bills in 1965, including identical legislation to plug the jurisdictional gap opened up by *Toth v. Quarles*. In 1965 the wording of the background memorandum to this bill, S. 761, was identical to that in the memorandum accompanying the 1963 bill, right down to the exasperated reference to the armed services' study of the problem of the jurisdictional gap's becoming "bogged down."[31]

In explaining the benefits of the bills, Ervin referred to President Johnson's call for an improvement in the status of military personnel, saying that in order to be treated as first-class citizens they had to be accorded the same rights, privileges, and protections guaranteed to every American citizen under the Constitution. He drew attention again to inadequacies in the operation of the UCMJ and in administrative discharge proceedings. Focusing on the research that had led up to the drafting of the legislation, Ervin said that in addition to the hearings in 1962 the Subcommittee on Constitutional Rights had conducted extensive field investigation in military establishments in Europe to assess the operation of the military justice system. Despite the vital need for the legislation, Ervin said he was not wedded to any specific language and acknowledged that it might be necessary to revise the wording of some of the measures: all eminently reasonable, but the reasoning was as fruitless in 1965 as it had been in the previous Congress.[32]

If any revision of the UCMJ was to be enacted, there would have to be counterpart bills in the House of Representatives. The armed services exerted their influence through the strongly promilitary House Armed Services Committee, which was amenable to their views about what laws were and were not needed. Rather than simply respond to Ervin's eighteen bills, the Department of Defense and the armed services sought legislative support for the code committee's "G" and "H" bills intended to reform the UCMJ.[33]

The effect of those bills would have been to bring special and general courts-martial procedures more closely in line with those of federal district courts, to enhance the procedural authority of the law officers, full-time legal officers whose role included ensuring due process in courts-martial, and to guarantee defense counsel in special courts martial. Proponents of these bills later referred to them as basic housekeeping measures to improve the operation of the UCMJ.

In November 1964 the armed services' code committee had found a champion for these bills in Rep. Charles E. Bennett of Florida, a Democrat and a resolute supporter of the armed forces who had by then racked up a decade and a half of service in the House Armed Services Committee. He put the armed services' draft bills forward as H.R. 273 and H.R. 277, intended as substitutes for five of Ervin's eighteen bills.[34] Ervin responded by proposing his own alternative versions of the House bills similar in scope to H.R. 273 and H.R. 277. He explained that while there were already eighteen Senate bills under consideration, the new, parallel bills would allow the views of the Department of Defense to be evaluated while efforts were made to resolve the differences between the two sets of proposals.[35] None of the relevant legislation was reported out of committee in the 89th Congress, and Bennett again proposed a version of the Department of Defense–sponsored "G" and "H" bills in 1966.[36] Thereafter, until 1972, when Ervin gave up on his effort to close the jurisdictional gap, Bennett's House bills would form a counterpoint to Ervin's work in the Senate.

To say that the armed services' efforts were designed to preempt or undermine Ervin's efforts would be simplistic; suffice it to say that the services sought to shape events rather than simply to respond to them. Although Bennett's bills did not go as far as Ervin's, they were perfectly respectable legislative proposals that contained various provisions dealing with the role of the law officer and court-martial procedures which paralleled Ervin's proposals.[37] The Senate Judiciary and the House Armed Services Committees agreed to concert their actions on the proposals in the two chambers and held joint hearings on the bills the next year.[38] The House bills won the approbation of the Federal Bar Association and of the American Bar Association's special committee on military justice, which regarded them as addressing the most urgent of the reforms of the UCMJ and preferred them to their Senate counterparts.[39] The Department of Defense also favored them, and it appeared to the armed services that the swiftest way to achieve some of the desired reforms was for the Senate to adopt the House bills' language.[40] In contrast, the armed services failed to propose any legislation that would have achieved the purposes of Ervin's bills to close the jurisdictional gaps. Because of the "burdensome administrative problems" they would impose, the Pentagon opposed Ervin's S. 761 and S. 762, which were identical to S. 2014 and S. 2015, the bills he had proposed in the previous Congress.[41] The code committee's selective drafting of bills, coupled with the Pentagon's established objections to the legislation designed to plug the jurisdictional gaps, indicates the armed services' uncertainty over what to do about the generally acknowledged problem, coupled with their opposition to the solutions Ervin proposed.

Once again, though, a number of individuals and organizations endorsed the bill to close the jurisdictional gap opened up by *Toth*. The American Veterans Committee said, "There is no justification for people accused of crimes to go free without trial, simply because no court has jurisdiction to hear the case."[42] Frederick Bernays Wiener said, "Plainly, S. 761 is desirable legislation; without it, persons committing serious offenses will regularly escape, not on the merits, but because there is no tribunal competent to try them." As he had observed in 1962, "It is a very undesirable situation where a crime can be committed with impunity so that there is nobody to try the person."[43]

The Department of Defense, however, requested that action be deferred on S. 761 and S. 762, the bills that closed the jurisdictional gap affecting, respectively, veterans and civilians accompanying the armed forces. Brig. Gen. Kenneth J. Hodson, the army's assistant judge advocate general for military justice, explained that there was no agreement about a legislative remedy and that the department itself was preparing its own draft bills.[44] However, the air force judge advocate general who accompanied Hodson spoke rather more candidly when he admitted that, insofar as S. 762 was concerned, after various practical and constitutional objections to the department's draft bills, "We are hopeful that we *some day may be able* to come up with some kind of proposed legislation or that somebody else will which will kind of bail us out of a hole on this thing [emphasis added]." The most difficult problem in his view was that of bringing witnesses from overseas to testify in U.S. courts. As he saw things, a constitutional amendment was probably necessary, but that was unlikely, so no solution was in the offing.[45] One can infer that the purpose of the amendment would be to overcome the Supreme Court's rulings in *Covert* and the related cases in order to reinstate jurisdiction over civilians accompanying the armed forces in courts-martial. Ervin responded in colorful but opaque language that the legislature would have to "unscrew the inscrutable" to find a solution to the constitutional problem.[46]

Others testified against S. 761 and S. 762. The president of the Judge Advocates Association approved the principle that a happenstance in status should not affect an individual's liability for punishment for criminal offenses but questioned the constitutionality of the bills.[47] The Federal Bar Association concurred in the objectives of the two bills, seeing the closing of the jurisdictional gaps as "essential," but nevertheless objected to their detailed provisions, especially those in S. 762.[48] Seymour W. Wurfel, like Wiener a retired army judge advocate, drew attention to some practical difficulties as well as to the poor drafting of S. 762, about which several others commented.[49] He was one of a number who testified to the difficulty of compelling witnesses residing overseas to appear in U.S. courts. A further obstacle was the expense of transporting foreign witnesses and U.S. military personnel serving overseas to a court in the United States. There was no obvious solution to such problems, even though they had been contemplated for several years.[50]

The chairman of the New York City Bar Association's subcommittee to amend the UCMJ expressed similar views when asked for his opinion of S. 761 and S. 762. He said he preferred federal district court to court-martial jurisdiction over civilians but thought it was hardly a pressing problem. Overlooking the *Toth* decision and the issue of jurisdiction over veterans, he added that the jurisdictional problem emerged in 1957 with the *Covert* decision: "At that time there was great hue and cry. However, it is now 1966. We seem to have managed without legislation."[51] His opinion ignored the possibility that a particular kind of crime that was not committed yesterday might nevertheless be committed tomorrow; and that one should not await the event in order to enact measures to deal with it, given that there were certain crimes that could not be tried in any U.S. court.

The American Civil Liberties Union (ACLU) argued that if S. 761 was passed, it would allow a suspect to be tried thousands of miles from the scene of the offense. This would create insurmountable problems in the defense's investigation of the facts, preparation of the case, and compelling of witnesses who were still overseas to attend. Few defendants would have the economic means to conduct effective defenses, and the term *due process* would become meaningless. The ACLU acknowledged a jurisdictional hiatus but, it asked, how often was the sort of case the bill contemplated likely to arise? "How compelling is the need to fill the breach?" the ACLU asked. "How many persons would this legislation in reality affect?"[52]

These responses echoed the executive branch's response to the legislation of 1963, which had argued that because the measures proposed by the bills, if enacted, would rarely be used they would have "limited impact." The difference was that in 1966 the United States was engaged in a large-scale shooting war in Vietnam. Given that what transpired in Vietnam is now well known, it is easy to say that the ACLU and the bar association subcommittee chairman showed a lack of imagination about what might happen in war. But even at the time, no one who was paying attention to the news could have missed the potential for legal cases involving civilian casualties arising from the Vietnam War.

The ACLU offered its testimony on March 1, 1966. Two weeks earlier Neil Sheehan reported in the *New York Times* on the "appalling destruction" of South Vietnamese civilian dwellings and their occupants wrought by U.S. artillery, naval gunfire, and aerial napalm attacks.[53] The previous year the *Times* had published Sheehan's report on "ferocious" American naval gunfire and air raids on five prosperous fishing hamlets, attacks which resulted in hundreds of civilian deaths and forced the majority of the inhabitants to flee to areas controlled by the South Vietnamese government.[54] A national television audience had already seen a CBS news broadcast showing U.S. marines conducting a "Zippo raid," using their cigarette lighters to set thatched roofs alight and burn Vietnamese civilians out of their houses.[55] American reporters had observed incidents in which U.S. troops fired on defenseless civilians and made up false pretexts for killing them.[56] By the time of the ACLU testimony, American jet fighter bombers had been bombarding ground targets in South Vietnam for over a year, and 730,000 people had fled into refugee camps as a result of a deliberate strategy to force civilians to move into areas under South Vietnamese government control.[57] To claim at this stage, as the ACLU did, that there was no likelihood that new crimes like Toth's—and worse—might occur showed more than a willful lack of imagination. It betrayed a resolute imperviousness to credible reports of questionable military conduct in Vietnam. The problem Ervin later described as executive and legislative apathy was not, therefore, confined to the legislative and executive branches of government. Apathy and moral blindness were all around.

The effect of the jurisdictional gap in the war in Vietnam was underlined by a congressional report in 1967. In hearings that focused largely on the question of court-martial jurisdiction over civilians accompanying the U.S. armed forces in Vietnam, the committee found that "U.S. military personnel are in no way subject to the jurisdiction of the courts of the Republic of Vietnam [South Vietnam] nor does that Government undertake to exercise jurisdiction over military personnel."[58] Under the terms of the mutual defense treaties into which the United States and South Vietnam had entered in the 1950s, all U.S. troops in Vietnam were regarded as members of the diplomatic mission and accordingly enjoyed diplomatic immunity. These agreements were signed when the United States had only a small force in South Vietnam and were not updated when the troop levels rose into the hundreds of thousands.[59] Whereas the United States had negotiated SOFAs with other allies whose judicial processes it regarded as adequate to try Americans, no such arrangements applied to the client state of South Vietnam—and in any case, SOFA arrangements generally prevailed only in peacetime. The United States never relinquished its jurisdiction over its armed forces in Vietnam.[60] The congressional committee also observed that, as a practical matter, "police and judicial officials of the Republic of Vietnam are apparently reluctant to exercise jurisdiction over any U.S. personnel."[61]

In the same month the subcommittee presented its report, Ervin proposed an Omnibus Military Justice Bill, S. 2009, which, with two notable exceptions, covered the same ground as the eighteen bills he had proposed in the 89th Congress the year before. Having bundled together most of the matters pertinent to the protection of the constitutional rights of military personnel, Ervin separated out the two bills intended to close the jurisdictional gaps. S. 2006 closed the gap opened up by *Toth,* and S. 2007 closed the gap affecting civilians accompanying the armed forces.[62] These two bills, identical to S. 761 and S. 762 introduced in the previous Congress, were referred to the Judiciary Committee and hence to the Constitutional Rights Subcommittee, which Ervin chaired, whereas the omnibus bill went to the Armed Services Committee. One can speculate that the segregation of the bills intended to close the jurisdictional gaps was a tactical measure, one which made it less likely that the seemingly intractable problems identified by their critics would impede the passage of the omnibus bill, but its result was that whereas the omnibus bill progressed through a series of drawn-out negotiations, S. 2006 and S. 2007 remained at a standstill.

One searches in vain throughout the record of the 90th Congress for evidence of a change of heart by any of those who had opined that plugging the jurisdictional gap would serve no useful purpose. By the time Ervin proposed his bills there was, however, mounting international and domestic dismay that American forces in Vietnam were visiting large-scale death and injury on Southeast Asians. Clergy and Laymen Concerned spoke out early in 1967 against the "immorality of the warfare in Vietnam in which civilian casualties are greater than military; in which whole populations are deported against their will; in which the widespread use of napalm and other explosives is killing and maiming women, children, and the aged."[63] An article published in *Ramparts* magazine early in the lifetime of the 90th Congress said there had been at least a million child casualties in South Vietnam since 1961.[64] Sen. Edward Kennedy predicted there would be one hundred thousand civilian casualties in South Vietnam in 1967.[65] Deputy Secretary of Defense Cyrus Vance admitted that U.S. artillery and aircraft made "errors" that caused civilian casualties.[66] On April 4, 1967, three enlisted men murdered a Vietnamese peasant whom their commander suspected of being a Viet Cong guerrilla. At their court-martial they claimed they were following orders, although their commander was acquitted by a jury of fellow officers.[67]

On the same day the murder took place, Martin Luther King Jr. criticized the war in a speech at Riverside Baptist Church in New York, condemning the United States for its "sins and errors" in Vietnam, comparing its conduct of the war to the actions of Germany's leaders in the Second World War, and calling on the nation to atone.[68] Other church people began to articulate their moral criticisms of American policy in Vietnam by decrying the death and injury inflicted on civilians and propounding the idea that the United States was violating the tenets of international justice. A thousand American divinity students wrote to Secretary of Defense Robert McNamara denouncing the war, which they said was neither in the tradition of just wars nor in the national interest.[69]

A nonjudicial international tribunal convened by the British philosopher Bertrand Russell declared that the United States was guilty of the crimes of aggression and of "widespread, deliberate and systematic" bombardment of civilian targets in Vietnam.[70] This finding had no practical judicial effect: the tribunal was not recognized by the United Nations and had no means of enforcing its judgments. Yet the declaration carried moral force: the tribunal served as a forum for the gathering and presentation of facts; the prestige of its sponsors brought international media attention to its proceedings; and its very impotence to enforce its judgments focused attention on the absence of any authoritative international judicial forum in which American policymakers and troops could be held accountable.

The passage of the omnibus bill was a story of compromise that helps illuminate just what it would take to enact a reform of the UCMJ. Ervin, who had seen successive bills with the same goals fail, recognized the pointlessness of proposing measures that ran up against the determined opposition of the armed services. He was aware that the Department of Defense backed the House legislation Bennett proposed, and it appeared at first as though Bennett's proposals would close the jurisdictional gaps—at least until the armed services objected. Bennett introduced a single bill that, among other things, contained measures to close the jurisdictional gaps opened up by *Toth, Covert,* and the other Supreme Court decisions that denied court-martial jurisdiction over civilians.[71] The Department of the Army, responding on behalf of the Department of Defense, said it recognized "the need for a solution to the present lack of jurisdiction in such cases." However, in view of the "lack of consensus" regarding the desirability of the legislation or the form it would take, it requested "that the [House Armed Services] committee defer consideration of this matter pending further study and resolution within the Executive Branch of the issues involved."[72]

Bennett discussed the Pentagon's objections to the bill in detail with the Department of Defense's point man for the legislative negotiations, Kenneth

Hodson, a career officer who had served with the artillery before being trained at the Judge Advocate General School. As the American chairman of the U.S.–Japan Criminal Jurisdiction Committee, he was in post when the Girard case blew up and had therefore been acquainted with the difficult issues of jurisdiction in military-related cases for a decade.[73] As assistant judge advocate general for military justice, Hodson had assured legislators in 1966 that the armed services were drafting legislation to close the jurisdictional gap. In July 1967 Hodson was promoted to judge advocate general of the army at the rank of major general and immediately began to engage in discussions with legislators about the revision of the UCMJ.[74] He proceeded to give new impetus to the armed services' efforts to get a version of their "G" and "H" bills passed. According to Hodson's account, the chief counsel of the House Armed Services Committee, a retired major general of the Marine Corps Reserve, advised him "to get a bill drafted with the noncontroversial housekeeping provisions" in it "but to keep it as short as possible." Hodson said he would send Bennett a new draft bill as soon as it was ready.[75]

This episode is revealing of the degree of influence Hodson had over the legislative process: it is not surprising that the committee's chief counsel should have an opinion on the bill or that he should discuss it with the judge advocate general of the army, but it is striking that he was advising Hodson, not elected officials or their legislative staff, "to get a bill drafted."

Soon after the discussions with Hodson, Bennett introduced a shortened version of the bill from which the provisions related to the jurisdictional gap were stricken; Bennett said the bill "contains the minimum changes in the present law which the Judge Advocate General of the Army felt necessary at this time."[76] This revised bill had the support of the Department of Defense and the armed services, and Hodson spoke in favor of it at both hearings of the House Armed Services Committee.[77] Hodson then demonstrated his support for the revised language by defending the House bill against its few remaining critics.[78] Bennett consulted Hodson when a new idea for the language of the bill was considered, asking for Hodson's opinion about whether or not it should be accomplished and, if so, how.[79] The House Armed Services Committee passed the so-called clean bill, redesignated as H.R. 15971, in May 1968, and the full House passed it the following month.[80]

Ervin thought the revised bill lacked the "minimum reforms necessary in any meaningful military justice legislation," but it had the advantage of having passed the House of Representatives.[81] In contrast, there was "enormous opposition" to Ervin's omnibus bill in the Pentagon.[82] For the purposes of this discussion, the specifics of the disagreements are less important than how the argument developed and was resolved. Because the Pentagon supported the "watered-down" House bill, Ervin believed that bill to be the most promising vehicle for a more extensive reform measure.[83] For their part, Bennett's legislative staff and the Department of Defense saw that they needed to work out a compromise with Ervin because without it Bennett's bill would be "dead in the Senate."[84]

Bennett had asked Richard Russell, the chairman of the Senate Armed Services Committee, to schedule hearings on H.R. 15971.[85] Russell had responded courteously by telling Bennett that his committee had quite a few House-passed bills before it but that he would do his best to schedule consideration of some of them in the current session. This was hardly a firm commitment to hold hearings, and Russell pointedly reminded Bennett that his colleague Ervin, a strong ally in the Democratic Party's southern contingent, had also sponsored legislation in the military justice field and had held hearings on these bills in earlier Congresses. Russell concluded, "I shall talk with him about the possibility of hearings on H.R. 15971."[86] The unmistakable message was that without Ervin's say-so, Bennett's bill was a dead duck. In case there was any misunderstanding, the counsel of Ervin's Constitutional Rights Subcommittee let it be known that Russell would move on the military justice bill "whenever Senator Ervin gave the word."[87]

Rather than attempt to have the Senate pass S. 2009 and then try to work toward a compromise in a House–Senate conference committee, on which the Department of Defense could lower the boom at any time, Ervin attempted to preempt any wrangles and win the Pentagon's support in advance for alterations in the bill. Ervin had asked the judge advocates general of the armed services for their comments and suggestions about his proposals in the summer of 1967, but the negotiation proceeded in earnest after passage of the House bill.[88] Ervin held a number of informal conferences with Hodson to work out a series of compromises.[89] Based on their understandings, he tailored amendments to the bill which were then "carefully studied and discussed by each of the armed services and informally approved by them."[90] Tactically, this was an astute approach and was perhaps the only way Ervin could achieve some of what he wanted. Bennett, however, pleaded with Ervin to accept H.R. 15971 as it stood, saying that by then, the fall of 1968, there was no time to convene a conference committee to reconcile the two versions if the language of the House bill was "greatly amended." Bennett asserted that, while his bill did not go as far as he and Ervin wanted, there was "nothing wrong about it, and nothing more than that will be passed in this Congress." Signing his letter "Your devoted friend," Bennett promised to support further legislation the following year and begged Ervin to "please help!!!"[91]

By September 1968 Ervin had thrashed out all the issues with Hodson and modified or withdrawn some of the amendments he initially proposed. All of the remaining amendments Ervin intended to submit to the Senate Armed

Services Committee had been approved by Hodson.[92] The counsel of the House subcommittee that had approved the bill in May 1968 reported to its members that "Ervin added amendments in areas not directly related to matters that we had considered" and that Bennett, who now had no practical alternative, approved them. The subcommittee chairman did not like the "method of operation" that was forced on the subcommittee, but he could hardly object to the amendments once Bennett declared that he had studied them and recommended that they be approved by the House.[93] Although the bill could have been referred back to the House Armed Services Committee, there was by now little chance to schedule hearings and convene a conference—which, as Ervin told his Senate colleagues, the House committee chairman, L. Mendel Rivers, had declined to do—and Bennett asked the leadership to bring the bill up on the floor and adopt the Senate amendments.[94]

Despite whatever reservations anyone may have had about the results, the compromise bill enjoyed virtually universal support from the organizations that had testified in the hearings in 1962 and 1966, and to that extent it was uncontroversial; some of the rights it accorded defendants had by this time already been recognized by the U.S. Court of Military Appeals.[95] In October 1968 the Senate Armed Services Committee reported favorably on H.R. 15971, and the Senate passed the bill unanimously.[96] After Bennett and Hodson expressed their support for the Senate amendments, the House of Representatives also unanimously accepted the amended H.R. 15971.[97] The Military Justice Act of 1968 became law on the president's signature on October 24, 1968.[98] Enacted as Pub. L. No. 90-632, the act established the Courts of Military Review to review court-martial convictions in cases in which the sentence exceeds one year of confinement, involves the dismissal of a commissioned officer, or results in the punitive discharge of an enlisted person.[99] It further stipulated that the Court of Criminal Appeals may review findings of fact and findings of law and may reduce the sentence, dismiss the charges, or order a new trial.[100] The act expanded on the requirement that the accused have legally qualified counsel and reinforced the independence of the armed services' judiciary from control by line commanders. The armed services' code committee now considered its agenda to have been fulfilled: it said that passage of the Military Justice Act of 1968 "completes the passage of legislation affecting military justice and the U.S. Court of Military Appeals" that the committee had advocated.[101] Ervin disagreed. Although he said that passage of the act was a vital step forward in the reform of military justice, he declared his intention to introduce new legislation early in the next year "to take care of the loopholes."[102]

What the act never set out to do was to plug the jurisdictional gap—and the hurdles Ervin had to jump to ensure the passage of the reforms he advocated help explain why. Lacking the support of the armed services and the Pentagon and absent any counterpart House legislation once Bennett had shortened his bill, S. 2006 and S. 2007 became dead letters. There was no procedural activity on the bills, such as reports or hearings.[103] Their archival bill files are empty of correspondence, save for a letter from the ACLU saying that it wanted to testify about one of the bills.[104]

Although it was irrelevant as a measure to close the jurisdictional gap, the Military Justice Act of 1968 does cast light on the story because it gives a vivid picture of the effort required and the balance of forces involved in passing any bill related to military justice. It reveals that the impetus for the legislation came from the legislative branch, that the White House played no role whatever in pushing the legislation along, and that the armed services exerted so much influence that they were able to block legislative proposals to which they were strongly opposed, such as the House bills that closed the jurisdictional gap. Hodson played a leading role in the drafting of the House legislation and in negotiating with Ervin about its amendment once Ervin realized he needed the armed services' stamp of approval for his revisions, without which they were unlikely to pass. Bennett went along with the compromises Ervin and Hodson negotiated once he saw that, unless Ervin was satisfied, the House legislation would stall in the Senate. The leaders of the legislative efforts in the Senate and House did not act in perfect accord with one another but were able to achieve sufficient cooperation to get some basic reforms passed.

As the Military Justice Act was being debated in Congress, a legislator began a correspondence with Secretary of Defense Clark Clifford. Their exchanges are another telling indication of what Ervin was up against in Congress. Rep. John M. Slack, a Democrat from West Virginia, wrote to Clifford on behalf of Pfc. Charles W. Keenan, a marine convicted by a court-martial of shooting and killing two elderly Vietnamese noncombatants, a man and a woman. The corporal in command of Keenan at the time of the killings had already shot Nguyen Thi Co when he ordered Keenan to "finish her off," even though the wound she had suffered was so serious that she would have died anyway. Keenan complied and a little later also shot and killed her cousin, Nguyen Qua, at point blank range after the corporal had shot the Vietnamese man. Neither of the victims was armed, acting in a suspicious or unusual manner, or giving the marines any reason for concern when the patrol came across them.[105] Slack could not believe Keenan could be convicted of premeditated murder while on patrol and under orders. He called the charge preposterous and demanded instead a commendation for Keenan from the commandant of the Marine Corps and an admission of error on the part of the secretary of defense.[106] The case was noteworthy in three senses: first, it highlighted a legislator's incomprehension of the basics of military law. Keenan's trial, in particular the instruction to the jury, bore out the principle that a serviceman must refuse a clearly illegal order, a legal tenet that had been affirmed by the war crimes tribunals after the Second World War and remained effective in U.S. courts-martial arising from the Vietnam War.[107] Slack's legal illiteracy and his strong resistance to prosecuting an American infantryman, even one with blood on his hands, was bound to be an obstacle for anyone hoping to win his vote, or those of legislators with similar views, to help pass military justice legislation allowing the prosecution of Americans charged with crimes committed while they served in or accompanied the armed forces. Second, the court-martial jury (or panel) in the case took account of military conditions in Vietnam and yet did not accept them as mitigation.[108] Finally, the judicial aftermath was a harbinger of the reduction in sentences that troops convicted of war crimes could often expect. Keenan's life sentence was reduced by the convening authority to twenty-five years; after appellate review, one of the convictions was dismissed and the remaining sentence reduced to five years. Clemency action further reduced Keenan's confinement to two years and nine months.[109] As we shall see, this degree of leniency in a case of a U.S. serviceman convicted of the premeditated murder of Vietnamese civilians was not exceptional.

The Military Justice Act took effect shortly before the presidential and congressional elections of 1968. Bennett and Ervin were both reelected. Ervin stood on a conservative anticrime position that hardly differed from that of the Republican presidential candidate, Richard Nixon. It included the goal of overturning the Supreme Court's decision in the *Miranda* case, signaling that his position on procedural protections for suspects and defendants was by no means an absolutist one.[110] Bennett had told Ervin that H.R. 15971 was the best that could have been achieved during the 90th Congress but said that "from 1969 forward you would expect me to cooperate with you to bring about much other [*sic*] needed reforms" to military justice.[111] True to his word, almost as soon as the new Congress began its first session Bennett resumed his efforts to plug the jurisdictional gap by proposing H.R. 4225, a bill intended to achieve that purpose.[112] Bennett reminded the Armed Services Committee chairman Rivers that it was now eighteen months since the Department of Defense had asked Bennett to remove the provisions related to the jurisdictional gap from his previous bills so as to allow the armed services time to prepare their own draft bill, and that it was time for the Pentagon to come through. He asked that Rivers request departmental reports on H.R. 4225 "to determine whether the [controversial] issues have been resolved or are at least being studied and whether the Congress should act. Based upon the limited information I have at hand, I feel action should be taken immediately by the Congress to fill the jurisdictional gaps that now exist."[113] Rivers accordingly referred H.R. 4225 to the Department of Defense and the Department of Justice for reports.[114] In a sign that the executive departments in the Nixon administration were no more enthusiastic about the legislative proposals to close the jurisdictional gap than the Johnson administration had been, they issued no such reports throughout 1969.

Despite his stated intention to close the loopholes in military justice, Ervin did not propose a new bill relevant to the jurisdictional gap for most of 1969. Perhaps he was exhausted by his efforts to pass the omnibus law the previous year; perhaps he was biding his time while observing how H.R. 4225 fared. Ervin always had a full legislative agenda and was pursuing a number of other issues in 1969, so it may be he was simply occupied by these other calls on his attention.[115] Be that as it may, before the year had ended the lacuna in the legislation assumed a new and unmistakable magnitude as a result of a train of events that originated in the massacre at My Lai.

CHAPTER FOUR

"Uncharted Legal Waters"

The My Lai Massacre and the Jordan Memorandum

In the spring of 1969 a Vietnam veteran named Ronald Ridenhour acted on some painful knowledge that had been weighing heavily on his conscience: while he was still in Vietnam some of his fellow soldiers had told him of the massacre of a whole village. He was aware of incidents in which villagers had been killed in twos and threes, but this was different. Initially disbelieving, he made a point of questioning his service buddies and acquaintances while in Vietnam until he was certain in his own mind that a large-scale atrocity had taken place, and he continued his inquiries with fellow veterans once in the United States. Ridenhour decided to reveal what he learned, and he turned out to be an unusually eloquent and effective witness. His report not only divulged that a crime had taken place and prompted an investigation and legal proceedings against certain suspects; it also validated the long-held fears that in the absence of legislation closing the jurisdictional gap perpetrators who had left the armed forces could literally get away with murder.

The massacre of which Ridenhour had learned took place on March 16, 1968, when Task Force Barker, a unit of the Americal Division, attacked the village of Son My, located near the coast of Quang Ngai province.[1] The plan was to surprise the 48th Viet Cong Local Force Battalion, a unit that had fought the South Vietnamese and the Americans tenaciously during the previous three years, in one of their village strongholds.[2]

Task Force Barker, commanded by Lt. Col. Frank A. Barker, consisted of three companies.[3] Charlie Company's target in the first phase of the operation was a place the Americans identified as My Lai (4), a subhamlet of Son My. The majority of the killings took place in My Lai (4). Elements of Bravo Company entered another hamlet marked on maps as My Khe (4), as part of the operation directed at the nearby My Lai (1), which was reputed to be the Viet Cong stronghold. A second massacre took place at My Khe (4). Alpha Company acted as a blocking force and took little direct part in the killings that day.

The day before the attack, Barker addressed the gathered troops, telling them he wanted all the buildings in the Son My area burned, the foodstuffs destroyed, and the livestock killed.[4] The army's review of the massacre, the Peers Inquiry, later found that these orders "were clearly illegal" and conveyed to a sizable number of the soldiers engaged in the assault that everyone in the village was the enemy and that the enemy was to be destroyed. The orders were repeated in briefings by the commanders of Bravo and Charlie Companies and "in that context were also illegal."[5] The assault on My Lai (4) began with preparatory artillery fire, delivered without warning. When the villagers heard the artillery striking, most of them fled to bunkers, although some remained in their houses.[6] Helicopter gunships attacked the subhamlet with rockets and machine-gun fire, and the door gunners of the helicopters airlifting the troops to My Lai (4) shot up the tree lines surrounding the landing zone.[7]

Several helicopter lifts brought Charlie Company onto the landing zone. Before entering My Lai (4), the soldiers killed several Vietnamese fleeing the area. The Viet Cong battalion they sought was not present, however. As the Peers Inquiry found, "No resistance was encountered at this time or later in the day."[8] As 1st and 2nd Platoons of Charlie Company entered My Lai (4) and approached its houses, they broke into smaller units: squads and even smaller groups consisting of just a few men. Members of the two platoons intermingled rather than remaining with their units.[9] Because of the vegetation that separated groups of houses from each other, the various groups were often out of eyesight of one another and were acting to a large extent independently of one another.[10] Members of both platoons roved through the village and killed everyone they encountered, from the very young to the very old. In parts of the village the killings were organized and systematic; elsewhere the soldiers ran wild. Some of the GIs raped or gang-raped women and girls, sexually mutilated several of the victims, and mutilated other corpses. The troops burned the houses by lighting their thatched roofs. They planted dynamite and other explosives to destroy brick buildings and threw animals they had killed down wells in order to pollute the water supply.[11]

Some of the villagers hid in bunkers and were killed by grenades; others were shot or stabbed to death in their houses or on pathways as they tried to escape. In at least three places, groups of five to ten villagers were gathered and shot on the spot. Most of the villagers knew better than to run, as they were aware that the Americans fired on those who ran away.[12]

Lt. William Calley, the commander of 1st Platoon, instructed his soldiers to round up and guard large groups of villagers. One such group consisted of several dozen villagers whom the Peers Inquiry later estimated to number between twenty and fifty people. After leaving the scene for a few minutes, Calley returned and told the soldiers he wanted the Vietnamese people dead. The troops fired their automatic weapons at the group, killing them all.[13] Members of Calley's platoon gathered another group of about seventy to eighty Vietnamese, almost exclusively women and children, near one of the two canals skirting My Lai (4). They were quiet and obeyed the Americans' instructions.[14] Calley directed several groups of villagers into the canal and ordered each group in turn to be shot and hand-grenaded, shooting a number himself. The dead included infants. Calley had by then come to the conclusion that all Vietnamese people were enemies and that even the babies were Viet Cong or would be in a few years' time.[15] A soldier named Michael Terry was passing by just as the shooting started. "They had them in a group," he said, "standing over a ditch—just like a Nazi-type thing."[16]

Calley was not the only platoon commander in My Lai (4). Lt. Stephen Brooks, the commander of 2nd Platoon, was also there and ordered his men to kill unarmed civilians. Brooks ordered Varnado Simpson, a rifleman in the 2nd Platoon's third squad, to shoot a woman. When Simpson turned over her corpse he found that she was carrying a small child, whom the bullets had also killed. At that point, in Simpson's words, "I just went." He roamed around the village and killed some two dozen of its inhabitants, scalping and mutilating some of them.[17] Brooks and his men in the 2nd Platoon in the northern part of My Lai (4) systematically ransacked the subhamlet, slaughtered the population, and killed the livestock.[18] As Richard Hammer writes, Brooks's platoon "did no less than Calley's," and Brooks himself was "no laggard in joining them," although he could not be tried, as Calley eventually was, because he was killed later in his tour of duty in Vietnam.[19] The Peers investigation found that Charlie Company's 2nd Platoon was responsible for killing up to a hundred civilians, almost as many deaths as it attributed to 1st Platoon.[20] None of 2nd Platoon's killings resulted from the actions or orders of Lieutenant Calley. After Calley's and Brooks's platoons had gone through the village, 3rd Platoon, led by Lt. Geoffrey LaCross, "mopped up." Its rifle squads killed most of the remaining Vietnamese people they encountered.[21] In effect, not just Calley's but all three of Charlie Company's platoons were responsible for the deliberate killing of civilians in My Lai.

While Charlie Company was assaulting My Lai (4), Bravo Company was moving toward its objective of My Lai (1), the subhamlet thought to be the headquarters and hospital area of the 48th Viet Cong Battalion. However, My Lai (1) was heavily guarded by mines and booby traps, and Bravo Company's 2nd Platoon suffered several casualties as a result of explosions. The platoon commander, 1st Lt. Roy B. Cochran, was killed by the first of the mines. The surviving GIs refused to continue with their assault on My Lai (1), and Barker called off the attack. First Platoon, commanded by 1st Lt. Thomas Willingham, pressed on with its attack on My Khe (4), initially sending mortar shells into the subhamlet, several of which turned out to be duds. The troops then used an M-60 machine gun to shoot into My Khe (4), killing dozens of civilians. Some of the soldiers later claimed they had been shot at and that, on a trail near My Lai (1), one or two hand grenades had been thrown at them, but they suffered no casualties. The hand grenade or grenades did not explode and could not be found; rifle squad leaders did not recall receiving any fire.[22] The story of incoming fire may have been a fabrication intended to mitigate any accusations that the soldiers had attacked My Khe (4) and caused numerous civilian deaths without provocation or military purpose. It is also possible that some troops mistook the sound of rifle shots from Charlie Company and bullets landing in Bravo Company's area as sniper fire. The troops then approached the subhamlet, and the lead squad opened fire with an M-60 machine gun and M-16 automatic rifles when they were about seventy-five to one hundred yards away. Inhabitants, mostly women and children, "were cut down as they ran for shelter or attempted to flee."[23] The men of Bravo Company's 1st Platoon then entered the subhamlet, machine-gunning its inhabitants, mostly women, children, and elderly men, at close quarters, just as the troops of Charlie Company had done at My Lai (4). One said later, "We were out there . . . having a good time. It was sort of like being in a shooting gallery." A helicopter flew in extra supplies of dynamite and TNT, and the men of 1st Platoon used it to destroy dozens of houses as well as tunnels and bunkers, some with people inside them. A soldier said, "We just flattened that village, and that was it." A Vietnamese survivor said that the troops killed ninety to one hundred inhabitants.[24] When the deaths were reported by Bravo Company, the Task Force Barker logs recorded thirty-eight Vietnamese dead, none of whom were said to be women or children.[25] First Platoon captured no weapons and suffered no casualties, and there were no indications that the platoon was engaging an enemy force. These circumstances should have prompted inquiries from higher headquarters, but apparently none was made.[26] Knowledge of the massacre was held close by members of Bravo Company, and talk of it soon died out. As Peers reports, "It was an almost total coverup."[27]

Charlie Company's killings at My Lai (4) were also covered up successfully until Ridenhour made his complaint. The combat action report Barker submitted on March 28, 1968, was misleading in suggesting that there had been return fire from a substantial enemy force at My Lai (4). Nevertheless, the report should have alerted Barker's superiors to the possibility that Charlie Company had caused an unusual number of civilian casualties: Charlie Company had supposedly inflicted 128 "enemy losses" but had captured only three weapons and had suffered one casualty, from a self-inflicted wound.[28] Maj.

Gen. Samuel Koster and his assistant Brig. Gen. George Young of the Americal Division were informed of the killing of civilians and should have reported the matter to Military Assistance Command, Vietnam (MACV) and conducted an official investigation but did not take these actions.

In late March 1968 Koster ordered Col. Oran Henderson, the commander of the 11th Infantry Brigade, to whom Barker reported, to conduct an investigation into possible civilian deaths. Having heard of complaints about a "bloodbath" from Warrant Officer Hugh Thompson, a helicopter pilot who had been flying above My Lai during the operation (and who was responsible for rescuing a number of Vietnamese civilians from attack), Henderson had questioned some of the men in Charlie Company on March 16, 1968, the day of the incident, and had found no evidence of excessive civilian deaths. His later investigation also appears to have been perfunctory and turned up no evidence of wrongdoing.[29]

Henderson claimed that the civilian casualties had resulted from cross fire between the Viet Cong defenders of the village and the American soldiers and from "preparatory fires" by artillery and helicopter gunships; the log of the 61st Artillery Battalion was stripped of its pages covering March 16, 1968, in an apparent attempt to conceal relevant evidence. Records in several locations, at the divisional, task force, province, and district levels, disappeared as well.[30] Interviews Henderson said he conducted with Barker and other officers in Task Force Barker revealed that "at no time were any civilians gathered together and killed by US soldiers." His report makes no mention, though, of Thompson's eyewitness allegations about the mass killing of civilians.[31]

No brigade, divisional, or MACV officers showed any determination to pursue the facts about civilian casualties. Although the discrepancy between the number of alleged enemies killed in action and the number of weapons captured should have set off alarm bells, the MACV commander, Gen. William Westmoreland, was delighted by the operation.[32] Impressed by the high body count Charlie Company had achieved, Westmoreland congratulated them for an "outstanding action" that had dealt the enemy a "heavy blow."[33] For their part, Americal Division commanders were more interested in sending on favorable reports about their operations than in asking awkward questions about civilian deaths.[34] They appear to have been following the "mere gook rule": "If he's dead and Vietnamese, he's Viet Cong."[35] The Peers Inquiry found that "within the Americal Division, at every command level from company to division, actions were taken or omitted which together effectively concealed from higher headquarters the events which transpired in TF Barker's operation of 16–19 March 1968."[36] Peers also commented, "People were apparently so interested in favorable reports that they sometimes overlooked the obvious and failed to check into questionable reports from subordinate commands. . . .

Only a few . . . seemed to care that Vietnamese noncombatants (women, children, and old men) had been killed."[37] The cover-up succeeded in concealing the events for over a year.

On March 29, 1969, Ridenhour wrote letters to President Nixon, Secretary of Defense Melvin Laird, the chairman of the Joint Chiefs of Staff, and numerous senators and congressmen informing them of a massacre of Vietnamese civilians in a place he knew as Pinkville (the name his fellow soldiers called it because of its color on U.S. military maps), a few miles north of Quang Ngai city in the province of the same name.[38] Other veterans had written to elected officials with denunciations of the illegality of the war, but their complaints were usually dismissed. This letter was detailed, factual, and authoritative; it had the ring of truth. Rep. Morris Udall, a Democrat from Arizona and a member of the House Armed Services Committee, asked permission to circulate it to his committee colleagues and pressured Chairman Rivers to request an investigation.[39] Rivers asked the Department of the Army to carry it out.[40]

Ridenhour's letter was already circulating in the higher reaches of the Pentagon. Gen. Earle Wheeler, the chairman of the Joint Chiefs of Staff, forwarded it to Westmoreland, until recently the commander of U.S. ground forces in Vietnam and now the army's chief of staff, who ordered an inquiry. The Office of the Inspector General (IG) began to investigate the allegations of a massacre less than two weeks after Ridenhour sent his letter, and during the summer of 1969 investigators interviewed some three dozen troops and officers of Task Force Barker. The IG investigator established that there was credible evidence of numerous unlawful killings and recommended that the Criminal Investigation Division (CID) take over the investigation. On August 6 the White House was informed that the testimony confirmed that an atrocity had taken place at Son My, and then Sen. John Stennis, Sen. Barry Goldwater, Sen. Edward Brooke, and Rep. Rivers were briefed about the progress of the investigation. The CID conducted sixty additional interviews between August and November 1969.[41]

By September 1969 the CID had gathered sufficient evidence to charge Calley with premeditated murder.[42] In an unusual move with respect to an ongoing investigation, army representatives continued to brief the House Armed Services Committee counsel and select congressional leaders about its progress.[43] The government was all too aware of the potential political repercussions of the disclosure of the crime. A White House aide gave the president a detailed report on the progress of the CID investigation just before the charges were preferred against Calley. Anticipating a court-martial, he warned, "Publicity attendant upon such a trial could prove acutely embarrassing to the United States."[44] The White House and the Pentagon set out to adopt a joint approach to dealing with the media.[45]

How long the government intended to hush up the legal proceedings is not clear, but the announcement of the charges against Calley was cryptic. The officially worded release downplayed the crime, giving no indication of its scale. Officials at the Defense Department braced themselves for a barrage of questions from the media, but none came.[46] The announcement was treated as a routine news story, and reports were buried in the inside pages of most newspapers, except for those in Georgia, where Calley was confined, which gave it more prominence.[47] No further stories were published for the next two months, until November 1969.[48]

Although the investigation and the charges against Calley received little publicity at first, a number of newspapers had reporters working on the story. On November 12, 1969, two papers, the *Alabama Journal* and the *Detroit News*, published reports of the investigation of Calley's role in the deaths of around one hundred Vietnamese civilians.[49] The following day Dispatch News Service fed the account of the massacre by the investigative reporter Seymour Hersh to the *Chicago Sun Times* and some thirty other newspapers. The story was also reported on the front pages of the *New York Times* and the *Washington Post*. The army announced that a second member of Charlie Company, S.Sgt. David Mitchell, had been charged in the incident, and it emerged that he had been a squad leader in Calley's platoon.[50] Then came a flood of further revelations.

Photographs of the massacre shocked the public into fuller awareness. An army reporter, Jay Roberts, and a combat photographer, Ron Haeberle, had documented the attack on My Lai (4) and, along with the official black-and-white photographs of a routine operation, Haeberle had used his own camera, loaded with color film, to take photographs of numerous women, children, and old men the soldiers had killed. To ensure that the photographs could not serve as evidence against any individual, Haeberle made a point later of destroying all those that showed any American in an act of violence.[51] Although Haeberle therefore became an incidental participant in the cover-up, his photographs ultimately brought the horror of the massacre home to the American public. On November 20, 1969, the *Cleveland Plain Dealer* published some of the photographs on its front page, CBS News showed the paper's photo spread as the lead item of its nightly news broadcast, and Hersh's interviews with eyewitnesses to the massacre were published.[52]

Once the media blew open the news of the massacre, Nixon asked National Security Adviser Henry Kissinger to make sure both that the Defense Department had a "game plan" to deal with the repercussions and that the White House and the Pentagon could concert themselves around some "unified line." Defense Secretary Laird said that Haeberle's pictures were "pretty terrible" and admitted that, if he could, he would find some way to "sweep the whole thing under the rug." The photographs, however, belonged to Haeberle and could not be impounded, and, besides, they had already been published.[53]

Shortly thereafter, the general court-martial convening authority announced that Calley was being prosecuted for the murder of at least 109 Vietnamese civilians.[54] A special CID task force was established to expedite the investigation already under way.[55] The first public statement by a high-ranking official of the administration came when Secretary Laird said he was "shocked and sick" when he first heard about the killings.[56] H. R. Haldeman, the White House chief of staff, advocated the establishment of a "My Lai planning group to figure out how best to control the whole problem—which is, as of now, pretty well out of hand."[57]

Because of the year-long cover-up, most of the members of Charlie Company had left the armed forces, and the Department of Defense contemplated how it might be able to prosecute the perpetrators of the My Lai massacre who were no longer in uniform. According to one theory, the department could recall to active duty anyone who still had a connection to the military, for example, because they were in the inactive Reserves or because they were receiving a military pension. Unnamed Pentagon officials had decided, though, that this would be a bad policy and determined that all those who had left active duty would be treated alike. The reporter to whom these officials spoke wrote, "Unless a way can be found to try all who appear culpable, none will be tried."[58] The personnel who were still in the armed forces presented no such quandary because they could be tried by court-martial; the question was, in what forum could the government try those who had returned to civilian life?

In late November 1969 the army general counsel, Robert E. Jordan III, appearing on all three television networks, held a press conference to announce the findings to date of the CID investigation.[59] He said that a small group of Americans had shot many Vietnamese civilians, possibly as many as 100, although the press reported that the number might be considerably higher: the Vietnamese survivors of the massacre said that 587 of their fellow inhabitants of Son My had been killed. Jordan revealed who was currently being investigated: eleven servicemen who were still serving in the army and about fifteen former soldiers. He explained the legal complexities of the UCMJ, including the problems involved in prosecuting former servicemen. Jordan referred to the "kind of uncharted legal waters" the government would be entering.[60] By January 22, 1970, the number of suspects had increased to fourteen serving soldiers and nineteen former servicemen.[61] By February 4 the number of veterans suspected of having committed war crimes at Son My had increased to twenty-two, all former enlisted men.[62]

Along with Secretary of the Army Stanley Resor and Maj. Gen. Richard G. Stilwell, the deputy chief of staff for operations, Jordan briefed members of the Senate Armed Services Committee on November 26. On the same day, Resor also briefed the House Armed Services subcommittee convened to investigate the massacre, and Rivers brought together the full House Armed Services Committee to hold the first of four hearings in executive session on My Lai.[63] Resor led the elected representatives through the basic facts of the massacre, telling them how it had come to the attention of the army and how the investigation had progressed from that point on. Resor said the event was "wholly unrepresentative" of the conduct of the armed forces in Vietnam and that the troops operated under detailed directives prohibiting them from killing unarmed noncombatants. The overall record of the troops with regard to Vietnamese civilians, he proposed, was one of "decency, consideration, and restraint."[64]

The politicians he briefed, some of them Second World War veterans familiar with the horrors of combat, saw Haeberle's slides of the massacre and afterward declared themselves to be shocked and dismayed. Senator Stennis, chairman of the Senate Armed Services Committee and a determined war hawk, said, "War is war, and it's a rough go. Sherman said war is hell and that's about as good a description as you can find. But these were civilians—and women and children too." His fellow Democratic Party senator Daniel Inouye of Hawaii, who lost an arm in combat in the Second World War, said, "I thought I would be hardened, but I must say I am a bit sickened."[65] Rep. Leslie C. Arends, a senior Republican from Illinois first elected in 1934, left the equivalent House briefing complaining that the pictures were "pretty gruesome." The congressman explained, "That's why I walked out. I have one of those queasy stomachs."[66]

During the intense discussions that day representatives of the Defense, State, and Justice Departments and the acting judge advocate general of the army met to discuss whether there was a way, consistent with the requirements of the Constitution, to prosecute the former servicemen; they promised to let the Department of the Army know within a week whether they would support the army's plan to assert jurisdiction over the veterans suspected of committing war crimes.[67] The solution they contemplated was to ask President Nixon, as commander in chief, to invoke existing law and the inherent constitutional power of the presidency to create military commissions or tribunals.[68] This course of action was not without constitutional difficulties, however, and legal scholars continue to challenge the idea that the president has any such inherent powers.[69] The question of presidential powers could have been rendered irrelevant by having Congress pass a law authorizing the creation of a military tribunal for the purpose of prosecuting the veterans (as Congress did decades later in passing the Military Commissions Act to prosecute "unlawful enemy combatants" fighting for or with the Taliban and Al Qaeda). There is no evidence that anyone in the government advocated such a step and little likelihood, given the legislative record I have chronicled, that Congress would have voted to approve such a measure.[70]

Senator Ervin proposed a different legislative solution. On December 1, 1969, a few days after Jordan briefed members of Congress, Ervin introduced S. 3188 and S. 3189, bills intended, respectively, to plug the jurisdictional gap affecting veterans and the one affecting civilians accompanying the armed forces.[71] Ervin reminded Laird of the assistance the Department of Defense had lent to his previous legislative efforts but pointed out that no satisfactory solution had yet been found. He appealed for Laird's support.[72]

Ervin declared on the Senate floor that the My Lai massacre had prompted him to propose these bills again. As he said, "Recent disclosures of the alleged killing of Vietnamese civilians by American forces in the village of My Lai have brought to public attention once more a serious problem of jurisdiction which has existed since 1955. At present, there is no apparent jurisdiction in any American court, either State, Federal, or military, to try offenses committed by former U.S. servicemen while they were in military status." Ervin summarized the legislative efforts to close the jurisdictional gap and said that the Constitutional Rights Subcommittee had wrestled with the problem for years and had tried, along with the Departments of Justice, Defense, and State, to fashion a satisfactory legislative solution.[73]

This statement put the most favorable gloss on things: Ervin might more accurately have said that the three executive departments had paid lip service to the need to find a legislative solution but that for a decade, if there was any wrestling going on, it was between the chairman of the Constitutional Rights Subcommittee and the executive branch, and he had never managed to pin the departments down to agree on any specific language. But Ervin was trying to rally his fellow legislators at a time when it seemed to him that the massacre must surely have tipped the nation's conscience into action. "Now it is apparent," he said, "that the issue is very critical. The My Lai incident poses this problem in glaring terms."[74] Accordingly, Ervin wrote to the three executive departments to obtain their "present thinking." The press reported his renewed combative mood: Ervin "wanted to know what the Defense, Justice and State departments proposed to do about the 14-year-old gap in military law that has left the government with no court in which to try former servicemen who might be accused of atrocities in Vietnam."[75] He said he would wait for responses from the executive branch before deciding whether to hold hearings on his bills, which had "gone nowhere in past sessions."[76] He did not need to spell out why new thinking on the subject was required. The *Congressional Record* reproduced the departmental response to S. 761, proposed in the previous Congress, which opposed the bill because of the "burdensome administrative problems" it would pose.[77]

S. 761, the bill Ervin had proposed in the 89th Congress to close the jurisdictional gap opened up by *Toth*, had been controversial enough. Its replacement in the 90th Congress, S. 3188, had another crucial feature that Ervin downplayed in his remarks to his Senate colleagues but that was included in the press release his office issued, namely, the bill no longer contained the restriction that would make the legislation apply only to future offenses, ones committed after the enactment of the law.[78] This aspect of the bill opened up a whole new area of controversy. Ervin presented the matter to legislators as though it were an open question. "Whether the legislation, if enacted," he said, "should or properly could be made retroactive to cover prior offenses is only one of the many very difficult questions which must be resolved."[79]

Was it the constitutional problem of retrospective jurisdiction that persuaded Ervin to skirt the issue?[80] Or was it the more immediate legal and political question about whether the My Lai veterans should be prosecuted, which must have been part of the bill's purpose in vesting retrospective jurisdiction in the federal courts? Either issue on its own posed problems, but evidently the combination of a complex constitutional problem with a legal–political one was sufficient to make Ervin bring up the matter obliquely.

There was considerable room for debate on the matter: some held that the prohibition against ex post facto laws applied only to the creation of new crimes, not to establishing the power of courts to try existing crimes; but there was sufficient uncertainty to raise serious questions about whether the My Lai veterans might come under the scope of S. 3188, should it be passed.[81]

The day after Ervin introduced S. 3188 and S. 3189 Jordan wrote a memorandum to William Rehnquist, who at that time, three years before his elevation to the federal bench, was assistant attorney general in the Office of Legal Counsel. This role has been termed "the president's lawyer's lawyer."[82]Among other things, the Office of Legal Counsel renders opinions on the constitutionality of the administration's actions and policies.[83] By writing to Rehnquist, Jordan was communicating with the executive department that would take the lead in any decision about the prosecution of former servicemen. In the memorandum, Jordan laid out how the former servicemen who were suspects in the My Lai massacre might be prosecuted. The memorandum is important because it reflects the thinking of a high-ranking government lawyer on the possibility of prosecuting the My Lai veterans and demonstrates that there was a serious proposal in the upper echelons of the Pentagon to enable such prosecutions. Jordan recalled years later that he "hammered out the legal issues" with Rehnquist. Jordan's statement "Bill Rehnquist and I worked on this" refers to conversations before and after he wrote the memo, including a flurry of talks between November 6 and 14, and a meeting on December 19 attended by Jordan, Rehnquist, legal representatives of the Defense and State Departments, and someone Rehnquist's diary describes as a "two-star general," presumably Hodson.[84]

By sending the memo Jordan was going through the correct departmental channels to reach the attorney general, John Mitchell, who had enormous respect for Rehnquist's legal acumen.[85] Mitchell had a strong personal connection to the president, founded in their membership in the same law firm in the 1960s and in Mitchell's service as manager of Nixon's presidential campaign in 1968, a role he would repeat four years later. John Dean, the White House counsel, called Mitchell Nixon's "most intimate adviser."[86]

The memorandum follows the line of reasoning reportedly devised by "Pentagon legal sources," presumably Jordan himself.[87] Jordan and his colleagues at the Defense Department gave the press detailed briefings about the memo's arguments and recommendations. A well-informed story in the *Washington Star* reported that the army was about to send the Justice Department a memorandum laying out possible approaches to prosecuting the My Lai veterans. Demonstrating a level of knowledge that goes beyond the content of the Jordan memorandum itself, it disclosed some of the alternative means of prosecution that army lawyers had considered—extraditing the suspects for trial in Vietnam, prosecuting them at courts-martial on the grounds that the veterans' reserve status meant they were not truly civilians, and trying them in regular civilian courts—before Jordan settled on the recommendation to convene a military commission.[88] Other Defense Department press briefings included detailed accounts by the Pentagon spokesman Jerry Friedheim of the constitutional problems and the relevant Supreme Court precedents.[89]

Jordan begins by setting out the basic facts of the massacre and saying that charges were being lodged against two individuals. He then explains the constitutional problem arising from *Toth v. Quarles*. Moreover, he establishes that there was no statutory authority allowing the recall of any former servicemen in the Reserves for the purpose of subjecting them to military jurisdiction.[90] Nor was there a federal statute that made their alleged conduct a crime punishable in the civilian courts, and the federal courts possessed no common law jurisdiction.[91]

Hence the question was, What law could the veteran suspects be accused of violating? There were two plausible answers: first, they could be charged with a violation of one or both of the Geneva Conventions governing the treatment of civilians in wartime and prisoners of war. An obvious objection to this approach was that statutory authority would still be required for the purposes of a prosecution, as the Geneva Conventions, which required legislative enactments in order to be enforced, were not self-executing. The other solution was to try the suspects under the power granted to Congress to define and punish offenses against the law of nations and thereby to provide for the prosecution of violations of the law of war.[92]

As a part of the law of nations, the law of war is a combination of treaty obligations and the custom and practices of states, which gradually obtained universal recognition and formed the basis for the general principles of justice applied by jurists and practiced by military courts.[93] Article 6 of the Charter of the Nuremberg Tribunal states that soldiers would be held individually responsible for war crimes in violation of the laws and customs of war.[94] As Jordan acknowledges, the intentional killing of noncombatants within the custody of a belligerent had been recognized as a criminal act contrary to the customs of war. He explains that whether or not the conflict in Vietnam was considered an international armed conflict, a determination which would decide whether the inhabitants of Son My were "protected persons" within the meaning of the Geneva Conventions, the killing of the civilians at My Lai would constitute an offense against the law of war.[95]

Jordan proposes that existing statutory authority would allow the president to convene a military tribunal or commission to prosecute a suspect for a violation of the law of war. According to Jordan's theory, Congress did not need to pass a law authorizing the formation of such a tribunal or commission to try the My Lai veterans because the statutory authority for such prosecutions already existed in the UCMJ.[96] Jordan thus finessed the question of whether the president's war power or any other implied or inherent power under the Constitution allowed him to convene a military commission or tribunal to try the My Lai veterans: according to Jordan, Congress had approved the president's power to convene military commissions through the enactment of the UCMJ, whose Articles 18 and 21, respectively, give a general court-martial jurisdiction to prosecute offenses against the law of war and provide for concurrent jurisdiction by military commissions.[97] According to Jordan, these articles therefore brought the provisions of the law of war into American domestic law and gave the president statutory authority, without further congressional enactment, to convene a military commission or tribunal to exercise jurisdiction over offenses against the law of war.[98] Constitutionally, such a body would exist neither through the grant of powers to the courts under Article III of the Constitution nor solely under the president's war powers and authority as commander in chief of the armed forces, but under the Article I powers of Congress to "make rules for the government and regulation of the land and naval forces," to "discipline" the militia, and to "define and punish . . . Offenses against the Law of Nations."[99]

The Nixon administration might, according to Jordan's theory, have created a tribunal or commission, taken steps toward the prosecution of the veteran suspects in the My Lai massacre in anticipation of a legal challenge, and, in response to any such challenges by the accused, allowed the courts to judge whether the trials were constitutional. It remains unclear what the outcome would have been, and there is no certainty the courts would have accepted the constitutionality of a military tribunal or commission, although settled constitutional law made that appear unlikely.[100] The Supreme Court's striking down of Article 3(a) of the UCMJ served as a precedent denying court-martial jurisdiction over veterans who committed offenses enumerated in the UCMJ. The court's decision did not refer to the prosecution in military courts of those suspected of "grave breaches" of the Geneva Conventions, which would constitute violations of the law of war.[101] As Jordan recognizes, the problem was that "whatever the source of Congress' authority—whether under the grant of power to punish offenses against the law of nations or under the grant of power to make rules for the government of the armed forces—the same constitutional limitations [arising from *Toth*] would seem to apply."[102]

The unnamed "Pentagon lawyer" who was briefing the press (presumably Jordan himself) said he believed there was "great flexibility" in the concept of a military commission and that trials could be held in Washington, using jurors from the civilian jury panels. As he pointed out, the Court of Military Appeals consists of civilian judges, who might be brought together to conduct the trials.[103] Unnamed lawyers told the same journalist that if Congress passed a law to permit trial of veterans in federal district courts, it would not violate the constitutional ban on ex post facto laws, as long as the court was trying a crime that existed in military law at the time of the massacre.[104] It appears that Jordan—or whoever was speaking to the press on his behalf—was busy promoting the same argument he was presenting in the memorandum, simultaneously working inside and outside the bureaucracy to win support for the course of action he advocated.

Jordan refers in the memorandum to the possible significance of the recent Supreme Court decision in *O'Callahan v. Parker*.[105] In many respects that case provides unpromising grounds for Jordan's effort to find a way to try the My Lai veteran suspects. The defendant in *O'Callahan* was, at the time of his prosecution, a member of the armed forces and hence in a position different from that of the My Lai veterans. The *O'Callahan* court strongly reaffirmed the superiority of Article III courts over military trials and reasserted the *Toth* doctrine that, to be tried by a court-martial, a defendant must have been a member of the armed forces at the time of both the offense and the trial.[106] Justice Douglas's opinion for the court expressed "palpable disdain" of military justice.[107] *O'Callahan* thus did not appear to be the most obvious ground for believing that the court would countenance the creation of a military commission to prosecute civilians. However, Jordan found at least the kernel of a principle from which to develop the position he was expounding: the court, as he described its judgment, had ruled that a strong "military interest" might create an exception to the normal constitutional requirements of a jury trial, after grand jury indictment, before an Article III judge.[108]

This part of Jordan's argument, though, rests on a misreading of the phrase "military interest": "In *O'Callahan*," Jordan argues, "the problem was whether the military had sufficient interest to justify creating an exception to the normal constitutional requirements of a jury trial, grand jury indictment, and trial by an Article III judge."[109] In *O'Callahan*, however, the word *interest* does not mean a motive or purpose but has a specialized meaning: the degree of connectedness between a criminal act and military affairs.[110] Jordan ignores the court's definition of *interest* and proceeds in a line of reasoning that relies on another meaning of the word: "In this case, there is no doubt that the military has a vital interest in the proper conduct of military operations in a friendly country and in obedience to general standards of conduct."[111] The armed services and the nation may have had this sort of interest in prosecuting the My Lai suspects, but this is quite different from the concept of military interest (meaning service-connectedness) outlined in *O'Callahan*.[112] The meaning of the court's service-connectedness holding caused no problems for other interpreters. The fact that Jordan strains to find some constitutional basis for prosecuting the My Lai veterans is the most telling feature of this passage in his memorandum. It demonstrates both the difficulty of the task he was undertaking and the effort that the army's top civilian lawyer was then devoting to the purpose of trying the suspected murderers.

Jordan's memorandum goes on to remind his Justice Department colleagues of the nation's international obligations under the Geneva Conventions, but, as with his reference to *O'Callahan*, the argument is at best equivocal. Jordan says that through its adherence to the conventions the United States undertook to enact legislation required to punish "grave breaches": acts such as those alleged to have occurred at My Lai.[113] He says that when the Senate held hearings about the ratification of the conventions, the executive branch took the position that existing legislation was sufficient to enforce the requirement to punish grave breaches—but his qualification "albeit prior to *Toth*" is crucial. The *Toth* ruling opened up a jurisdictional gap, and Black's opinion for the court underlined that the onus was now on Congress to remedy that situation; yet the executive branch had failed to propose the legislation required to fulfill the obligation of the United States under the Geneva Conventions, and Congress had failed to close the gap with such a statute. Jordan observes that there were now legislative proposals in Congress to plug the jurisdictional gap, but that remark simply redoubles the point that no such statute currently existed. Although one might readily agree that the United States ought to have resolved the discrepancy between its treaty obligation and the actual state of things, the irremediable fact was that this discrepancy still existed.

Jordan concludes powerfully by proposing that prosecutions at least be attempted under existing statutes. The logic of this argument is that then the

United States could not be accused of shirking its legal responsibilities in the eyes of the world. If the courts ruled the prosecutions unconstitutional, no one could say that the government had not tried. "Given the status of our international obligations," Jordan argues, "there might be some difficulty about discarding our existing authority [to conduct the prosecutions] as worthless without even trying to invoke it." In other words, the United States should make an honest effort to try and punish the perpetrators of the atrocity.[114] Jordan was an astute political actor as well as a lawyer, and it may appear he was engaged in part in an exercise in international public relations, but that is not all it was. Jordan was convinced that the route to prosecution he proposed would not just bolster the international image of the United States but also prove to be legally sound: "There is existing statutory authority which would allow discharged servicemen to be tried for violations of the law of war which are alleged to have occurred at My Lai. . . . the fact that war crimes are involved may well provide a sufficient basis for the invocation of military jurisdiction in this particular case. . . . If you agree with this view of the law, I would suggest that we attempt to obtain Executive Branch agreement on the propriety of trial by military tribunal in this factual situation." There is circumstantial evidence that Jordan advocated this approach in his briefing of legislators. After hearing Jordan testify in the closed Senate session, Sen. Peter H. Dominick of Colorado said he favored the creation of a military commission if there was no other way of bringing the veteran perpetrators to trial—although he was quick to add that he was not pressing for the creation of such a commission.[115]

A "decent respect to the opinions of mankind" might have seemed to dictate that there was both a national interest in preventing the My Lai veteran suspects from getting away with murder and a powerful imperative for testing whether that interest might overcome the limitations of what appeared to be settled law. One is left to speculate on what might have occurred had the matter been submitted to the Supreme Court's judgment. A quarter century after the events, when a journalist reminded him of the stance he had taken and sent him a copy of his memorandum to prompt his recollections, Jordan said he was proud to stand behind the document: "In my judgment a very strong case was available for trying the My Lai folks."[116]

A number of press articles published shortly before and after the date of the Jordan memorandum reported that the constitutional problems involved in prosecuting the My Lai veterans were being investigated. The stories were sufficiently well informed to suggest that government lawyers were telling the press about their approaches—in other words, leaking the stories to help muster sufficient political momentum to overcome constitutional scruples about the prosecutions.[117] Hersh, who broke the My Lai case in the press and was following the events as carefully as any observer, said, "Pentagon correspondents were fed information pointing out that the Army was doing everything possible to get jurisdiction over former Charlie Company members in order to prosecute some of them for murder." Hersh seems to believe the news stories were intended to pressure the veterans not to speak to the press, although the seriousness of Jordan's effort to find a constitutional means of prosecution signals that if that was a goal, it was not the only one.[118]

The matter came to the attention of various interested parties, including the My Lai veteran suspects and the White House. In January 1970 an attorney for Varnado Simpson contacted the army to ask for a copy of his CID interview (in which he had admitted to killing eight villagers) and for information about whether Simpson was a suspect in any offense. He also inquired if the army had a legal opinion as to whether any military or civilian body had jurisdiction to try a person who was honorably discharged but who remained in reserve status for offenses committed while on active duty. An army representative denied the attorney a copy of Simpson's interview, explaining that it was held in a file for "law enforcement purposes." The attorney was told that the jurisdictional matter was under consideration in the Department of the Army and "as yet, no decision has been made."[119]

Three days after the date of the Jordan memorandum, the White House staff member Patrick Buchanan laid out a public relations strategy for dealing with the massacre. It dealt with such questions as how to "fudge" the matter of what the president knew in April 1969, when the White House received Ridenhour's letter and the government ordered an investigation of the allegations, and it contained a number of model questions and answers that might be used in response to press queries. Among them was the following: "Q. Mr. President: what does the government plan to do about prosecution of civilians involved in the My Lai case? A. As you may know, the prosecution of an American citizen who, while under the jurisdiction of the military in a foreign nation, commits an act in violation of the military code presents the most difficult legal problems, some of them possibly unique. I don't have the answer to that now, but the Department of Defense has been consulting with the Justice and the State Departments on the matter."[120]

The Department of the Army and the Department of Defense were in no doubt about the question of jurisdiction over former servicemen. Secretary of the Army Resor said on NBC's *Meet the Press* on December 2 that Jordan had sent the Department of Justice proposals for trying the former servicemen by general court-martial or military commission: "I think it is important that we pursue that and that we try any [former serviceman] if the facts justify it." He explained the constitutional problem, Supreme Court precedents that he believed allowed the trials, and the articles of the UCMJ that permitted them to take place.[121] Secretary Laird announced to the press a week later that "any present or former U.S. serviceman" who was responsible for the killing of civilians at My Lai "will be brought to trial."[122]

On December 24, 1969, the Department of Justice responded to Jordan's memorandum by stating that it would support the army if the veteran suspects were to be tried by military tribunal. That was a breakthrough, but it did not settle the matter. On January 2, 1970, a meeting of representatives of the executive departments that would have to agree on a course of action took place: the legal adviser and others from the State Department met with the acting judge advocate general and representatives of the Department of Defense and of the army general counsel. The State Department representatives said they would prefer trial in a civilian court pursuant to enabling legislation, but they would not object to trial by military tribunal "if such trial would not lessen the likelihood of future legislation." The State Department approach was quite logical: a stopgap measure such as a trial by military tribunal might undermine legislative proposals to pass a law closing the jurisdictional gap by making it appear that there was a nonlegislative solution to the problem. This was not an unequivocal endorsement of a military tribunal but, following the Justice Department's unreserved endorsement of a military tribunal prosecution, a second executive department gave qualified consent to Jordan's proposal.[123] A later document corroborates that the "Departments of State and Justice indicate [that] trial by military tribunal [is] unobjectionable."[124] The judge advocate general and the Office of the General Counsel (Jordan's department) undertook to study the possible ways of implementing a decision "to try these persons by military tribunal."[125] They concluded that, despite the constitutional problems, "either [a] general court-martial or [a] military commission may exercise jurisdiction in this case."[126] Yet another document conceded that the scope and constitutionality of Articles 18 and 21 of the UCMJ, which provided for prosecution of offenses against the law of war by court-martial or military commission, had not been tested. It reported that some people believed that the army was empowered to try by court-martial or military commission offenses against the law of war that former soldiers may have committed at My Lai.[127]

All the public comment and not-for-attribution briefings about the exploration of ways to prosecute the veterans came from the Department of Defense and from the army. As we have seen, in late November and December 1969 the sources were either official statements by Resor, Jordan, and the Defense Department spokesman, Jerry Friedheim, or briefings by unnamed "Pentagon lawyers" or "Pentagon legal sources."[128] After the agreement of January 2, 1970, with the Departments of Justice and State, though, the public commentary by army and Defense Department sources dried up: for the next fifteen months there were no more leaks, no more announced visits to Congress, and no more press releases about the prosecution of former servicemen. The stories were soon forgotten, to the extent that a well-informed legal source referred to the possibility of prosecuting the My Lai veterans as "the most interesting and least publicized problem" surrounding the massacre.[129]

One way of interpreting this silence is that Jordan and his colleagues ended their media campaign because it was no longer needed now that the State and Justice Departments had agreed to support the prosecution of the veterans. The Pentagon lawyers had their hands full in early 1970 planning for the release of the results of the official investigation into the massacre conducted by the Peers Inquiry, handling the prosecutions that would follow the recommendations it was planning to make in March 1970, and coming up with a media strategy to deal with the inevitable fallout from the cases—all of which involved a new approach to the media centering on reticence, not leaks.

There was another possible explanation of the new silence regarding the prosecution of the veterans: Jordan and his colleagues were taking a wait-and-see approach in anticipation of the court-martial prosecutions of the suspects still in the armed forces, which would allow a rehearsal of the cases that would be made against the My Lai veterans. They were also contending with the broadening of the scale of the events of which they were aware: the government had learned about the second massacre in Son My, had broadened the Peers investigation to encompass that event, and had begun to recognize that Bravo Company's 1st Platoon had been responsible for dozens of civilian deaths at My Khe (4). Most of the suspects were out of uniform, thereby expanding the possible scope of the prosecutions by military commission. Prosecutions of former members of Bravo Company against whom a prima facie case existed would draw attention to the second massacre and heighten the political repercussions of the planned military commission trials. Once Jordan, his Pentagon colleagues, and the representatives of the other executive departments had seen how the prosecution of the enlisted men in the My Lai courts-martial had gone, they could assess whether to confront the sticky problem of conducting the prosecution of similar crimes in a military commission. In June 1970, in his testimony to the House subcommittee conducting an investigation of the My Lai massacre, General Westmoreland still reported the view of the secretary of the army and the army judge advocate general that "there probably is a way" that the former servicemen could be tried and said that Resor and Jordan were "working diligently" on the matter with the Department of Justice. But this assertion came before the verdicts began to arrive in the My Lai courts-martial.[130]

CHAPTER FIVE

A "Tragedy of Major Proportions"

The Peers Inquiry and the House Subcommittee Report

The disclosure of the atrocity at My Lai, the widespread publicity attending the publication of the photographs and interviews, and the realization of the effects of the jurisdictional gap spurred Senator Ervin to redouble his efforts to close the gap at the same time the army general counsel was trying to work around it. Meanwhile, in the flurry of political activity accompanying the disclosure of the atrocity, two investigations commenced. One, initiated by the army, was headed by Lt. Gen. William Peers, who had commanded a division in Vietnam, and the other was led by Rep. Edward Hébert of Louisiana, who prided himself on his extreme hawkishness regarding the conduct of the war. Hébert's subcommittee released a report that surprised some by advising the passage of a law to fill the jurisdictional gap, and the Defense Department responded positively to that recommendation. This moment turned out to be the closest the nation came in a generation to securing a legislative remedy to the jurisdictional gap.

In November 1969 the Department of the Army sent Ervin a series of documents briefing him on the My Lai case and the charges being preferred against Calley.[1] Ervin responded by raising the "exceedingly difficult problem" of trying any former servicemen for what he called "improprieties" while they were in uniform. He grilled representatives of the Department of the Army about why the army had not acted sooner and learned that it had not yet secured legally admissible evidence for use in a court-martial.[2]

On the day Secretary of the Army Resor and Robert Jordan briefed Congress, Resor and the army's chief of staff issued orders to General Peers to begin an investigation into the adequacy of the original army inquiry into the massacre and the "possible suppression or withholding of information by persons involved in the incident": in other words, to investigate the cover-up as well as the massacre itself. That same day Congressman Rivers, the hawkish chair of the House Armed Services Committee, announced that his committee's investigative subcommittee, chaired by Hébert, would begin its own inquiry into the massacre.[3] The coincidence in time of the two investigations—and the fact that both would be calling witnesses, the subcommittee with subpoena powers at its disposal, even while criminal investigations and the preliminary stages of court-martial proceedings were under way—demonstrated the degree of rivalry between the two investigative efforts.[4] As Hébert later remarked, "Mendel [Rivers] merely had called the investigating subcommittee to see what it was all about. He wanted an explanation of it. . . . And that's when Resor comes in. He beat us to the punch."[5]

Both of the investigations, that of General Peers and that of the House subcommittee, had problems of credibility. Some congressmen doubted that an inquiry initiated by the army and conducted by a general could impartially investigate the service. It was equally doubtful that an investigation commissioned by as avid a supporter of the troops as Rivers would come anywhere near the truth.[6] As it turned out, Peers's reputation for integrity won over many of the skeptics. As Michael Bilton and Kevin Sim state, he and the civilian lawyers who assisted him shared a basic philosophy: "a fundamental belief in the truth as an absolute."[7] Rivers, in contrast, made unfortunate remarks during the subcommittee's investigation that undermined his credibility. For example, he stated in December 1969 that he was unsure that a massacre had taken place at My Lai at all, even though the army investigation had by then established that a mass killing had indeed occurred.[8]

Senator Stennis, the chairman of the Senate Armed Services Committee, warned the White House against possible congressional and press "tub-thumping" and about the "circus" that might develop if "garish and overlapping" congressional and army investigations proceeded.[9] These concerns explain why, although the dovish Democratic Senate majority leader, Mike Mansfield, called for the Armed Services Committee to hold hearings, Stennis merely sent investigators to Vietnam and did not hold his own separate hearings. Stennis advised Nixon to create a blue ribbon commission on the model of the Warren Commission, which investigated John F. Kennedy's assassination. The establishment of such a commission would, he suggested, eliminate the need for any further investigations, and he repeated that advice publicly. Similar calls for a civilian commission rather than the army investigation led by Peers had begun soon after the establishment of the Peers Inquiry, but the Nixon administration resisted them.[10] Nixon told his aides to contact the top leadership in the House and Senate who supported the administration to get such calls "knocked off."[11] The advantage of having an inquiry headed by an army general is that the Department of the Army could retain control of the scope of the investigation and the release of its findings. As Kendrick Oliver comments, "The Peers investigation was an exercise in institutional damage limitation, not independent historical enquiry. Its principal purpose—albeit one which was not specified in formal directives—was to demonstrate that the army did in fact have standards of conduct, that its command did not take the view that massacre was an allowable excess."[12] To this one can add another purpose: to deflect the demands for a civilian commission outside the control of the armed services and the government. While there were legitimate reasons for their wanting to retain control—namely, so that the Peers Inquiry could dovetail with the CID investigation and so that the premature disclosure of its findings would not jeopardize any prosecutions—both the army and the Nixon administration wanted to exercise control for political and public relations purposes. They would not have had such authority over an independent citizens' commission or one involving legislators.

By January 1970 Peers had determined that the massacre at My Lai (4) was only one of several attacks on the same day, another being Bravo Company's assault on the subhamlet marked on army maps as My Khe (4).[13] After Terry Reid, a member of Bravo Company, had been interviewed in the press about the killings at My Khe (4), the White House attempted to discover whether there would be additional revelations. The president asked Secretary Laird if there was any factual basis to the story and "if similar stories are expected to surface."[14] Kissinger told his aide Alexander Haig to "make sure we get a reply as soon as possible. It will affect our attitude on [whether to convene a] Presidential Commission."[15] Kissinger recommended riding out the hue and cry and avoiding the creation of a commission unless credible new allegations came to light.[16] Laird told Kissinger there might be a scattering of such stories by people with a variety of motives and that the secretaries of the armed services would investigate them expeditiously in order to stop false reports from mushrooming.[17] What Laird did not say was telling: he did not say that the service secretaries would conduct expeditious investigations in order to ensure that prosecutions would follow whenever necessary. The matter was still treated largely as a political issue to be handled by judicious news management, not as a moral and legal one that might demand judicial redress. Peers, though, was instructed to broaden his inquiry to include the events at My Khe (4).[18]

The scope of the investigation was accordingly expanded to cover all the events at Son My village.[19] In February 1970 Capt. Thomas K. Willingham, the commander of Bravo Company's 1st Platoon, was charged with the unpremeditated murder of twenty Vietnamese civilians, making false official statements, and misprision of (failing to report) a felony for his part in the massacre in My Khe (4) and its cover-up. Like Calley, he was charged just before his scheduled separation from the armed forces.[20] Other veterans who were being investigated had been released from service between March and September 1969.[21] The army was legally entitled to embargo the discharge from military service of anyone suspected of offenses in the massacre at Son My so as to prevent them from slipping out of the judicial net.[22] The government, however, did not flag the first suspects on active duty to prevent their being separated from the army without the approval of the Department of the Army's headquarters until December 22, 1969.[23]

Peers announced the outcome of his investigation at a press conference in March 1970. One of its intended results was the preferring of charges against military personnel, so it had to be ready by March 15, 1970, because of the two-year statute of limitations on most military offenses.[24] Secretary Resor, who had been keeping track of the progress of the investigation, urged Peers to tone down the report's language by describing the Vietnamese who had been killed as "noncombatant casualties" rather than as women, children, babies, and old men. Maj. Gen. Winant Sidle, the army's chief of information, insisted that Peers not use the word *massacre.* At the press conference Peers replaced *massacre* with the phrase "tragedy of major proportions."[25] (Forty years later there was an eerie familiarity to the script a military spokesman followed when he described the killing of an unarmed, wounded Iraqi captive in a mosque in Fallujah as a "tragedy" that was "understandable.")[26]

The severely abridged version of the Peers Inquiry report issued on March 17, 1970, excluded references to the massacre at My Khe (4), which allowed the hierarchy of the army, from Secretary Resor on down, to recite the lie that the massacre at My Lai (4) was an isolated event.[27] The withholding of large parts of the report was justified on the basis that releasing the bulk of the thousands of pages of evidence gathered could lead to damaging pretrial publicity concerning the accused. By the time someone inside the Pentagon leaked the unpublished parts of the report to Hersh as well as volumes of testimony and other documents, the remaining suspects in the My Khe (4) massacre had all left the armed forces, and it was too late to prosecute them by court-martial.[28]

Peers announced that Koster, Young, Henderson, and ten other officers in addition to Calley and Willingham would be charged as a result of the events of March 16, 1968. Like Brooks, the leader of Charlie Company's 2nd Platoon, the commanding officer of Task Force Barker was no longer alive to face criminal charges: Barker had been killed in a helicopter accident in Vietnam.[29] The offenses of which the higher-ranking officers were accused, such as dereliction of duty, false swearing, making a false statement, and misprision of a felony, showed that the charges pinpointed their role in the cover-up, not their responsibility for the massacre itself.[30] Charges of murder and assault were directed at the officers who had been directly involved in the assault on Son My. Capt. Ernest Medina, the commander of Charlie Company, who a number of witnesses and participants in the massacre said had ordered the destruction of My Lai (4), was charged with murder. Witnesses had also seen Medina kill a young boy and a wounded Vietnamese woman by shooting them at close range.[31] Charges of assault and maiming were brought against Capt. Eugene Kotouc, the Task Force Barker intelligence officer.[32] Except for Medina and Willingham, the other officers faced possible Article 32 investigations—similar to a civilian grand jury process—and were transferred to Fort Meade for that purpose. The decision to locate them there and not in Fort Benning along with Calley was deliberately made in order "to clearly separate in the public mind" those directly charged with atrocities from those who commanded them but were not present at Son My.[33]

Nixon told Kissinger that Peers was "trying to make himself look good while he kicks his colleagues around." The president regarded it as a "pretty cheap shot to allow the generals to be put on the rack" for the "delay" in the disclosure of the massacre. "We know why it was done," Nixon said. "It was covered up because it was in the interest of the country," a statement that foreshadowed Nixon's distinctive concept of the national interest when he presided over the subsequent cover-up of the Watergate crimes and justified abuses of power as long as the president sanctioned them. He explained that "these boys" were being killed by women using satchel charges. When Kissinger discussed Haig's thoughts about a way of "getting rid of" the matter, he said that Haig thought "somebody had to go": in other words, someone had to take the rap for an event that could not be brushed under the carpet. Nixon concurred: "Let's get it out of the way."[34]

A number of enlisted men who were still in uniform were also charged with murder both before and after the release of the Peers Inquiry report: Sgt. Charles E. Hutto, Sgt. Esequiel Torres, Cpl. Kenneth Schiel, Spec. 4 William F. Doherty, Spec. 4 Robert W. T'Souvas, Pvt. Gerald A. Smith, and Pvt. Max D. Hutson.[35] Charges of assault with intent to kill were filed against S.Sgt. David Mitchell and S.Sgt. Kenneth L. Hodges, who was also charged with rape. Reflecting the continuing uncertainty over whether there was any way of conducting constitutionally acceptable prosecutions of veterans, the government did not prefer charges against former members of Charlie Company who were no longer in uniform, even those who had confessed to killing unarmed civilians.

The thirteen-member investigating subcommittee of the House Armed Services Committee began its investigation into the massacre in December 1969. When the committee chairman Rivers began leaking distorted reports of the testimony the subcommittee heard—for example, reporting that the testimony of the helicopter pilot Hugh Thompson proved there had been no massacre, an interpretation of Thompson's testimony that other committee members denied—his actions prompted one of his colleagues in the House to fear that the subcommittee's investigation would lead to a whitewash, redoubling the call for an independent civilian investigating commission.[36] Laird tried to persuade Rivers to call off the subcommittee investigation. As a result of the brouhaha Rivers announced the creation of a four-person panel headed by Congressman Hébert, to proceed with the investigation. The panel conducted hearings in April, May, and June 1970 and visited My Lai (4).[37]

Both Rivers and Hébert were southern Democrats, opponents of the civil rights movement, and militarists, Rivers representing a district in South Carolina, and Hébert one in Louisiana. They were long-standing allies, having entered Congress on the same day in 1941. Both were critics of the Johnson and Nixon administrations' conduct of the war. Rivers had convened a subcommittee to investigate whether the Johnson administration had a "plan for victory" in Vietnam and whether there were sufficient troops there to win the war. He guaranteed that he would find the subcommittee's findings agreeable by ensuring that every one of its members was, like him, a hawk.[38] Rivers's stance identifies him as one of the prowar enthusiasts who believed the Johnson administration was showing too much restraint and that it should fight all out for victory. On the war in Vietnam, he said, "Words are fruitless, diplomatic notes are useless. There can be only one answer for America: retaliation, retaliation, retaliation! They say, 'Quit the bombing.' I say, 'Bomb!' "[39]

Strongly protective of the constitutional prerogatives of the House of Representatives, Rivers regarded it as his responsibility not just to raise but to oversee the tens of billions of dollars it cost to fund the armed forces, a position that sometimes brought him into conflict with the Department of Defense. As chairman of the Armed Services Committee, he "brought under his wing every man, woman and institution engaged in the defense effort and thought its importance entitled them to ask for a certain leeway and forgiveness." Soldiers in the field frequently wrote to him confiding their troubles, and he often took up their cause and challenged their commanders.[40]

It was said that there was "not a dime's worth of difference" ideologically between Hébert and Rivers, and Hébert was known, if anything, to be an even harsher scourge of witnesses before the committee. He built a reputation as "anti-Administration (any Administration)."[41] Hébert had a "virtually unblemished record in support of a strong military and against civil rights legislation, welfare programs, and other issues he saw as evils of a permissive society."[42] In the late 1960s, when Rivers was ailing, Hébert was "unofficial chairman" of the committee, and his press secretary recalled, "Nothing went into or came out of committee without his stamp of approval."[43] He declared himself to be "the loudest of the Hawks."[44] Hébert complained that Johnson and McNamara had shown too much restraint in their policy in Vietnam, and by 1968 he was advocating the use of tactical nuclear weapons there.[45] He told McNamara that the United States should send four million troops to Vietnam if that would hasten victory.[46]

For his part, Rivers could not bring himself to believe that his beloved troops had done what they were accused of: "I just don't believe any American boys went into any hamlet and murdered any 109 civilians—I just don't believe that. . . . These men have already been lynched in the news media, but we got jurisdiction over this, and I don't know how guilty they are, but we gonna find out how innocent they are too, if we can."[47] Rivers was appalled by the number of charges against U.S. officers. On March 19 he was reported as saying that the "arrest" of fourteen officers marked "one of the darkest days in U.S. military history." On April 11 he declared that none of the soldiers should have been charged because the army as an institution was responsible for any crimes that may have been committed. And, he vowed, they're "not going to get away with it. . . . I'm going to have something to do with stopping this."[48] By this time the CID had established that Charlie Company had slain some 347 Vietnamese men, women, and children at My Lai (4) and had reported this finding to the Peers panel, but this number—far greater than the number about which Rivers had expressed his doubts—was not reported to the public, in an apparent attempt to minimize the scale of the atrocity.[49]

While the feasibility of prosecution by a military tribunal was being assessed and while the House subcommittee was conducting its investigation and preparing its report, Ervin continued to lobby for S. 3188. In April 1970 a "legal spokesman" for the Senate Constitutional Rights Subcommittee attempted to rekindle media interest in the issue of the jurisdictional gap by chronicling the efforts made by the subcommittee since 1957 to pass a law closing the gap.[50] The spokesman, possibly its counsel, Robinson Everett, said that "administrative apathy" was the main reason the bills had remained bottled up in the subcommittee. Ervin, it was reported, had been trying to summon congressional enthusiasm for the legislation. The same article reported that Ervin's colleague Sen. Edward Brooke, one of those to whom Ridenhour had sent his letter disclosing the massacre, said that what had happened at My Lai was a war crime and came within the scope of international law. Brooke, a senator from Massachusetts, was a member of the now-extinct tribe of liberal Republicans. (Nixon felt closer to conservative Democrats, who were more reliable supporters of his legislative proposals, than he did to Brooke.) On the basis of the Nuremberg precedent, Brooke said that the United States was "firmly committed" to prosecuting such cases. Although Brooke may have exaggerated the nation's determination to live up to the Nuremberg standard, Ervin was said to be "hopeful, if not optimistic," that the My Lai case might give sufficient impetus to executive and congressional support for the necessary legislation.

"Unfortunately, it may have taken a massacre to achieve such interest," said the congressional aide.[51]

The recommendations of the House Armed Services Subcommittee's investigation of the My Lai massacre, contained in the report issued on July 15, 1970, fulfilled Ervin's hopes but took others by surprise. As noted earlier, the Department of Defense had treated the House Armed Services Committee as a bulwark against unwanted military justice legislation. The subcommittee's recommendation of a law to close the jurisdictional gap finally shook loose from the Pentagon the specific legislative proposal that the Department of Defense had been promising for years but had long deferred producing.

Like the Peers Inquiry report, the subcommittee used a euphemism to refer to the events at My Lai, describing it not as a massacre or an atrocity but as a "tragedy of major proportions."[52] The report contained three recommendations, one of which was that in future the army should appoint qualified investigators from outside the chain of command to investigate alleged war crimes. Another recommendation implicitly criticized the conduct of witnesses of whom the committee disapproved. For the purposes of the discussion here, the most important recommendation was the second, which addressed the jurisdictional gap. As members of the House Armed Services Committee, the lawmakers on the subcommittee had long been aware of the legislative proposals to close the gap. They were also aware of Jordan's arguments, which had been brought to their attention in his memorandum that said that, although there were constitutional problems, "it is believed that the Army is empowered to try by general court-martial or military commission former members of the military who may have committed offenses at My Lai in violation of the law of war."[53] In language that echoed the relevant bills that had been repeatedly proposed in Congress, the subcommittee advised that "consideration should be given to amending Section 803 (a), Title 10 of the United States Code to provide for trial in the United States District Courts, of persons charged with having committed offenses while on active military duty, who are no longer subject to military jurisdiction as a result of having been discharged."[54] Rivers sent the report to Secretary Laird with a brief note, asking him to respond to the recommendations.[55] Laird asked the armed service secretaries to respond to the first and third recommendations, while the documentary record shows that the Department of Defense undertook no such interdepartmental consultation before stating that it favored the purposes of the second recommendation, to plug the jurisdictional gap.[56]

Hébert's motives are difficult to fathom. His questioning of some of the witnesses at the hearings seemed to flow from his prowar position. He also seems, however, to have been dismayed both by the failure of Task Force Barker's commanders and their divisional superiors to investigate the killings properly and by the "blanket of silence" with which State Department personnel and Americal Division officers covered up the massacre. The subcommittee criticized the MACV inspector general. A fierce defender of the army in normal times, Hébert did not produce the favorable assessment of the army's handling of the matter that it had pressured him to produce, and he seems genuinely to have been disturbed not only by the massacre but also by the existence of the jurisdictional gap that allowed some of the perpetrators to go unpunished.[57] Indeed, the army pressure—in Hébert's account not far short of harassment—coupled with the conflict over access to witness testimony and other documents, seems to have provoked the subcommittee to voice criticisms of the army that its members might otherwise have stifled. Rivers was surprised by the strength of Hébert's disapprobation of the army, a result he did not expect when he appointed his fellow conservative as its chair.[58]

Hébert's concern about the effects of *Toth* was complex. He was troubled not only that some veterans might likely get away with murder but also that, being immune from prosecution themselves, veterans were free to make accusations that might implicate anyone, in or out of uniform, against whom they had a grudge. Mark Carson argues that what disturbed Hébert was that veteran immunity meant that career soldiers, still in the service, were more likely than others to be liable to prosecution.[59] It is not clear whether the predominant worry was that some veterans were escaping justice or that, once free of the fear of prosecution, they might point the finger of blame against others or profit from their experiences by sensationalizing their stories.[60] Most significant, irrespective of Hébert's reasoning, this "loudest of the Hawks" now favored the remedial legislation that had never been voted out of the House Armed Services Committee. The Department of Defense, which had promised to present its own draft bills to achieve the same purpose as the ones Congressman Bennett had repeatedly proposed, could no longer defer living up to its commitment.

The Pentagon finally engaged constructively with the legislative proposals to fill the jurisdictional void opened up by *Toth.* As discussed in chapter 3, Bennett had resumed his efforts to plug the jurisdictional gap by introducing a new legislative proposal to achieve that purpose, H.R. 4225, almost as soon as the new Congress began its first session in January 1969. Laird told Rivers that the Department of Defense would meet the subcommittee's second recommendation by proposing two bills substituting for Bennett's proposal.[61] On the same day, the department responded to the request for a report on H.R. 4225 and, shortly thereafter, to Ervin's counterpart Senate legislation.[62] The Pentagon "generally favor[ed]" the objectives of the bills, namely, to fill the jurisdictional voids opened up by *Toth, Covert,* and the later cases dealing with civilians accompanying the armed forces. It found certain technical deficiencies in H.R. 4225. Consequently, it proposed the substitute legislation that Laird mentioned, intended to achieve essentially the same ends.[63] One of the new bills, H.R. 18857, closed the jurisdictional gap opened up by *Toth* by conferring jurisdiction over the relevant offenses on federal district courts;[64] the other bill, H.R. 18547, allowed for the apprehension, restraint, removal, and delivery of the suspects so that they could be tried.[65] A favorable report was received from the Department of Defense, as one might expect given that the department had drafted the bills.[66]

The legislation the Department of Defense proposed to plug the jurisdictional gap would have had only a prospective effect: in the Pentagon report, Fred Buzhardt, the recently appointed general counsel of the Department of Defense, observed that the question of retrospective application was closely related to the issue of asserting jurisdiction under present law to try veterans who were suspects in the My Lai massacre. As he said, the possibility and desirability of applying Articles 18 and 21 of the UCMJ to the My Lai veterans was currently "under review." He observed that difficult constitutional questions were involved and that once a final decision on this question was reached it would be possible to evaluate whether separate legislation to vest retrospective jurisdiction in the civilian courts was needed.[67]

Reports on H.R. 18547 and H.R. 18857 were requested from the Department of Justice, but it failed to respond, just as it had declined to submit a report on H.R. 4225.[68] It appeared, judging from his department's continuing unresponsiveness to these requests, that Attorney General Mitchell remained opposed to the legislation. The State Department had promised to give "careful consideration" to S. 3188 but did not follow through with a report to this counterpart bill to H.R. 4225.[69] No congressional hearings were held, and, once again, the legislation died.[70] As Lawrence Rockwood observes, the petering out of the legislative effort was a signal failure of the government to "adhere to its own Nuremberg-era precedents." The suspects were not retained in or returned to uniform for trial by court-martial, and the Congress "did not have the political will to pass enabling legislation to try them as civilians."[71]

The impunity of the My Lai veterans is not simply an anomaly. It accords with the striking leniency shown toward U.S. troops for crimes they committed in Vietnam. Such leniency falls into several categories: first, the inexplicable decisions not to bring court-martial prosecutions despite overwhelming evidence of the suspects' guilt; second, the command decisions to order administrative action rather than a court-martial, leading to light sanctions relative to the gravity of the offenses with which the suspects were charged; third, when a court-martial was convened and resulted in a verdict of guilt, the instances of extraordinarily light sentences in proportion to the seriousness of the offense of which someone was convicted; finally, the perverse acquittals by court-martial panels (military juries) consisting of military personnel, usually officers, despite overwhelming evidence of the accused's guilt. A few examples from the case files of the Vietnam War Crimes Working Group in the U.S. National Archives are instructive. In Case 112 it was proven that a murder had been committed by U.S. troops when a lieutenant ordered a staff sergeant to kill a Vietnamese prisoner. The staff sergeant was convicted of murder but served less than two years in confinement for the point-blank shooting as well as reduction in rank and the loss of pay and allowances; the lieutenant who ordered the murder was acquitted by a general court-martial.[72] In Case 124 the investigators established that an American perpetrator had committed "electrical torture" by wiring the "sensitive areas of the bodies" of three men and a woman to a field telephone, but he refused to accept an administrative punishment, and no further action was taken.[73] In Case 147 a platoon sergeant in the 173rd Airborne Brigade shot three Vietnamese men at close range, arrayed their bodies together on the ground, detonated a grenade to disguise the source of their fatal injuries, and planted weapons near their bodies to support his claim that they were Viet Cong. He was convicted of manslaughter for this carefully thought out crime but suffered no custodial punishment, being sentenced only to a reduction in rank and a loss of pay for six months.[74] The records of Case 150 disclose that in November 1966 members of a long-range reconnaissance patrol kidnapped a young Vietnamese woman and then raped and murdered her. Two of them were convicted of the crime: one served a little more than three years in confinement, the other less than three years.[75] In Case 39 the platoon sergeant of a unit of the 4th Infantry Division pleaded guilty to unpremeditated murder after killing two Vietnamese men, but the court-martial, which found him guilty, imposed no sentence on him.[76]

The disposition of these cases is consistent with the many reports by ex GIs of troops who were found guilty of killing and assaulting civilians but who were merely reduced in rank and returned to their units. Illustrating the leniency of sentences, Hersh writes that every one of the life sentences imposed on the twenty-one army officers and troops convicted of premeditated murder of a Vietnamese victim between 1964 and 1971 was reduced by military review boards; marines convicted of a total of thirty-one murders, one rape, and one attempted rape were ordered to serve, after all reviews and appeals, a total of thirty-five years at hard labor, slightly more than one year's imprisonment for each crime.[77]

In the Vietnam war crimes cases he reviewed, Gary Solis finds that marines convicted of murder and manslaughter for killing Vietnamese noncombatants were sentenced to substantial terms of confinement, and there was no appreciable difference between the sentences imposed for killing Vietnamese and those for killing fellow American servicemen. However, the punishments imposed on those who killed Vietnamese noncombatants were often reduced by clemency or parole hearings, sometimes massively. A senior marine judge advocate remarked that there was a feeling in Washington of "congressional pressure to cut back on a lot of the sentences." A marine lance corporal was found guilty of executing four Vietnamese noncombatants within the space of two days and of cutting the throat of a fifth. Convicted of five murders, he was sentenced to confinement at hard labor for life, but his sentence was successively reduced by the convening authority and by clemency action. He ultimately served less than three years in confinement. Others ordered to serve life terms for unlawful killings served even shorter sentences, in one case less than a year in confinement.[78]

The failure of S. 3188 and H.R. 4225 may seem extraordinary. In the aftermath of the My Lai massacre, the Nixon administration, legislators, and the public were confronted by the results of over a dozen years of legislative inaction. The numerous warnings issued over the years by advocates of remedial legislation were no longer abstract, hypothetical possibilities: now it was clear that veterans might escape trial for crimes, even serious ones, they committed while in uniform; this eventuality had become a reality with the disclosure that over twenty veterans had escaped trial after having collectively participated in hundreds of killings.[79] That even this revelation failed to prompt legislative action might seem beyond belief, until one reminds oneself of the gentleness with which military judicial authorities customarily treated Americans accused of crimes against Vietnamese civilians; the years of indifference many legislators had shown toward the problem of veteran immunity; and the total silence, amid all the chatter about justice and the law, that was the persistent and abiding response to the legislative proposals from the Nixon administration's Department of Justice.

CHAPTER SIX

"Inexcusable and Terrible"

The Calley Conviction and the Abandonment of the Effort to Try the My Lai Veterans

The trial of Lt. William Calley was not just a legal process but also a political event. The Nixon administration monitored the progress of the trial and strategized about how to manage its political repercussions. Apart from the potential damage to the reputation of the armed forces and the erosion of public support for the war, an overriding preoccupation of the White House was how its handling of the case would affect the president's popularity and his chances of reelection in 1972.

During Nixon's first year in office White House staff gathered in two strategy groups to plan how to win Republican control of the Senate in the midterm elections of 1970.[1] Soon after the midterms, in which the Republican Party gained a couple of Senate seats but remained well short of achieving a majority, the White House established a reelection strategy that relied on the president's projecting an image of personal rectitude in order to develop public confidence in the presidency as an institution and in President Nixon himself. A memorandum written for the president reads, "We've got to create and *maintain* an impression of rectitude, of honor, of decency—and I can't stress the word decency too strongly: a person considerate of others, with a sense of high purpose above self, generous of impulse, firm but forgiving, who encourages 'the better angels of our nature' by appealing to those better angels."[2] The president, Nixon's speechwriter William Safire said, was never likely to become the object of public affection but should project an image of firmness, calmness, and decisive leadership.[3] Creating this image required careful stagecraft, though, as the record captured by memoranda and presidential annotations to documents reveals that Nixon the person was calculating, suspicious, vindictive, and completely lacking in the qualities the White House was trying to promote. Far from being driven by decency and rectitude, the White House and the president himself tended to see every issue in terms of its partisan political impact and its consequences in regard to his reelectability.

Nixon was shocked by reports of the My Lai massacre, calling the killings "inexcusable and terrible" and "a sickening tragedy."[4] However, he was reluctant to allow the massacre to undermine the war effort by demoralizing the public, believing that opponents of the war would use the atrocity to increase the pressure on the government to hasten the withdrawal of U.S. forces from Vietnam. Accordingly, he called for a public relations effort to counter the negative effects of the story.

The measures the White House contemplated came straight out of the Nixon playbook. The administration's operatives were instructed to come up with dirty tricks to discredit one witness and to "get out facts on Hue," where the Communists had committed atrocities during the Tet Offensive. To counterbalance the association of U.S. troops with atrocity the White House assembled records of the humanitarian activities of American troops and evidence about "Communist terror tactics" in 1968 and 1969. Sure enough, amid the reports on My Lai, other writings by journalists and editorialists in early December 1969 referred to Communist atrocities at Hue and elsewhere. When the media tried to pin responsibility for the massacre on American generals, Kissinger reassured Gen. Earle Wheeler, chairman of the Joint Chiefs of Staff, that Nixon would "see to it that [the generals] don't get ruined. . . . He will not permit the military to be kicked around in this country."[5]

In his early public pronouncements about the massacre Nixon managed to sound statesmanlike. The Pentagon's general counsel advised him to be cautious in his statements, making sure he simply said that the matter would be determined in court, as any comment on factual matters could undermine the Pentagon's approach to news management.[6] At his news conference of December 8, 1969, Nixon declared that one of America's goals in Vietnam was to protect the people of South Vietnam from having a government imposed on them that "has atrocity against civilians as one of its policies. We cannot ever condone or use atrocities against civilians in order to accomplish that goal." The president pointed out that many of the U.S. troops in Vietnam had helped the people by building roads, schools, churches, and pagodas. He went on to say, "Now this record of generosity, of decency, must not be allowed to be smeared and slurred because of this kind of an incident. That is why I am going to do everything I possibly can to see that all of the facts in this incident are brought to light and that those who are charged, if they are found guilty, are punished."[7] Although public responses to Nixon's statement were "relatively light," editorials in the press praised him for an "impressive performance" in his "most successful press conference." At the beginning of December 1969 Nixon's job approval rating was higher than it had been at any time since the start of his presidency, largely because of his policy of withdrawing troops from Vietnam. A CBS News poll showed that after the press conference his approval rating rose even higher to an extraordinary 81 percent nationwide.[8]

While the president was acting the statesman on the public stage, behind the scenes the Nixon White House went into action to investigate and, if need be, discredit those who played the main roles in exposing the facts of the massacre. Nixon wanted to know who was "backing" Ridenhour.[9] A "confidential investigator" interviewed Ridenhour to find out if he was "aligned with left-wing elements" or had a close relationship with Hersh. It turned out, however, that Ridenhour believed Hersh to be a "no-good son of a bitch" who had manipulated and profited from his story. In a reversal of identities better suited to a stage farce than to a "sickening tragedy," Ridenhour claimed that Hersh, an investigative journalist, had pretended to be a government representative; conversely, the White House's confidential investigator impersonated a journalist when interviewing Ridenhour. Nixon annotated the report that Ridenhour wished to sue Hersh with the handwritten comment "Good" and proposed, "Shouldn't a good news reporter be put to work on this?"[10] A few days later a memo chivvied the White House staff member Alexander Butterfield to follow up on the president's exhortation.[11]

Early the next year Robert Jordan approached Ridenhour less deceptively than the White House, that is, he did not pretend to be anyone other than the army general counsel, although, like the administration, he seems to have wanted to manipulate Ridenhour. Aware that Hersh was writing a book about the massacre, Jordan tried to impress on Ridenhour the difficulties that publicity might pose for ensuring a fair trial of the suspects. Jordan expressed the hope that Hersh could be persuaded to delay publication of his investigation until after all courts-martial had been completed, but, given the brevity of their acquaintance and the reported tensions in their relationship, Ridenhour was hardly the most likely candidate to exert influence over Hersh. Ridenhour told Jordan there was little chance Hersh could be slowed.[12]

Hersh's article in *Harper's* magazine titled "My Lai 4: A Report on the Massacre and Its Aftermath" appeared in May 1970, in the context of the massive nationwide demonstrations that took place following the American invasion of Cambodia and the killings of students by the National Guard at Kent State University in Ohio and by the state police at Jackson State University in Mississippi.[13] The article was an excerpt from a book of the same title that appeared in print the same year.[14] Hersh's revelations about the massacre and its cover-up provoked renewed public and congressional interest in the atrocity.

The army had been carefully monitoring Hersh's plans to follow up *My Lai (4)* by publishing articles in the *New Yorker* in which he claimed that the government had suppressed information about the massacre at My Khe (4).[15] The army went into overdrive to find ways of countering the argument and minimizing its impact. It weighed inviting Hersh for a briefing at which he would be asked to furnish any additional facts he had obtained beyond what the army already knew. An army memorandum read, "We would then be on record as having approached Hersh and sought his cooperation in discovering any evidence pertinent to this matter."[16] The army considered but decided against a preemptive release of information, reasoning that "if we publish now that we are clean" but Hersh then produced evidence that an atrocity had indeed occurred at My Khe (4), the army would have to publish a retraction of its denial. Moreover, if it tried to preempt his publication by releasing a new statement, it risked "opening a can of worms."[17] The chief of information for the general staff, Winant Sidle, lamented that the army did not yet know what Hersh would publish. Consequently, "he did not present a sufficiently precise target for us to shoot at now."[18]

At first, an army general staff memorandum suggested that a broad refutation should be issued in response to damaging statements in Hersh's article. It asked whether the Peers Inquiry and surrounding material should be published by a commercial publishing house; whether any of Hersh's points that did not bear on the guilt or innocence of suspects should be rebutted before the completion of judicial proceedings; what the public should be told about publication of the army's account of the massacre; whether the army should publish a monograph on the My Lai massacre itself; and a host of other questions.[19] In the event, the army decided that addressing the Hersh article would simply give him more publicity without doing any good.[20]

In June 1970 Lt. Gen. Jonathan Seaman and Lt. Gen. Albert Connor, the commanding generals under whose authority some of the officer suspects had been placed, dismissed the cases against a number of them, including Willingham, the commander of Bravo Company's 1st Platoon. The charges against him were dropped for "lack of evidence."[21] The army did not bar the reopening of the case against him, though, "if warranted."[22] Willingham was soon released from active duty and allowed quietly to leave the armed forces.[23] Upon his discharge from the army, the motives for withholding the Peers Inquiry report on My Khe (4) diminished. Jordan explained that the decision to withhold the relevant parts of the report was made in order to avoid pretrial publicity, but Willingham was the only member of Bravo Company charged with an offense.[24] An army document says that withholding sections of the Peers report safeguarded the privacy of the individuals concerned, but none of the other Bravo Company suspects was named in the report.[25]

Although initially the plan was to publish the whole report by the end of April, the government changed its mind.[26] It was very worried not only that

"Public Affairs hazards" might arise from any disclosure but also that a release of information even to certain congressional committees would lead to leaks.[27] A month after the publication of an abridged version of volume 1 of the report, Jordan approved the further release only of its chapter 5, which described the Son My operation from March 16 to 19, 1968, and only to the House subcommittee. Chapter 5, however, contains an innocuous description of Bravo Company's activities. It describes the killings by Bravo Company in language that does not hint at the death of civilians, referring to the killing of "several groups of enemy," "a total of 30 enemy KIA," and so on. Not until a later chapter does the Peers report redescribe those events as "the possible commission of war crimes" and the death of "80–90 noncombatants, including women and children." Jordan withheld this chapter, with its dramatically contrasting content and language, from the subcommittee as well as from the public.[28] It was among several chapters "purposely not included in the three copies furnished to Congress on 17 March 1970."[29]

The administration's abiding worry after the release of the Peers report lay in whether and how the My Lai cases would affect the president's political standing. A memo of August 1970 to a military assistant to the president said that "recent events" indicated that the military justice system would come under increasing attack in the next few months and could become a major national issue "which will sooner or later involve the President." It asked if contingency plans were being developed and, "assuming that there are problems with the military justice system, what kind of activity is taking place to recommend changes and improvements in the system?" This vague, woolly question could have elicited any number of responses, each of which could have begun with the words, "Please straighten up and pay attention!" After all, the judge advocates general issued annual reports on new developments in the field of military justice and their recommendations for any changes in legislation; only a month earlier the House Armed Services Subcommittee had issued its report containing three recommendations, one of which involved the jurisdictional gap. The Secretary of Defense immediately followed up with legislative proposals. Whether or not the White House perceived the congressional proposal and the Pentagon response to be a national issue, it certainly pointed to a "problem with the military justice system." Yet the administration's anxiety stemmed not from the details of any problem which might exist but from how it might play out in public debate and affect Nixon. The memorandum ended as follows: "Is anyone thinking about action that should be taken to keep this issue from reaching a boiling point and surrounding the President?"[30]

Problems in the administration of military justice, although not the sort provoking White House agitation, were certainly evident in the My Lai prosecutions. Like the cases against the officers, the cases against two enlisted men, David Mitchell and Charles Hutto, collapsed. In Mitchell's trial the military judge announced he would not allow any testimony by soldiers who had appeared at the House subcommittee hearings because the subcommittee had refused to make available a transcript of the hearings, as the government is required to do under the Jencks Act.[31] As Michal Belknap observes, "By classifying its hearings, the House Armed Services Committee wrecked the government's case against Mitchell."[32] One of Rivers's tactics to undermine the prosecutions of the My Lai defendants thus succeeded. That left the prosecution almost bereft of witnesses, and the prosecutor did not make a convincing case. The military panel, or court-martial jury, quickly made up its mind to find Mitchell not guilty.[33]

Next came the trial of Hutto, who admitted to using his M-60 machine gun to shoot a number of villagers. His statement to the CID said he had received orders to kill all the people, destroy all the food, and kill all the animals in My Lai (4). His lawyer defended him by saying that Hutto had never thought to question whether the order was illegal and that he had been trained to obey orders without question. The six officers on the panel acquitted Hutto in less than two hours.[34]

After the failure of the prosecutions of Mitchell and Hutto, the government concluded it would be impossible to win a conviction in the case of any enlisted man still in uniform: "There seemed to be a penchant of officers on military juries to accept the plea that obedience to orders was a total defense for an enlisted man, despite what international law and the Army's own rules said, and if that plea were made . . . , then the officers would acquit, no matter the evidence and no matter the law."[35] Consequently, having already dismissed the cases against several enlisted men the previous year, on January 21 and 22, 1971, the government dropped the remaining cases against the ones who were still in uniform.[36]

The army explained the decision not to charge any Bravo Company soldiers and to release them from the service by saying there was insufficient evidence on which to base a charge—but a primary reason for the scant evidence was that the principal suspects refused to talk to investigators. The army showed a determined willingness to believe any scrap of information they could use to avoid proceeding with any cases arising from the killings at My Khe (4). For example, an army general staff document reported that there was some evidence, namely, the exculpatory statements of some the perpetrators themselves, that the troops had received fire from the village and returned fire. However, the most straightforward and credible testimony given to the Peers Inquiry did not mention receiving any fire from My Khe (4) before the troops went in shooting.[37] Even the statements that mention sniper fire do not record that 1st Platoon was returning fire when the soldiers attacked My Khe (4) and its inhabitants because they had not established where the sniper shots came from and no sniper was sighted, so there was no reason to suppose the sniper was in My Khe (4).

The general staff document goes on to say that Bravo Company "had a known reputation for stressing the safeguarding of noncombatants and avoiding indiscriminate fire. Consequently, insufficient evidence exists to support either criminal or administrative action."[38] This line of reasoning has the same validity as arguing that so long as an accused murderer had a "known reputation" for not previously murdering anyone, he is probably innocent. On this ground, everyone gets a free pass to commit one major crime, and only serial killers with a known reputation for prior murders need fear a rigorous investigation. In any event, the general staff document misses an important detail: it was Capt. Earl Michles, the company commander, who was said to have stressed often the importance of avoiding indiscriminate firing in order to avoid producing noncombatant casualties.[39] This fact was irrelevant for several reasons: Michles was not present and was out of touch with 1st Platoon except for intermittent radio contact; once it entered My Khe (4), 1st Platoon's rifle and machine-gun fire was not indiscriminate but deliberately targeted at the inhabitants of My Khe (4); and, irrespective of the preferences of the company commander, it was "common knowledge" among Bravo Company that the point element "had shot many people indiscriminately" even before March 16, 1968.[40] Moreover, Willingham's radio-telephone operator testified to the CID that during the assault on My Khe (4) Willingham had ordered his platoon to "level the village."[41]

Despite the evidence against Willingham, the judge advocate general of the army concluded that he met the standards expected of an officer of his position, grade, and experience.[42] A few days before this judgment, a CID summary of the evidence against a member of the point team of Bravo Company's 1st Platoon—one of the group believed to have committed the majority of the killings—was completed. The evidence included the soldier's admission that he had killed women and children, an eyewitness statement that he had shot a boy in the head, and various corroborating statements. The investigators concluded that the soldier, discharged from the army in October 1968, had committed premeditated murder.[43] By this time, though, it had evidently been decided that nothing further would be done about the killings at My Khe (4). With the approval of the chief of staff of the army, the judge advocate general recommended to the secretary of the army that no administrative action be taken against Willingham.[44] Peers found it "difficult to understand" why charges against Willingham and certain others were dismissed without an Article 32 investigation.[45] Toward the end of his military career Peers was asked whether there was anything about the inquiry he would have done differently, and he replied that he wished he had looked with "a little greater depth into the activities of Bravo Company."[46]

Had the facts of the My Khe (4) massacre been connected with events at My Lai (4), it would have been difficult to escape the conclusion that the troops who said they were following orders from their commanders were telling the truth; otherwise one would have had to accept the implausible idea that two groups of men operating in geographically close proximity happened to engage in spontaneous rampages of violence at the same time without encouragement from above. Such a possibility is rendered even more implausible by the realization that all three of Charlie Company's platoons took part in the massacre at My Lai (4), and one of the two Bravo Company platoons that came into close contact with the civilian inhabitants of Son My acted in the same way.[47] These circumstances suggest that the commanders of these platoons believed they were acting with a common purpose and thus implicate the officers who planned the operation and gave the illegal orders that the whole village be destroyed. The army, in an internal document carefully monitoring Hersh's reporting, quoted one of his articles in the *New Yorker*: the My Khe (4) atrocity is important because of "its vital connection with the My Lai 4 tragedy; the American public's ignorance of it; the total, detailed knowledge of it among the Peers investigators, the Department of the Army, and higher Pentagon officials; and the failure of any of these agencies to see that the men involved were prosecuted."[48]

The possibility that people might put the two massacres together and conclude they were part of a deliberate, coordinated attack establishes a motive for the acrobatics the army's military justice authorities were performing in order to keep the geographic extent of the killings on March 16, 1968, out of public view. In the event, by the time the details of the My Khe (4) massacre emerged, very few had the will to follow the facts to where they logically led, and the whole issue of command responsibility and the continuing cover-up, with the army's military justice apparatus implicated in it, was evaded.

The cases against higher officers were also withdrawn or ended in administrative sanctions.[49] In late January 1971 General Seaman at Fort Meade, where several officers awaited prosecution, announced that all charges against Maj. Gen. Samuel Koster would be dropped "in the interest of justice," even though there was "some evidence" that he knew civilians had been killed at My Lai and failed to investigate.[50] Charges against the other officers who had been accused of offenses such as dereliction of duty and failure to obey lawful regulations were also dismissed by Seaman, on the advice of staff judge advocates who said there was insufficient evidence to justify prosecutions.[51] Brig. Gen. George Young's and Koster's records were flagged, along with those of Col. Oran Henderson, Col. Nels Parson, and twenty others, including some of the enlisted men who had been acquitted or against whom the cases had collapsed. This action effectively wrecked the officers' military careers.[52] The negative reactions in Congress encouraged further administrative sanctions against Koster and his second in command, Young. Koster was reduced in rank and, on May 19, 1971, both he and Young were stripped of their Distinguished Service Medals and had letters of censure placed in their files for their failure to investigate the My Lai massacre properly.[53]

The decision to end the prosecutions of the enlisted men still in uniform restricted the scope of the remaining prosecutions to four officers, Calley, Kotouc, Medina, and Henderson. The first to be tried was the lowest ranking of the four, the hapless Calley. His was the sole prosecution that took place at Fort Benning, Georgia. The fact that he seemed to have been singled out for special treatment and that he was the first (and, as it transpired, only) suspect convicted for his role in the massacre after higher officers had received only administrative sanctions helps to explain the public outcry against his conviction.

Calley's court martial began on November 12, 1970, and lasted four months. He was charged with having murdered a number of "Oriental human beings," a phrase that grated on some and caused the chief of military justice of the army to tell his staff that future criminal charges arising from the massacre should refer simply to "human beings."[54] Several witnesses stated that Calley had ordered groups of unarmed, unresisting Vietnamese civilians killed. First Platoon members Dennis Conti, Charles Sledge, and Thomas Turner said that Calley had killed a substantial number himself.[55] The evidence against him was overwhelming. His defense team argued that he had been obeying Medina's orders, believing he could be shot for failing to obey his commander.[56]

On March 29, 1971, after thirteen days of deliberation the court-martial jury found Calley guilty of murdering at least twenty-two civilians and of assault with the intent to murder a child. Two days later he was sentenced to life imprisonment at hard labor. The failure up until then to hold higher officers criminally accountable for their role in ordering and covering up the massacre increased the widespread public repugnance to Calley's life sentence, a circumstance from which the White House tried to gain political advantage.

As soon as the Calley verdict was announced, the White House commissioned a survey by Opinion Research Corporation to test various possible responses to the Calley conviction, allowing it to fine-tune its actions to suit the public mood. "Let's keep our eye on the ball," Nixon said to his aides. The ball was not military justice; it was maintaining public backing of the war. Nixon continued, "Let's see if this time there isn't a way that we can be on the side of the people for a change, instead of always doing what's cautious, proper, and efficient."[57] There was also a "bigger cause": "how we can hold enough support for a year and a half [until the presidential election] to maintain our conduct of the war."[58]

As Lawrence Jacobs and Robert Shapiro note, public opinion was a "guiding concern" of the Nixon White House, and early on in his presidency Nixon had established an apparatus for keeping abreast of the polls in order to track "what moves and concerns the average guy." Nixon favored private polls commissioned by the White House because they could drill down into the nuances of opinion in greater depth than published polls.[59] The first White House polls on the Calley verdict were conducted on April 1, 1971, and demonstrated overwhelming public sympathy for Calley. In response to a question about his sentence, 78 percent of the respondents disagreed with the verdict, and, of those, 65 percent thought he should be set free and 75 percent that the president should intervene in the case.[60] Nixon and his aides spent most of the day debating what he should do. Some staff members wanted immediate action to free Calley or lighten his sentence, while others opposed a radical reversal so soon after the sentence.

The legal research the White House had commissioned established that to intervene in the case would be a derogation of the military justice system's review process, and that it could not properly begin until a trial transcript was prepared, which would take at least two months. Nixon was afraid of making a misstep: as Haldeman observed, public opinion "runs high on this," and the public's "awareness level" of 96 percent was higher than on any other issue on which the White House had polled. The administration decided on a course of action carefully calibrated to satisfy the groundswell of sympathy for Calley without inviting the charge of excessive interference with the course of justice. Nixon instructed Assistant to the President for Domestic Affairs John Ehrlichman to consult with the secretaries of several executive departments so that the White House could say it had acted with deliberation and taken advice from many quarters.[61]

The next day, a Saturday, Ron Ziegler, the White House press secretary, and Ehrlichman announced from San Clemente, where Nixon resided during his visits to California, that "before any final sentence is carried out in the case of Lt. Calley, the President will personally review the case and finally decide it." Military officers involved in legal affairs saw the announcement as undermining the military justice system.[62] The administration, though, had determined it would meet the wishes of the public and of promilitary members of Congress. Nixon acted then because he wanted his actions to dominate the stories and analysis in the Sunday newspapers and news magazines, which went to press on Sundays.[63] The White House Office of Legal Counsel continued thereafter to investigate the legal and constitutional niceties that would constrain the president's power to interfere with the execution of the sentence.[64]

The White House followed up its immediate post-verdict temperature taking with a new privately commissioned poll. It asked respondents whether Calley should be set free or have his sentence reduced; whether they agreed with Nixon's decision to review the case before final sentencing; and whether they agreed with the action of releasing Calley from the stockade and confining him to quarters at Fort Benning. The poll established that an overwhelming majority of the public favored the president's intervention in the case. Three-quarters of the respondents approved of Nixon's decision to review the case, and four out of five people agreed that Calley should be confined to quarters. Half the sample, though, would have been even more lenient: 51 percent thought Nixon should free Calley, and a further 28 percent that Nixon should substantially reduce his sentence.[65]

In Washington, two White House staff members added to the picture by visiting and telephoning fifteen members of Congress from all regions of the country to obtain a sense of how their constituents' mail was running. The universal response was that the public disapproved of the verdict, and most of the elected representatives reported that the numbers were hugely skewed in favor of leniency toward Calley. For example, of one hundred telephone calls and thirty-five to forty letters to Rep. Peter Frelinghuysen, a Republican from New Jersey, all were said to have been pro-Calley and referred to him as a victim and scapegoat. Of two hundred letters written to Rep. Bob Stafford, a Republican from Vermont, all but two approved of the president's decision. Several of the representatives said that the president's moves—releasing Calley from the stockade and announcing his decision ultimately to review the outcome of the trial—had quieted the public reaction.[66]

Members of the public who wrote directly to the White House also favored leniency toward Calley, the letters at first running one hundred to one in his favor.[67] For example, Bartlett L. Kennedy of Santa Monica, California, wrote that his youngest son, a marine, had been killed in Vietnam when his platoon commander had led him into a supposedly friendly village. Had his son's commander acted the way Calley did, Kennedy said, his son might be alive today: "This is a war where the ordinary rules do not and cannot apply. I do not condone what Lt. Calley did—but surely it was not premeditated murder!"[68] Pauline Small of Cahokia, Illinois, who described herself as a "sad mother" of a soldier serving in Vietnam, asked, "Why are they taking all our boys away from home and teaching them to KILL and then when they do what they are ordered to do they get punished over and over again[?]"[69] Julia Breidenstein, of Wheatridge, Colorado, wrote that Calley did not ask to go to Vietnam. The crime of which he was convicted was an act of war: "War is war, and incidents like these have happened in all wars."[70]

The Department of Defense set up two phone lines, one for those opposing the verdict and sentence and one for those approving them. At the end of the first day, not a single caller had approved the verdict or commended the army for holding the trial.[71] Within a month after the verdict the Pentagon and the Department of the Army had received 2,153 telegrams, 75 of which favored the trial and verdict, the remainder being sympathetic to Calley; of 12,000 letters and postcards, 350 endorsed the verdict and sentence.[72] The army felt itself to be under so much pressure to justify the decision to prosecute Calley that it put out a fact sheet saying that although the legal action was "painful and difficult" the army would have failed to meet its obligation to the law had it not acted.[73] It began to devise a media strategy both to cultivate known "military friends" regarding the topic of civilian casualties and to gain the backing of others.[74]

The president had gauged the public's mood well. Louis Harris and Associates established that the majority of respondents did not believe Nixon had undermined the system of military justice by showing sympathy for Calley; that he went as far as he could in showing he disagreed with the decision in the case; and that he was right to have Calley removed from the stockade and confined to quarters while Calley appealed the judgment. Fifty-eight percent rated Nixon's handling of the case as "excellent" or "pretty good."[75] Nixon's approval ratings jumped by 13 percent as soon as the White House announced that he intended to review the verdict and that Calley had been released from the stockade.[76] This upsurge was welcome because by April 1971, following a catastrophic South Vietnamese invasion of Laos, approval of Nixon's handling of the war had sunk to 41 percent, and the administration was seeking by any means possible to bolster his policies.[77] Nixon considered this period to be the low point of his first term of office, and he began to doubt not just whether he could win reelection the following year but whether he could win his party's nomination as its presidential candidate.

In Nixon's estimation the Vietnam War was likely to be the main issue in the presidential election in 1972.[78] He established a My Lai working group to determine how to control the political repercussions of the My Lai cases, keeping abreast of the continuing legal proceedings and monitoring public opinion polls.[79] The White House counsel, John Dean, enjoined all White House staff to be circumspect in their responses to any public queries about the Calley case.[80] A few months later Egil "Bud" Krogh, who, like Dean, achieved notoriety as a result of Watergate, told Dean he was worried about leaks from judge advocate generals' offices in the armed services. He recommended that Dean communicate with the Department of Defense through an intermediary in order to "hide our trail" and avoid adverse stories.[81]

Peers criticized Nixon for his lack of moral leadership and for his failure to inform the American public about the proper conduct of its armed forces: "Instead of treating the public clamor over Calley's conviction as a short-term political problem to be 'defused' by promising to review the matter, the President could well have taken the occasion to remind the American people of this country's obligations to punish those who commit war crimes, of the overwhelming evidence of Calley's guilt as adduced at the trial, and of the fact that he had been found guilty after a long trial, not by anti-military war protesters but by a panel of his peers."[82] Facing the likelihood, as he saw it, of a tough reelection campaign in 1972, Nixon failed in a typically Nixonian way, by seeking political advantage. His administration did not rest at trying to gain popularity by promising to intervene in the Calley case; the popular outcry in favor of Calley also afforded an opportunity to settle the long-standing issues about the prosecution of the My Lai veterans.

On April 8, 1971, the Pentagon announced that it could find no way of prosecuting its former servicemen and that a number of suspects were free from the threat of a court-martial, even ones who had publicly admitted to being personally responsible for killing unarmed civilians at My Lai (4). As a result, it said, some fifteen veterans who had been investigated for their part in the massacre would not be prosecuted. The Pentagon spokesman, Jerry Friedheim, said that the Departments of Defense and Justice "had discussed the question for 18 months" but could find no constitutional means to try the men. Friedheim reported, "It has turned out to be, as a practical matter, an insoluble problem at this time.... At the moment, nobody's trying any more." However, as the *New York Times* reported, Friedheim said the Department of Defense did not rule out future attempts at prosecution.[83] The *Washington Post* reported that it was finally decided that military tribunals or commissions would have no legal jurisdiction over former servicemen but that "some lawyers in the Defense Department were divided on the issue," a recognition that Jordan and the army's judge advocate general believed the contrary. "Defense officials," the *Post* reported, had determined that the army has no jurisdiction over civilians for crimes they committed while in active service.[84] Soon after, an internal document of the Judge Advocate General's Corps, referring to Friedheim's announcement, confirmed this was the situation.[85] Friedheim's announcement does not tell the whole story, though, because it omits an important step on the way: the decision to forego the prosecutions of the veterans was made in large part because of the outcome of the earlier courts-martial.

As we have seen, Jordan had obtained the agreement of the relevant executive departments that the prosecutions of the veterans were legally possible, and the judge advocate general of the army had agreed. While they could not be confident that the constitutional problems would be satisfied, they had decided that trying the veterans by a general court-martial or a military commission was feasible. They decided not to pursue the prosecutions for a practical reason: the judge advocate general and the army general counsel determined that the prosecutions "may not be warranted in view of acquittals and dismissals of charges against others involved."[86] In other words, because the courts-martial of the enlisted men had ended in failure, there was no point in taking on the constitutional problems in mounting trials of veterans that were likely to end in the same way.

Years later, when interviewed by a journalist, Jordan said he did not recall hearing back from secretary of the army or from Nixon administration officials after submitting his memorandum, and, as far as he knew, it was not pursued further. The reason the government did not proceed with the plan to prosecute the veteran suspects was, as he remembered, the lack of endorsement at the highest echelons of government: "We would have needed the president's support to proceed," he recalled. "We didn't have much support upstairs."[87] Jordan's recollection appears to be incomplete in that it omits any reference to the discussion with the other executive departments and the judge advocate general—such a lapse is understandable given an interval of over thirty years.[88] The straightforward reason, namely, that there was little point in conducting the prosecutions given the court-martial acquittals of the enlisted men in uniform and the dismissal of the charges against those still awaiting trial, requires little explanation. Convening a military commission to prosecute the veterans would have produced a no-win situation: either the trials would have resulted in further acquittals or, if they had succeeded, they would have cast doubt on the effectiveness of the system of military justice that had failed in the prosecution of the enlisted men still in uniform. What that explanation leaves a bit mysterious, though, is why the government waited until after the Calley verdict to declare that it had given up its attempts to try the veteran suspects; and why it explained this decision by means of a cover story, a reference to a constitutional problem that it had concluded in January 1970 was not insuperable. Why did the Defense Department not simply declare that it had decided not to prosecute the My Lai veteran suspects in January 1971 when, after the acquittal of Hutto, Lt. Gen. Connor dismissed the charges against the remaining enlisted men awaiting prosecution at courts-martial?

It seems plausible that the outcry against the Calley sentence and verdict was a final deterrent to the prosecution of the veterans. Many of the protests expressed anger at the leniency shown to high-ranking officers in contrast to the treatment of Calley. Prosecuting former enlisted men would have exacerbated the appearance that the low men in the military hierarchy were being punished while their superiors were escaping responsibility for the massacre. Seen in this light, Friedheim's statement that the Defense Department and the Justice Department had discussed the matter for eighteen months but had found it legally impossible to bring the suspects to court may be a more respectable sounding way of saying that, having given up on the idea of pursuing the prosecution of the My Lai veteran suspects, the administration had been awaiting the opportune moment to bury the issue. If so, the government used a legal excuse to cover what was essentially a political decision. But this does not tell the whole story. Friedheim's announcement had political repercussions that reveal that at least some parts of the state had an ulterior motive for keeping alive the possibility that the veterans might be prosecuted.

An antiwar organization called the Citizens' Commission of Inquiry into U.S. War Crimes (CCI), greeted Friedheim's announcement "with enthusiasm." The CCI believed the announcement would "encourage thousands of Vietnam veterans to come forward and relate their own experiences in Vietnam without fear of criminal prosecution." This development opened the door for a "full exposure of the extent and scope of U.S. war crimes in Southeast Asia."[89] The army's general staff was equally aware that veterans might now speak freely about their knowledge of war crimes and greeted this prospect with far less enthusiasm. It was less concerned with what thousands of veterans might say than with the potential testimony of a handful of former members of Bravo Company of the 4th Battalion of the 3rd Infantry, the company that carried out the attack on My Khe (4) on March 16, 1968.

The army's investigation had established that Bravo Company's 1st Platoon was under strength on March 16, 1968, consisting of only twenty-two men. These included the most likely suspects in any crime that had taken place at My Khe (4). Mario Fernandez, one of those who provided what Peers considered the "best information," testified that about half the men in 1st Platoon had engaged in the killing of villagers.[90] Two of the members of the platoon had been killed in later actions, and eight had left the army and either refused to talk to the Peers Inquiry or said they did not remember anything about the killings.[91] The general staff's greatest worry was about the possible testimony of the four members of the point element of Willingham's platoon, only one of whom testified to the Peers Inquiry and provided little information in doing so. All four enlisted men had left the armed forces.[92] In addition, some of those who did testify "had poor memories or were deliberately misleading."[93] Their silence had weakened the case against their platoon commander, Willingham. Any new statements by the veterans might bring pressure on the army to reopen the case, and the My Khe (4) case potentially could bring new and unwelcome attention to the events of March 16, 1968.

Amidst the discussion of the army's response to Hersh's articles, a general staff memorandum to Westmoreland, now the army chief of staff, and his deputy, Vice Chief of Staff Bruce Palmer, complained that, encouraged by Friedheim's "ill-timed" announcement, "B/4/3 [Bravo Company] witnesses—previously silent—may reveal to Hersh testimony re the killings at My Khe (4)."[94] The complaint was not about the decision to abandon the prosecution of the veterans but about the timing of its announcement, meaning that the general staff would have preferred the announcement to be delayed. Why?

This memorandum establishes an ulterior motive in the army's decision not to announce earlier that the plans to prosecute the veteran suspects had been dropped. There was no better way to encourage the silence of the My Khe (4) veterans than to leave them in fear of being prosecuted or to raise the chance that their testimony might reopen the case against Willingham, who was no longer in active service. The atrocity at My Khe (4), the second massacre on March 16, 1968, was the event that would potentially point the finger of responsibility upward because it would establish that the massacre at My Lai (4) was not an isolated event and that elements of two companies that belonged to Task Force Barker had swept into villages believed to be inhabited by Viet Cong sympathizers and had deliberately attacked their unarmed and unresisting inhabitants. These circumstances would make it impossible to pin the responsibility for the massacre solely on a single lieutenant and the platoon he commanded. Members of the general staff and Westmoreland had a twofold reason for being anxious: not just about the reputation of the army as a whole but about Westmoreland's own reputation and legal position. As Telford Taylor had argued, the finger would eventually have pointed not only to brigade and divisional commanders but also to the MACV commander, Westmoreland. Leaving a deliberate, strategic ambiguity about whether the government had discovered a constitutional means of prosecuting military veterans served the interests of anyone who might wish to prevent further disclosures about the massacre at My Khe (4).

Westmoreland took a personal interest in the review of the actions of Bravo Company once he learned of Hersh's publication plans. He wanted to be sure the army had demonstrably done everything it could to investigate the killings at My Khe (4). He recommended publishing the whole of volume 1 of the Peers Report as soon as possible, although he acknowledged the difficulties of doing so with prosecutions still pending. He also advised issuing a press release to "diminish or destroy the credibility of Hersh's claims." Given that all or most of the potential witnesses were out of the army, Westmoreland's advisers fretted that Hersh might have "uncovered one or more of them who has since 'remembered' events of the B/4/3 operation." Westmoreland observed that chapter 7 of the Peers Report, which dealt with Bravo Company's actions at My Khe (4), tells of the shooting and rape of noncombatants. "The question is to explain how this report jibes with subsequent actions taken by the Army," he said.[95] Well might he have been agitated, given that the sole result of the investigation of Bravo Company to date was the preferral and then the dismissal of charges against one platoon commander and a concerted effort to prevent information about the extent of the alleged crimes from entering the public domain.

Following a television appearance by Hersh in which he described the planned article, Westmoreland's deputy, Palmer, approved sending the secretary of the army a report by the judge advocate general about the My Khe (4) killings, with an annotation from the general staff.[96] Westmoreland, however, edited the annotation to delete the following statement: "The 8 Apr 71 OSD [Office of the Secretary of Defense] announcement—that discharged soldiers implicated in the Son My Incident would not be prosecuted by DoD or DoJ [the Department of Defense or the Department of Justice]—tends to encourage the disclosure of testimony from previously uncooperative witnesses through the media." The document went on to explain the possible repercussions of Hersh's further reporting on the matter, but this passage too was deleted.[97] Westmoreland's general staff appeared to be playing a complicated game, urging caution and orchestrating a departmental response to the possible revelations it anticipated Hersh's articles would make, while determining not to confide in the secretary of the army a frank account of the reason for its uneasiness. Sidle said he had known Hersh for many years and found him to be "totally unpredictable . . . , an indefatigable worker and digger for information." He had little doubt Hersh had dug up some new information. Sidle went on, "I am already working with the General Counsel and ASD (PA) [Assistant Secretary of Defense for Public Affairs] on being prepared for allegations of a massacre by Willingham's platoon."[98] The army general staff prepared a "talking paper" on Hersh's allegations and carefully drafted and redrafted a position statement downplaying the connection between the killings at My Lai (4) and My Khe (4).[99]

Between the Calley verdict in April 1971 and the end of the year the remaining prosecutions of officers arising from the My Lai massacre (Kotouc, Henderson, and Medina) resulted in acquittals. After the last of these trials had ended (albeit Calley's appeals would run until they reached the Supreme Court in 1976), Taylor wrote an article in the *New York Times* drawing attention to the obligations of the United States as a signatory of the Geneva Conventions. By then, Hersh had written articles in the *New Yorker* disclosing the parts of the Peers report that had been kept confidential while the trials were going on. Now that it was clear that Calley's was not the only platoon that had perpetrated the massacre and that members of two companies had been involved in the mass killings at Son My, Taylor said it was absurd for Calley alone to be held criminally responsible. He also drew attention to the continuing problem of the jurisdictional gap. The government, he said, had failed to enact a legislative response to the Supreme Court decision of 1955 that immunized former servicemen from prosecution for crimes they were alleged to have committed while in service. That decision, he wrote, should have stimulated legislative action to confer jurisdiction on either federal courts or other suitable tribunals. The government's failure to take that action was a "plain breach of our obligation, under the Geneva Conventions," to enact legislation to effectuate penal sanctions for war crimes. "The consequence of this failure," Taylor wrote, "was that those involved in Mylai who had left the service before the disclosures were immune."[100] He might have added that those who remained in the army at the time of the disclosures but who were allowed to leave before the government preferred charges against them also became immune.

Taylor proposed a number of actions as a result of the lessons of My Lai, among which was "enactment of legislation authorizing appropriate tribunals to try ex-servicemen accused of crimes committed while in service outside the United States." The article was discussed in the White House (a copy is in Dean's papers at the Nixon Library), but the administration took no steps to implement Taylor's recommendation.[101] Army officers at a high level of command redoubled their effort to mount an effective defense against Taylor's charges.[102] The acting judge advocate general of the army counseled against stirring up more public debate and suggested that any letter responding to Taylor must be well written, meeting the high standard established by the Office of the Deputy Chief of Staff for Operations, while also being coordinated with the efforts of the Office of the Deputy Chief of Staff for Personnel, which was managing the army's response to the massacre.[103]

Dean wrote a memorandum about legal issues surrounding the Calley court-martial and recognized the jurisdictional gap arising from *Toth v. Quarles,* which meant that the My Lai veterans could not be tried. He said the hiatus in the UCMJ had existed since 1955 and "should be corrected." He also mentioned Ervin's long-standing effort to plug the gap and, intriguingly, said that in 1970 the Defense, State and Justice Departments had agreed on a legislative alternative to Ervin's proposal, "but no action has been taken since."[104] Perhaps Dean knew more than appears in the record. It is plausible he was referring to the Defense Department–approved replacements for H.R. 4225, but there is no evidence they had gained the sanction of the other executive departments.

Dean seems therefore to have mistakenly exaggerated the degree of departmental support for the proposed legislation. Such a level of inattention to detail appears to be at odds with the compulsive wonkiness of the White House staff, that is, until one recalls that the awareness of minutiae by Nixon's men was selective and often driven by a narrow political agenda. One may recall as well that Dean reported his staff to be "hopelessly overworked" by early 1971, the period in which it began to research the legal issues related to My Lai.[105] Thus, it is entirely possible that while looking into the constitutional and procedural issues having to do with presidential intervention in a court-martial, Dean's staff had only a sketchy understanding of the circumstances that had allowed some twenty suspects in the My Lai massacre to go unprosecuted for want of a jurisdiction in which to try them. Such a lapse by the White House counsel is a telling sign of just how disengaged the Nixon administration was from the investigation of the legal and constitutional measures being contemplated in order to prosecute the My Lai veterans.

Most striking about the Dean memorandum is its detachment from the substantive issues, which is revealed by its phrasing. He says, "Reportedly, many servicemen involved in the My Lai incident cannot be proceeded against because of lack of jurisdiction." The key word here is *reportedly:* it implies this is an issue someone has told Dean about and signifies that there may even be some doubt about the matter. It is not the sort of definite statement one would expect from someone who had been involved in researching the issue or trying to do something about it. The description of the legal conundrum, with its reference to Ervin's legislation, treats it as part of a discussion going on elsewhere, even though the executive branch had been wrestling with it for the past eighteen months. The memorandum appeared just five weeks after the Pentagon announced it was abandoning its effort to prosecute the servicemen, and the broad brushstrokes in which it paints the matter contrast with the exquisite detail with which various members of the Army and Defense Departments were engaging in intrigue. In that Dean was the White House's legal point man on the My Lai cases, one may infer that the White House was uninvolved in the debate in which the executive departments were engaged.

Such indifference might seem astonishing but for the record of the Nixon administration's overall response to the My Lai massacre and its aftermath. As Peers observed, the White House regarded it as a political problem to be "defused" rather than as an occasion for moral leadership, public education, and the rigorous defense of justice. The Nixon administration seems to have determined—with some justification—that the public had no appetite for further prosecutions of low-ranking troops, as the "scapegoat" argument would be even stronger in the case of enlisted men than it was in Calley's case. The administration's decision resolved the long-standing constitutional matter by ensuring that the suspects, including confessed killers, would get away with their crimes.

Consistent with the public preference for leniency, Calley's life sentence was reduced by the reviewing authority to twenty years. Calley's appeals were heard by the Army Court of Military Review in February 1973 and the U.S. Court of Military Appeals in December 1973. Both affirmed the verdict. The secretary of the army affirmed the conviction but reduced Calley's sentence to ten years, which made him eligible for parole in the summer of 1974. In May 1974 Nixon considered the final review he had promised to conduct. He could have pardoned Calley or further reduced his sentence, but such a decision would have been controversial and pointless as Calley would soon be eligible for parole. Nixon decided not to intervene.[106] In November 1974, after a confinement of three and a half years, Calley was paroled.[107] A few days later the undisclosed parts of the Peers Report were at last published.

Some considered the publication overdue. In 1972, once the My Lai courts-martial had ended with one conviction, five acquittals in further cases, and the dismissal of the remaining charges, Rep. Samuel Stratton, a member of the four-person House Armed Services investigating subcommittee panel, had demanded, to no avail, the publication of all sections of the Peers Inquiry report not bearing on Calley's appeals.[108] Not even a lawsuit by Rep. Les Aspin could pry the full report from the army's grip, and it was not until November 1974 that the unreleased sections began to be published.[109] Comparing the version released to the public and to Congress in March and April 1970 against the version withheld from them, it is difficult to escape the conclusion that the team of officers who determined which parts of the report to release perpetrated a new cover-up, or at least prolonged the cover-up that the members of Bravo Company had begun.[110]

There was no public outcry over the announced abandonment of the effort to find a constitutional means to prosecute the My Lai veteran suspects, demonstrating that, whatever his failings as a moral leader, Nixon led an administration that had an astute sense of political timing and an accurate measure of the public's mood. It appears, though, that for once the White House, disengaged from the details of the jurisdictional gap, was outdone in its manipulativeness. After Jordan had led a serious effort to find a means of prosecuting the My Lai veterans by means of a military commission, the existence of the jurisdictional gap intertwined with a strategic calculus by military authorities prompted by the discovery of a second massacre on March 16, 1968. The jurisdictional gap initially served the interests of the army, who wished to be seen to have pursued the case exhaustively but who also wanted to manage the bad news and contain the story by minimizing the number of prosecutions. Once it had been determined that a military commission would not be convened to prosecute the veterans, high-ranking officers in the army general staff wished nevertheless to prolong the uncertainty over whether or not veterans could be prosecuted. It is difficult to draw any inference from this examination of the documentary record than the one proposed above: that strategic ambiguity served the interests of protagonists who wanted the Bravo Company veterans to remain silent.

Ervin received only one letter from a disgruntled constituent: G. C. Slack of High Point, North Carolina, sent him a copy of a letter he wrote to Calley's civilian attorney, George Latimer, complaining that the courts did not have jurisdiction over veterans and expressing disgust at what he justifiably called "immunity upon discharge." He condemned the inaction of the Senate Constitutional Rights Subcommittee and launched a diatribe against Ervin, which he continued on the back of the envelope he mailed to Ervin. The scrawled letter, cantankerous and peppered with folksy sayings, seems to contain the ravings of a crank; yet it is the only constituent letter I have seen in the course of my research in several archives that seems both knowledgeable about the responsibilities of the relevant congressional committee and dismayed over the lack of action to close the jurisdictional gap.[111]

The matter received scant media attention. In one telling instance, in a round-table discussion on the Calley case broadcast in May 1971, Rep. Robert F. Drinan brought up the jurisdictional gap, the effect of which had been confirmed by the Pentagon the month before: "The unfortunate point is that once a person is out of the military . . . he is not really accountable to any court. The federal courts have no jurisdiction over the matter." Drinan, a Massachusetts Democrat, was a lawyer and the first Catholic priest elected to Congress, and he believed the war in Vietnam was "genocidal."[112]

If the interviewer understood the force of Drinan's statement about the lack of jurisdiction, he gave no indication of it. He responded by turning to another guest, a Vietnam veteran, and asking him for his view. The veteran entirely missed or ignored the point of Drinan's statement, expressed his hurt that all Vietnam veterans were lumped together, and said that most veterans had not committed crimes in Vietnam. The issue of whether veterans who *had* committed crimes could be prosecuted in any court was overlooked. The discussion moved on. When someone working for the Army Judge Advocate General's Corps wrote a summary of the broadcast, the issue of jurisdiction did not figure among the topics it mentioned.[113]

Ervin, as we have seen, had been a staunch supporter of legislative proposals to close the gap, submitting them again and again for consideration by the Constitutional Rights Subcommittee, but his call to conscience was decidedly the minority view. The majority of the legislature was content to leave the jurisdictional lacuna that allowed 90 percent of the perpetrators of the My Lai massacre immunity from prosecution. Robinson Everett writes that the issue was later "routinely raised in oversight hearings of the House and Senate Armed Services Committees."[114] What Everett neglects to say is that after one last throw of the dice, Ervin's heart seems to have gone out of the effort to close the jurisdictional gap affecting veteran offenders. Was Ervin discouraged by the failure of the legislative effort, having expressed the hope in 1970 that the massacre might prompt some legislative action? Certainly his attitude to the rights of defendants was unchanged.

Consistent with his frequently stated concern for the rights of those accused of military crimes, it turned out that Ervin's natural sympathy lay with Calley. He wrote to one constituent that a soldier does not have to obey a manifestly illegal order but that he himself was reluctant to see that principle invoked "because I do not believe it is practical for a soldier to pass on [i.e., to vet] the legality of the orders he receives before he carries [them] into execution." This statement implies that Calley would have needed to consult a lawyer or a legal treatise to determine that massacring civilians was a violation of the law.[115] Ervin wrote to another constituent who opposed Calley's conviction, "Like you, I had entertained the hope that the military jury would acquit Lt. Calley." Ervin supposed that Calley had been under a degree of tension that precluded his having killed with premeditation or had been acting "in obedience to orders of a superior which he determined to be valid."[116]

The majority of constituents who wrote to Ervin about the verdict also sympathized with Calley, and Ervin's staff seems to have overlooked the possibility that any of the correspondents actually favored it. This led to an embarrassing result when Ervin signed his standard reply to three supporters of the verdict, telling them, "Like you, I had entertained the hope that the military jury would acquit Lt. Calley," a view in which they did not concur. They wrote back to Ervin suggesting he tell his staff to read his letters before sending a rote reply. One of them told Ervin that the senator's reply nauseated him and that he drew comfort only from the fact that there were "six honest men in the army," the court-martial panel members who convicted Calley.[117]

Ervin's views about the Calley trial show that, in proposing legislation to close the jurisdictional gap, he was above all focused on guaranteeing the constitutional rights of defendants accused of crimes committed while in uniform, not on assisting in their prosecution. The arguments he made on these lines were not sugarcoating to make the prosecution of veterans more attractive to his fellow legislators: he meant what he said, and he believed American legal forums to be superior to foreign and international ones. Indeed, since the 1950s these concerns had led him to oppose the Genocide Convention and "treaty law," just as Bricker had done. Although southerners like Ervin opposed the Genocide Convention in the 1950s as an infringement on state's rights involving racial questions, Ervin continued to oppose the measure because it might subject U.S. citizens to trials before foreign and international tribunals. In a speech of 1985 that confirmed his abiding sympathy for the legal predicaments of U.S. troops, Ervin again opposed the Genocide Convention, asking, "How can any intelligent Senator who loves our country vote to ratify a Convention which sanctions the trial and punishment in the court of a foreign foe or an [international] penal tribunal of an American soldier whose only offense is that he killed or wounded an enemy of the United States while fighting for his country in a land beyond the seas?"[118] Ervin's zeal to pass laws plugging the jurisdictional gap did not arise from his determination to ensure the prosecution of those who had once worn the nation's military uniforms; it arose from his adamant desire to ensure that when U.S. troops and veterans were prosecuted they would enjoy all the legal rights that the Constitution and American trial procedures promised to U.S. citizens.

Ervin wished Calley had been acquitted. One could reasonably suppose that he felt the same sympathy for the discharged troops who might have been prosecuted had his legislative proposal to close the jurisdictional gap been passed. After all, they were of even lower rank than Calley, and Ervin's reflections on the effects of strain or of a superior's orders might have applied at least as much to them as to the platoon leader. But no such view diminished Ervin's efforts to close the jurisdictional gap affecting veteran suspects.

On May 3, 1971, less than a month after expressing his disappointment that the court-martial jury had convicted Calley, Ervin once again proposed a pair of bills, S. 1744 and S. 1745, which would have vested jurisdiction in federal courts to try veterans and civilians accompanying the armed forces.[119] And while the jurisdiction of the courts under S. 1745 would be prospective only, jurisdiction under S. 1744, the law covering veteran offenders, would have been retrospective.

Ervin explained his renewed proposal of the bills by saying that the recent conviction of Calley as well as allegations of other crimes committed by former servicemen (principally a fraud involving NCO clubs and post exchanges around the world) had brought attention to a "serious defect in criminal jurisdiction" which had existed since 1955.[120] After "extensive consultation" between the Departments of Defense and Justice, "no solution could be found to the problem," and therefore others implicated in the My Lai massacre could not be prosecuted. Ervin spells out the legislative consequences of inaction and the embarrassing judicial result: "The situation in which we find ourselves today, and the embarrassment of the Army and the Justice Department in not being able to bring to trial the individuals involved in Mylai or the PX scandals, is a direct result of procrastination and indecision by the Justice Department and the Defense Department for over a decade."[121]

Despite the discouraging circumstances, Ervin, far from giving up, redoubled his efforts to justify passage of the legislation, grappling even more firmly with the difficult issue of its retrospective application. As Ervin set out the matter, Article I, § 9 of the Constitution prohibited ex post facto laws, and the Supreme Court had made judgments that set out which laws came within that prohibition. A law was defined as ex post facto if it made an action a crime that was not a crime before the law was enacted, if it aggravated the crime by making it more serious than it had been, if it made the punishment of the crime more severe, or if it altered the legal rules of evidence.[122] The Supreme Court had decided, however, that a change of place of trial for an offense after its commission was not an ex post facto law. As Ervin read the relevant case, it involved not just a change in jurisdiction but the creation of a new jurisdiction where none had previously existed.[123] Ervin therefore regarded the case as "almost identical to the situation presented by this proposal."[124] Ervin's presentation of the matter constituted a forceful justification for the retrospective application of the law he proposed, and it is difficult to see why that matter had become so urgent as to demand the legal research his staff performed except for the purposes of prosecuting the My Lai veteran suspects.

Both S. 1744 and S. 1745 were referred to the Constitutional Rights Subcommittee on May 13, 1971. Reports were requested from the attorney general and secretary of state, but the new legislative proposals were met with the same indifference as the previous versions of the bills were, in that no reports were received. There was no further legislative action, and the bills died on the adjournment of the 92nd Congress.[125]

This was the moment when the heart finally went out of Ervin's decade and more of campaigning to close the jurisdictional gap. He had convened hearings; he had admonished his colleagues; he had nagged the executive departments; he had trained his staff on the constitutional problems. For year after year, not just the Constitutional Rights Subcommittee but a subcommittee of the Armed Services Committee had taken note of the jurisdictional gap.[126] Every time, his efforts came to naught, and without some change in the political environment or the motives of the key actors there was no reason to expect a different result. Soon Ervin was to take the stage under the full glare of national publicity when he became one of the central players in the national agony of Watergate. Following the failure of S. 1744 and S. 1745, for over two decades the numerous efforts to fill the jurisdictional void failed again and again.

The jurisdictional gap actually widened around the time Ervin gave up his legislative effort when a military court ruled that the UCMJ's applicability to civilians accompanying the armed forces "in time of war" was limited to *declared* wars. Up until 1970 it seemed clear that the Vietnam War was a war for the purposes of military law. The judge advocate general of the army had come to an opinion on this matter in order to decide (in line with the Supreme Court decisions restricting courts-martial of civilians to "time of war") whether civilians accompanying the armed forces could be prosecuted by courts-martial. In memoranda of November 1966 and February 1967, he determined that the stipulation "in time of war" did apply to the conflict in Vietnam, despite the absence of a declaration of war.[127] In a memorandum on the same subject, the chief of the Department of the Army's Military Justice Division said that a formal declaration of war is not necessary to initiate a time of war. The conflict in Vietnam, he argued, met all the tests set out in the relevant precedents; the president, the secretary of state, and other high officials had repeatedly declared the conflict in Vietnam to be a war. Thus, insofar as the issue of court-martial jurisdiction over civilian employees and contractors was concerned, the conflict in Vietnam had reached the state of time of war within the meaning of the UCMJ.[128] Consistent with this finding, in 1968 the Court of Military Appeals in *United States v. Anderson* held that the United States was in time of war in Vietnam in November 1964 for the purpose of tolling the statute of limitations in relation to the offense of desertion.[129] Citing *Anderson,* Jordan, in his memorandum, assumed that the United States was at war in Vietnam for the purposes of military law.[130]

In 1970 the Court of Military Appeals, by a narrow majority and with a strong dissent by Chief Judge Robert Quinn, overturned *Anderson.* In *United States v. Averette* it determined that the designation "in time of war" did not apply to the Vietnam War because Congress had not formally declared war.[131] This case had enormous repercussions for the jurisdictional questions I have been discussing. In its 1960 decisions the Supreme Court held that courts-martial could try civilian dependants, employees, and contractors accompanying the armed forces in time of war. The *Averette* ruling narrowed the scope of that holding by specifying that it applied only to wars declared by Congress—something that had occurred only five times in the nation's history and not since 1942.[132] There was no avenue to appeal *Averette* because at the time there was no right to seek a writ of certiorari from the Supreme Court over a decision of the Court of Military Appeals.[133] Federal courts could review courts-martial proceedings and judgments only under habeas corpus proceedings, with a limited right to examine the trials for jurisdictional issues and illegal punishments.[134] Later military court decisions followed the *Averette* precedent.[135] Recognizing that further attempts to court-martial civilians would fail because of the *Averette* decision, the armed services determined that they could not exercise criminal jurisdiction over civilians and stopped mounting further cases.[136]

Despite the apparent incongruence of the decisions in *Anderson* and *Averette,* the court distinguished the two holdings by saying that the desertion case involved a member of the armed forces, whereas the larceny case involved a civilian, and that the earlier case involved a procedural matter whereas the later case involved a jurisdictional one.[137] *Averette* deepened the jurisdictional gap opened up by the *Covert* line of cases.[138] The judgment foreclosed the exercise of court-martial jurisdiction over civilians in the subsequent decades, and it continued to define the limits of the UCMJ's applicability in the new century, when legislators began to contemplate ways of bringing civilian contractors and government employees supporting the "war on terror" within the reach of U.S. law.[139]

CHAPTER SEVEN

"Why Can't We Just Shoot Them All?"

MEJA and the First Prosecutions in Federal District Courts

The government finally closed the jurisdictional gaps arising from *Toth, Covert,* and their progeny with the passage of the Military Extraterritorial Jurisdiction Act (MEJA) of 2000 and of an amendment to the National Defense Authorization Act of 2006. These two legislative measures take different routes to plug the gaps I have considered. MEJA fulfilled the half-century-old proposal by Army Judge Advocate General Thomas H. Green by providing for federal district court jurisdiction over acts committed by civilians that would have been violations of the UCMJ had the perpetrators been subject to that law and by allowing military veterans to be tried in civilian courts for acts they committed overseas while in the armed forces. The 2006 law takes a different approach by expanding the reach of the UCMJ. Confronting the reality that a substantial proportion of the U.S. military mission in Iraq and Afghanistan was being performed by private contractors, the amendment to the National Defense Authorization Act for Fiscal Year 2007 changed the language of Article 2(a)(10) of the UCMJ, which had provided for court-martial jurisdiction over civilians accompanying the armed forces "in time of war." This phrase was changed to "in time of declared war or contingency operations."[1] By expanding the reach of the UCMJ to "contingency operations," i.e., military operations other than declared wars, Congress nullified *Averette.* MEJA and the amended UCMJ establish concurrent jurisdiction over civilian contractors serving with the armed forces, and, as such, they require civilian and military authorities to decide the best venue—a military or civilian court—in which to try civilian contractors and others serving alongside the armed forces in operations like those in Iraq and Afghanistan.[2]

There have been very few prosecutions under MEJA, and skeptics believe this can be explained in large part because of the burden on the budgets and energies of the U.S. district attorneys who would have to conduct the prosecutions and because of the numerous obstacles posed by having to conduct investigations in war zones thousands of miles from the United States.[3] Experience seems to bear out the concerns expressed decades earlier in the debates about the bills Ervin proposed, namely, the administrative strains those measures would have imposed on the government. Courts-martial in the vicinity of alleged crimes will not be hampered in the same way, but a judgment of the constitutionality of extending court-martial jurisdiction over civilians serving alongside the armed forces in "contingency operations" may rest on whether there is a sufficiently compelling interest to override the *Covert* line of precedents. Although the extension of court-martial jurisdiction over civilian contractors offers an alternative means of prosecuting those who are suspected of committing crimes in overseas operations, the existence of MEJA will make it more difficult to demonstrate the necessity for court-martial jurisdiction over civilian contractors who come within the reach of MEJA because that law makes available another path to prosecution, that of civilian courts.[4]

After Ervin's last initiative, a number of bills were proposed to close the jurisdictional gaps affecting military veterans and civilians accompanying the armed forces.[5] For example, Bennett offered H.R. 763, to be designated the "Foreign Crimes Act of 1977," whose language met the previous Department of Defense (DoD) objections and recommendations and addressed both jurisdictional gaps—the ones arising from *Toth* and *Covert*—in a single bill.[6] Bennett's new bill, however, fared no better than his and Ervin's earlier proposals.

Bennett and his colleagues were baffled about why the bill did not pass. Bennett remarked, "In all of the years I introduced it, I have never had anyone tell me it shouldn't be passed. Obviously someone who commits murder and gets by with it, that is something we should not allow." The Yale University law professor Eugene Fidell, a leading expert in military law, similarly expresses surprise (leavened with irony) that an issue that had excited a good deal of scholarly commentary escaped a legislative fix for decades: "It would seem—*shockingly*—that our legislators do not read the law reviews, since nothing happened in Congress." Some legislators were just as nonplussed as Fidell. Rep. Joshua Eilberg, a Democrat who represented a district in Philadelphia, said, "It is remarkable that Congress hasn't moved to close this gap yet." Bennett's response, "Everybody is so busy," may explain Congress's being preoccupied for a few weeks or months; it hardly suffices as an excuse for the two decades of legislative failure up to then.[7]

Benjamin Forman, assistant general counsel of the DoD, testifying in favor of Bennett's proposal in 1977, underlined the seriousness of that record of inaction when he pointed out, "The My Lai incident is a quite recent and dramatic instance where this bill would have been quite helpful."[8] Although the language of the bill had now coalesced into a consistent set of proposals, and although it was said that it had "consistently received the support of the Departments of State and Defense," the Pentagon continued to dither about specific aspects, first asking for particular amendments and then canceling the request.[9] A number of tricky questions of detail arose over the provision of court-appointed counsel for defendants, but nothing that ought to have sunk the bill had there been the will to overcome them.[10] Once again, the bill failed to pass.

In 1979 the General Accounting Office (GAO) produced a report detailing the dangers of the restricted jurisdiction over civilians accompanying the armed forces outside the United States. The GAO reported that the United States had sent 343,000 civilian personnel and dependants accompanying the armed force overseas from 1960 to 1979 but had no power to prosecute them for any crimes they committed.[11] The judicial background to this report remained as it had been for about a decade: first, the *Covert* decision of 1957 and the Supreme Court cases decided in 1960 that had determined that court-martial jurisdiction existed only for civilians accompanying the army in the field in time of war; then the *Averette* decision of 1970, which had specified that "in time of war" meant only wars declared by Congress. Following *Averette* it had no longer been possible to prosecute civilians accompanying the U.S. forces in Vietnam because Congress had not formally declared war in that conflict. At the height of American involvement in Vietnam some 10,000 civilians were accompanying the armed forces, a ratio of civilian to military personnel of about 1 to 50. If any of them were alleged to have committed an offense after *Averette,* generally the worst the suspect would suffer was debarment, that is, removal of military privileges, leading to the loss of employment.[12] Although, as we shall see, the civilian component was considerably smaller than the number of civilian employees and contractors the United States has sent into military operations in recent years, it was still a substantial number, and the GAO proposed that Congress should enact legislation providing for the prosecution by American authorities of all overseas civilian employees and dependants of the armed forces.[13]

In 1983, after a yearlong study, the Wartime Legislation Team established by the judge advocate general of the army produced a report that made similar recommendations for an extension of court-martial jurisdiction over civilians and former service personnel.[14] It also advised that Congress extend the jurisdiction of the UCMJ to cover civilians in both declared and undeclared wars.[15] No such legislation was enacted in the 1980s. The issue of what to do about civilian personnel sent overseas with the troops faded into the background in part because the deployments of U.S. forces in combat operations during the 1980s were few and relatively brief, albeit the jurisdictional issues surrounding civilians deployed alongside military personnel remained unchanged.[16]

Another major reform of the UCMJ, the Military Justice Act of 1983, was enacted, but the issue of the jurisdictional gap had been forgotten or appeared so hopeless that the bill contained no relevant provisions: the Senate and House reports do not mention the *Toth* case or the issue of jurisdiction over veteran suspects.[17] The act did have one potential consequence in regard to the judicial position, though: as we recall, the Supreme Court could not review the *Averette* decision because at the time it lacked certiorari over the judgment of the U.S. Court of Military Appeals, the highest court to which a court-martial judgment could be appealed. That situation was corrected by the Military Justice Act.[18]

By 1983 the composition of the Supreme Court had undergone substantial change, and the Warren Court justices who had been most skeptical about the quality of military justice were no longer on the bench. Moreover, procedural changes had brought military courts increasingly into line with civilian courts.[19] After passage of the Military Justice Act, military courts remained likely to abide by the *Averette* precedent, but the military authorities might have set up a test case in which the Supreme Court could review the "time of war" definition in *Averette*. Such a move would, however, have involved a substantial effort in mounting the case. As John O'Connor remarks, "Given the military's focus on defending the country instead of engineering test cases, no such effort to revisit *Averette* occurred."[20] The jurisdictional gaps survived the 1980s largely intact.

In 1986 a provision of the National Defense Authorization Act adjusted the UCMJ's jurisdiction over members of the Reserve components by, for example, allowing a member of the Reserves who was not on active duty to be returned to active duty for the purposes of an investigation or court-martial.[21] While not immediately consequential with respect to the constitutional precedents of *Toth*, *Covert*, and their successors, this legislation is notable because it appears to be the first occasion when a National Defense Authorization Act was used to make an amendment relevant to the UCMJ's jurisdictional provisions, as I have discussed them. Legislators used National Defense Authorization Acts in the first decade of the new millennium to make further adjustments in vexing jurisdictional arrangements.

At the end of the 1980s determined members of Congress continued to propose measures to close the jurisdictional gaps opened up by the *Toth* and *Covert* line of cases. Senator Inouye, one of those who had been shocked by Haeberle's photographs when they were shown to him and his colleagues in

1969, proposed S. 147 in 1989. He patiently explained to the Senate that the Supreme Court held that civilians may not be court-martialed for offenses against the UCMJ they may have committed abroad while they were members of the armed forces or while they were serving with, employed by, or accompanying the armed forces.[22] Inouye proposed similar legislation again in 1993, and the following year Rep. William M. Thomas of California proposed a bill in the House that would have closed the gap opened up by *Covert.*[23] Like their predecessors, these bills died. In 1995 legislators introduced three bills to extend federal court jurisdiction over service members and civilians serving with or accompanying the military outside the United States and, like their precursors, all three died.[24]

The War Crimes Act of 1996 finally met the obligation to define penalties in U.S. law for violations of the Geneva Conventions. It subjects any suspects, whether U.S. nationals or members of the U.S. armed services, to the jurisdiction of U.S. courts for such breaches, whether the alleged crimes occurred inside or outside the United States.[25] As the legislative report on the bill said, while it constituted the overdue implementing legislation required by the Geneva Conventions, it filled another gap in military law: it would allow for the prosecution of members of the armed forces even after their discharge.[26] The War Crimes Act has had little practical effect, although it formally provides for penalties in cases of grave breaches of the Geneva Conventions. At the time of writing, it appears that no prosecutions have taken place under the statute;[27] prosecutions of U.S. troops and veterans are unlikely to occur because the United States has a policy of not prosecuting its nationals for war crimes.[28] As we shall see in the conclusion, though, the rationale for passage of the statute is revealing of the purposes of the United States in filling the jurisdictional gaps.

Legislators recognized that the War Crimes Act left jurisdictional gaps to be filled. As originally passed, it did not cover major crimes other than grave breaches of the Geneva Conventions. A year after its passage Congress passed the Expanded War Crimes Act, which replaced the term *grave breach* with *war crime.*[29] The amended language did not, however, allow for the prosecution of crimes such as rape, sexual assault, and crimes of violence other than those identified as war crimes; arson; robbery; larceny; drug distribution; embezzlement; and fraud.[30] Moreover, the statute arguably does not apply in nonconflict contexts.[31] Although many crimes committed by civilians accompanying the armed forces abroad could be prosecuted by the host countries where they were stationed, and service personnel were also punishable under the laws of those countries (subject to the terms of SOFAs), the local authorities often declined to prosecute them and in some cases lacked jurisdiction to do so.[32] In 2006 the Military Commissions Act amended the War Crimes Act to limit its application by criminalizing only specified violations of Common Article 3 of the Geneva Conventions.[33]

The jurisdictional gap opened up by *Averette* became an increasingly important lacuna in the law as the government began to employ a growing number of private employees and contractors in military operations encompassing such activities as peacekeeping, humanitarian assistance, and disaster relief in places like Somalia, the former Yugoslavia, and Haiti. At the end of the Cold War the administrations of George H. W. Bush and Bill Clinton drastically downsized the nation's military forces, eventually cutting the active-duty force by 30 percent. Reluctant to cut frontline combat units, the Pentagon disproportionately reduced the number of support troops and came to rely more and more on contractors for support roles.[34] Budgetary considerations reinforced this trend. A GAO report stated that using civilian support employees and contractors cost considerably less than employing similarly graded uniformed personnel.[35] A GAO official pointed out that it was always "much easier to add contractors" because funding was more readily available and there were fewer rules involved in filling civilian positions.[36] The use of contractors rather than military personnel circumvented congressional limitations on the number of troops deployed in a theater of operations.[37] Increasingly, military planners outsourced certain functions to private military contractors, who fulfilled quasi-military roles such as providing security for diplomatic staff.[38]

During the 1990s the United States undertook one major military operation, Operation Desert Shield and Desert Storm (the operation against Iraq in 1991). The United States used some 4,500 DoD civilian employees during Desert Shield and Desert Storm and some 3,000 government civilian employees and private contractors in the 1990s operations in Somalia, Haiti, Kuwait, Rwanda, and the Balkans.[39] Contractors performed militarily vital functions such as maintaining technologically sophisticated weapons systems.[40] There was also a complement of employees and contractors in nonmilitary support roles. By the end of the 1990s there were 58,600 civilian employees of the Defense Department working overseas, in addition to the 193,000 dependent family members of military personnel living with them abroad.[41]

The bill that became MEJA emerged from a study that recognized the legal responsibilities arising from the deployment of so many civilians overseas. In 1996 the secretary of defense and the attorney general jointly appointed a committee, the Overseas Jurisdiction Advisory Committee, to review and make recommendations regarding the appropriate forum for criminal jurisdiction over civilians accompanying the armed forces in the field. Its work was motivated by the renewed attention to the problem of jurisdiction over civilians that arose from the deployment of thousands of civilians during the peacekeeping, humanitarian, and military operations of the 1990s.[42] The committee was charged with the task of determining whether to establish court-martial jurisdiction over such persons, extend the jurisdiction of Article III courts over them, or establish a military court to exercise criminal jurisdiction over them. In April 1997 the committee submitted its report to the secretary and the attorney general, who in turn transmitted it to Congress.[43] The report said it was vital that the UCMJ be extended over civilians because of the integration of civilians into military operations.[44] The committee made two recommendations: first, that court-martial jurisdiction cover civilians accompanying the armed forces during "contingency operations" as designated by the secretary of defense; second, that the jurisdiction of federal courts be extended to reach offenses committed by civilians accompanying the armed forces abroad.[45] Following the advisory committee's review, a report by the Pentagon's inspector general found that civilians accompanying the armed forces were committing serious crimes at the rate of several hundred a year, the vast majority of which went unprosecuted as a result of the jurisdictional gap and host nations' lack of interest in prosecuting offenses in which the victims were U.S. citizens or entities.[46] The legislative recognition of the problem is evident in a series of unsuccessful bills proposed in the late 1990s that would have closed one or both of the jurisdictional gaps.[47]

In April 1999 Sen. Jeff Sessions, a Republican from Alabama, adopted the Overseas Jurisdiction Advisory Committee's language almost verbatim and proposed S. 768, the bill that became MEJA, to meet both of the committee's objectives by extending court-martial jurisdiction over civilian employees and contractors deployed in contingency operations and establishing federal courts' jurisdiction over civilians accompanying the armed forces.[48] At this stage there was no counterpart House legislation. Lawyers in the Pentagon were worried, however, that extending the jurisdiction of the UCMJ to cover civilians participating in contingency operations would be overturned on constitutional grounds. Both the State and Defense Departments wrote to legislators stating their opposition to Sessions's version of the MEJA bill, the Pentagon recommending language that extended federal courts' jurisdiction over the civilians rather than applying the UCMJ to them.[49] Lawyers in the DoD began to work with members of the House to draft legislation that would stand up to the anticipated constitutional challenges. The result was H.R. 3380, the House version of the MEJA bill, which called for civilian court jurisdiction over civilians and over members of the armed forces, once the latter ceased to be subject to the UCMJ. The House language was substituted for the Senate version, although ultimately the bill that came up for approval retained its original designation as S. 768.[50]

While the MEJA bill was working its way through Congress, a court judgment in 2000 focused the attention of legislators on the need to close the jurisdictional gap. The U.S. Court of Appeals for the Second Circuit was obliged, because of the lack of jurisdiction arising from the *Covert* line of cases, to set aside a conviction in an especially egregious criminal case, *United States v. Gatlin,* involving an adult man who was married to a member of the armed forces and was found to have had sex with his wife's minor daughter.[51] The court's opinion in *United States v. Gatlin* included an account of the judicial history of the extraterritorial application of U.S. law and a chronicle of the unsuccessful legislative efforts to close the jurisdictional gap. Circuit Court Judge José Cabranes summarized the matter by saying, "In short, for over fifty years, there has been a consensus—among all three branches of the federal government as well as academic commentators—that, notwithstanding the existence of [18 U.S.C. § 7(3), which defines the 'special maritime and territorial jurisdiction of the United States'] and its precursors, United States courts lack jurisdiction over crimes committed by civilians accompanying the military overseas."[52] Judge Cabranes then took Congress to task in a manner reminiscent of Justice Black's opinion of 1955 that had held it was fully within the power of Congress to enact legislation to fill the jurisdictional gap opened up by *Toth.* Cabranes went on, "Congress has not responded to this call for legislation [by commentators, government officials, commissions, and scholars], though its inaction hardly can be blamed on a lack of awareness of the gap. Indeed, Congress has held several hearings on the matter, and, over the last four decades, has entertained more than thirty bills aimed at closing the gap."[53] Cabranes took the unusual step of directing the clerk of the court to send copies of his judgment to the Armed Services and Judiciary Committees of the House and Senate, apparently with the goal of spurring Congress into action. This act drew the attention of lawmakers to the jurisdictional lacunae that had by then existed for decades. Evidently, the message got through, as the House Judiciary Committee cited the opinion and quoted Cabranes's admonition to Congress in its legislative report on MEJA.[54]

The MEJA statute signed into law in November 2000 provides for the prosecution of former military personnel and private contractors in federal district courts.[55] It states, "Whoever engages in conduct outside the United States that would constitute an offense punishable by imprisonment for more than 1 year if the conduct had been engaged in within the special maritime and territorial jurisdiction of the United States (1) while employed by or accompanying the Armed Forces outside the United States; or (2) while a member of the Armed Forces subject to chapter 47 of title 10 (the Uniform Code of Military Justice), shall be punished as provided for that offense."[56] The acts punishable under MEJA were ones that would be punishable if committed within the jurisdiction of a state, commonwealth, territory, possession, or district of the United States.[57] The bill finally provided for federal civilian courts' jurisdiction over veteran offenders for crimes they committed while in military service overseas.

The availability of MEJA became important after the United States–led coalition's invasions of Afghanistan in 2001 and Iraq in 2003 because of the burgeoning number of private contractors supporting the U.S. armed forces. The heavy reliance on contractors was redoubled by Secretary of Defense Donald Rumsfeld's approach to operations in Iraq, when he deployed far fewer troops than the number military experts advised would be required for a successful military operation and occupation of the country.[58] Unlike the signing on of technicians and maintenance personnel, the use of armed contractors in Iraq and Afghanistan was alleged by members of Congress to be more financially costly than employing equivalent members of the armed forces. But the calculus favoring their use was political rather than economic: private military contractors could be hired to deliver greater force levels with no politically costly admission that the initial estimate of troop requirements had been too low and no need of a further call-up of the National Guard or Reserves.[59] By 2007 there were 180,000 private military contractors stationed in Iraq, outnumbering the 165,000 military personnel in country. By 2009 the number of contractors in Iraq and Afghanistan working for the DoD alone numbered some 240,000.[60]

Among the contractors were some 20,000 to 30,000 armed personnel, including employees of Blackwater, a private security firm, in quasi-military roles such as escorting U.S. officials through Baghdad.[61] The behavior of these security contractors brought opprobrium onto the use of such firms, not just from the foreign populations among whom they operated but from legislators and military officers, who feared the disrepute that trigger-happy civilians could bring to American operations. A House committee memorandum of 2007 found that Blackwater and the four next-largest private security firms operating in Iraq were all guilty of unacceptable practices, being responsible for dozens of shooting incidents, the vast majority of which involved contractors shooting first, without having been fired on.[62] Blackwater was said to have a "sense of impunity in dealing with Iraqis."[63] The U.N. special rapporteur on extrajudicial, summary, and arbitrary executions found that private contractors' use of indiscriminate or otherwise questionable force in Iraq had led to civilian casualties conservatively estimated to be in the hundreds, perhaps thousands.[64] The Congressional Research Service found that by abusing civilians and acting in other objectionable ways, private security contractors may have been undermining the allied missions in Iraq and Afghanistan.[65] Military officials described them as "out-of-control cowboys."[66]

Despite well-documented abuses by private military contractors, for several years after President Clinton signed MEJA into law, "the Justice Department

. . . seemed to take little interest in bringing to trial cases that fall within MEJA."[67] The Department of Defense took a considerable time to generate the implementing regulations intended to satisfy due process concerns, which did not appear until March 2005.[68] The statute did not prohibit MEJA prosecutions before the regulations took effect, but the House Judiciary Committee strongly discouraged them until that time.[69] The Defense and State Departments and other federal agencies were supposed to plan for a coordinated approach to implementing MEJA but failed for a decade to do so. Victor Hansen observes that MEJA did not appear to be living up to its intended purpose in extending federal criminal jurisdiction to civilians accompanying U.S. forces overseas.[70] In 2010 another commentator expressed a pessimistic view of MEJA's worth: "Given the lack of guidance as to how and when to apply MEJA, it is practically a dead letter law today."[71] Although the legal architecture exists to deter and punish contractors who commit illegal acts, the problem lies in the mobilization of the political will to enforce the pertinent laws.[72]

MEJA did not, in any event, entirely close the jurisdictional gaps arising from *Averette*. Insofar as it reached civilian employees of the United States, MEJA applied exclusively to those employed by the DoD, and consequently it reduced but did not eliminate the jurisdictional gap. MEJA could not be used to prosecute the civilians involved in prisoner abuse in Iraq because they were employed not by the DoD but by the Central Intelligence Agency (CIA). The scandal that emerged from detention sites in the aftermath of the United States–led campaign in Afghanistan and the invasion of Iraq drew attention to this problem.

In 2004 reports of prisoner abuse at Abu Ghraib, a prison in Iraq where U.S.-led coalition forces held Iraqi detainees, surfaced.[73] Their American captors subjected the prisoners to torture, sleep deprivation, sexual humiliation, and a variety of other harsh "enhanced interrogation techniques." In the wake of the publication of photographs documenting the mistreatment, there were reports of similar techniques being used at the American detention facility at Bagram Air Force Base in Afghanistan, at the detention facility at Guantánamo Bay in Cuba, and at a number of international "black sites" to which coalition captives were secretly transported. The harsh treatment of prisoners was not, therefore, the product of a few bad apples, as originally recounted, but was widespread and systematic. High-ranking government officials and lawyers gave it a legal and philosophical foundation in a number of opinions and policy directives. For example, a series of memoranda by Justice Department lawyers produced idiosyncratic standards according to which torture was narrowly defined so as to exclude the interrogation techniques the American personnel were using.[74] Credible accounts indicated the involvement of CIA personnel in at least five custodial deaths arising from torture or ill treatment.[75] Military personnel who went beyond the permitted forms of prisoner treatment were subject to the UCMJ and could be prosecuted by court-martial. DoD employees could, at least in theory, be prosecuted for violations of MEJA. Employees of the CIA and other non–DoD government agencies who were involved in prisoner abuse outside the United States and its special maritime and territorial jurisdiction were beyond the reach of any U.S. court.

After the revelations about prisoner abuse Congress held hearings and considered various measures to amend MEJA in order to provide for prosecution of non–DoD employees accompanying the armed forces overseas. For example, H.R. 4390, the MEJA Clarification Act, was introduced in the House.[76] It would have extended MEJA's extraterritorial jurisdiction over civilian employees and contractors of the DoD and other federal agencies as well as specifying that MEJA covered war crimes. Ultimately, the National Defense Authorization Act for Fiscal Year 2005 extended federal court jurisdiction over employees and contractors of any government agency or provisional authority "supporting the mission" of the DoD.[77]

Although the act broadened the applicability of MEJA to cover employees and contractors of U.S. government agencies other than the DoD there was still plenty of uncertainty about the scope and limits of this extension of jurisdiction: to begin with, there was room for debate about what the terms *supporting* and *mission* meant in this context.[78] The geographical proximity of the civilian employee or contractor to the nearest military unit might be relevant, but so too might the degree of connectedness between that individual's role and the military campaign. Ultimately, these would offer someone convicted under the law with a possible avenue of appeal, and the courts would have to sort out the nuances of what "supporting the mission" means.

MEJA has been used rarely—in preferring charges against or initiating prosecutions of fewer than two dozen civilian employees and contractors and of two former service members as of 2010.[79] One might explain the current small number of prosecutions of veterans as a reflection of the small number of serious crimes that are committed by uniformed personnel and remain undetected during the perpetrator's military service and for which there is sufficient evidence to provide subsequently for prosecution. This does not, however, explain the low rate of prosecution of contractors in Iraq.[80] The minimal number of arrests and prosecutions appears disproportionate to the large number of contractors and employees serving in Iraq and Afghanistan. Underlining the lack of investigative and prosecutorial will, there were reported rapes and gang-rapes by private contractors deployed with the U.S. forces in Iraq that did not lead to effective investigations and prosecutions under MEJA.[81] As one legal expert observed in 2007, given the number of civilian employees and contractors in Iraq at that time, it was as though in a town of one hundred thousand people there had not been a single arrest for an act of violence in three years.[82] Fidell reported to legislators the following year, "I've been baffled why there hasn't been more activity under that statute."[83]

The number of successful prosecutions under MEJA supposedly increased thereafter, but not by much. In May 2011 Assistant Attorney General Lanny Breuer testified that since MEJA was enacted, "the Justice Department has successfully prosecuted numerous MEJA cases involving former Department of Defense employees or individuals accompanying them overseas." However, Breuer cites only six successful prosecutions of military veterans and DoD private contractors—a record that seems small in proportion to the number of contractors serving with U.S. forces and that therefore bolsters the argument of MEJA skeptics—as well as an unspecified number of convictions of non-DoD contractors.[84]

The implementing regulations require a complex rigamarole of consultation among a number of federal departments and agencies in deciding whether to proceed with an investigation geared to a MEJA prosecution.[85] The responsibility to organize an investigation falls on the individual U.S. attorney's office that is allocated the case. In the case of a prosecution in Iraq or Afghanistan, this is likely to involve multiple trips to a war zone thousands of miles away.[86] Decisions regarding the investigation and recommendations for prosecution are made at a higher level of command than equivalent decisions for prosecution under the UCMJ, which may well cause delays in decision making.[87] Because there is no designated theater investigative unit to serve in such circumstances, there is likely be a hiatus before the FBI and the Department of Justice's Criminal Division gird themselves up for their investigative and prosecutorial tasks. Investigators must operate in a distant location days or even weeks after the alleged crime occurred, posing problems for gathering physical evidence from often unsecured crime scenes. An investigation in a foreign war zone is bound to involve an element of danger. Sometimes the investigators may find themselves in the uncomfortable position of having to rely on the services of civilian contractors, perhaps from the same security firm alleged to have committed the crime being investigated. The investigators will often have to overcome language barriers in deposing witnesses. If a case proceeds in a federal court, the government's subpoena power does not reach foreign witnesses and evidence, and the government will have to use extradition treaties or other means to return suspects to the United States for trial. This concatenation of problems will predictably lead to a "lack of prosecutorial motivation."[88]

Financial pressures present another hurdle because whichever U.S. attorney's office is assigned a case must fund the prosecution from its own budget. The expense of having to mount an international investigation might strain, if not exhaust, the budget of a district attorney's office.[89] Because of the vagaries of allocating a case to a particular district attorney's office, it is impossible to predict such an event and hence to budget for it.[90] As P. W. Singer put the problem, "The reality is that no U.S. Attorney likes to waste limited budgets on such messy, complex cases 9,000 miles outside their district, even if they were fortunate enough to have the evidence at hand."[91]

The effectiveness of the amended MEJA met its first major test in the prosecutions arising from the so-called Bloody Sunday incident of September 16, 2007, at Nisour Square in downtown Baghdad, when five Blackwater contractors were accused of multiple counts of manslaughter after killing Iraqi noncombatants. As State Department contractors, they were the first non–DoD civilians charged under the statute.[92] In this incident a Blackwater convoy serving as the advance guard for another group of vehicles carrying U.S. officials became snarled in traffic. A Blackwater contractor shot one Iraqi driver, and, as he slumped over the wheel of his car, it kept rolling toward the convoy. Fearing they would be vulnerable to attack, the Blackwater employees turned their vehicles around and sped away while spraying nearby vehicles with automatic weapons fire. A total of seventeen Iraqi men, women, and children were killed in the shooting spree and another twenty-four wounded.[93]

The Blackwater personnel claimed they had been shot at, but the subsequent investigation indicated that this was probably untrue and that they adopted a "shoot first, ask questions later" approach. If so, this was just one incident among many in which private contractors used indiscriminate force against innocent bystanders.[94] A senior military official said that Blackwater was creating resentment among Iraqis that "may be worse than Abu Ghraib." Rep. Tom Davis said of Blackwater's actions, "Iraqis understandably resent our preaching about the rule of law when so visible an element of the U.S. presence there appears to be above the law."[95] The Blackwater contractors could not be prosecuted under Iraqi law because of an immunity agreement signed by the Coalition Provisional Authority, the governing authority installed by the invaders after they took control of Iraq.[96] The strongest sanction Blackwater used against its employees was to dismiss or fine them: it had no authority to impose other penalties.[97] It therefore fell to the United States to prosecute the suspects.

The Bloody Sunday investigation "provides a prime example of the difficulties in applying MEJA to civilian contractors."[98] Although the State Department, the U.S. military, and Iraqi forces began to conduct an investigation immediately after the incident, their efforts were improperly coordinated with those of the FBI investigative team, which arrived in country two weeks after the incident. Delay is bound to undermine the effectiveness of a criminal investigation. Contrasting the situation in Nisour Square with the aftermath of a shooting in the United States, a former federal prosecutor said that in the

United States "within minutes you would have police there securing the crime scene, interviewing witnesses. . . . You'll have a secure chain of evidence. . . . All that requires people on the scene almost simultaneously."[99] The crime scene at Nisour Square was unsecured, and Blackwater personnel themselves tampered with physical evidence: before the FBI could examine the vehicles the Blackwater employees had shot up, the company had repaired and repainted them. Those conducting the official Department of State inquiry found that Blackwater was providing them with protection.[100] These difficulties are precisely the kind that commentators have said are likely to impede any MEJA-related criminal investigation.

When the Department of Justice charged five Blackwater contractors with manslaughter and weapons violations for their part in the Bloody Sunday shootings, a federal judge dismissed the case, criticizing the prosecution for having utilized tainted testimony that had been compromised by compelled and immunized statements. Prosecutors committed other improper acts as well, such as withholding exculpatory evidence from the grand jury that indicted the suspects.[101] The district court's dismissal of the case was vacated by the appeals court, although the government acknowledged that prosecutors had used tainted evidence.[102]

This is not the only prosecution that has ever been damaged by prosecutorial errors. The outcome of the case will not therefore prove a general point about the effectiveness or otherwise of MEJA. MEJA did, however, create the situation in which interdepartmental and interagency cooperation was required among investigative and prosecutorial entities that do not have as much experience in coordinating their work as military investigative and legal personnel do: once the Diplomatic Security Service had taken its statements and passed them on to the FBI and the Department of Justice Criminal Division, those in charge of the investigation and prosecution had gingerly to step around or overlook the tainted evidence, a challenge to which they were evidently unequal.

Contractor misconduct understandably came under increased scrutiny after the Bloody Sunday incident.[103] The MEJA Expansion and Enforcement Act of 2007, introduced in the aftermath of the incident, would have extended the reach of MEJA over all contractors "in an area, or in close proximity to an area . . . where the Armed Forces [are] conducting a contingency operation." This amendment would have brought contractors not technically supporting the mission of the DoD within reach of MEJA. Pointing out that in the absence of the legislation, felonies conducted by those working for other federal departments and agencies would go unpunished, Rep. Betty Sutton said, "This Congress must act to ensure that justice is not a selective American principle," adding, "Nobody should be immune from the law."[104] The bill was passed by the House of Representatives on October 4, 2007, but it failed to pass in the Senate and consequently died.[105]

In 2006 Congress provided another route to the prosecution of civilians accompanying the armed forces by broadening the reach of the UCMJ to cover civilian employees and contractors supporting the armed forces. An amendment to a military spending bill, the Defense Authorization Act for Fiscal Year 2007, allows courts-martial to prosecute employees and contractors accompanying the armed forces during contingency operations as well as declared wars.[106] There were no hearings and no recorded floor debate before the passage of the amendment, so it is difficult to know what legislators had in mind.[107] In light of earlier legislative proposals, one can discern that the amendment met one of the recommendations of the Overseas Jurisdiction Advisory Committee and realized the purpose of the original Senate MEJA bill, which would have allowed court-martial jurisdiction over civilians during war and contingency operations.

The amendment to the UCMJ's Article 2(a)(10) now makes available a second avenue, the extended UCMJ, through which most crimes by civilian employees and contractors can be prosecuted. A Defense Department memorandum lays out the sequence of events now that two alternative routes to prosecution of a private military contractor coexist, requiring the Department of Justice to decide whether to pursue a prosecution or to allow the Pentagon to do so.[108] The memorandum advises the circumstances in which court-martial prosecution of a civilian should proceed, including whether the civilian's misconduct is adverse to a "significant military interest."[109]

The amendment of the UCMJ raises serious constitutional questions. The Fifth Amendment to the Constitution allows Congress to make rules for the government and regulation of the "land and naval forces." Unlike the wives of military personnel in the *Covert* case, civilian security contractors deployed in a war zone or an area occupied by the United States and its allies are arguably, for practical purposes, members of those forces. Some of them are armed, and most dress in uniforms indistinguishable from those of regular troops, fighting the same enemies as the U.S. armed forces are fighting, on the same battlefields.[110] "The activities that security contractors engage in," Matthew Dahl argues, "blur the line between civilian and soldier to the point where distinguishing the two can be nearly impossible."[111] Now that contractors are such a significant portion of deployed military forces, a strong argument can be made that they constitute part of the "land and naval forces."[112] However, because they are not literally *in* the land and naval forces, the extension of the UCMJ's jurisdiction to civilian employees and contractors is susceptible to constitutional challenge.

The Sixth Amendment guarantees the right to jury trial after indictment by a grand jury. Although an Article 32 procedure is similar in function to a grand jury—and affords the defendant certain procedural rights which a grand jury does not—their rules and procedures are different. Juries in civilian courts are larger than court-martial panels, and juries in criminal trials must achieve unanimity.[113] The processes by which juries and panels arrive at verdicts are also different. A civilian defendant convicted by a court-martial could challenge the verdict on those grounds.

If we look at the wording of the amended UCMJ, there are further arguments to be made regarding the applicability of the law to any particular defendant. The revised Article 2(a)(10) says that the jurisdiction of the UCMJ extends "in time of declared war or a contingency operation" to "persons serving with or accompanying an armed force in the field." Just as the MEJA statute's meaning rests on the definition of "supporting the mission," the wording of the extended UCMJ will require courts to tease out the meanings of "serving with," "accompanying," and "in the field." To take only the example of "in the field": courts might well examine the history of the meaning of the phrase, which throughout the nineteenth century meant operations in areas where U.S. armed forces were likely to encounter an enemy; it did not apply to military bases outside war zones. One could therefore anticipate numerous grounds for challenge with respect both to the constitutional protections the amendment to the UCMJ may face and to the interpretation of the statute itself.[114]

Moreover, there are technical challenges in applying the UCMJ to civilians because civilian status does not fit the circumstances contemplated by the UCMJ. A number of military offenses, such as mutiny, dereliction of duty, and desertion, have no counterpart in criminal law.[115] The apparently simple answer to this problem is that one would not expect a civilian contractor to be charged with an offense that did not fit his status. There are, however, more complex problems regarding the criminal procedures surrounding the possible court-martial of a civilian. Normally the immediate commander of someone suspected of a court-martial offense conducts the preliminary inquiry, but this requirement is difficult to apply to a civilian suspect, who does not have a position in the chain of command. Reduction in pay grade and punitive discharges are not options for civilian defendants.[116]

The government has proved reluctant to permit the UCMJ's expansion to be tested in the courts. The air force made an abortive attempt to prosecute a civilian contractor but dropped the case after he sought habeas corpus relief.[117] In several other cases, as soon as a defendant's lawyer petitioned for a writ of habeas corpus, the government dropped the charge, thus avoiding a judicial test of the constitutionality of court-martialing a civilian.[118] The administration of President Barack Obama "trod carefully" in implementing the new law.

The amendments made to the *Manual for Courts-Martial* in 2010 admonish prosecutors to be aware of the constitutional issues surrounding court-martial jurisdiction over civilians and ask them to examine carefully "relevant statutes, decisions, service regulations, and policy memoranda" before initiating the prosecution of a civilian.[119] As Fidell remarks, in light of the government's tentative approach, "no one should expect widespread use of this controversial authority to court-martial civilians."[120]

Because of the questionable effectiveness of MEJA arising from the practical and budgetary obstacles to a successful prosecution under the law, many criminals are likely to escape justice for want of the will or resources to prosecute them. Susan Gibson states that because the military is used to conducting investigations overseas and foreign nations are accustomed to allowing courts-martial to operate on their soil, "court-martial jurisdiction is in many ways the best method for exercising jurisdiction over civilians overseas."[121] Yet, as Dahl argues, the availability of MEJA as a means of prosecution increases the burden on the government to justify court-martial prosecution of a civilian: "Showing that there is no reasonable, less intrusive path will be more difficult because another path [to prosecution] already exists in the form of the MEJA statute."[122] MEJA allows a prosecution to proceed in an Article III court with all the constitutional protections that such a forum affords. But, as Dahl suggests, the existence of an *ineffective* MEJA might have a paradoxical result insofar as jurisdiction over private military contractors is concerned: it sets the bar higher in justifying court-martial prosecutions in cases where an alleged crime could also be prosecuted under MEJA and may thereby provide for a greater constitutional challenge to a means of prosecution that appears more likely in practice to succeed.

If Dahl's interpretation is valid, it is so in large part because the government has neither brought about effective coordination among the departments and agencies required to enforce the law nor established an efficient investigative mechanism and appropriated the financial resources required to implement the law around the world. The MEJA Expansion and Enforcement Act of 2007 would have required the FBI to create an investigative unit for contingency operations and theater investigative units to pursue allegations of misconduct by contractors around the world. The bill would also have required the director of the FBI to ensure that the unit had adequate personnel to investigate allegations of criminal conduct by contractor personnel and would have authorized the attorney general to request additional personnel and resources from various executive departments. After the bill failed, no further congressional discussion of the establishment of an FBI theater investigative unit occurred.[123] In the absence of such a dedicated unit, the Department of Justice merged two existing entities to form the Human Rights and Special Prosecutions

Section, whose responsibilities include MEJA cases, but the effectiveness of its operations is still to be objectively assessed.[124] Although some of the barriers to effective prosecution of overseas crimes in the United States—such as the fact of geographical distance—are structural, others could be remedied by improved coordination among the entities involved in enforcing the law, the provision of adequate financial and personnel resources, and a governmental commitment to enforce the law. As Gibson argued before the passage of MEJA, the enormous expansion of jurisdiction it entailed "would require an equally enormous expansion of resources to effectively exercise that jurisdiction."[125] Although it may be premature to judge from the results, there is no indication that a sufficient expansion of resources has yet taken place.

The government subjected the extension of the UCMJ's jurisdiction to its first meaningful judicial test in a case involving a suspect whose citizenship placed him beyond the reach of MEJA and therefore precluded a challenge based on the defendant's entitlement to a civilian trial. This appears to be the government's way of initiating the first constitutional test of the UCMJ extension on the most propitious factual grounding. Alaa Mohammad Ali, an interpreter working for U.S. military forces in Iraq, was convicted by a court-martial of stabbing a fellow interpreter and was sentenced to imprisonment by the army (although, according to a pretrial agreement that resulted in his guilty plea, his sentence was satisfied by time served before his conviction).[126] Ali is the first civilian tried by a court-martial since the Vietnam War era. The military judge found that he fell within the scope of Article 2(a)(10) of the UCMJ because he was "serving with or accompanying an armed force" and was "in the field" within the meaning of the law. Among the factors helping to determine this status were that Ali lived with the troops, went on operations with them in which his contributions played an integral part, and wore the same uniform, body armor, and helmet they wore, including the same unit patch. In response to Ali's claim that he was entitled to indictment by a grand jury, the military judge ruled that because this was a case "arising in the land or naval forces," the Fifth Amendment exception applied.[127]

Ali's sentence did not meet the threshold for automatic review in the military appellate courts, just as the sentences handed down in all the cases involving private military contractors in Iraq were below the threshold for normal review in the military appellate courts.[128] The judge advocate general of the army, however, set the case on the course to judicial review by referring it to the Army Court of Criminal Appeals, which upheld the conviction.[129] This court found that a court-martial was the only U.S. forum that could have tried him because, as an Iraqi citizen, he was immune from prosecution under MEJA.

The U.S. Court of Appeals for the Armed Forces (C.A.A.F.), the renamed U.S. Court of Military Appeals, reviewed the case and found that the conviction did not violate the Constitution. It rejected Ali's challenges based on the Fifth and Sixth Amendments' guarantees of jury trial after indictment by a grand jury because, it said, these protections do not apply to noncitizens in judicial proceedings outside the United States.[130] The debate about whether the application of U.S. law to extraterritorial matters can be judged in black-and-white constitutional, or "formal," terms or whether it demands the contemplation of particular facts and circumstances seems to revive the issues with which Black, Harlan, and Frankfurter wrestled in *Covert* and *Krueger* (see chapter 2).[131] This case therefore seemed to reanimate not only the constitutional issues with which the court had grappled in *Covert* but also the divergences in jurisprudential philosophy that underpinned the decades-old judicial debates. Although the C.A.A.F. accepted that MEJA might reach noncitizens, who could be brought to the United States for prosecution in an Article III court, it recognized that MEJA did not apply to citizens of the host country such as Ali (who held dual citizenship of Canada and Iraq).[132] Notably, however, MEJA immunizes host country nationals from prosecution not in order to allow them to be prosecuted by court-martial but to allow the host nation to exercise criminal jurisdiction over its citizens and residents. Whatever the legislators' intent, though, Ali could not be prosecuted under MEJA, so there was no federal court alternative to court-martial prosecution.[133] The Supreme Court denied Ali's certiorari petition in May 2013, thereby allowing his conviction to stand.[134] The peculiar features of the Ali case, especially those arising from his citizenship, mean that one should not yet draw any general conclusions about the viability, in constitutional terms, of court-martial prosecution of civilian contractors under the UCMJ.

While the constitutionality of the UMCJ's expansion remains uncertain, the record of MEJA prosecutions of military veterans has been mixed. The first such trial was that of Jose Luis Nazario Jr., an honorably discharged marine veteran who had been decorated for valor for actions during his service in Iraq. Nazario was acquitted by a jury in the federal district court for central California, in Riverside, in 2009. The criminal complaint read, "On or about November 9, 2004, in Fallujah, Iraq, defendant Jose Luis Nazario Jr., in heat of passion caused by adequate provocation, unlawfully and intentionally killed two unarmed male human beings, without malice." The charges of voluntary manslaughter, abetting murder, assault with a deadly weapon, and felonious discharge of a firearm arose from an incident in house-to-house fighting in dwellings forming a "maze of interlocking fortresses" during Operation Phantom Fury, a ten-day assault on the city of Fallujah, west of Baghdad.[135] This "brutal operation" saw some of the heaviest fighting of the whole Iraq campaign.[136] An eyewitness summed up one unit commander's instructions to his troops: "We'll go house to house, killing anyone we find and destroying the weapons and ammo."[137] Before the operation began, the U.S.-led coalition forces warned the inhabitants of Fallujah, known as a redoubt of Al Qaeda and the Iraqi insurgency, to leave the city in order to avoid the assault by the marines. Some twenty-five thousand people remained behind, the majority of whom were perceived by the troops and their commanders to be insurgents.[138] On November 9, 2004, after a member of their unit had been killed by a sniper earlier that day, a marine squad led by Nazario, part of Kilo Company, 3rd Battalion, 1st Marine Regiment (Kilo 3/1), entered a house in the insurgent-held Jolan neighborhood and killed four insurgents they captured. Nazario was said to have killed the Iraqis or ordered them killed.

The prosecution resulted from the admissions made by one of Nazario's subordinates, Sgt. Ryan Weemer, to a secret service job interviewer. As a result, Weemer, a member of the Reserves, was recalled to active duty in order to face a court-martial murder charge. His fellow marine Sgt. Jermaine Nelson faced court-martial prosecution for the same charge, whereas a federal case was brought in the district court in Riverside against Nazario, a civilian.[139] (The MEJA statute allows the cases of current and former military personnel to be combined in a civilian court, but the prosecutions in this instance diverged.) Weemer's taped interview stated that Nazario and his squad received orders to kill the Iraqis and that they did so. The military tape-recorded Nelson's interview with an agent from the Naval Criminal Investigation Service (NCIS), in which Nelson said his squad shot the captives dead. Nelson said Nazario became angry on finding assault rifles in the house, after the detainees had insisted there were no weapons. On the tape Nelson said Nazario shot a kneeling captive at point-blank range and then said, "I'm not doing all this by myself. You're doing one, and Weemer is doing one." Nelson said Weemer then drew his nine-millimeter sidearm and killed one of the detainees.[140]

Two other members of Nazario's squad testified to hearing the shots and seeing the corpses but not to witnessing the shootings. Assistant U.S. Attorney Jerry Behnke, leading the prosecution team, said the killings were not acts of self-defense but executions.[141] The only men alleged to have seen the killings—Nelson, Weemer, and Nazario—refused to testify. Nelson and Weemer, facing court-martial murder charges in the same incident, were held in contempt in June 2008 and jailed until a judge ordered their release the following month. The district court jury was required to come to a verdict on the basis of secondhand accounts of the killings and the previous statements Nelson and Weemer had made.[142] Of the former marines who did testify at the trial, one said he saw Nazario holding an M-16 automatic weapon while standing over the body of one of the Iraqi victims. Another testified that Nazario tried to persuade him to help kill the captives, and a third said he saw four dead bodies in the house after Nazario had left. None of these witnesses saw Nazario kill the Iraqis.[143]

The law firm Pepper Hamilton represented Nazario pro bono, and the defense was also funded by several hundred donors. "That is what the Brotherhood of Marines is all about," said the lead counsel, Kevin McDermott, a retired Marine Corps major.[144] In large part because of the perception that the case involved a politically motivated prosecution of a marine veteran, the case rallied former members of the corps and others to Nazario's cause. They saw Nazario, as some had seen Calley, as a scapegoat. Three marine veterans were part of Nazario's defense team. Vincent Barbera, the only member of the so-called Marine Dream Team who is not a veteran, commented that the case "was purely politically driven to support some still-unknown government agenda—most probably, the appeasement of anti-American Iraqi factions. Unfortunately, this young hero [Nazario] was the government's guinea pig."[145] For his part, sounding much like the American citizens who protested the Calley verdict and sentence, Nazario told a reporter, "They train us, and they expect us to rely back on that training. Then when we use that training, they prosecute us for it?"[146] Douglas Applegate, one of Nazario's defending counsel, said of McDermott that he has "a special fondness for the young grunts that seem to always take the beating when things go wrong in the front office."[147] Applegate himself had retired from the military as a colonel after spending considerable time in Iraq, and he provided the defense with insights into the rules of engagement and battlefield context.

The prosecution tried to inculcate in the jurors a sense of the realities of combat, but their efforts may have been counterproductive. In order to give the jurors some insight into what the marines experienced, they called as a witness Maj. Daniel Schmitt, who ran marine training sessions in a mock village. Schmitt testified that during combat a marine's senses can fail to function or, conversely, can become extraordinarily acute. He said that many marines lose their ability to hear when the bullets start flying. Some suffer tunnel vision. "There is little room for discussion or debate," he said. Marines depend reflexively on their training and trust their buddies to do the same. Knowing when not to shoot "is the difficult part of our profession."[148]

This disquisition on the turmoil of combat and the fog of war may have been perfectly valid as a description of the circumstances of pitched battle, but it does not match the situation Nazario's squad were alleged to have been in. The bullets had indeed been flying, and one of their number had fallen, but by the marines' own account they held the Iraqis as captives before shooting them. The marines' obedience at that moment was not the reflexive, unhesitating trust in a commander that troops are trained to observe in combat. It may, however, have expressed equally powerful sentiments: the collective wish to deliver some payback after the enemy had shed a comrade's blood; the loyalties forged in battle; the code of silence that unites partners in crime; and the widespread disinclination of marines in Iraq to report abuses by their comrades.[149] If, as Nelson reported, Nazario had the presence of mind to tell the others that each one must shoot a captive, neither his command nor his troops' obedience arose in the heat of battle: they came from the cold realization that the best safeguard against an informer in one's midst is to ensure that each member of the gang has killed his own man. If so, in cementing this blood pact, Nazario demonstrated the leadership qualities that had earned him the solid allegiance of his men. Much as one might want to believe that only the highest causes bind men in unbreakable loyalties, sometimes their bonds are forged from darker alloys.

Benefiting from his formidable legal and moral support, Nazario was acquitted on August 28, 2008. One of his defenders spoke of the obstacles the government must surmount in achieving the successful prosecution of a veteran defendant. McDermott said, "In addition to playing Monday morning quarterback, MEJA prosecutions in general, and the Nazario case in particular, present insurmountable challenges to successful prosecutions. . . . Removing military aspects completely from the Nazario case, the U.S. government sought to convict a man of killing another human being without producing a body, the alleged victims' I.D., any eyewitness testimony, or a shred of physical evidence. The Constitutional implications were and continue to be enormous, as long as MEJA remains on the books."[150] Applegate said, "At the end of the day, this jury of civilians simply wasn't willing to second[-]guess a Marine and resented being placed in a position of having to do so."[151] Echoing him, one of the cheerleaders for the accused said that the acquittal "sends a warning to federal prosecutors about second-guessing warriors in combat."[152]

Some commentators expressed surprise that MEJA could be used at all to prosecute veterans. Retired Rear Adm. Don Guter, the navy judge advocate general from 2000 to 2002, recalled that MEJA had been proposed in order to prosecute civilians accompanying the armed forces overseas: "I don't ever remember [its] being contemplated that [the law] would cover ex-military people."[153] Sen. Jeff Sessions, who proposed the original Senate version of the bill that, as amended, became the MEJA statute, said that the bill's principal purpose was not the prosecution of veterans. Indeed, the original Senate proponents of the bill had not contemplated the possibility that MEJA could be used for prosecuting military veterans for combat-related actions. Although the text of the amended bill makes such a prospect unmistakable, prosecution of veterans was hardly mentioned in the congressional debates leading to its passage, which concentrated almost exclusively on the establishment of federal jurisdiction over civilian employees of the armed forces and dependants of members of the armed forces.[154] After the government had embarked on Nazario's prosecution, Sessions said, "I don't fault the Department of Justice for using what legal authority they have if a clear criminal act has been committed. But I do think that it would be preferable for crimes committed on active duty to be prosecuted by court martial rather than in civilian courts." Sessions's statement reflected the proposals of the Overseas Jurisdiction Advisory Committee and the similar proposal for the extension of UCMJ jurisdiction contemplated by S. 768, as originally drafted, as well as the perception that MEJA was not living up to its intentions and might need reconsideration. Sessions went on, "I think maybe what it says is we need to rethink the question of military personnel who are subject to prosecution."[155]

What significance should one attach to Nazario's acquittal? Does it mean that a civilian jury will generally be unwilling to convict veterans, hence perpetuating in a practical sense the de jure immunity that the *Toth v. Quarles* precedent once conferred on them? Several jurors stated that they were uneasy about civilians' judging the actions of troops in a combat zone. "Who are we to decide what men in war are doing?" asked the juror Nicole Peters, a high school guidance counselor, after the jury had delivered its verdict. "My father was a military man in Belgium who went through World War II fighting the Germans. He understands." After delivering the verdict, Peters approached the defendant and hugged him. "I never thought he was guilty," she said. "When we went in, it was nine to three for not guilty. By lunch there was only one juror who thought he was guilty," she added. The lone holdout kept saying, "But he killed somebody." Peters said she could not understand why only Nazario, and not Weemer and Nelson, was facing trial. Evidently she had not grasped or had not been told that, as serving marines, they were facing charges of murder and dereliction of duty at courts-martial.[156] Peters's reaction to the case bore out the apprehension expressed at the start of the proceedings by a senior marine officer who was in Fallujah: that the jury in a civilian court might not "understand the reality of combat, understand the reality of Falluja."[157]

Far from acting against Nazario's interests by leading to a lack of sympathy with the troops' actions, this situation seems to have served the interests of the defense because civilians felt themselves unable to judge the actions of troops in a war zone. This understandable civilian diffidence raises a question about the provision of MEJA that veterans be tried in federal district courts—and reminds one of the misgivings expressed by Everett and others soon after the *Toth* judgment that the facts of a case might be less comprehensible outside the war zone to those who were not there.

Nazario's defense team pointed to a solution that revisited the old debates about the merits of civilian over military jurisdiction: "We believe the Uniform Code of Military Justice should be expanded beyond its standard limit, so that former military personnel can be tried only by the military," said the former sergeant Joseph Preis, an advocate for Pepper Hamilton. "Currently, the typical enlistment provides the UCMJ with jurisdiction for eight years, which often includes four years of active service and four years of inactive reserve service. In the latter four years, military personnel can be recalled to active duty and then prosecuted under the UCMJ. However, after eight years of service, the military no longer has jurisdiction over former service members."[158] They proposed an amendment to the law to allow former members of the armed services to be recalled in order to face trial at courts-martial.[159]

Olivia Miller agrees that a civilian jury is simply not equipped to understand, far less judge, the actions of troops in "the fury of combat." Such a jury is likely either to acquit the defendant "because of a hesitation to judge a soldier's wartime decisions" or to condemn the defendant "due to an ignorance of essential combat actions." In contrast, a jury composed of Nazario's military peers, "who possess an innate understanding of combat actions," could have evaluated the charges against him more knowledgeably. Although patriotism and promilitary sentiments are bound to permeate a military courtroom, Miller believes that a military panel "strives to uphold the reputation of the military profession and will not hesitate to convict a renegade soldier for unauthorized conduct that shames the United States military."[160]

Yet coming to such a conclusion based on the limited experience of the prosecutions so far conducted under MEJA would be hasty. The specific features of the Nazario case make it unwise to extrapolate from its outcome and generalize it to others. The evidence presented—marred by an evidentiary gap resulting from the refusal of the three witnesses to the killings (who were also the alleged perpetrators) to testify about what they saw—may have made a conviction impossible by any legal forum. The trial judge promised Sergeants Weemer and Nelson that their testimony could not be used against them in their own trials, but they nevertheless refused to testify and were willing to face the additional charge of contempt of court as a result.[161] Because the defense would be unable to cross-examine Weemer, the trial judge granted a defense motion to suppress his taped confession that he, Nelson, and Nazario killed the Iraqi men. Weemer and Nelson said they would not testify against Nazario under any circumstances because they owed him their lives for his actions during the Iraq deployment; after the trials were completed, prosecutors dropped the contempt charges "in the interests of justice" even though the two men's silence had thwarted the prosecution of their comrade and leader.[162] The jurors did hear the recording of a telephone call between Nazario and Nelson, recorded at the behest of the NCIS, in which Nazario appeared to admit ordering the killings.[163] Two jurors thought that the tape-recorded evidence raised questions, though, about who gave the orders, Nazario or some other person. Ted Grinnell, a thirty-six-year-old real estate agent and navy veteran (the only veteran on the jury and the last holdout favoring a conviction before joining the others in their verdict), said, "I was actually looking for something from the government to sway me the other way. . . . We had no idea about what happened before the trigger was pulled. We didn't get to hear the whole story." He said he would have voted to convict Nazario to "send the military the message it is not above the law," except the evidence was just not there.[164]

A comparison of the trial in federal district court with the courts-martial of Nazario's alleged accomplices does not lead to the firm conclusion that a military court is a better forum in which to prosecute crimes committed by U.S. troops in combat. In his trial Sergeant Nelson pleaded guilty to two counts of dereliction of duty. The plea agreement spared him any jail time and allowed him to be honorably discharged from military service, with reduction in rank to lance corporal and a suspended sentence of 150 days.[165] "I gave in to the peer pressure and now I have to live with it for the rest of my life," Nelson said in an unsworn statement during the sentencing phase of his court-martial, expressing remorse for having followed Nazario's order to shoot rather than leaving the house and asking his superiors for help. "It's like I slapped my own family in the face," he said.[166]

Sergeant Weemer was acquitted of second-degree murder and dereliction of duty by a jury consisting entirely of veterans of Iraq and Afghanistan. Paul Hackett, a marine reservist who served on Weemer's defense team, honored the marines' esprit de corps and its motto, *Semper Fidelis* ("always faithful," colloquially abbreviated as Semper Fi) in his spirited advocacy of Weemer's cause: "You take a 22-year-old American, you shoot at him all day long, you make him see his buddies being killed, he has their blood on his boots and blouse, and when you don't see perfection in his decisions you court-martial him? It's absurd."[167]

The court-martial panel had heard a tape recording in which Weemer confessed that he and the other marines had shot dead four Iraqis after his squad suffered its first fatal casualty.[168] Weemer's defense, however, maintained that the man he admitted killing had lunged for his weapon during a chaotic few minutes inside the home. (Captain Medina similarly justified his killing of an unarmed, wounded Vietnamese woman outside My Lai (4) by saying she had made a threatening move before he shot her.)[169] Weemer had not specifically raised that defense in two taped interviews with investigators in 2006. Gary Solis, a former Marine Corps prosecutor and military law expert, said that Weemer's acquittal follows a pattern: "What you appear to have had here was a sympathetic military jury unwilling to find a young man guilty for something that happened in combat."[170] The acquittal was another setback for prosecutors at Camp Pendleton, who struggled to win convictions of marines accused of wrongdoing in Iraq. It came soon after the Marine Corps's failure to achieve the conviction at court-martial of several suspects in a massacre committed by Kilo 3/1, although not by the same individuals, at Haditha in 2005.[171]

The leniency shown in the case of the Fallujah killings mirrors the outcome of similar events in Vietnam. Public reactions to these prosecutions also echoed the sympathy many Americans felt toward the perpetrators of the My Lai massacre. A complaint about Weemer's prosecution, in response to an article about his acquittal, could have come from four decades earlier:

> Oo-Rah! Justice at Last for our Boys!!!! As the mother of a Marine it just burns me that we are charging our boys with murder for shooting the ENEMY. When you are fighting an enemy that refuses to identify themselves by wearing a uniform, act like they are your friend one minute and blow you up the next, the only way to stay alive is to work with the premises that EVERYONE is the ENEMY until proven otherwise. . . . when someone (other than an American) gets killed, everyone wants to call it Murder? It's WAR, and sometimes non-combatants die, sometimes you do things that, in another time, another place, you wouldn't do. But it's War! And that is why they call it HELL.[172]

In response to a suggestion by another participant in the discussion that the Iraqis in the Fallujah killings should have been treated as prisoners and not summarily shot, another member of the public wrote, "They were ordered to kill them, you are a Marine, you follow orders PERIOD! Besides they killed one of ours! Should have taken out the entire town!" And sounding like the draft board members and veterans who, in the wake of the My Lai prosecutions, said they could not countenance sending more young Americans into the armed forces, Jerry, a Vietnam veteran, said,

> I'm amazed that any young american, will volunteer for service, in the military. We take thes[e] young people[,] spend [s]ome months, teaching them how to kill and destroy. We saddle them with rules of engagement, that get them killed for no reason except politicians, want to wear a white hat, awarded by the rest of the world. . . . I am an ex marine, who, served in Viet Nam, one of the things I was always confident about, was that, my officers, would take care of me. Now, I have my doubts. I couldn't with a clear conscience, recommend to a young person, that they go into the corps.[173]

It is difficult to condemn these American citizens for their allegiance to the troops their nation sent into harm's way or for the relative value they place on the well-being of those troops against the lives of the Iraqi people, who remain strangers and abstractions to most Americans. When all most American civilians know about Iraq is the dusty, sun-baked battle scenes on the television news, stories of corrupt governments and ethnic cleansing, and the threat of roadside bombs and fanatical insurgents, one ought not to be surprised when the public places its loyalty to its family members and compatriots on a higher plane than any concerns about Iraqis. But this recognition cannot help but be a reminder of how little has changed in the decades since another generation of Americans respected the same scale of values in saving all their sympathy for the perpetrators of the massacre at My Lai while devaluing the lives of the Vietnamese civilians they killed.

Given that it proved difficult to persuade a jury of marines to convict a fellow marine for his actions in a combat zone, one cannot conclude, as Preis does, that the outcome of the Nazario trial is explained by its being heard before a civilian jury. Although the totality of the evidence, including the interviews that were barred from consideration by the jury, seems to prove that the marines killed unarmed captives, it was problematic to determine precisely what happened, above all because of the *omertà* practiced by the only living witnesses, the alleged perpetrators. The record in case law is not yet sufficient, therefore, to establish whether the civilian courts are in general an effective forum in which to try crimes alleged against military veterans.

Although the first, the Nazario case is not the only trial of a veteran under the provisions of MEJA. A second MEJA case tried by a federal district court is that of former Pfc. Steven Dale Green, a veteran of the 101st Airborne Division and an admitted perpetrator of an especially brutal crime in Mahmudiya, Iraq, on March 12, 2006. That day Green and three other soldiers entered the home of an Iraqi family, gang-raped Abeer Qassim Hamza, a fourteen-year-old girl, then killed her and burned her body, and at some point in the attack killed her parents and her six-year-old sister in order to leave no witnesses behind. They attempted to disguise their crime by using the household's AK-47 weapon to kill the family and make the killings appear to have been committed by insurgents. One reason the killings aroused the suspicion of other American troops who investigated the scene was that the AK-47 jammed, and Green used a shotgun, a weapon used almost exclusively by Americans in Iraq, to kill two members of the family.[174]

There were repeated warnings that Green was likely to commit such a crime. He repeatedly told his superiors about his desire to kill Iraqi civilians. In December 2005, at a meeting with his brigade commander, a colonel, Green asked, "Why can't we just shoot them all?" He told a psychiatric nurse practitioner with the rank of lieutenant colonel that he was obsessed with killing Iraqis. Yet he was declared fit to return to combat "with little more than a pep talk and a pat on the back." The sequence of events demonstrates a lack of accountability by higher officers for the crimes committed by the troops they supervise and command.[175] During the sentencing phase of the trial one of the officers who had declared Green fit to return to duty said that such murderous sentiments had been expressed by other members of the unit and were not uncommon among troops in combat.[176]

When Sgt. Tony Yribe heard Green confess to having been the sole perpetrator of the crime, he told Green he should report to the so-called Stress Tent with a psychiatric problem and leave the military. Yribe did not want to probe further in an investigation of the crime, even though it appeared unlikely Green had committed it alone. Diagnosed with a preexisting psychiatric disorder, Green was sent home to the United States and honorably discharged from the army in May 2006.

This did not end the matter, though. A fellow soldier, Pfc. Justin Watt, heard about the killings and was dissatisfied with Yribe's attempt to sweep the matter aside. He gathered evidence sufficient to allow the other perpetrators to be identified. The matter was taken up by Watt's commanders. Soon the confessions of several conscience-stricken soldiers established their guilt. Still in uniform when the crime was officially investigated, they were tried at court-martial, convicted, and sentenced to long terms of detention: ninety years and one hundred years in the military's maximum-security prison at Fort Leavenworth, although all will be eligible for parole in ten years or less.[177] These sentences seem to indicate that the leniency shown to troops serving during the Vietnam War may become a thing of the past, although the recent record in this area is mixed.

In May 2009 the civilian jury in Green's district court prosecution under the MEJA statute found him guilty of aggravated sexual abuse, murder, and other crimes.[178] Green's defense team had tried, unsuccessfully, to have him reinducted into the army so that he could face trial by court-martial—an indication that in the minds of his lawyers, even though the evidence against Green was overwhelming, he faced the prospect of getting a lighter sentence if he was judged before a panel of his former peers in the armed forces. In this they made a well-founded bet, first, because under the UCMJ convicts have a chance of obtaining parole after ten years, an option not always available under federal law; and, second, because since 1961 the army has not executed anyone convicted and sentenced to death by a court-martial.[179] In the district court Green did face the death penalty, and the Justice Department refused to take it off the table in return for the offer of a guilty plea. Perhaps that decision was made out of concern for the image of the U.S. military in the eyes of Iraqis, since the relatives of the murdered family were saying that nothing less than capital punishment would suffice for the crimes Green committed.[180] Solis remarked that the decision to prosecute Green in the federal district court "undoubtedly reflects political pressure to ensure the most severe punishment for the crime's alleged ringleader."[181] In the event, Green was sentenced to life in prison.[182] Watt, the whistle-blower, received death threats after Green and the other perpetrators were sentenced, just as the helicopter pilot Hugh Thompson once had for reporting to his superiors the bloodbath he saw taking place at My Lai.[183]

The convictions in the Mahmudiya case were made almost inevitable because Green and the others confessed to their crimes before and during the investigation; the acquittal in the Nazario case was similarly a near foregone conclusion because of the suspects' refusal to confess to the alleged crimes and because the perpetrators left no remaining eyewitnesses who might have described what happened. It is therefore difficult to draw any certainties about the likelihood of successful prosecution of military veterans by civilian courts. The weakness of the case against Nazario, the statement by the veteran juror after that trial, and the verdict in the Green trial rule out the easy assumption that civilian juries will be unwilling to convict military veterans; yet the overwhelming strength of the evidence in the Green case should also warn against assuming that civilian juries will be ready to second-guess the actions of troops when the facts of the case leave room for doubt about the justification of their actions. As far as a general assessment of the effectiveness of MEJA in prosecuting veterans is concerned, metaphorically the jury is still out.

CONCLUSION

"The One Significant Holdout"

Why was MEJA finally passed at the end of the twentieth century after decades of legislative inaction? And how can one square the further closing of the jurisdictional gap through the extension of the UCMJ with the Bush administration's repudiation of international legal standards in its approach to the "war on terror," its use of torture, and its congressionally endorsed resistance to the International Criminal Court (ICC)? The record reveals that the wish of the United States to retain primary jurisdiction over its troops, private security personnel, and veterans led it finally to pass laws that permitted the enforcement of generally acknowledged legal standards in its own courts lest an international or foreign court invoke its jurisdiction over their offenses. The new legislation did not emerge from a new attitude on the part of legislators; rather, in passing laws that allowed the assertion of primary jurisdiction over U.S. nationals, Congress demonstrated the same attitude of skepticism and hostility toward foreign and international courts that was evident throughout the decades considered by this book.

The motives leading to the passage of MEJA are already apparent in the congressional hearings and scholarly commentary preceding the passage of the War Crimes Act and in the testimony and commentary regarding the potential jurisdiction of the ICC. In the mid-1990s, as the War Crimes Act was moving toward passage in Congress, the initial support of the United States for the creation of a permanent, United Nations–sponsored international criminal court had begun to waver. The ICC, unlike the International Court of Justice, which adjudicates conflicts among nations and makes judgments to which nations, not individuals, are subject, would be able to try individuals who violated international humanitarian law and the law of war. Despite its initial favorable interest in the creation of the ICC, the United States soon began dragging its feet regarding the proposed court. One of the principal points of contention was whether U.S. nationals would ever be subject to prosecution by the court.

Robinson Everett had never stopped arguing the need to fill the jurisdictional gap by providing for an American forum in which war crimes could be prosecuted.[1] He "worked closely" with legislators to enact the War Crimes Act, which would allow at least some currently unprosecutable suspects to be tried in U.S. courts, while also fulfilling the decades-long obligation of passing legislation that implemented the Geneva Conventions.[2] In congressional hearings Everett argued that the prospect that Americans might be prosecuted by an international tribunal made it imperative to establish a judicial forum in the United States in which the same alleged crimes could be prosecuted and suspects would enjoy the procedural and constitutional protections familiar in American law: "Our having jurisdiction may protect us in situations where we need to be able to say we want to deal with our people; we don't want to surrender them to an international court or to extradite them somewhere else."[3] The motive could not have been more clearly stated: the creation of a judicial forum that closed the jurisdictional gap, by allowing for prosecution of American defendants in a U.S. court, would "protect us" by providing a rationale on which to refuse to surrender those nationals or allow them to be extradited "somewhere else."

Everett reminded Congress of the long-standing efforts by Ervin to fill the jurisdictional void and contemplated occasions not only when an American national or a person in American custody would be accused of having violated treaty provisions, but also when demands would be made that the suspect be delivered for trial in the courts of the foreign country where the alleged crimes occurred or in an international criminal court. He pointed out that in such a situation, "if American courts have jurisdiction to try the accused for the alleged offense, a basis exists for conducting the trial in our own courts, where important procedural protections exist. However, *if our courts lack jurisdiction, treaty obligations may require the United States to surrender the accused or detain the accused for trial elsewhere.* In short, I believe that broadening the jurisdiction of American courts may in some instances assure procedural protections for any of our own citizens who are accused of grave breaches of international law and may allow our country to 'wash its own dirty linen.'"[4] Thus the longtime concern with the constitutional and procedural rights of U.S. troops and citizens with which Ervin had been preoccupied encouraged the passage of legislation that would begin to plug the jurisdictional gap.

Michael Mathesan, the principal legal adviser for the State Department, said in the hearing preceding passage of the War Crimes Act that "the United States has played a leading role in international efforts to bring to justice those who have committed war crimes and other violations of international humanitarian law."[5] He reminded Congress, however, that the United States had not immediately passed legislation required to enforce the Geneva Conventions' prohibition of grave breaches because it believed at the time that the United States already possessed laws necessary to prosecute those who committed such acts. He recounted how the courts had arrived at decisions that struck down military courts' jurisdiction over offenders who were not in active military service. This, he said, appeared to impose on the United States an obligation to correct that anomaly. Like Everett, he suggested that passage of the War Crimes Act would also allow the United States to reinforce its claim to primary jurisdiction over U.S. citizens accused of grave breaches of the convention.[6]

The as-yet-unconstituted ICC was not the only international legal forum in which war crimes prosecutions might be conducted. The United Nations had shown a new propensity in the 1990s to set up ad hoc tribunals, such as those covering the former Yugoslavia and Rwanda, when a nation-state was unable or unwilling to prosecute its citizens.[7] This new situation rendered the continued existence of pockets of national-jurisdictional immunity increasingly incongruous and potentially susceptible to assertions of foreign-country or international jurisdiction. Moreover, the United States, until it passed the War Crimes Act, could have found itself in an embarrassing situation: it claimed Geneva protections for its civilians in foreign war zones; it therefore seemed anomalous that it had failed to pass legislation allowing it to comply with the conventions' requirements regarding the control of those civilians.[8]

There were thus multiple motives for the passage of the War Crimes Act: first of all, the statute would fulfill the overdue responsibility to pass legislation implementing the Geneva Conventions; it would also allow the United States to assert the jurisdiction of its courts over any of its nationals who might be accused of war crimes rather than surrendering them to a foreign or international court. These twin purposes combined with a concern for the United States's international image. Bringing it into line with international legal standards by allowing it to prosecute its own troops and nationals would sustain its image as an upholder of the law. A high-ranking Pentagon lawyer said in recommending passage of the War Crimes Act, "The United States, as a political matter, should be seen as fully in conformity with its international obligations in this very sensitive area."[9]

After Congress passed the War Crimes Act in 1995, the United States vacillated between supporting the ICC, while trying to modify its mode of operation in order to protect U.S. interests, and withdrawing its support. After President Clinton made some favorable references to the ICC, his administration was insisting the court be controlled by the U.N. Security Council, which would have allowed the permanent members, including the United States, the right of veto over prosecutions.[10] After unsuccessfully seeking guarantees that U.S. nationals would never be subject to its jurisdiction, Clinton refused for a considerable time to sign the Rome Statute, which founded the ICC.[11] The United States managed to increase the deferral to national jurisdictions in the regime of complementarity (apportioning jurisdiction to national courts and the ICC), but not as much as it sought. It successfully defeated the attempt to establish universal jurisdiction, but it did not manage to delete the provision of the Rome Statute that would allow the troops of a nonsignatory country to be prosecuted if they committed crimes on the territory of a signatory.[12]

The Justice Department, the Defense Department, and conservatives in Congress were suspicious of the court because of worries that it might infringe on America's sovereignty. In hearings on the ICC, Sen. John Ashcroft expressed concern that "Americans could be dragged before this court and denied the protection of the Bill of Rights." If there is one critical component of sovereignty, he argued, "it is the authority to define crimes and punishments."[13] Ashcroft was repeating decades-old arguments used in the fifties about the intrusion of "treaty law" on U.S. sovereignty. Likewise, the former defense secretary Caspar Weinberger cited the constitutional rights that any American defendants brought before the ICC would no longer enjoy: trial by jury, protection against self-incrimination, and the right to cross-examine prosecution witnesses. He said the concept of the court "tests whether the idea of sovereignty exists any longer. And it is a very major step along the road toward wiping out individual national sovereignty."[14]

By 1998 opposition by the United States to the ICC coalesced around the firm conviction that there should not be even the slightest possibility that any American should be subject to judgment or even oversight by the court. The U.S. ambassador-at-large for war crimes issues, David Scheffer, recalling the obstacles posed by the Washington bureaucracy, writes, "Every deliberation turned on the fear of prosecution of American soldiers and officials rather than considering the larger picture of ending atrocity crimes in our time."[15] This "absolutist" stance of opposition to the ICC was shared by the Pentagon and by Jesse Helms, the chair of the Senate Foreign Relations Committee, which would have received any proposal to ratify the treaty founding the court. Scheffer, who led the American delegation negotiating the terms of the treaty establishing the ICC, chafed against statements by Helms and his aides that undercut the position of the United States in the negotiations over the treaty that would establish the court; he, too, however, stated that the troops of the sole remaining superpower had a "unique peacekeeping role" and are "uniquely subject to frivolous, nuisance accusations by parties of all sorts."[16] However, a more serious problem for the United States than "frivolous" accusations was that a state party might bring a well-founded accusation against an American national, one that could not be swept under the rug; and that any failure to cooperate with a prosecution that the United States was unable, because of gaps in the law, to try in its own courts would have diplomatic repercussions.

After the president signed the War Crimes Act into law, Everett specified one of its benefits: according to the principle of complementarity, the existence of the act allowed the United States to assert its primary jurisdiction over an alleged war crime committed by a U.S. soldier or citizen. "If an American servicemember or civilian is charged with conduct that falls within the [War Crimes Act]," Everett wrote, "the principle of complementarity would authorize the United States to demand that the accused be tried in a federal district court, rather than in the ICC." But the War Crimes Act had not fully plugged the jurisdictional gaps and did not cover all the crimes that are the subject of the Rome Statute establishing the ICC. Everett pointed out that Congress needed to legislate further in order to prohibit crimes coextensive with those covered by the Rome Statute.[17]

The fears of an invasion of American jurisdiction if the United States joined the court were largely exaggerated. The ICC's rules established that it would exercise jurisdiction over an alleged crime only when the state that would normally exercise jurisdiction was unable or unwilling to carry out an investigation and prosecution. A case would be inadmissible if the crime was being investigated or prosecuted by that state. But this principle obviously could apply only in cases in which a state had jurisdiction. This circumstance introduced an additional motive for the United States to close the jurisdictional gaps which denied its courts jurisdiction over certain crimes and suspects.

The articles of the Rome Statute dealing with issues of jurisdiction and the admissibility of cases to the court applied equally to nonsignatories of the statute (referred to in the treaty as states) as to signatories (states parties). The United States rejected altogether the jurisdiction of the ICC over the citizens and nationals of nonsignatories as a matter of principle. Nevertheless, the passage of laws plugging the jurisdictional gaps would install an additional safeguard against an ICC prosecution of U.S. nationals. If the United States could assert its primary jurisdiction over alleged crimes committed by its troops or the private contractors serving with them, and if it made a plausible claim that it had investigated or would investigate the allegation, the ICC would regard a case against an American national as inadmissible.[18]

This circumstance was plainly recognized by Scheffer several years after the founding of the court. He stated that under the principle of complementarity, a nation's ability to prosecute the same crimes found in the ICC's jurisdiction "essentially shields that nation's nationals from ICC scrutiny." Because they had passed laws incorporating genocide, crimes against humanity, and war crimes into their domestic penal codes, he said, "paradoxically, some of America's allies, as states parties to the Rome Statute of the ICC, now are more insulated from ICC investigation than is the United States, even as a non-party to the Rome Statute." While Scheffer's article advocated laws penalizing "atrocity crimes," the logic he laid out applied to any gap in jurisdiction.[19] The important point for my argument is the acknowledgment that the principle of complementarity provides a motive for the United States to shield its nationals from the ICC by establishing its jurisdiction over crimes not already covered by its domestic laws. This line of reasoning was articulated in the period immediately preceding the passage of MEJA. As Everett argued in 2000, "The ability of the United States to prevent the trial of American servicemembers by the ICC will be greatly enhanced if U.S. courts have jurisdiction to try servicemembers for any crime that falls within the ICC's jurisdiction."[20]

By the time the House of Representatives held hearings on MEJA in 2000, the international legal context afforded further reasons for asserting jurisdiction by the United States over Americans suspected of breaches of international law. The universal jurisdiction that existed under a number of treaties, like the Geneva Conventions, enabled any state party to try anyone accused of the crimes in question, and that principle was now beginning to be seriously applied. Plaintiffs and criminal complainants were also asserting the extraterritorial applications of national laws.[21] In the 1990s, for example, courts in Germany and Denmark invoked universal jurisdiction to try defendants for crimes committed in the former Yugoslavia.[22] The precedent-setting example of a court's attempting to enforce international law against a former national leader under the principle of universal jurisdiction was the action of Judge Baltasar Garzón of Spain, who issued an international warrant against Augusto Pinochet for crimes he committed in Chile. The warrant led to Pinochet's arrest in London in 1998.[23] Such events, coupled with the imminent founding of the ICC, augured the advance of universal jurisdiction. As Wolfgang Kaleck argues, the arrest of Pinochet a few months after the Rome conference in which the statute establishing the ICC was negotiated "motivated and empowered human rights organizations, lawyers, prosecutors, and judges all over the world to prosecute human rights violations in domestic and international fora and to apply transnational strategies of using criminal law to bring dozens of war criminals and perpetrators of crimes against humanity to justice."[24] Even if the United States succeeded in blocking the establishment of universal jurisdiction in the ICC, which it was determined to do, the concept of justice without borders appeared to be advancing.[25]

In the context of opposition by the United States to international and foreign court jurisdiction over its nationals, the inability of American courts to prosecute defendants who fell outside their jurisdiction was both anomalous and unappealing: Robert E. Reed, the associate deputy general counsel for the Department of Defense, stated at the House hearing on MEJA that "the inability of U.S. authorities to adequately respond to serious misconduct within the civilian component of the U.S. Armed Forces, presents the strong possibility for embarrassment in the international community, increases the possibility of hostility in the host nation's local community where our forces are assigned, and threatens relationships with our allies."[26]

The wish to protect the rights of American defendants by plugging the jurisdictional gap and hence shielding them from prosecution by a foreign or international court is unmistakable in other testimony given at the House hearing on MEJA: "Individuals accused of [serious criminal offenses overseas] are entitled to no less due process and fairness and other constitutional protections than they would if they were accused in the United States;"[27] "This legislation actually provides those U.S. constitutional protections and due process guarantees that these civilian employees and others accompanying our forces overseas would not otherwise enjoy, such as when jurisdiction to investigate and prosecute rests with the foreign country in which these employees find themselves assigned;"[28] "We have civilian employees, contractor personnel, in over 100 countries around the world. It is in our interest . . . to ensure that they are not subjected to the potentially draconian jurisdiction of whatever state we happen to be operating in."[29] Plugging the jurisdictional gap by passing MEJA would, according to this reasoning, establish a U.S. forum in which accused Americans could be tried, and, just as important, it would permit the jurisdiction of a U.S. court to be invoked, whether or not a prosecution eventuated, sparing the defendants the "potentially draconian" jurisdiction of a foreign court.

This historical record adds depth to the view that Judge Cabranes's prompting of Congress in *Gatlin* was the precipitating event spurring passage of MEJA. Fidell regards Cabranes's order that his opinion be sent to the congressional committees as the act that goaded Congress into passing MEJA.[30] As he points out, the jurisdictional gap had existed for decades, and there had been numerous legislative proposals to fill it as well as extensive discussion in law reviews, all to no avail.[31] Cabranes's action sparked legislative action. A circuit court similarly finds that *Gatlin* "prodded Congress" to act.[32] But Glenn R. Schmitt, who helped draft the MEJA bill and played a crucial role in its passage, says that the circuit court is "simply wrong" about this matter. Cabranes may have encouraged legislators to vote for the bill, but his opinion played no part in the committee process that drafted the bill and brought it before Congress. As Schmitt points out, the Senate Judiciary Committee reported the MEJA bill favorably to the full Senate in June 1999, "long before we learned about *Gatlin*."[33] By the time the *Gatlin* case was decided in the summer of 2000, the House Judiciary Committee's Subcommittee on Crime had already voted favorably on the bill.[34]

If *Gatlin* encouraged legislators to pass MEJA, the historical context in which Cabranes delivered his opinion helps explain its impact. The need to close the jurisdictional gaps arising from *Toth* and the *Covert* line of cases was unchanged, in legal terms. What had altered was the surrounding situation. The most crucial political and diplomatic precondition for passage of the law was the implicit pressure coming from the imminent creation of an international criminal court and the risk to American servicemembers of prosecution in foreign courts, which was repeatedly cited in the hearings leading to the enactment of the gap-closing laws. The most significant military circumstance was the increased number of U.S. troop deployments overseas in the 1990s, coupled with the expanding reliance on civilian employees of the armed services and private security contractors. In principle, the courts in the nations where U.S. forces were engaged might have exerted jurisdiction over the civilians, but in some countries that was not a practical or politically attractive possibility. For example, in Somalia there was no functioning court system; in Saudi Arabia the local courts functioned under Islamic law.[35]

On the last day of the period allowed for signature and shortly before leaving office, President Clinton signed the Rome Treaty establishing the ICC, but he made it clear he did not recommend that his successor, George W. Bush, submit the treaty to the Senate for ratification "until our fundamental concerns are satisfied." Among these were the wish to protect U.S. officials from "unfounded charges" and Clinton's objection to the court's possessing jurisdiction over American personnel before the United States ratified the treaty. The reason for his signing, he explained, was that the United States, as a signatory, would be able to influence the evolution of the court.[36]

In May 2002 President Bush formally renounced the Rome Treaty that established the ICC. Conservative Republican opponents of the court introduced the American Servicemembers' Protection Act (ASPA, nicknamed the Hague Invasion Act), which empowered the president to send in the U.S. military to rescue any American soldiers held by or on behalf of the ICC.[37] The legislation set out to sabotage the court by prohibiting military assistance to any country that was party to the ICC, although it exempted NATO members and other major non-NATO allies from the sanctions. In August 2002, Bush signed ASPA into law.[38]

Echoing the decades-old concerns expressed by Ervin and by opponents of "treaty law," the ASPA statute includes a passage that establishes its motive: "Any American prosecuted by the International Criminal Court will, under the Rome Statute, be denied procedural protections to which all Americans are entitled under the Bill of Rights to the United States Constitution, such as the right to trial by jury." The wording of the statute asserts the right of members of the U.S. armed forces to be free of the risk of prosecution by the ICC and affirms the obligation of the U.S. government to protect them from such prosecutions.[39] The statute repudiates the jurisdiction of the ICC over U.S. nationals: "It is a fundamental principle of international law that a treaty is binding upon its parties only and that it does not create obligations for non-parties without their consent to be bound. The United States is not a party to the Rome Statute and will not be bound by any of its terms. The United States will not recognize the jurisdiction of the International Criminal Court over United States nationals."[40]

ASPA prohibited the United States from participating in peacekeeping operations unless the country in which the troops were to be deployed was not a party to the ICC or unless it had signed an Article 98 agreement with the U.S. government preventing the ICC from moving against U.S. troops stationed in that country.[41] The Bush administration threatened to cut off development assistance to any nation that refused to guarantee Americans immunity from prosecution at the tribunal.[42] The cut-off of military assistance took effect in July 2003, and the Nethercutt Amendment made good on the threat of cutting off economic assistance to any country that was a party to the ICC and that did not guarantee to immunize U.S. troops stationed in that country from prosecution by the court.[43] The United States managed to pressure one hundred nations into signing Article 98 agreements, bilateral agreements in which each state promised it would not surrender citizens of the other to the ICC and which were a condition of the United States resuming economic and military assistance.[44] Such bullying and blackmail tended to provoke resentment and countermeasures by U.S. allies.[45] The conflict over the ICC is thus one indication of the diplomatic and political difficulties that beset the United States as a result of its exemptionalist position regarding international law.

The ICC has been a disappointment to those who foresaw in its founding a new era in the administration of international justice. In practice, the operation of the court has been vastly expensive, slow, and limited in its achievements. These criticisms would not be so serious were it not for the fact that the ICC has demonstrated partiality in the meting out of justice: the accused and the convicts have for the most part been the leaders of African governments and rebel movements.[46] The court did not list the crime of aggression under its prosecutable offenses until 2010, and, despite its refusal to join the court, the United States was able to persuade the delegates at the ICC review conference to defer any prosecution of this crime until 2017 at least.[47] Consequently, absent from the court's penal sanctions have been such malefactors as George W. Bush and Tony Blair, whose crimes include the launching of aggressive and preventive war lacking the sanction of the United Nations. So long as such delinquency remains immune from the operation of international justice, the ICC's claim to administer the law impartially and evenhandedly will ring hollow.[48]

Under the Obama administration the United States has softened its opposition to the ICC. In its National Security Strategy of May 2010 the administration summarized its position toward the court in the following way: "From Nuremberg to Yugoslavia to Liberia, the United States has seen that the end of impunity and the promotion of justice are not just moral imperatives; they are stabilizing forces in international affairs. The United States is thus working to strengthen national justice systems and is maintaining our support for ad hoc international tribunals and hybrid courts."[49] The attraction of ad hoc tribunals and hybrid courts is that they target particular classes of defendant and do not seek the broad jurisdiction that might bring U.S. nationals and troops within the reach of international justice.

The statement continues, "Although the United States is not at present a party to the Rome Statute of the International Criminal Court, and will always protect U.S. personnel, we are engaging with State Parties to the Rome Statute on issues of concern and are supporting the ICC's prosecution of those cases that advance U.S. interests and values, consistent with the requirements of U.S. law." The statement that the United States will "always protect U.S. personnel," without regard for the possibility that there might be a valid criminal case against them, represents a continuation of the country's insistence on immunity from prosecution in foreign and international courts for its citizens and troops. The spirit of the Hague Invasion Act lives on.

The Obama administration states that it supports the ICC's prosecutions and offers assistance in response to specific requests from the ICC prosecutor and other court officials, consistent with American law, when it is "in U.S. national interest" to do so. Since November 2009 the United States has participated in an "observer capacity" in meetings of the ICC Assembly of States Parties.[50] Stephen J. Rapp, the U.S. ambassador at large for war crimes issues, stated, "While we have not made the decision ourselves to ratify the Statute of Rome, . . . we have offered to assist the Prosecutor and Registrar in each of the current cases of the ICC, seeking ways consistent with our law to help with witness protection and relocation, information-sharing, and the arrest and transfer of fugitives."[51] Indeed, a sort of middle ground, "cooperating behind the scenes, assisting in detentions, sharing intelligence, and providing other sorts of background support" without joining the court or accepting its jurisdiction over Americans, had been a long-planned-for outcome of the negotiations if other states did not agree to the concessions the United States demanded.[52]

The selective cooperation of the United States with the ICC perpetuates the situation of asymmetry that was the starting point of this book's argument. Why should the United States be allowed to participate in the operation of the court when it refuses to join the court and opposes the court's jurisdiction over its nationals and troops? To the extent that the United States currently cooperates in the court's operation, it acts on the side of the prosecutor. It is unacceptable for an entity to administer justice when it is not accountable to that justice. For the ICC and the signatories of the Rome Treaty to cooperate with a nonsignatory United States that pursues "U.S. interests" while continuing to "protect its personnel" is to acquiesce in a situation of legal asymmetry and to legitimize the American exemption.

Offers of prosecution-related assistance to a court that lacks a police force of its own may inveigle the signers of the Rome Treaty into allowing the United States to play an in-between role, half in and half out of the international court, lending the weight of its military apparatus to the enforcement of international law while keeping a distance commensurate with the special international responsibilities it claims. Some may feel convinced by the argument that America's role as global enforcer makes it a target for politically motivated prosecutions and that the international community benefits from allowing it a monopoly over the prosecution of its own; others may wish to believe that allowing the United States a measure of involvement in the ICC will encourage it to re-sign the Rome Treaty and become a full participant in the court. The history of the past half century and more cautions against any such belief.

If the United States is permitted to adopt a sort of halfway involvement in the ICC—cooperating in "information-sharing, and the arrest and transfer of fugitives" without joining the court and hence embracing the possibility that its own nationals will be subject to ICC prosecution—no one knows how the story will end, but one can predict the next chapters. The halfway status is likely not to be a transitional stage but will perfectly suit American policymakers. Its prolongation and eventual permanency will sediment the American exemption and American immunity. As we recall from the discussion of customary international law, a set of institutional arrangements, if unchallenged, assumes the status of custom, and there is no affront to justice that cannot imaginably become normalized when it is backed up by the unchallenged military capability of a self-satisfied superpower. The decades in which U.S. veterans could get away with murder because year after year the U.S. government allowed a jurisdictional gap to exist remind us of this basic truth about the capacity of an unrivaled power distractedly to tolerate its own delinquency, while the world looks on.

The availability of an inadequately resourced MEJA is the perfect complement to this sort of halfway arrangement. Insufficient as a means of exercising jurisdiction over the large numbers of private security contractors who serve alongside U.S. troops, and likely to be used therefore to prosecute only selected, egregious crimes, it nevertheless is a bulwark against the assertion of a foreign or international court's jurisdiction over U.S. nationals. No matter how infrequently and ineffectively it is used, the mere fact that it might be used will allow the United States to assert its primary jurisdiction over such defendants. To recall the army judge advocates' reported view in 1957: a U.S. statute, although not aimed at actual trials, would allow the United States, under SOFA arrangements, to assert its jurisdiction over U.S. nationals it wished to spare a trial in a foreign court. One need not be a cynic to see this as the controlling principle according to which the United States ultimately closed the jurisdictional gaps: by retaining its jurisdiction over its nationals, it preserves its sovereign autonomy from infringement by foreign and international laws. Having asserted its jurisdiction, the United States may choose when and when not to prosecute. Plugging the jurisdictional gap thereby serves as a stratagem to prevent prosecutions as much as to allow them.

The history of the jurisdictional gap discloses a covert truth about the U.S. government's attitude to the standards of law it has enforced on others and professes to respect. Presidents, lawmakers, and judges tolerated a tear in the fabric of U.S. law through which murderers passed with impunity. This injustice ought to have brought on international opprobrium, but the scandal is that there was no scandal. The world raised not a peep of protest, while American power was so overwhelming that it not only shielded U.S. citizens' rights, as its judges proclaimed them, but also consequently immunized criminals from prosecution by any court. If we want to understand the tolerance for injustice that lies behind the attitude of the United States toward the ICC, we need only look back at the half century preceding the court's establishment and the complacency with which America's leaders for year after year allowed the jurisdictional gap to remain unfilled.

A mature international community will vindicate the emerging concept of sovereignty as responsibility by resolving not to allow the participation in the ICC's operations of any nation that does not subject its citizens and troops to the court's jurisdiction. The nations of the world stand now at a crossroads: one way lies a recognition of universal human rights and respect for universally acknowledged standards of justice; the other way lies the lasting disfigurement of the system of international justice scarred by the American exemption. The current situation of asymmetry is unsustainable. The world will become one thing or the other: it will be a place where justice is possible or one where power prevails and hides its wrongdoing behind the cloak of sovereignty. American citizens, officials, legislators, and nongovernmental organizations should recognize that the United States has a national interest in strengthening, not undermining, institutions of international justice. The United States should not await the moment when its global hegemony has been challenged and surpassed before discovering the benefits of full membership of the concert of nations.[53]

Given the persistent failure of American politicians to take steps to ratify the Rome Treaty, the public's views appear to be ahead of their leaders' regarding membership of the ICC. In a survey of opinions about foreign policy conducted in 2002, 71 percent of a sample of American respondents said the United States should participate in the court. More significant, even when another sample in the same survey was primed by being told that U.S. soldiers on peacekeeping operations might be brought before the ICC on "trumped-up charges," 65 percent supported the court.[54] In a follow-up survey in 2006, 71 percent continued to support the ICC, despite the years of fearmongering by some of the nation's leading diplomats and its president.[55] The figure was almost unchanged, at 70 percent, in 2012.[56]

Revealing though these surveys are, the polls that actually count are those that result in the election of members of Congress and the president. Like their predecessors in the 1950s, these officials may well perceive that a respect for international law has not been a certain vote-winner on which the results of elections turn. The situation is surely ripe for change, though, because unilateralism and lawlessness damage the international standing of the United States and concentrate a justified sense of popular grievance onto the chief enforcer of an asymmetrical international order. As the *New York Times* pointed out when the United States began to hedge against involvement in the ICC, "It looks bad for the U.S. to lecture other countries on human rights and international standards of decent behavior and then be the one significant holdout against a mechanism to uphold those standards."[57] American immunity from foreign and international legal judgment comes at a high cost: resentment breeds insecurity; legal immunity heightens political danger. Citizens of the United States and of other nations thus share an interest in finally repudiating the tyranny constituted by unaccountable power.

ABBREVIATIONS

APP	American Presidency Project, Online by Gerhard Peters and John T. Woolley, www.presidency.ucsb.edu/
AR	*Annual Report of the U.S. Court of Criminal Appeals and the Judge Advocates General of the Armed Forces and the General Counsel of the Department of Transportation Submitted to the Committees on Armed Services of the Senate and the House of Representatives and to the Secretary of Defense and Secretary of the Treasury and the Secretaries of the Departments of the Army, Navy, and Air Force Pursuant to the Uniform Code of Military Justice for the Period* [dates].
ASC	Armed Services Committee
CEB	University of Florida, Smathers Library, Special Collections, Charles E. Bennett Collection, Legislative Services—Military Justice
EA	Eckhardt Archives, Documents Donated by William G. Eckhardt, in the custody of the Regimental Historian, the Judge Advocate General's Legal Center and School, Charlottesville, Virginia
EB	Library of Congress, Manuscript Division, The Papers of Edward W. Brooke
EW	Library of Congress, Manuscript Division, The Papers of Earl Warren
FFP	Library of Congress, Manuscript Division, The Felix Frankfurter Papers, American Legal Manuscripts from the Harvard Law School Library, University Publications of America microfilm edition. The original documents can be found in The Felix Frankfurter Papers, Historical and Special Collections, Harvard Law School Library.
GPO	U.S. Government Printing Office
HLB	Library of Congress, Manuscript Division, The Papers of Hugo L. Black
IHT	*International Herald Tribune*
LHC	Four Hours in My Lai Collection, Liddell Hart Centre for Military Archives, King's College London
MACV	Military Assistance Command, Vietnam
MLM	Records Pertaining to the My Lai Massacre, 1969–74
NA	National Archives
NPM	Nixon Presidential Materials, Nixon Presidential Library, Yorba Linda, California

NSCF National Security Council (NSC) Files
NYT *New York Times*
OCC U.S. Army Judiciary, Office of the Clerk of the Court, Records of the Calley General Court-Martial, 1969–74
ODCSPER Office of the Deputy Chief of Staff for Personnel
OSD United States Department of Defense, Office of the Secretary of Defense Historical Office, Subject Files, box 278a, Congressional Investigation, My Lai Incident
PI–AC Records of the Peers Inquiry, Records Created After the Completion of the Peers Inquiry, 1969–75
PI–CI Records of the Peers Inquiry, Administrative and Background Materials, Closed Inventory, 1967–70
PI–OI Records of the Peers Inquiry, Administrative and Background Materials, Open Inventory, 1967–70
RC Roper Center for Public Opinion Research, University of Connecticut, Storrs
RG 46 Record Group 46: Records of the United States Senate
RG 127 Record Group 127: Records of the United States Marine Corps
RG 153 Record Group 153: Records of the Judge Advocate General (Army)
RG 233 Record Group 233: Records of the United States House of Representatives
RG 267 Record Group 267: Records of the United States Supreme Court
RG 319 Record Group 319: Records of the Army Staff
RG 472 Record Group 472: Records of the U.S. Forces in Southeast Asia, 1950–75
SJE Samuel James Ervin Collection, Southern Historical Collection, University of North Carolina at Chapel Hill, Wilson Library
SMOF Staff Member and Office Files
THC Senator Thomas Hennings Collection C3000, The State Historical Society of Missouri
TPI Testimony to the Peers Inquiry, *Report of the Department of the Army Preliminary Investigations into the My Lai Incident,* Volume 2: "Testimony" (Washington, D.C.: Department of the Army, March 14, 1970)
VWCWG Records of the Vietnam War Crimes Working Group
WHCF White House Confidential Files
WHSF White House Special Files

NOTES

Introduction: The American Exemption

1. For an account of the growing recognition of universal jurisdiction in U.S. federal courts and the courts of other nations, see Mark Zaid, Prepared Statement, U.S. Congress, House, 104th Cong., 2nd Sess., Committee on the Judiciary, *Hearing before the Subcommittee on Immigration and Claims of the Committee on the Judiciary on H.R. 2587, War Crimes Act of 1995,* June 12, 1995, 33–38. International humanitarian law regulates the conduct of armed conflicts.

2. *U.S. ex rel Toth v. Quarles,* 350 U.S. 11 (1955).

3. K. Elizabeth Waits, "Avoiding the 'Legal Bermuda Triangle': The Military Extraterritorial Jurisdiction Act's Unprecedented Expansion of U.S. Criminal Jurisdiction over Foreign Nationals," *Arizona Journal of International and Comparative Law* 23 (2005–6): 494, 513.

4. See, for example, the testimony by the American Civil Liberties Union (ACLU) in the hearings on S. 761 in 1966. U.S. Congress, Senate, 89th Cong., 2nd Sess., Committee on the Judiciary, Subcommittee on Constitutional Rights, and Committee on the Armed Services, Special Subcommittee, Joint Hearings, *Military Justice,* January 18, 19, 25, and 26, March 1, 2, and 3, 1966 [hereafter 1966 Joint Committee Hearings], 343.

5. William G. Eckhardt, Ron Ridenhour, Hugh C. Thompson Jr., "Experiencing the Darkness: An Oral History," in *Facing My Lai; Moving beyond the Massacre,* ed. David L. Anderson (Lawrence: University Press of Kansas, 1998), 43; William G. Eckhardt, "My Lai: An American Tragedy," *University of Missouri Kansas City Law Review* 68 (1999–2000): 680.

6. Muriel Dobbin, "My Lai Revives Legal Issue," *Baltimore Sun,* April 26, 1970. A few years later a member of the Judge Advocate General's Corps was still expressing this rather forlorn hope, at around the time Senator Ervin abandoned his legislative efforts: "The need for legislative reform to cure this jurisdictional problem has not gone unnoticed, and My Lai may provide the incentive for legislation which has in the past been proposed but not imposed as law." Norman G. Cooper, "My Lai and Military Justice—To What Effect?" *Military Law Review* 59 (Winter 1973): 110.

7. Paul R. Clancy, *Just a Country Lawyer: A Biography of Senator Sam Ervin* (Bloomington: Indiana University Press, 1974), 236.

8. For the effects of his eloquence on his Senate colleagues, see, e.g., Dick Dabney, *A Good Man: The Life of Sam J. Ervin* (Boston: Houghton Mifflin, 1976), 240–41.

9. Thomas Jefferson, *Notes on the State of Virginia,* ed. William Peden (New York: Norton, 1972), 163.

10. Michal R. Belknap, *The Vietnam War on Trial: The My Lai Massacre and the Court-Martial of Lieutenant Calley* (Lawrence: University Press of Kansas, 2002) deals with the decision not to pursue the cases against the suspects no longer in uniform in less than two

pages; Michael Bilton and Kevin Sim, *Four Hours in My Lai: A War Crime and Its Aftermath* (New York: Penguin, 1992); Kendrick Oliver, *The My Lai Massacre in American History and Memory* (Manchester: Manchester University Press, 2006).

11. For a theorization of American exemptionalism and double standards, which Ignatieff identifies as variants of exceptionalism, see Michael Ignatieff, "Introduction: American Exceptionalism and Human Rights," in *American Exceptionalism and Human Rights,* ed. Michael Ignatieff (Princeton: Princeton University Press, 2005), 1–26.

12. Costas Douzinas, *Human Rights and Empire: The Political Philosophy of Cosmopolitanism* (Abingdon: Routledge-Cavendish, 2007), 27–28; see also Costas Douzinas, *The End of Human Rights* (Oxford: Hart Publishing, 2000), 118.

13. *The Responsibility to Protect: Report of the International Commission on Intervention and State Sovereignty* (Ottawa: International Development Research Centre, 2001), 13. One must note, however, the growing challenge to the concept that the nation-state is the only relevant actor in the creation of international law. Austen L. Parrish, "Reclaiming International Law from Extraterritoriality," *Minnesota Law Review* 93 (2008–9): 829–30.

14. Louis Henkin, "That 'S' Word: Sovereignty, and Globalization, and Human Rights, Et Cetera," *Fordham Law Review* 68 (1999–2000): 2. In *McCullough v. Maryland,* 17 U.S. 316 (1819), the U.S. Supreme Court upheld the validity of federal laws passed in pursuance of the Constitution over against any attempted prohibitions by the states because the people ratified the Constitution; the powers of the federal government were not delegated by the states but derived from the sovereign people.

15. For a discussion of the equality of sovereigns and the mutual recognition of sovereign dignity, see Carl Schmitt, *The* Nomos *of the Earth in the International Law of the* Jus Publicum Europaeum, trans. G. L. Ulmen (New York: Telos Books, 2006), 101–6, 147, 153, 159, 163–64.

16. For the theorization of "the exception," see Carl Schmitt, *Political Theology: Four Chapters on the Concept of Sovereignty,* trans. George Schwab (Chicago: University of Chicago Press, 2005), 5, 7. See also Giorgio Agamben, *Homo Sacer: Sovereign Power and Bare Life,* trans. Daniel Heller-Roazen (Stanford: Stanford University Press, 1998), 9, 12.

17. For the overwhelming preponderance of U.S. military spending over that of other nations in recent times, see Michael Mann, *Incoherent Empire* (London: Verso, 2003), 18. See also Timothy L. H. McCormack, "Selective Reaction to Atrocity: War Crimes and the Development of International Law," *Albany Law Review* 60 (1996–97): 719.

18. Telford Taylor states that in 1907, when the Fourth Hague Convention was enunciated, the reference in its preamble to "civilized" nations (the "usages established among civilized peoples") implied that "savage tribes may not be held to standards of conduct unfamiliar to them." Telford Taylor, *Nuremberg and Vietnam: An American Tragedy* (New York: Quadrangle Books, 1970). Common Article 3 of the Geneva Conventions similarly refers to "judicial guarantees which are recognized as indispensable by civilized peoples." With the accession of more and more nations to the conventions, the pockets of territory where universal standards of international law do not prevail can be considered to have dwindled to close to zero in the post–Second World War period addressed in this book. Perversely, at the moment universal jurisdiction could claim in a practical sense to encompass the globe, the U.S. government attempted to carve out in its detention camp at Guantánamo Bay a jurisdictional void under its effective control but standing outside the reach of regularly constituted courts. This move was resisted by its own highest court. *Hamdi v. Rumsfeld,* 542 U.S. 507 (2004); *Rasul v. Bush,* 542 U.S. 466 (2004); *Boumediene v. Bush,* 553 U.S. 723 (2008).

19. Schmitt contrasts the Europeans' concept of those who stood outside of humanity and

therefore do not enjoy legal rights with the concept of *justi hostes,* who were recognized as legally equivalent even though enemies. See, e.g., Schmitt, *The* Nomos *of the Earth,* 52, 55. Schmitt's argument concerns the dignity of sovereigns, but the nonrecognition of sovereign equality was consequential for populations, not just for their rulers: members of societies not regarded as being equal to the Europeans in civilization and who refused to accept the dominion of a European monarch were susceptible to being dispossessed of property and enslaved. See, for example, Lewis Hanke, *The Spanish Struggle for Justice in the Conquest of America* (Philadelphia: University of Pennsylvania Press, 1949), 32; Hanke, "The Requerimiento and Its Interpreters," *Revista de Historia de América* 1 (March 1938), 25–34.

20. Michael Ignatieff, "We're So Exceptional," *New York Review of Books,* April 5, 2012, 6. Numerous others have commented on the same phenomenon. See, for example, Parrish, "Reclaiming International Law from Extraterritoriality," 835n96.

21. Paul W. Kahn, *Political Theology: Four New Chapters on the Concept of Sovereignty* (New York: Perseus Books, 2011), 2.

22. Joseph S. Nye Jr., "The Way to Trim the U.S. Military Budget," *IHT,* August 6–7, 2011.

23. Lyndon Johnson, "Peace without Conquest," March 8, 1965, www.lbjlib.utexas.edu/johnson/archives.hom/speeches.hom/650407.asp. Richard Nixon, "Address to the Nation on the Situation in Southeast Asia," April 7, 1971, APP, www.presidency.ucsb.edu/ws/?pid=2972.

24. Barack Obama, "Remarks at Fort Bragg, North Carolina," December 14, 2011, APP, www.presidency.ucsb.edu/ws/?pid=97764.

25. For a critique of this line of thought promoted as "state fantasy," see Donald E. Pease, *The New American Exceptionalism* (Minneapolis: University of Minnesota Press, 2009), 162–66.

26. David Scheffer, *All the Missing Souls: A Personal History of the War Crimes Tribunals* (Princeton: Princeton University Press, 2012), 22.

27. Ibid., 4.

28. A political scientist who says that "unrestrained hypocrisy" undermines the legitimacy of power finds that the "judicious use of hypocrisy" can provide "crucial strategies for melding ideals and interests." Martha Finnemore, "Legitimacy, Hypocrisy, and the Social Structure of Unipolarity: Why Being a Unipole Isn't All It's Cracked Up to Be," *World Politics* 61 (January 2009): 61.

29. James W. Ceaser, "The Origins and Character of American Exceptionalism," *American Political Thought* 1 (Spring 2012): 4.

30. Francis Fukuyama, *After the Neocons: America at the Crossroads* (London: Profile Books, 2007), 101.

31. Sen. Rod Grams, Statement, U.S. Congress, Senate, 106th Cong., 2nd Sess., Hearing before the Committee on Foreign Relations, "The International Criminal Court: Protecting American Servicemen and Officials from the Threat of International Prosecution," June 14, 2000, 3.

32. Aldo S. Zilli, "The Human Rights Committee, the U.S. and the ICCPR," *Santa Clara Journal of International Law* 9 (2011): 420.

33. Ignatieff, "Introduction: American Exceptionalism and Human Rights," 21–22.

34. Mann, *Incoherent Empire,* 37.

35. Samantha Power, "Boltonism," *New Yorker,* March 21, 2005, 23, quoted in Ivo Daalder and James M. Lindsay, *America Unbound: The Bush Revolution in Foreign Policy* (John Wiley and Sons, 2005), 199. See also the discussion of "sovereigntists" in Parrish, "Reclaiming International Law from Extraterritoriality," 823.

36. John R. Bolton, "Is There Really 'Law' in International Affairs?," *Transatlantic Law and Contemporary Problems* 10 (2000): 6. States appear to have pushed the boundaries of customary law by deliberately violating the law in an attempt to normalize their customs, for example, with respect to targeted killings. Daniel Reisner, an Israeli legal authority, said in 2009, "International law progresses through its violations. We invented the targeted assassination thesis and we had to push it. At first there were protrusions that made it hard to insert easily into the legal molds. Eight years later it is in the center of the bounds of legitimacy." George Bisharat, "Taking Israel to Court in The Hague," *IHT,* January 31, 2013.

37. Bolton, "Is There Really 'Law' in International Affairs?," 4.

38. Ibid., 48.

39. Charles Simic, "Connoisseurs of Cruelty," *New York Review of Books,* March 12, 2009, 23.

40. See, for example, Richard Falk and Andrew Strauss, "On the Creation of a Global People's Assembly: Legitimacy and the Power of Popular Sovereignty," *Stanford Journal of International Law* 36 (2000): 191–220; Richard Falk and Andrew Strauss, "Bridging the Globalization Gap: Toward a Global Parliament," *Foreign Affairs* 80 (2001): 212–20.

41. Falk and Strauss, "Global People's Assembly," 193.

42. Jacques Derrida, *Rogues: Two Essays on Reason,* trans. Pascale-Anne Brault and Michael Naas (Stanford: Stanford University Press, 2005), 97.

43. For examples of explicit uses of the epithet and of the presentation of evidence demonstrating it is well deserved, see William Blum, *Rogue State* (London: Zed Books, 2002); William Blum, *Killing Hope* (London: Zed Books, 2003); Michael Mandel, *How America Gets Away with Murder* (London: Pluto Press, 2004); Stephen Kinzer, *Overthrow* (New York: Henry Holt, 2006).

44. See, for example, "Adding Definition to Common Article 3 of the Geneva Conventions," in "Fact Sheet: The Administration's Legislation to Create Military Commissions," September 6, 2006, APP, www.presidency.ucsb.edu/ws/?pid=82688. The development of novel definitions of the Geneva Conventions' prohibitions on the abuse of prisoners followed the determination by the Bush White House counsel, Alberto Gonzales, that Geneva standards are undefined: Memorandum for the President, January 25, 2002, in Karen J. Greenberg and Joshua L. Dratel, *The Torture Papers: The Road to Abu Ghraib* (Cambridge: Cambridge University Press, 2005), 119; and Assistant Attorney General Jay Bybee's novel definitions of torture: Memorandum for Alberto R. Gonzales, August 2, 2002, in ibid., 214. See also A. O. Schwarz Jr. and Aziz Z. Huq, *Unchecked and Unbalanced: Presidential Power in a Time of Terror* (New York: New Press, 2007), 73.

45. G. John Ikenberry, *Liberal Leviathan: The Origins, Crisis, and Transformation of the American World Order* (Princeton: Princeton University Press, 2011), 244–45; Mark Danner, "After September 11: Our State of Exception," *New York Review of Books,* October 13, 2011, 44.

46. Pease has pointed to President Harry Truman's declaration of a "national emergency" in 1950 and suggested, "After World War II, America became a State of Exception." Pease, *The New American Exceptionalism,* 62, 219n23. He also says that the "State of Exception is marked by absolute independence from juridical control and any reference to the normal political order" (24). One wonders, then, how the Supreme Court was able to overturn Truman's emergency order in the steel seizure case, *Youngstown Sheet & Tube Co. v. Sawyer,* 343 U.S. 579 (1952). Truman claimed the president had the inherent power to act in a national emergency on behalf of the people's welfare but stated he would abide by the court's decision

if it declared the seizure of the steel plants unconstitutional. Harry S. Truman: "The President's News Conference," May 22, 1952, APP, www.presidency.ucsb.edu/ws/?pid=14124.

47. Godfrey Hodgson, *America in Our Time* (New York: Vintage Books, 1978), 40–47; M. J. Heale, *American Anticommunism* (Baltimore: Johns Hopkins University Press, 1990), 145–90; H. W. Brands, *The Devil We Knew: Americans and the Cold War* (New York: Oxford University Press, 1993); John Dumbrell, "Cold War America," in *American Century,* ed. Iwan W. Morgan and Neil A. Wynn (Teaneck, N.J.: Holmes and Meier, 1991), 139.

1. "A Very Simple Provision"

1. Enacted as Pub. L. No. 81-506, May 5, 1950, 64 Stat. 107; 10 U.S.C. 47, the UCMJ, became effective on May 31, 1951.

2. U.S. Congress, House, 81st Cong., 1st Sess., *Hearings before a Subcommittee [No. 1] of the Committee on Armed Services on H.R. 2498, Uniform Code of Military Justice* (1949), 566. For a brief history of the motives leading to the drafting of the bill, see U.S. Congress, Senate, 81st Cong., 1st Sess., *Report to Accompany H.R. 4080: Establishing a Uniform Code of Military Justice,* June 10, 1949; U.S. Congress, House, 81st Cong., 1st Sess., *Report to Accompany H.R. 4080: Uniform Code of Military Justice,* April 28, 1949, 3–5; and Robert J. White, "The Uniform Code of Military Justice—Its Promise and Performance (The First Decade: 1951–1961), A Symposium," *St. John's Law Review* (May 1961), reproduced in 1966 Joint Committee Hearings, 714–19.

3. Arthur E. Farmer and Richard H. Weis, "Command Control—Or Military Justice?" *New York University Quarterly Review* (April 1949), reproduced in U.S. Congress, Senate, 81st Cong., 1st Sess., *Hearings before a Subcommittee of the Committee on Armed Services on S. 857 and H.R. 4080, Uniform Code of Military Justice,* April 27, May 4, 9, and 27, 1949, 64–65.

4. Statement of Rep. Carl Vinson, *Congressional Floor Debate on the Uniform Code of Military Justice* (Washington, D.C.: Department of the Navy, Judge Advocate General, 1949), www.loc.gov/rr/frd/Military_Law/pdf/congr-floor-debate.pdf. Solis states that there were 1.7 million court-martial convictions during the Second World War, although this figure presumably includes those following summary courts-martial (or deck courts in the navy). Gary D. Solis, *Marines and Military Law in Vietnam: Trial by Fire* (Washington, D.C.: Department of the Navy, Headquarters United States Marine Corps, n.d. [c. 1988]), 1-7, NA, RG 127, Headquarters Marine Corps, Headquarters Division, Marines Trial by Fire, box 1. Although the work has been published, references in this book are to the archival typescript.

5. Fred P. Graham, "Reforms Sought in Military Code" *NYT,* May 18, 1967.

6. *[Senate] Report to Accompany H.R. 4080: Establishing a Uniform Code of Military Justice,* June 10, 1949, 6. For a statement concerning the UCMJ's place in the reorganization of the military establishment, see Harry Truman, "Special Message to the Congress on the Reorganization of the National Military Establishment," March 5, 1949, www.trumanlibrary.org/publicpapers/index.php?pid=1066.

7. Secretary of Defense James Forrestal to the Speaker of the House of Representatives, February 8, 1949, in *[House] Report to Accompany H.R. 4080: Uniform Code of Military Justice,* April 28, 1949, 41. His successor took the same view. Secretary of Defense Harold Johnson to Senator Millard E. Tydings, June 8, 1949, in *[Senate] Report to Accompany H.R. 4080: Establishing a Uniform Code of Military Justice,* June 10, 1949, 38–39.

8. The original Article 3(a), "Jurisdiction over Certain Personnel," stated, "Reserve personnel of the armed forces who are charged with having committed, while in a status in

which they are subject to this code, any offense against this code may be retained in such status: or, whether or not such status has terminated, placed in an active-duty status for disciplinary action, without their consent, but not for a longer period of time than may be required for such action." U.S. Congress, House, 81st Cong., 1st Sess., *Hearings before a Subcommittee of the Committee on Armed Services on H.R. 2498, Uniform Code of Military Justice* (1949), 567.

9. U.S. Congress, House, 81st Cong., 1st Sess., *Hearings before a Subcommittee of the Committee on Armed Services on H.R. 2498, Uniform Code of Military Justice* (1949), 882.

10. Joseph W. Bishop Jr., *Justice Under Fire: A Study of Military Law* (New York: Charterhouse, 1974), 58.

11. U.S. Congress, House, 81st Cong., 1st Sess., *Hearings before a Subcommittee of the Committee on Armed Services on H.R. 2498, Uniform Code of Military Justice* (1949), 882.

12. U.S. Congress, House, 81st Cong., 1st Sess., *Hearings before a Subcommittee of the Committee on Armed Services on H.R. 2498, Uniform Code of Military Justice* (1949), 800. In later testimony to Congress, Wiener declared his personal involvement in the Hirshberg case, 1966 Joint Committee Hearings, 316. *United States ex rel. Hirshberg v. Malanaphy,* 168 F.2d 503 (2nd Cir. 1948).

13. U.S. Congress, House, 81st Cong., 1st Sess., *Hearings before a Subcommittee of the Committee on Armed Services on H.R. 2498, Uniform Code of Military Justice* (1949), 882. The same two cases, the "Durant jewel case" and the Hirshberg case, were referred to in the *[House] Report to Accompany H.R. 4080: Uniform Code of Military Justice,* 5; and in Millard E. Tydings, chairman, Senate Armed Services Committee, to Pat McCarran, chairman, Senate Judiciary Committee, July 13, 1949, in *Congressional Floor Debate on the Uniform Code of Military Justice,* 231. For a brief account of the two cases, see Robinson O. Everett and Laurent R. Hourcle, "Crime without Punishment—Ex-Servicemen, Civilian Employees and Dependents," *U.S.A.F. Judge Advocate General Law Review* 13 (1971): 184–85. See also *U.S. ex rel. Hirshberg v. Cooke,* 336 U.S. 210 (1949).

14. Unlike the Supreme Court, whose powers are set out in the Constitution, the inferior federal courts were established by act of Congress (originally, the Judiciary Act, signed into law on September 24, 1789), and their powers had accordingly to be specified by Congress. Justice Johnson's *per curiam* opinion stated, "The legislative authority of the Union must first make an act a crime, affix a punishment for it, and declare the Court that shall have jurisdiction of the offence." *United States v. Hudson and Goodwin,* 11 U.S. 32 (1812), at 34.

15. Seymour W. Wurfel, Testimony, 1966 Joint Committee Hearings, 144. For the extraterritorial jurisdiction of civilian courts over veterans who had committed frauds against the government while in the armed services, see Charles Fairman, "The Supreme Court 1955 Term," *Harvard Law Review* 70 (November 1956): 108; Everett and Hourcle, "Crime without Punishment," 198–99. For a summary of the broad principles of extraterritorial jurisdiction, see, e.g., *Rocha v. United States,* 288 F.2d 545 (1961), para. 24n. 4; *Chua Han Mow v. United States,* 730 F.2d 1308 (1984), para. 24; K. Elizabeth Waits, "Avoiding the 'Legal Bermuda Triangle': The Military Extraterritorial Jurisdiction Act's Unprecedented Expansion of U.S. Criminal Jurisdiction over Foreign Nationals," *Arizona Journal of International and Comparative Law* 23 (2005–6): 530–33.

16. *U.S. v. Bowman,* 260 U.S. 94 (1922).

17. U.S. Congress, House, 95th Cong., 1st Sess., Committee on the Judiciary, Hearing before the Subcommittee on Immigration, Citizenship, and International Law on H.R. 763, H.R. 6148, and H.R. 7842, "Extraterritorial Criminal Jurisdiction," July 21, 1977, 122; Memorandum on Extraterritorial Criminal Jurisdiction of the United States, November

2, 1977, 1, 3, NA, RG 233, 95th Cong., Judiciary Committee, Legislative Files, box 11, H.R. 733–H.R. 896; Jordan J. Paust, "Non-Extraterritoriality of 'Special Territorial Jurisdiction' of the United States: Forgotten History and the Errors of *Erdos*," *Yale Journal of International Law* 24 (1999): 308n9. The Supreme Court held that the "legislation of the Congress, unless the contrary intent appears, is construed to apply only within the territorial jurisdiction of the United States." *Blackmer v. United States*, 284 U.S. 421 (1932), at 437. One should note, however, the growing tendency of plaintiffs to seek and courts to accept the extraterritorial applicability of national laws. Austen L. Parrish, "Reclaiming International Law from Extraterritoriality," *Minnesota Law Review* 93 (2008–9): 815–74.

18. U.S. Congress, House, 81st Cong., 1st Sess., *Hearings before a Subcommittee of the Committee on Armed Services on H.R. 2498, Uniform Code of Military Justice* (1949), 881.

19. U.S. Congress, House, 81st Cong., 1st Sess., *Hearings before a Subcommittee of the Committee on Armed Services on H.R. 2498, Uniform Code of Military Justice* (1949), 881–84. The revisions were incorporated into H.R. 4080, which replaced H.R. 2498. U.S. Congress, House, 81st Cong., 1st Sess., *Report to Accompany H.R. 4080: Uniform Code of Military Justice* (1949), April 28, 1949, 2.

20. *Report to Accompany H.R. 4080: Uniform Code of Military Justice*, 11; *Congressional Floor Debate on the Uniform Code of Military Justice*, 8.

21. Testimony of Maj. Gen. Thomas H. Green, U.S. Congress, Senate, 81st Cong., 1st Sess., *Hearings before a Subcommittee of the Committee on Armed Services on S. 857 and H.R. 4080, Uniform Code of Military Justice* (1949), May 9, 1949, 256.

22. *Congressional Floor Debate on the Uniform Code of Military Justice*, 126.

23. Oral History Interview with Felix E. Larkin, conducted by Jerry N. Hess, New York, New York, September 18, 1972, transcript, 24, NA, Harry S. Truman Library and Museum, www.trumanlibrary.org/oralhist/larkin.htm.

24. Green Testimony, 257.

25. Ibid.

26. "Subject to the provisions of article 43 [the statute of limitations], any person charged with having committed, while in a status in which he was subject to this code, an offense against this code, punishable by confinement of five years or more and for which the person cannot be tried in the courts of the United States or any State or Territory thereof or of the District of Columbia, shall not be relieved from amenability to trial by courts-martial by reason of the termination of said status." 10 U.S.C. § 803, Art. 3 "Jurisdiction to Try Certain Personnel," subsection (a).

27. For the Reserve Components' objections to the revised Article 3(a), see *Congressional Floor Debate on the Uniform Code of Military Justice*, 125–32.

28. *[House] Report to Accompany H.R. 4080: Uniform Code of Military Justice*, 5.

29. Statement of Capt. Edwin A. Jerome, Proceedings before the U.S. Court of Appeals for the District of Columbia, Transcript of Record of the Supreme Court of the United States, October Term, 1954, No. 3, *U.S. Supreme Court Records and Briefs* 350 (October Term 1955), 59.

30. "National Affairs: A Crucial Case of Murder," *Time*, August 31, 1953.

31. The U.S. District Court for the District of Columbia in 1953 granted a writ of habeas corpus on the ground that certain procedures necessary to Toth's removal to Korea had not been complied with. On March 25, 1954, the U.S. Court of Appeals for the District of Columbia Circuit found these procedures unnecessary and sustained the constitutionality of Article 3(a). Fairman, "The Supreme Court 1955 Term," 108; see also briefs for the petitioner and respondent in *U.S. Supreme Court Records and Briefs* 350 (October Term 1955).

32. Luther A. Huston, "Court Frees Toth and Bars Military Trials for Ex-G.I.'s," *NYT,* November 8, 1955.

33. The case was initially heard as *Toth v. Talbott* in the court's October term, 1954. Talbott was Harold E. Talbott, the secretary of the air force at the time of the initial hearing. Quarles was Donald A. Quarles, who succeeded Talbott as secretary of the air force. *Journal of the Supreme Court of the United States October Term 1955,* 32. For the various drafts of Black's opinion, with memoranda indicating when it won the support of the justices making up the majority following the October 1955 rehearing, see HLB, box 327, case file no. 3, October 3, 1955, Toth v. Quarles I and Toth v. Quarles II. See also Warren to Black, October 29, 1955; and Frankfurter to Black, October 26, 1955, EW, box 432, folder: no. 3—Toth v. Quarles.

34. James F. Simon, *The Antagonists: Hugo Black, Felix Frankfurter and Civil Liberties in Modern America* (New York: Simon and Schuster, 1989), 71, 76–77.

35. Ibid., 82, 83, 86, 98, 155, 210.

36. Carl Brent Swisher, "History's Panorama and Justice Black's Career," *Hugo Black and the Supreme Court: A Symposium,* ed. Stephen Parks Strickland (Indianapolis: Bobbs-Merrill, 1967), 8.

37. Wallace Mendelson, *Justices Black and Frankfurter: Conflict in the Court* (Chicago: University of Chicago Press, 1961), 116.

38. Noah Feldman, *Scorpions: The Battles and Triumphs of FDR's Great Supreme Court Justices* (New York: Twelve, 2010), 145–46; Simon, *The Antagonists,* 99–100, 103.

39. Simon, *The Antagonists,* 54.

40. Ibid., 127.

41. Ibid., 127, 236–37.

42. Mendelson, *Justices Black and Frankfurter,* 119; Simon, *The Antagonists,* 114, 118, 179, 249; Fred Rodell, "Foreword," *American University Law Review* 10 (January 1961): 5.

43. Hugo Black, "Absolutes, Courts, and the Bill of Rights," in *The Supreme Court: Views from Inside,* ed. Alan F. Westin, 173–90 (New York: Norton, 1961). Although the talk on which the essay is based was delivered in 1960, it summarizes views that Black had articulated since his first term on the court. See also Hugo Black, "The Bill of Rights," The James Madison Lecture, New York University, February 17, 1960, EW, box 347, folder: Earl Warren Correspondence, Associate Justice Hugo L. Black, Oct. 5 1952–1962. For the circumstances of the talk, which can be seen as implicitly a rebuttal of Frankfurter's views, see Simon, *The Antagonists,* 243.

44. *Korematsu v. United States,* 323 U.S. 214 (1944); Feldman, *Scorpions,* 243–45. For the history of the case and a federal court's eventual recognition of a fundamental injustice through the granting of a writ of error *coram nobis,* see Peter Irons, ed., *Justice Delayed: The Record of the Japanese American Internment Cases* (Middletown, Conn.: Wesleyan University Press, 1989).

45. Simon, *The Antagonists,* 108, 200.

46. George Kaufmann, "The Federal Civil Rules and the Pursuit of Justice," *Hugo Black and the Supreme Court: A Symposium,* 224–25. For relevant cases, see ibid., 327n17.

47. *United States v. Lovett,* 328 U.S. 303 (1946), at 317–18; *Duncan v. Kahanamoku,* 327 U.S. 304 (1946), at 322; dissents in *Madsen v. Kinsella,* 343 U.S. 341 (1952), at 372; and *Johnson v. Eisentrager,* 339 U.S. 763 (1950), at 791. The Kinsella whose name appears in a number of cases discussed in this and the next chapter is Nina Kinsella, the warden of the federal reformatory where the female convicts in those cases were confined. See also Swisher, "History's Panorama and Justice Black's Career," 16–17; Feldman, *Scorpions,* 332; Brian C. Baldrate,

"The Supreme Court's Role in Defining the Jurisdiction of Military Tribunals: A Study, Critique, and Proposal for *Hamdan v. Rumsfeld*," *Military Law Review* 186 (Winter 2005): 74.

48. Article III, § 1.

49. 327 U.S. 322. The Supreme Court had affirmed this doctrine in *Ex Parte Milligan,* 71 U.S. 2 (1866): "The discipline necessary to the efficiency of the army and navy required other and swifter modes of trial than are furnished by the common law courts," and anyone in the military or naval service "surrenders his right to be tried by the civil courts. *All other persons,* citizens of states where the courts are open, if charged with crime, are guaranteed the inestimable privilege of trial by jury. . . . Martial rule can never exist where the courts are open and in the proper and unobstructed exercise of their jurisdiction." 71 U.S., at 123, 127.

50. *Burns v. Wilson,* 346 U.S. 137 (1953), at 150–55.

51. 346 U.S., at 142. Vinson also recognized that the system of military justice was distinct from that of the civilian courts: "This Court has played no role in its development; we have exerted no supervisory power over the courts which enforce it; the rights of men in the armed forces must perforce be conditioned to meet certain overriding demands of discipline and duty, and the civil courts are not the agencies which must determine the precise balance to be struck in this adjustment." 346 U.S., at 140. This doctrine was significant in precluding the Supreme Court's review of a military court judgment of 1970 that deepened the jurisdictional gap (see chapter 6). For Frankfurter's perception of shades of gray in this case where Black saw matters in black and white, see 346 U.S., at 149–50.

52. "Airmen Hanged in Guam," *NYT,* January 28, 1954.

53. *U.S. ex rel Toth v. Quarles,* 350 U.S. 11, at 17–18.

54. 350 U.S., at 21–22, 23. The principle of "the least possible power adequate to the end proposed," which was invoked in a number of later cases citing *Toth,* was enunciated in *Anderson v. Dunn,* 6 Wheat. 204, 19 U.S. 204 (1821), at 231.

55. 350 U.S., at 22.

56. See, e.g., the reference to *Ex Parte Milligan,* above.

57. Statement of Rep. Carl Vinson, *Congressional Floor Debate on the Uniform Code of Military Justice,* 20, 21.

58. See, e.g., William Winthrop, *Military Law and Precedents,* 2nd rev. ed. (Washington, D.C.: GPO, 1920), 93, 105. In *Toth,* Black cites the passage in which Winthrop states, "This class of statutes, which . . . subject persons formerly in the army, but [who have] finally and legally separated from it, to trial by court-martial, are all necessarily and alike unconstitutional" (107).

59. Robinson O. Everett, "Military Jurisdiction over Civilians," *Duke Law Journal* 9 (Summer 1960): 374–75. Everett had made a similar argument soon after the court rendered its judgment: Robinson O. Everett, *Military Justice in the Armed Forces of the United States* (Westport, Conn.: Greenwood Press, 1956), 30–35.

60. 350 U.S., at 39.

61. "Conference of February 12, 1955," *The Supreme Court in Conference (1940–1985): The Private Discussions behind Nearly 300 Supreme Court Decisions,* ed. Del Dickson (New York: Oxford University Press, 2001), 549. Although the record is not a verbatim transcript of what was said and was based on notes that may not have been entirely accurate, Black and Frankfurter are recorded as having confused matters further by garbling the phrase as "arising from" and "arising under."

62. Ibid. See also Reed's dissent. 350 U.S., at 39–41.

63. Solicitor General Simon E. Sobeloff said that the language of the Constitution was broad enough to permit court-martial jurisdiction. NA, RG 267, Records of the United

States Supreme Court, 267-4, Case # 3 (Reel 1 of 2), Toth v. Quarles, argued October 13, 1955, NA, Audiovisual Archives Division. This was the most persistent matter germane to the eventual disposition of the case which the justices and the solicitor general discussed in the reargument of October 1955. See also Simon E. Sobeloff, Solicitor General et al., Brief for the Respondent, U.S. Ex Rel. Toth v. Talbott No. 150 (January 1955), 38, in *U.S. Supreme Court Records and Briefs* 350 (October Term 1955).

64. 350 U.S., at 44.

65. 350 U.S., at 21, 22. Article I, § 8, cl. 18 states that Congress has the power "to make all Laws which shall be necessary and proper for carrying into Execution the foregoing [enumerated] Powers, and all other Powers vested by this Constitution in the Government of the United States, or in any Department or Officer thereof."

66. Justice Stanley F. Reed, joined by Justices Harold H. Burton and Sherman Minton, dissenting, *Toth v. Quarles,* 350 U.S., at 24.

67. 350 U.S., at 28.

68. Everett, "Military Jurisdiction Over Civilians," 375; Scott L. Silliman, "Robinson O. Everett and National Security," *Duke Law Journal* 59 (2009–10): 1448.

69. Everett, "Military Jurisdiction Over Civilians," 380.

70. Everett, *Military Justice in the Armed Forces of the United States,* 33–34.

71. Robinson O. Everett, "*O'Callahan v. Parker*—Milestone or Millstone in Military Justice?" *Duke Law Journal* 18 (October 1969): 853–54; Robinson O. Everett, "Military Justice Is to Justice as . . . ," *U.S.A.F. Judge Advocate General Law Review* 12 (1970): 202n2.

72. "Report of the Judge Advocate General of the Army," *AR January 1, 1955 to December 31, 1955,* 17.

73. U.S. Congress, Senate, 84th Cong., 1st Sess., Committee on Foreign Relations, *Hearing: The Geneva Conventions for the Protection of War Victims,* June 3, 1955 [hereafter Senate Hearing on Geneva Conventions], 7.

74. Ibid., 1, 4, 12, 60.

75. "Geneva P.O.W. Code Approved by Senate," *NYT,* July 7, 1955.

76. Mr. Justice Black, Dissent A, No. 150—October Term, 1954, Toth v. Talbott, April—, 1955, 8, EW, box 426, folder: No. 150, Toth v. Talbott.

77. Article 146 of the Geneva Convention (IV) Relative to the Protection of Civilian Persons in Time of War required that "the High Contracting Parties undertake to enact any legislation necessary to provide effective penal sanctions for persons committing, or ordering to be committed, any of the grave breaches of the present Convention defined in the following Article." 6 U.S.T. 3516. The Third Geneva Convention, on Prisoners of War, contained a provision with a similarly worded passage, Article 129. 6 U.S.T. 3317. Passages in Article 49 of the First Geneva Convention, on the Wounded and Sick on Land, and in Article 50 of the Second Geneva Convention, on the Wounded, Sick and Shipwrecked at Sea, make identical commitments.

78. Senate Hearing on Geneva Conventions, 28, 58.

79. Statement of Wilber M. Brucker, General Counsel, Department of Defense, ibid., 11.

2. "Treaty Law" and "Murdering Wives"

1. James M. Burns, *Roosevelt: The Soldier of Freedom* (New York: Harcourt Brace Jovanovich, 1970), 502.

2. "Taft and Bricker Called Best and Worst Senators," *Washington Post,* September 3, 1949.

3. Gladwin Hill, "U.N. Rights Drafts Held Socialistic: Holman, Bar Association Head,

Warns They Would Renounce Many Basic U.S. Principles," *NYT,* September 18, 1948; Natalie Hevener Kaufman, *Human Rights Treaties and the Senate: A History of Opposition* (Chapel Hill: University of North Carolina Press, 1990), 19.

4. Kaufman, *Human Rights Treaties and the Senate,* 29. For debates about various versions of the amendment, see "National Affairs: The Bricker Amendment: A Cure Worse than the Disease?" *Time,* July 13, 1953; "'Treaty Law' Held Big Threat to U.S.," *NYT,* September 30, 1953; "Press of the Nation Divided on Merits of Bricker Amendment," *NYT,* January 31, 1954; "Bar Ex-Head Urges Bricker Proposal," *NYT,* February 4, 1954; "The Constitution: A New Bricker Amendment," *Time,* March 19, 1956.

5. The court's decision in *Missouri v. Holland,* 252 U.S. 416 (1920) affirmed the provisions of the Supremacy Clause but left ambiguous how far the treaty-making power could impinge on the constitutional prerogatives of Congress and the state governments. Kaufman, *Human Rights Treaties and the Senate,* 97–103. The Supreme Court extended the principle that international agreements could override state laws in a later decision, *United States v. Pink,* 315 U.S. 203 (1942).

6. L. A. Scot Powe, *The Warren Court and American Politics* (Cambridge: Belknap Press of Harvard University Press, 2000), 112.

7. Kaufman, *Human Rights Treaties and the Senate,* 64.

8. Ibid., 16.

9. Ibid., 45.

10. Adam Fairclough, *Better Day Coming: Blacks and Equality, 1890–2000* (New York: Penguin, 2001), 217; Mary L. Dudziak, "*Brown* as a Cold War Case," *Journal of American History* 91 (June 2004): 34; Mary L. Dudziak, *Cold War Civil Rights: Race and the Image of American Democracy* (Princeton: Princeton University Press, 2000), 100.

11. Powe, *The Warren Court and American Politics,* 112. For the use of segregationist arguments, see also Duane Tananbaum, *The Bricker Amendment Controversy: A Test of Eisenhower's Political Leadership* (Ithaca: Cornell University Press, 1988), 13–14.

12. Kaufman, *Human Rights Treaties and the Senate,* 47–48, 111.

13. Ibid., 95.

14. For Eisenhower's persuasion of the senators, see "The Congress: The Watered-Down Version," *Time,* February 1, 1954. For the text of various versions of the Bricker Amendment, see Kaufman, *Human Rights Treaties and the Senate,* 201–3. The version that failed by one vote was proposed by another senator and was weaker than Bricker's own proposal. Kaufman, *Human Rights Treaties and the Senate,* 105.

15. Kaufman, *Human Rights Treaties and the Senate,* 106, 116; Costas Douzinas, *Human Rights and Empire: The Political Philosophy of Cosmopolitanism* (Abingdon: Routledge-Cavendish, 2007), 30.

16. Monroe Leigh, Testimony and Prepared Statement, U.S. Congress, House, 104th Cong., 2nd Sess., Committee on the Judiciary, *Hearing before the Subcommittee on Immigration and Claims of the Committee on the Judiciary on H.R. 2587, War Crimes Act of 1995,* June 12, 1995, 25, 29.

17. U.S. Congress, Senate, 84th Cong., 1st Sess., Committee on Foreign Relations, *Hearing: The Geneva Conventions for the Protection of War Victims,* June 3, 1955, 23.

18. "National Affairs: Justice and Law in Status-of-Forces Agreements," *Time,* June 17, 1957. See also Arthur Krock, "Girard Case Reopens Treaties Controversy; Angry Senators Now Seek Changes in the Status of Forces Pacts with Foreign Governments," *NYT,* June 9, 1957.

19. S. J. Res. 163, "favoring trial by the United States, where primary jurisdiction is conferred upon it by treaty, of members of the Armed Forces for criminal offenses committed

in foreign countries," introduced by Sen. George Armistead Smathers (D, Fla.), July 15, 1957. Despite the conditional wording of the bill, Smathers said it expressed a preference that the United States always preserve its jurisdiction over its troops. "Smathers Urges U.S. Try Troops Abroad," *NYT,* July 16, 1957. The executive branch opposed this measure. Robert Dechert, Department of Defense general counsel, to Senator Theodore Francis Green, chairman of the Senate Foreign Relations Committee, September 6, 1957; John S. Hoghland II, acting assistant secretary of state for congressional relations, to Sen. Green, August 2, 1957. NA, RG 46, 85th Congress, Committee on Foreign Relations, box 167 (SEN 85A-E7), bill file on S. J. Res. 163.

20. H.R. 8658, introduced by Rep. Frank Bow (R, Ohio), July 11, 1957: "To amend sec. 802 of title 10 of the United States Code with respect to the jurisdiction of the military departments over crimes committed by members of the Armed Forces in foreign nations."

21. H.R. 8704, introduced by Rep. Paul Kilday (D, Tex.), July 15, 1957: "To prohibit the delivery of members of the armed services of the United States to the jurisdiction of any foreign nation."

22. See, e.g., testimony by Jack Smith, U.S. Congress, "Veterans' Testimony on Vietnam—Need for Investigation," 92nd Cong., 1st sess., *Congressional Record—Extensions of Remarks,* April 6, 1971, E 9969.

23. U.S. Congress, Senate, 85th Cong., 1st Sess., Committee on Armed Services, Special Subcommittee, *Hearing on the William S. Girard Case,* June 5, 1957 [hereafter Girard Case Hearing], 3.

24. "Armed Forces: The Girard Case," *Time,* June 17, 1957.

25. Robinson O. Everett, *Military Justice in the Armed Forces of the United States* (Westport, Conn.: Greenwood Press, 1956), 41.

26. The concept of SOFA arose in 1941 during the Second World War. Gary D. Solis, *Marines and Military Law in Vietnam: Trial by Fire* (Washington, D.C.: Department of the Navy, Headquarters United States Marine Corps, n.d. [c. 1988]), 1-30. The basic agreement was the NATO status of forces treaty signed in London in 1951 and ratified by the U.S. Senate in 1953. 199 U.N.T.S. 67. Signed, June 19, 1951. Entered into force August 23, 1953. Other nations thereafter entered into similar agreements with the United States, e.g., the agreement between Japan and the United States, signed September 29, 1953, effective October 29, 1953. Host nations nominally retained primary jurisdiction over certain offenses but were required to give "sympathetic consideration" to requests by the United States to exercise jurisdiction over its personnel where the United States regarded a waiver of jurisdiction "to be of particular importance." See, e.g., *Girard v. Wilson,* 152 F. Supp. 21 (D.D.C. 1957); 354 U.S. 524 (1957). R. Chuck Mason, "Status of Forces Agreement (SOFA): What Is It, and How Has It Been Utilized?," Congressional Research Service, Report for Congress 7-5700, January 5, 2011, 2nn9, 11; Everett, *Military Justice in the Armed Forces of the United States,* 41–42.

27. "Girard and the Larger Problem," *Life,* July 22, 1957, 46.

28. Walter H. Maloney, asst. counsel, to Charles H. Slayman Jr., chief counsel, Senate Constitutional Rights Subcommittee, December 24, 1957, NA, RG 46, Judiciary Committee, Subcommittee on Constitutional Rights 1957–1964, Military Justice Correspondence, folder: Military Corresp. 2 of 2 [hereafter Subcommittee Military Justice Correspondence].

29. U.S. Congress, Senate, 83rd Cong., 1st Sess., Committee on Foreign Relations, Supplementary Hearing on Status of Forces of the North Atlantic Treaty, June 24, 1953, 3.

30. Merwin K. Hart to Rep. Carl Vinson, chairman of the House Armed Services Committee, July 31, 1957, NA, RG 233, 85th Congress, Papers Accompanying Specific Bills and Resolutions, Committee on Armed Services, box 45, folder H.R. 8704–H.R. 8711.

31. May Craig, "The President's News Conference of January 27, 1954," *Public Papers of the Presidents of the United States—Dwight D. Eisenhower 1954* (Washington, D.C.: National Archives and Records Service, 1960), 204.

32. Costas Douzinas, *The End of Human Rights* (Oxford: Hart Publishing, 2000), 118.

33. "The jurisdiction of a nation within its own territory, is exclusive and absolute. It is susceptible of no limitation not imposed by itself. . . . All exceptions to the full and complete power of a nation within its own territories must be traced up to the consent of the nation itself." *The Exchange v. McFadden,* 11 U.S. 116 (1812).

34. John S. Hoghland II, acting assistant secretary of state for congressional relations, to Rep. Carl Vinson, Chairman, House Armed Services Committee, July 26, 1957, NA, RG 233, 85th Congress, Papers Accompanying Specific Bills and Resolutions, Committee on Armed Services, box 45, folder H.R. 8535 to H.R. 8772; *Wilson v. Girard,* 354 U.S. 524 (1957).

35. Major General Mickelwait, Deputy Judge Advocate General of the Army, Bulletin 18, *The Judge Advocate General Journal,* October 1954, 16, quoted in Everett, *Military Justice in the Armed Forces of the United States,* 43.

36. "Random Notes from Washington: Resounding Rhetoric on Rights," *NYT,* July 15, 1957.

37. "National Affairs: Justice and Law in Status-of-Forces Agreements."

38. Charles Fairman, "The Supreme Court 1955 Term," *Harvard Law Review* 70 (1956): 109n67. H.R. 81, "To Amend Title 18 of the United States Code to give U.S. District Courts Jurisdiction of Certain Offenses Committed by Americans outside the United States, and for Other Purposes," proposed by Rep. William S. Cole (R, N.Y.), January 5, 1955, referred to the Committee on the Judiciary. *Congressional Record—House* 101, January 5, 1955, 713. The Supreme Court first heard arguments in *Toth v. Talbott* on February 8–9, 1955, a little over a month after Congressman Cole submitted the legislation. For the original arguments and lower court rulings, see *U.S. Supreme Court Records and Briefs* 350 (1955), 3–45.

39. Austin Stevens, "Pentagon Defends Murder Accusal," *NYT,* August 18, 1951.

40. "Holohan Mystery: New Chapter," *NYT,* August 21, 1955.

41. Cole's initial bill, H.R. 9033, was introduced in the 83rd Congress and referred to the House Judiciary Committee's Subcommittee no. 3. Mr. [Thomas F.] Broden, counsel, House Committee on the Judiciary, Memorandum to Emanuel Celler, chairman, House Committee on the Judiciary, n.d. [February 1956] [hereafter Broden memorandum], in NA RG 233, Committee on the Judiciary, 84th Congress, box 152, H.R. 81 bill file.

42. "E.C." [Emanuel Celler], manuscript annotation to Broden memorandum, directed at "Bess" [Elizabeth Dick], staff director of the committee.

43. Broden memorandum.

44. See the relevant correspondence with the executive departments in NA, RG 233, Committee on the Judiciary, 84th Congress, box 152, H.R. 81 bill file.

45. S. 2791, Jan 5, 1956. A bill "to amend title 18 of the United States Code to provide for the trial in the Federal district courts of persons not subject to military jurisdiction for certain offenses committed by them while subject to such jurisdiction." *Congressional Record—Senate,* January 5, 1956, 75, 78.

46. The relevant bill file contains no such report. NA, RG 46, 84th Congress, Committee on the Judiciary, box 362, folder S. 2791–S. 2801 [hereafter S. 2791 bill file]. Nor was one received, according to the relevant entry in U.S. Congress, *United States Senate, Committee on the Judiciary, Legislative and Executive Calendar, 84th Congress, Final Edition* (Washington, D.C.: GPO, 1956), 388.

47. The Pentagon did not report those concerns directly to the Judiciary Committee, but they were later attributed to the Department of Defense in the *AR January 1, 1956 to*

December 31, 1956, 33; see also U.S. Congress, Senate, 87th Cong., 2nd Sess., Committee on the Judiciary, Subcommittee on Constitutional Rights, Hearings Pursuant to S. Res. 260, *Constitutional Rights of Military Personnel,* February 20 and 21, March 1, 2, 6, 9, and 12, 1962 [hereafter 1962 Subcommittee Hearings], 946.

48. Royal W. France, executive secretary, National Lawyers Guild, to Hennings, March 13, 1956, THC, folder 5046.

49. U.S. Congress, *United States Senate, Committee on the Judiciary, Legislative and Executive Calendar, 84th Congress, Final Edition* (Washington, D.C.: GPO, 1956), 388.

50. "Appendix I, Mutual Defense Assistance in Indochina," George S. Prugh, *Vietnam Studies: Law at War, Vietnam 1964–1973* (Washington, D.C.: Department of the Army, 1975), 145–50; see also "Mutual Defense Assistance in Indochina," August 1951–January 1952, U.S. Department of State, *United States Treaties and Other International Agreements* 5, Pt. 3, 1954 (Washington, D.C.: GPO, 1956), 2740–51. For a thorough account of U.S. policymaking in this period, see Fredrik Logevall, *Embers of War: The Fall of an Empire and the Making of America's Vietnam* (New York: Random House, 2012).

51. "The SEATO Treaty," in *America in Vietnam: A Documented History,* ed. William Appleman Williams, Thomas McCormick, Lloyd Gardner, and Walter LaFeber (Garden City: Anchor/Doubleday, 1985), 174–78.

52. Robert Alden, "Key Voting in South Vietnam," *NYT,* March 4, 1956.

53. Clauses 6 and 7 of the "Final Declaration of the Geneva Conference (July 21, 1954)," in *Vietnam and America: A Documented History,* ed. Marvin E. Gettleman, Jane Franklin, Marilyn B. Young, and H. Bruce Franklin, rev. ed. (New York: Grove Press, 1995), 75; Dulles cable to U.S. State Department, May 8, 1955, quoted in ibid., 133; Robert Alden, "Saigon Casts Off '54 Geneva Pact," *NYT,* March 9, 1956; Patrick Hagopian, *The Vietnam War in American Memory* (Amherst: University of Massachusetts Press, 2009), 48, 448n202.

54. "America's Stake in Vietnam, the Cornerstone of the Free World in Southeast Asia" [Remarks of Senator John F. Kennedy at the Conference on Vietnam Luncheon in the Hotel Willard, Washington, D.C., June 1, 1956], *Vital Speeches of the Day* 22, no. 17 (June 15, 1956): 618.

55. The troops did not die as a result of enemy action. On June 8, 1956, two air force sergeants died in Vietnam, one shooting the other before he fell to his death while being pursued by police. "Dead Sergeants Named," *NYT,* June 21, 1956. Lt. Col. A. Peter Dewey, serving with the Office of Strategic Services, was killed in 1945 by Communist Viet Minh fighters who apparently mistook him for a Frenchman. The killing occurred before the United States had thrown in its lot with the colonial French government. Stanley Karnow, *Vietnam: A History* (New York: Viking Press, 1983), 139–40.

56. Dwight D. Eisenhower, "Joint Statement Following Discussions with President Diem of South Viet-Nam," May 12, 1957, APP, www.presidency.ucsb.edu/ws/?pid=11033.

57. Logevall, *Embers of War,* 623–30, 665–73, 678, 699–701.

58. For the relevant briefs, see *U.S. Supreme Court Records and Briefs* 351 (1955), 470–92; *U.S. Supreme Court Records and Briefs* 354 (1956), 1–90. Consistent with his prior opinion in *Toth,* Justice Black's opinion for the court in *Reid v Covert* stated, "Traditionally, military justice has been a rough form of justice emphasizing summary procedures, speedy convictions and stern penalties with a view to maintaining obedience and fighting fitness in the ranks. Because of its very nature and purpose the military must place great emphasis on discipline and efficiency. Correspondingly, there has always been less emphasis in the military on protecting the rights of the individual than in civilian society and in civilian courts." *Reid v. Covert* and *Kinsella v. Krueger,* 354 U.S. 1 (1957), at 36. Justice Douglas's opinion for the

court in *O'Callahan v. Parker* quoted the passage distinguishing civilian and military law in *Toth* and another statement as well: "Military law has always been, and continues to be, primarily an instrument of discipline, not justice." 395 U.S. 258 (1969), at 262, 266.

59. *Kinsella v. Krueger,* 351 U.S. 470 (1956); *Reid v. Covert,* 351 U.S. 487 (1956). For an account of the underlying facts of the cases and the lower court decisions, see Brittany Warren, "The Case of the Murdering Wives: *Reid v. Covert* and the Complicated Question of Civilians and Courts-Martial," *Military Law Review* 212 (2012): 142–55.

60. *Kinsella v. Krueger,* 351 U.S. 470, at 479.

61. 351 U.S., at 481n 12.

62. 351 U.S., at 480. For the debate in Congress, see U.S. Congress, Senate, 94th Cong., 2nd Sess., Committee on the Judiciary, Report No. 1716, to Accompany S. J. Res. 1, "Constitutional Amendment Relative to Treaties and Executive Agreements," March 27, 1956.

63. *Reid v. Covert,* 351 U.S. 487 (1956), at 492.

64. Consular courts had been authorized by statute in 1878, and their validity was upheld in *In re Ross,* 140 U.S. 453 (1891). Justice Field's opinion for the court referred to the "uniform practice of civilized governments for centuries to provide consular tribunals in other than Christian countries." 140 U.S., at 462. For the history of the consular courts, and an illuminating account of the dynamics of legal universalism and particularlism, see Teemu Ruskola, *Legal Orientalism* (Cambridge: Harvard University Press, 2013).

65. See Frankfurter to "Fellow Brethren," May 20, 1957, and surrounding correspondence, HLB, box 327, folder: case file Nos. 701 & 713, October Term 1955, Reid v. Covert II. The same document, and the memorandum of June 5, 1957, cited in note 86, below, can also be found in FFP, part II, reel 18.

66. "Conference of February 12, 1955."

67. American participants in the relevant debates generally use the spelling *dependent* indifferently whether referring to the noun or the adjective. Here, I distinguish the two by using *dependant* as the spelling for the noun.

68. "Conference of May 4, 1956," *The Supreme Court in Conference,* 551. Of course the question was not whether they were considered members of the armed forces "for military purposes" but for the purpose of determining the appropriate forum for a prosecution.

69. Ibid.

70. Ibid., 552–53.

71. Frederick Bernays Wiener, Petition for Rehearing on Writ of Certiorari to the U.S. Court of Appeals for the Fourth Circuit, No. 701 Reid v. Covert, No. 713 Kinsella v. Krueger, July 1956, 3, *U.S. Supreme Court Records and Briefs* 354 (1956); Glenn R. Schmitt, "Closing the Gap in Criminal Jurisdiction Over Civilians Accompanying the Armed Forces Abroad—A First Person Account of the Creation of the Military Extraterritorial Jurisdiction Act of 2000," *Catholic Law Review* 55 (2001): 66n82.

72. Justice Sherman Minton's retirement was announced on October 16, 1956. He was replaced by William Brennan. Justice Stanley Reed's retirement was announced on February 25, 1957. He was replaced by Charles Evans Whittaker. *Journal of the Supreme Court of the United States October Term 1956,* 49, 159.

73. 351 U.S., at 482.

74. 351 U.S., at 483.

75. 351 U.S., at 481–82. William Winthrop, *Military Law and Precedents,* 2nd rev. ed (Washington, D.C.: GPO, 1920), 106. The attorneys for Audrey Toth had referred to the same passage from Winthrop in a petition filed on behalf of her brother, Robert Toth. Petition for a Writ of Certiorari to the United States Court of Appeals for the District of Columbia Circuit,

June 18, 1954, United States of America Ex. Rel. Audrey M. Toth, Petitioner, v. Harold E. Talbott, Respondent, *U.S. Supreme Court Records and Briefs* 350, October Term 1954.

76. Frederick Bernays Wiener, "Persuading the Supreme Court to Reverse Itself: Reid v. Covert," *Litigation* 14 (Summer 1988): 6–10. For an exposition of Harlan's evolving thoughts about the case, see Warren, "The Case of the Murdering Wives," 168–71, 179–80.

77. John Marshall Harlan III, Memorandum for Mr. Justice Reed, Mr. Justice Burton, Mr. Justice Clark, and Mr. Justice Minton [the associate justices who had joined Harlan in the judgment on the first hearing of *Covert* and *Krueger*], *Reid v. Covert* (No. 701) *Kinsella v. Krueger* (No. 713) [petition for rehearing], September 5, 1956, HLB, box 326, folder: case file nos. 701 & 713, October Term 1955, Reid v. Covert, Kinsella v. Krueger I.

78. *Reid v. Covert* and *Kinsella v. Krueger,* 354 U.S. 1 (1957), at 74.

79. 354 U.S., at 75.

80. For example, in his repudiation of the concept of substantive due process Black rejected the associated doctrine that the courts had a right to pass on the reasonableness or arbitrariness of legislation, which he regarded as a prerogative of the legislatures. John P. Frank, "The New Court and the New Deal," *Hugo Black and the Supreme Court: A Symposium,* ed. Stephen Parks Strickland (Indianapolis: Bobbs-Merrill, 1967), 53–56. For Black's deference to the Constitution only, not the legislature, see Bernard Schwartz, "Earl Warren as a Judge," *Hastings Constitutional Law Quarterly* 12 (1984–85): 188.

81. Charles A. Reich, "The Living Constitution and the Court's Role," *Hugo Black and the Supreme Court: A Symposium,* 147–48.

82. John M. Harlan, Memorandum for Mr. Justice Reed, Mr. Justice Burton, Mr. Justice Clark and Mr. Justice Minton, *Reid v. Covert* (No. 701) *Kinsella v. Krueger* (No. 713), September 26, 1956, HLB, box 326, folder: case file nos. 701 & 713, October Term 1955, Reid v. Covert, Kinsella v. Krueger I.

83. Memorandum by Mr. Justice Black, September—, 1956, Nos. 701 and 713, October Term, 1955, 11–12; undated "First Draft Memorandum," No. 701 Reid v. Covert and No. 713 Kinsella v. Krueger, 8. HLB, box 327, folder: case file nos. 701 & 713, Oct. Term 1955, Reid v. Covert III.

84. Frankfurter to Black, March 13, 1957, HLB, box 327, folder: case file nos. 701 & 713, Oct. Term, 1955, Reid v. Covert II. The same document can also be found in FFP, part II, reel 18.

85. Frankfurter, "Memorandum Re: Nos. 701 and 713 [the *Covert* and *Krueger* cases], O.T. [October Term] 1955," May 20, 1957, HLB, box 327, folder: case file nos. 701 & 713, Oct. Term, 1955, Reid v. Covert II.

86. Felix Frankfurter, "Memorandum for the Conference Re: Nos. 701 and 713 O.T. [October Term] 1955," June 5, 1957, HLB, box 326, folder: case file nos. 701 & 713, October Term 1955, Reid v. Covert, Kinsella v. Krueger I.

87. Girard Case Hearing, 26–27.

88. Frankfurter, Memorandum for the Conference Re: Nos. 701 and 713, June 5, 1957. Frankfurter had long experience of the treaty issue, having first addressed the question of whether an international agreement conflicted with the government's constitutional obligations when representing the State Department in the drafting of the charter of the International Labor Organization after the First World War. As counsel for the Bureau of Insular Affairs in the Law Department, he had also been responsible for reviewing, analyzing, and arguing questions of U.S. treaty obligations during the William H. Taft administration. James F. Simon, *The Antagonists: Hugo Black, Felix Frankfurter and Civil Liberties in Modern America* (New York: Simon and Schuster, 1989), 23.

89. "Supplemental Brief for Appellant and Petitioner for Rehearing," No. 701, Reid v. Covert, and No. 713, Kinsella v. Krueger, October Term, 1955, *U.S. Supreme Court Records and Briefs,* 354, 7–8, 12–13, 42–43. This argument was consistent with the language of the statute: Article 2(a)(11) of the UCMJ stated that persons serving with, employed by, or accompanying the armed forces of the United States were subject to the code "subject to the provisions of any treaty or agreement" to which the United States is party and to any accepted rule of international law.

90. 354 U.S., at 15–16. Black's reference is to the Constitution's "necessary and proper" clause, Article I, § 8, cl. 18. In this and the later cases in the same line, the argument involved a decision whether the UCMJ's coverage of civilians is in line with its constitutional power to "make rules" for the government of the land and naval forces, as conjoined with or supplemented by the "necessary and proper" clause. *Kinsella v. Singleton,* 361 U.S. 234 (1960), at 237–40.

91. 354 U.S., at 16–18.

92. 354 U.S., at 5–6.

93. 354 U.S., at 32.

94. 354 U.S., at 33.

95. 354 U.S., at 35. Winthrop, *Military Law and Precedents,* 107.

96. 354 U.S., at 16–17.

97. "Down Bricker's Alley," *Washington Post and Times Herald,* June 12, 1957.

98. 354 U.S., at 5–6, 12, 41nn10, 19. Congress had "buried" the consular system for trying Americans in 1956: 22 U.S.C. 141–43 (repealed August 1, 1956) 70 Stat. 773 (1956).

99. 354 U.S., at 14.

100. As such, the holding of the court would likely affect only a small number of cases. There had been only eleven court-martial cases in which a civilian was prosecuted for murder between 1950 and 1955. "Nature of Offenses for Which Civilians Were Tried by General Court-Martial 1950–55," attached to E. W. Sargent, Army Judge Advocate General's Corps, to Helen Newman, U.S. Supreme Court librarian, n.d., EW, box 575, folder: Supreme Court File Opinions, Chief Justice, O.T. [October Term] 1955, Nos. 701 and 713—Covert and Kinsella, Dissent.

101. 354 U.S., at 45, citing *Liverpool, New York, and Philadelphia Steamship Co. v. Emigration Commissioners,* 113 U.S. 33 (1885), at 39.

102. The precedential value of no-clear-majority decisions in this period sometimes depended on the numerical configuration of the plurality opinion, the concurrent opinion or opinions, and the dissent or dissents, as well as the persuasiveness and authoritativeness of the opinions. For a discussion of the precedential value of plurality decisions in the era of the *Covert* judgment, see "Supreme Court No-Clear-Majority Decisions: A Study in *Stare Decisis,*" *University of Chicago Law Review* 24 (1956–57): 99–156. See also Linda Novak, "The Precedential Value of Supreme Court Plurality Decisions," *Columbia Law Review* 80 (1980): 761–67.

103. Justice Charles Whittaker, who had replaced Reed, did not participate in the decision. The other new associate justice, William J. Brennan Jr., voted with the plurality.

104. Louis Fisher, *Military Tribunals and Presidential Power* (Lawrence: University Press of Kansas, 2005), 160.

105. 354 U.S., at 88.

106. 354 U.S., at 78n12.

107. In his dissent in *Covert* Clark saw no distinction in the Constitution between capital and noncapital cases and was dismayed that the court's ruling deferred the judgment

whether the requirement of trial in a civilian court applied also in noncapital cases. 354 U.S., 89–90. Unwilling to join Frankfurter and Harlan in making that distinction, he later aligned with the *Covert* plurality in noncapital cases in which the court considered the prosecution by courts-martial of civilian dependants and employees of the armed forces. Warren, "The Case of the Murdering Wives," 180–81.

108. The deputy judge advocate general for the navy reported a conversation between Chief Justice Earl Warren and Robert E. Quinn, the chief judge of the Court of Military Appeals (the civilian court the UCMJ had established to hear appeals against court-martial convictions), in which Warren said that the Supreme Court did not want to "upset the applecart completely" as far as trying civilians overseas but was using *Covert* and *Krueger* "as admonishment to Congress to come out with something." Maloney, Memorandum to Slayman, December 24, 1957. If so, the reverse transpired when congressional inaction seemed to encourage the court's continuation on the line it had established with *Covert:* three years later, the court in *Kinsella v. Singleton* noted that Congress had not passed legislation to close the jurisdictional gap opened up by *Covert* but that the subsequent failure to prosecute capital cases against military dependants had not had the least effect on discipline at armed services installations. 361 U.S. (1960), at 245.

109. "Trial of Civilians Abroad," *Washington Post and Times Herald,* June 12, 1957.

110. *Kinsella v. Singleton,* 361 U.S. 234 (1960), at 239. *Grisham v. Hagan* was also "controlled" by *Covert.* 361 U.S. 278 (1960), at 280. *Covert* was considered "binding" in *McElroy v. United States ex rel. Guagliardo,* 361 U.S. 281 (1960), at 283.

111. *Kinsella v. Singleton* determined that the court-martial of a military dependant was unconstitutional in a noncapital case as well as in capital cases; *Grisham v. Hagan* found that an armed services overseas civilian employee was not subject to court-martial jurisdiction in a capital case; *McElroy v. Guagliardo* found that an armed services overseas civilian employee was not subject to court-martial jurisdiction during peacetime.

112. 361 U.S., at 249.

113. Article 2(10) of the UCMJ. U.S. Congress, House, 90th Cong., 1st Sess., Committee on the Judiciary, *Report of Special Subcommittee on Application of the Uniform Code of Military Justice to American Civilians in the Republic of Vietnam,* June 1967, 2–3, 9–10.

114. In 1961 a federal court upheld court-martial jurisdiction over a retired officer for crimes he committed prior to his retirement. *Chambers v. Russell,* 192 F. Supp. 425 (N.D. Cal. 1961). In 1964 a federal court and the Court of Military Appeals upheld the jurisdiction of the UCMJ over another retiree, this time for postretirement crimes, although the state where the crime took place declined to prosecute him for actions that also violated state law. *Hooper v. United States,* 326 F.2d 982 (Ct. Cl. 1964); 26 C.M.A. 417 (C.M.A. 1958). Other cases affirmed the jurisdiction of courts-martial over retired enlisted men as well as officers for crimes committed both before and after their retirement. J. Mackay Ives and Michael J. Davidson, "Court-Martial Jurisdiction Over Retirees under Article 2(4) and 2(6): Time to Lighten Up and Tighten Up," *Military Law Review* 175 (2003): 21, 22–24, 28, 30–31. The Supreme Court referred to potential court-martial jurisdiction over retirees in a ruling in 1981. Eugene Fidell, "Ten Years On: Military Justice and Civil Liberties in the Post-9/11 Era," *New York Law School Law Review* 56 (2011): 106n10.

115. Walter H. Maloney to Charles H. Slayman, December 17, 1957, Subcommittee Military Justice Correspondence. Emphasis added.

116. Maloney to Slayman, December 24, 1957.

117. See, for example, correspondence in Subcommittee Military Justice Correspondence; 1962 Subcommittee Hearings, 552–54, 779, 882; 1966 Joint Committee Hearings, 349, 839.

118. S. Mase to B. Fensterwald, Memorandum on Senator Hennings' Bill—S. 2791, June 13, 1957, THC, folder 5046.

119. J. Lacey Reynolds to Charles H. Slayman, Memorandum on Status of Publicized Cases of Courts-Martial of Civilians, December 7, 1959, THC, folder 5046.

120. Gettleman et al., *Vietnam and America,* 156.

121. "South Viet Nam: Death at Intermission Time," *Time,* July 20, 1959. The names of Maj. Dale Buis and M.Sgt. Chester Ovnand initiate the sequence of names inscribed on the Vietnam Veterans Memorial in Washington, D.C. The names of the two sergeants who died in June 1956 were added after the memorial was dedicated. The Wall–USA, "The Vietnam Veterans Memorial," http://thewall-usa.com/information.asp.

3. "A Very Undesirable Situation"

1. Ervin titled his autobiography *Preserving the Constitution* (Charlottesville, Va.: Michie Company, 1984). Southerners like Ervin dominated the Senate Judiciary Committee, which had a reputation as the place where civil rights legislation went to die. Ervin ensured that the Constitutional Rights Subcommittee would continue this tradition of obstructionism. Karl E. Campbell, *Senator Sam Ervin, Last of the Founding Fathers* (Chapel Hill: University of North Carolina Press, 2007), 108, 113, 137.

2. Campbell, *Senator Sam Ervin, Last of the Founding Fathers,* 9–10, 78–79, 138, 254; "Random Notes from Washington: Resounding Rhetoric on Rights," *NYT,* July 15, 1957.

3. E. W. Kenworthy, "Eisenhower Sees Fair Girard Trial," *NYT,* June 6, 1957.

4. *Congressional Record—Senate,* August 29, 1957, 16509; Kenworthy, "Eisenhower Sees Fair Girard Trial."

5. "Subcommittee on Constitutional Rights," Guide to the Records of the U.S. Senate at the National Archives (RG 46), Chapter 13, Records of the Committee on the Judiciary and Related Committees, 1816–1968, www.archives.gov/legislative/guide/senate/chapter-13-judiciary-1947-1968.html#SCR.

6. Campbell, *Senator Sam Ervin, Last of the Founding Fathers,* 172.

7. Richard E. Mooney, "Senate to Send Observer; Issues Raised on Agreements," *NYT,* June 9, 1957; U.S. Congress, Senate, 88th Cong., 1st Sess., Committee on the Judiciary, Subcommittee on Constitutional Rights, Summary—Report of Hearings Pursuant to S. Res. 58, *Constitutional Rights of Military Personnel* (Washington, D.C.: GPO, 1963), iii. As we saw in the previous chapter, Ervin was critical about the agreement that allowed a Japanese court to assert its jurisdiction over the Girard case. U.S. Congress, Senate, 85th Cong., 1st Sess., Committee on Armed Services, Special Subcommittee, *Hearing on the William S. Girard Case,* June 5, 1957.

8. Campbell, *Senator Sam Ervin, Last of the Founding Fathers,* 38–42; Dick Dabney, *A Good Man: The Life of Sam J. Ervin* (Boston: Houghton Mifflin, 1976), 68.

9. Campbell, *Senator Sam Ervin, Last of the Founding Fathers* 172; U.S. Congress, Senate, 87th Cong., 2nd Sess., Committee on Rules and Administration, Report [No. 1141] to Accompany S. Res. 260, *Study of Constitutional Rights,* January 26, 1952, 3.

10. William Chapman, "Pentagon Can't Find Way to Prosecute Former Servicemen," *Washington Post,* April 9, 1971.

11. Campbell, *Senator Sam Ervin, Last of the Founding Fathers,* 173.

12. The subcommittee sent pre-hearing questionnaires to the Department of Defense to which the army, navy, and air force sent responses. Question 35 asked whether the armed services saw a need for legislation to close the jurisdictional gap opened by the Covert and

Guagliardo cases; the next questionnaire item was a similar question about the Toth case. Ervin sent the questionnaire to more than seven thousand reserve officers and others with experience in military law. William A. Creech, Subcommittee on Constitutional Rights chief counsel, "Congress Looks to the Serviceman's Rights," September 18, 1963, 4, SJE, folder 13850, Military Constitutional Rights, Series II: Subject Files.

13. "Report of the Judge Advocate General of the Army," *AR January 1, 1961 to December 31, 1961,* 67, 69–70. The Armed Services' Code Committee consisted of the chief judge and the judges of the U.S. Court of Military Appeals, the judge advocates general of the army, navy, and air force, and the general counsel of the Department of the Treasury (which, in time of peace, provided civilian leadership for the Coast Guard).

14. "Joint Report," *AR January 1, 1962 to December 31, 1962* [hereafter *1962 Annual Report*], 1.

15. 1962 Subcommittee Hearings, 2, 852.

16. 1962 Subcommittee Hearings, 910, 946. Comptroller General of the United States, *Report to the Congress of the United States: Some Criminal Offenses Committed Overseas by DoD Civilians Are Not Being Prosecuted: Legislation Is Needed,* Report No. FPCD 79-45, September 11, 1979, 16, http://archive.gao.gov/f0302/110369.pdf.

17. *1962 Annual Report; AR January 1 1963 to December 31, 1963* [hereafter *1963 Annual Report*].

18. "Joint Report," *1963 Annual Report,* 1. House bills numbered H.R. 8565 to H.R. 8582 identical to Ervin's Senate bills were introduced by Rep. Victor Wickersham (D, Okla.). *Congressional Record—House,* September 25, 1963, 18123–24.

19. H.R. 10048 and H.R. 10050, 88th Congress, 2nd Sess. The bills were precursors to H.R. 273 and H.R. 277, introduced in the 89th Congress. See Harold C. Warner, American Bar Association Special Committee on Military Justice, to Rep. L. Mendel Rivers, chairman, House Armed Services Committee, January 28, 1965, NA, RG 233, House of Representatives, Committee on Armed Services, Legislative Files, box 1, folder H.R. 273–H.R. 280 [hereafter H.R. 277 bill file].

20. *Gideon v. Wainwright,* 372 U.S. 335 (1963).

21. S. 2014, introduced August 6, 1963, "To provide for compliance with constitutional requirements in the trials of persons who are charged with having committed certain offenses while subject to trial by court-martial, who have not been tried for such offenses, and who are no longer subject to trial by court-martial," and S. 2015, "To provide for compliance with constitutional requirements in the trials of persons who, while accompanying the armed forces, outside the United States, commit certain offenses against the United States." The counterpart House bills were H.R. 8581 and H.R. 8582, introduced by Congressman Wickersham on September 25, 1963, and referred to the House Armed Services Committee. *Congressional Record—House,* September 25, 1963, 18123, 18131–32.

22. *Congressional Record—Senate,* August 6, 1963, 14144–45.

23. *1963 Annual Report,* 2–4.

24. Fred B. Smith, acting general counsel, Department of the Treasury, to Hon. James O. Eastland, chairman, Senate Judiciary Committee, February 11, 1965, NA, RG 46, 88th Cong., 1st Sess., Judiciary Committee, box 29, folder on S. 2014 [hereafter S. 2014 bill file].

25. Stephen Ailes, secretary of the army, to the Hon. James O. Eastland, April 10, 1964, S. 2014 bill file. Ailes's letter in response to the House legislation contained an identical statement. Ailes to Rep. Carl Vinson, chairman, House Armed Services Committee, April 24, 1964, NA, RG 233, House of Representatives, Committee on Armed Services, Legislative Files, H.R. 8565–H.R. 8861, H.R. 8582 bill file.

26. *AR January 1, 1964 to December 31, 1964,* 1. The report contains a brief description of the draft bills (2).

27. Nicholas deB. Katzenbach, deputy attorney general, to the Hon. James O. Eastland, April 15, 1964, S. 2014 bill file. Katzenbach opposed S. 2015 for the same reason. Nicholas deB. Katzenbach, Deputy Attorney General, to Hon. James O. Eastland, Chairman, Senate Judiciary Committee, April 15, 1964, NA, RG 46, Judiciary Committee, 88th Cong., 1st Sess., box 29, folder on S. 2015.

28. Smith to Eastland, S. 2014 bill file. 1962 Subcommittee Hearings, 554.

29. 350 U.S., at 43. According to the navy questionnaire response, the Department of Defense had proposed a constitutional amendment in its item 87-109, but this would not have extended court-martial jurisdiction over former service personnel. 1962 Subcommittee Hearings, 910. Creech confirmed that a constitutional amendment had been considered to allow the prosecution of civilians accompanying the armed forces overseas in time of peace, but that this had been deemed an impractical method of closing a jurisdictional loophole. Creech, "Congress Looks to the Servicemen's Rights," 15.

30. U.S. Congress, House, 95th Cong., 1st Sess., Committee on the Judiciary, Hearing before the Subcommittee on Immigration, Citizenship, and International Law on H.R. 763, H.R. 6148, and H.R. 7842, "Extraterritorial Criminal Jurisdiction," July 21, 1977, 52.

31. *Congressional Record—Senate,* January 26, 1965, 1272.

32. Ibid., 1255–56. For an account of how perceived shortcomings in the UCMJ led to calls for reform, see Edward F. Sherman, "The Civilianization of Military Law: Part I," *Maine Law Review* 22 (1970): 51–54.

33. For an account of the transition from the "G" and "H" bills to H.R. 273 and H.R. 277, see Warner to Rivers, January 28, 1965.

34. H.R. 273, 89th Cong., 1st Sess., "To amend chapter 47 (Uniform Code of Military Justice) of title 10, United States Code, by creating single-officer general and special courts-martial, providing for law officers on special courts-martial, affording accused persons an opportunity to be represented in certain special court-martial proceedings by counsel having the qualifications of defense counsel detailed for general courts-martial, providing for certain pretrial proceedings and other procedural changes, and for other purposes"; H.R. 277, 89th Cong., 1st Sess., "To amend chapter 47 (Uniform Code of Military Justice) of title 10, United States Code, to authorize the Judge Advocate General to grant relief in certain court-martial cases, to extend the time within which an accused may petition for a new trial, and for other purposes"; Joint Committee Hearings, 9–10. The bills were substitutes for Ervin's S. 747, S. 750, S. 751, S. 752, and S. 757. Ibid., 711. *AR January 1, 1965 to December 31, 1965,* 28.

35. S. 2906 and S. 2907 (whose purposes were worded identically to those of H.R. 273 and H.R. 277), introduced by Ervin and referred to the Senate Committee on Armed Services on February 9, 1966. *Congressional Record—Senate,* February 9, 1966, 2487–88.

36. H.R. 16115, 89th Cong., 2nd Sess., "To Amend the Uniform Code of Military Justice to broaden the protections afforded to members of the Armed Services, and for other purposes," July 11, 1966. *House Journal* 666, 89th Cong., 2nd Sess., 1618. *AR January 1, 1966 to December 31, 1966,* 47. This bill was not reported out of the House Armed Services Committee.

37. For a comparison of the House bills with their Senate counterparts pointing out the failings of the latter, see 1966 Joint Committee Hearings, 652–54; for a sectional comparison of the House and Senate bills with the existing language of the UCMJ, see ibid., 668–709.

38. L. Mendel Rivers to Sam Ervin, August 17, 1965, H.R. 277 bill file.

39. Warner to Rivers, January 28, 1965; Marshall C. Gardner, president, Federal Bar Association, to Ervin, January 13, 1966, in 1966 Joint Committee Hearings, 647–48.

40. Stephen Ailes, secretary of the army, to the Hon. L. Mendel Rivers, April 16, 1965, H.R. 277 bill file; Waldemar A. Solf, Judge Advocate General Corps, "Report of the Committee on Military Law and Justice Concerning S. 745 and S. 762, and Other Bills, Pertaining to the Administration of Military Justice and Administrative Board Proceedings," 1966 Joint Committee Hearings, 650.

41. "The Department" was said to oppose S. 761 and S. 762 because of the "burdensome administrative problems" they would impose. 1966 Joint Committee Hearings, 638, 640. Although the department is not identified, the phrase "burdensome administrative problems" is identical to the one the Department of Defense used in opposing S. 2014, and one can therefore infer that the quoted phrase is the Pentagon's.

42. John S. Stillman, national chairman, American Veterans Committee, attachment to testimony, January 25, 1966, 1966 Joint Committee Hearings, 202.

43. 1966 Joint Committee Hearings, 310; 1962 Subcommittee Hearings, 791.

44. Statements of Thomas D. Morris, asst. secretary of defense for manpower, and Brig. Gen. Kenneth J. Hodson, Asst. Judge Advocate General for Military Justice, Department of the Army, 1966 Joint Committee Hearings, 13, 21.

45. Maj. Gen. R. W. Manss, Judge Advocate General of the Air Force, 1966 Joint Committee Hearings, 63.

46. Ervin, 1966 Joint Committee Hearings, 63.

47. Testimony of Comdr. Penrose Lucas Albright, 1966 Joint Committee Hearings, 406.

48. 1966 Joint Committee Hearings, 837.

49. The problems with S. 762 were similar to those that had previously marred S. 2791: it included and excluded the wrong offenses. For example, S. 2791 had included soliciting to mutiny but not mutiny. It excluded misbehavior before the enemy but included an offense for which the maximum penalty was three years' confinement, contradicting the principle that it applied to offenses for which the punishment was a minimum of five years' confinement. New York County Lawyers' Association, Committee on Federal Legislation, Report No. F-11 on S. 2791, April 26, 1956, S. 2791 bill file. Similarly, S. 762 seemed to exclude a number of offenses, such as murder, manslaughter, rape, larceny, and robbery, while including offenses civilians were unlikely to commit, e.g., misbehavior of sentinel and dueling. Wurfel statement and testimony, 1966 Joint Committee Hearings, 144–45, 151–52; Wiener testimony, 1966 Joint Committee Hearings, 310; Gardner statement, 1966 Joint Committee Hearings, 648; Federal Bar Association statement, 1966 Joint Committee Hearings, 838.

50. 1966 Joint Committee Hearings, 148. The prohibitive nature of these problems vis-à-vis bringing to trial in the United States U.S. civilians accompanying the armed services in Vietnam was reaffirmed the next year. U.S. Congress, House, 90th Cong., 1st Sess., Committee on the Judiciary, *Report of Special Subcommittee on Application of the Uniform Code of Military Justice to American Civilians in the Republic of Vietnam,* June 1967 [hereafter 1967 Special Subcommittee Report], 9.

51. Donald J. Rapson, chairman of the subcommittee to amend the Uniform Code of Military Justice, Committee on Military Justice, Association of the Bar of the City of New York, 1966 Joint Committee Hearings, 126.

52. 1966 Joint Committee Hearings, 343.

53. Neil Sheehan, "Vietnam Peasants Are Victims of War," *NYT,* February 15, 1966.

54. Neil Sheehan, "Rubble Depicts the Agony of a Town in Vietnam," *NYT,* November 30, 1965.

55. In a famous segment broadcast on CBS News on August 5, 1965, the journalist Morley Safer reported on one such episode in the village of Cam Ne. Michelle Ferrari, with commentary by James Tobin, *Reporting America at War: An Oral History* (New York: Hyperion, 2003); the news package can be seen in *The Vietnam War with Walter Cronkite*, "Morley Safer's Vietnam" (CBS Television, 1989).

56. For example, in one incident early in the war the journalist David Halberstam had seen a helicopter door gunner shoot a farmer in a paddy field for no reason—the sort of incident that would be widely reported as the war went on—and in another, a deaf-mute young villager who did not hear an order to halt was shot and later described as a Viet Cong guerrilla. David Halberstam, *The Making of a Quagmire* (New York: Ballantine, 1989 [1964]), 88; Jack Raymond, "It's a Dirty War for Correspondents, Too," *NYT*, February 13, 1966.

57. "U.S. Death Toll in War Is 1,350 for 1965," *NYT*, January 2, 1966.

58. 1967 Special Subcommittee Report, 10.

59. George S. Prugh, *Vietnam Studies: Law at War, Vietnam 1964–1973* (Washington, D.C.: Department of the Army, 1975), 88. "B. Grant of Immunity from Jurisdiction": "Under Article 4 and Annex B of the Agreement, immunity from criminal and civil jurisdiction is granted to US military personnel in Vietnam along with certain categories of civilians." Appendix I: "Mutual Defense Assistance in Indochina," Prugh, *Law at War: Vietnam*, 150.

60. Ibid., 89.

61. 1967 Special Subcommittee Report, 10.

62. S. 2006, "A bill to provide for compliance with constitutional requirements in the trials of persons who are charged with having committed certain offenses while subject to trial by court-martial, who have not been tried for such offenses, and who are no longer subject to trial by court-martial"; S. 2007, "A bill to provide for compliance with constitutional requirements in the trials of persons who, while accompanying the Armed Forces outside the United States, commit certain offenses against the United States; to the Committee on the Judiciary"; S. 2009, "A bill to further insure due process in the administration of military justice . . ." [Omnibus Military Justice Bill], *Congressional Record—Senate*, June 26, 1967, 17321; U.S. Congress, *U.S. Senate, Committee on the Judiciary, 90th Congress, Legislative and Executive Calendar [Final Edition]* (Washington, D.C.: GPO, 1968), 233.

63. "A Position Paper Prepared by the Executive Committee of Clergy and Laymen Concerned about Vietnam," for distribution at the Washington Mobilization, January 31–February 1, 1967, 3. EB, box 498, folder: Vietnam, General 1965–69.

64. William F. Pepper, "The Children of Vietnam," *Ramparts* (January 1967): 44–67.

65. "Vietnam; The Wounded and the Dead Statistics Released," *NYT*, May 14, 1967.

66. "Vance Asks Calm in Debate on War," *NYT*, May 7, 1967.

67. Bernard Weinraub, "U.S. Captain Cleared in Vietnam Suspect's Death," *NYT*, July 28, 1967; Edward F. Sherman, "Military Injustice," *New Republic*, reproduced in *Congressional Record—House*, March 27, 1968, H. 2321–H. 2323.

68. Martin Luther King Jr., "Declaration of Independence from the War in Vietnam" (speech delivered at Riverside Baptist Church, New York, April 4, 1967), in *Vietnam and America: A Documented History*, ed. Marvin E. Gettleman, Jane Franklin, Marilyn B. Young, and H. Bruce Franklin, rev. ed. (New York: Grove Press, 1995), 310–18.

69. "Vance Asks Calm in Debate on War."

70. Dana Adams Schmidt, "'Tribunal' Finds U.S. Guilty in War," *NYT*, May 11, 1967.

71. H.R. 226, "A bill to amend the Uniform Code of Military Justice to broaden the protections afforded to members of the Armed Forces, and for other purposes," introduced by

Bennett on January 10, 1967. *Congressional Record—House,* January 10, 1967, 99. See also Charles E. Bennett, "A Solution to the Case for a Modern System of Military Justice," 5–6, in CEB, box 14, 1967, folder 2 of 2.

72. David A. McGiffert, acting secretary of the army, to L. Mendel Rivers, August 7, 1967, NA, RG 233, Papers Accompanying Specific Bills and Resolutions, Committee on Armed Services, 90th Congress, AS1, H.R. 226 (4 of 40); Bennett to L. Mendel Rivers, February 12, 1969, NA, RG 233, Papers Accompanying Specific Bills and Resolutions, Committee on Armed Services, 91st Congress, box 3, H.R. 2782–H.R. 5258, H.R. 4225 bill file [hereafter H.R. 4225 bill file].

73. "Kenneth Joe Hodson," Arlington National Cemetery Web site, www.arlingtoncemetery.net/kjhodson.htm.

74. The manuscript notes of Bennett's meeting with Hodson on August 18, 1967, contain his legislative staff's detailed analyses of the provisions to which the armed services objected, discussion of the differences between Ervin's and Bennett's bills, and a section headed "what we can possibly get," indicating that in practical terms the armed services, through Hodson, enjoyed the right to vet and approve the legislation. CEB, box 14, 1967, folder 2 of 2.

75. Paul J. Walstad (Bennett's legislative assistant), notes of a meeting with Hodson on the Military Justice Bill, August 23, 1967; Bennett to Hodson, August 23, 1967. CEB, box 14, 1967, folder 2 of 2.

76. Bennett to Wilfred C. Varn, September 5, 1967, CEB, box 14, 1967, folder 2 of 2. Bennett sent essentially the same message to the chairman of the House Armed Services Committee the next day, substituting the phrase "the Department of Defense" for "the Judge Advocate General of the Army," confirming that Hodson was taking the lead for the Department of Defense in the negotiations. Bennett to L. Mendel Rivers, September 6, 1967, CEB, box 14, 1967, folder 1 of 2. Ervin corroborates Hodson's fulfillment of this role in Sam J. Ervin Jr., "The Military Justice Act of 1968," *Military Law Review* 45 (July 1969): 81. Hodson stated that he was "spokesman for the Department of Defense's position on H.R. 15971" in Hodson to Bennett, October 7, 1968, CEB, box 15, 1968, folder 2.

77. Bennett introduced the bill as H.R. 12705 on August 30, 1967. *Congressional Record—House,* August 30, 1967, H. 11497. Hearings on H.R. 12705 were held before Subcommittee No. 1 of the Armed Services Committee on September 14 and October 26, 1967. H.R. 12705 was generally held to be noncontroversial, and the part of H.R. 226 that seemed to be viable was the provision creating a Judge Advocate General's Corps for the navy, to match those of the army and the air force. For the statements of support, see "Statement before the Committee on Armed Services, U.S. House of Representatives, by Major General Kenneth J. Hodson, The Judge Advocate General of the Army," CEB, box 14, 1967, folder 2 of 2; Robert E. Quinn, chief judge, U.S. Court of Military Appeals, to Philip J. Philbin, chairman of Subcommittee No. 1, House Committee on Armed Services, September 28, 1967; Stanley Resor, secretary of the army, to L. Mendel Rivers, chairman, House Committee on Armed Services, September 12, 1967, CEB, box 14, 1967, folder 1 of 2. The creation of the Judge Advocate General's Corps for the navy was ultimately accomplished by H.R. 12910, signed into law by the president on December 8, 1967. *AR January 1, 1967 to December 31, 1967,* 2.

78. "Reply to the Statement of the American Legion on H.R. 12705 dated 29 September 1967" (with manuscript annotation "Draft—Hodson's Explanation of Amendments"), CEB, box 14, folder 2 of 2; "Reply of Major General Hodson, The Judge Advocate General, Department of the Army[,] to the Objections to H.R. 12705, 90th Congress, by Various Organizations," CEB, box 14, 1967, folder 1 of 2.

79. Bennett to Hodson, November 9, 1967, and Hodson to Bennett, November 16, 1967, in CEB, box 15, 1968, folder 2.

80. "Factual and Historical Speech on H.R. 15971," CEB, box 15, 1968, folder 2. For the reference to H.R. 15971 as the "clean bill" replacing H.R. 12705, see, e.g., Bennett to Rep. Henry B. Gonzalez, March 28, 1968, in CEB, box 15, 1968, folder 2.

81. Ervin, "The Military Justice Act of 1968," 80–81.

82. William C. Selover, "Legal Frontier: Bill of Rights Umbrella Extended to Include Military Personnel," *Christian Science Monitor,* November 1, 1968, in CEB, box 15, 1968, folder 2.

83. Stanley Resor, secretary of the army, to Richard B. Russell, chairman, Senate Armed Services Committee, July 1, 1968, NA, RG 46, 90th Congress, Armed Services Committee, box 899, S. 2009 bill file; Ervin, "The Military Justice Act of 1968," 80–81. The phrase "watered-down" was used by a journalist who interviewed Ervin after the Military Justice Act of 1968 passed. Selover, "Legal Frontier."

84. Paul J. Walstad, "Discussion Sheet," July 1, 1968, CEB, box 15, 1968, folder 2. The sheet contains a useful summary of the major points of difference between the legislative measures favored by the Department of Defense and by Ervin.

85. Bennett to Russell, June 4, 1968, CEB, box 15, 1968, folder 2.

86. Russell to Bennett, June 12, 1968, CEB, box 15, 1968, folder 2.

87. Paul F. Walstad, notes of telephone conversation with Mr. Woodard, counsel, Senate Constitutional Rights Subcommittee, July 2, 1968.

88. Ervin to Hodson; Ervin to Rear Admiral Wilfred E. Hearn, Judge Advocate General of the Navy; Ervin to Maj. Gen. Robert W. Manss, Judge Advocate General of the Air Force; all letters dated June 26, 1967; Ervin to Robert E. Quinn, chief judge, U.S. Court of Military Appeals, June 27, 1967. SJE, folder 6686, J[udiciary] C[ommittee], Constitutional Rights Subcommittee, Correspondence Files, 1967.

89. Ervin, "The Military Justice Act of 1968," 81. For documents related to the relevant discussions, see Ervin to Hodson, June 28, 1968; Hodson, Memorandum for Roger M. Currier, special assistant for legislative affairs, Secretary of the Army, n.d.; Hodson to Ervin, July 2, 1968, S. 2009 bill file; Roger M. Currier to John R. Blandford, chief counsel, House Armed Services Committee, August 19, 1968; George Norris, counsel, House Armed Services Committee, to Philip J. Philbin, chairman of Subcommittee No. 1, House Armed Services Committee, August 26, 1968, CEB, box 15, 1968, folder 2. Numerous Department of Defense objections to S. 2009 were enumerated in a fourteen-page Department of the Army report to Richard Russell, chairman of the Senate Armed Services Committee, attached to James F. Senechal, Legislative Division, Department of the Army, to the Chief of Legislative Affairs, Department of the Navy, and the Director, Legislative Liaison, Department of the Air Force, May 16, 1968, in CEB, box 15, 1968.

90. Ervin, "The Military Justice Act of 1968," 81.

91. Bennett to Ervin, September 20, 1968, CEB, box 15, 1968, folder 2.

92. Ervin to Senator John Stennis, September 25, 1968, SJE, folder 7609, JC, Constitutional Rights Subcommittee, Correspondence Files 1968. Ervin sent a number of identical letters to his Senate colleagues on that date.

93. George Norris, counsel, House Armed Services Committee, Memorandum for Members, Subcommittee No. 1, Re: H.R. 15971, October 7, 1968; Bennett to Philip J. Philbin, October 3, 1968, CEB, box 15, 1968, folder 2.

94. For the tactical maneuverings, see, e.g., Bennett to Ervin, September 20, 1968, and memoranda prepared by Bennett's legislative liaison about the procedures for managing the bill. CEB, box 15, 1968, folder 2. See also Ervin to Rivers, October 4, 1968, SJE, folder

7609, JC, Constitutional Rights Subcommittee, Correspondence Files 1968, in which Ervin tells Rivers that all the Senate amendments of H.R. 15971 were approved by Hodson and the Department of Defense and expresses his hope that the bill would be accepted by the House of Representatives. The amendments are listed in "Memorandum: Sectional Analysis of H.R. 15971 with Amendments Proposed by Senator Ervin," NA, RG 46, 90th Cong., 2nd Sess., Committee on Armed Services, box 917, Legislative Files: Dockets, H.R. 15971–H.R. 16254.

95. For evidence of the broad consensus in favor of the legislation, voiced by the same bar associations, civilian institutions (such as the ACLU), and veterans organizations that had contributed to the hearings in 1962 and 1966, see CEB, box 14, 1967, folder 2 of 2. For the claim that with regard to certain due process protections, military courts were ahead of civilian courts, see *American Bar Association Journal* 53 (July 1967): 664–65; Fred P. Graham, "Reforms Sought in Military Code," *NYT,* May 18, 1967; Edward F. Sherman, "The Civilianization of Military Law: Part II," *Maine Law Review* 22 (1970): 64–65.

96. U.S. Congress, Senate, 90th Cong., 2nd Sess., Report No. 1601, To Accompany H.R. 15971, October 2, 1968. The Senate passed the bill the following day. Ervin, "The Military Justice Act of 1968," 44.

97. Charles E. Bennett to L. Mendel Rivers, chairman, House Armed Services Committee, October 3, 1968; Hodson to Rivers, October 7, 1968, NA, RG 233, 90th Congress, Armed Services Committee, Legislative Files, folder H.R. 15971 to H.R. 16060, H.R. 15971 bill file. The House passed the bill on October 10, 1968. Ervin, "The Military Justice Act of 1968," 45.

98. Lyndon B. Johnson, "Remarks upon Signing the Military Justice Act of 1968," October 24, 1968, APP, www.presidency.ucsb.edu/ws/?pid=29200. Library of Congress Military Legal Resources, "The Military Justice Act of 1968," www.loc.gov/rr/frd/Military_Law/MJ_act-1968.html.

99. UCMJ art. 66, 10 U.S.C. § 866.

100. "Military Law—Military Criminal Justice System," http://law.jrank.org/pages/8564/Military-Law-Military-Criminal-Justice-System.html; J. A. Mounts Jr. and M. G. Sugarman, "A Renaissance for Military Justice," *Military Review* (September 1969), in *Extensions of Remarks—Congressional Record,* September 19, 1969, 26430–31.

101. *AR January 1, 1968 to December 31, 1968,* 3.

102. Selover, "Legal Frontier."

103. U.S. Congress, Senate, Committee on the Judiciary, 90th Cong., *Legislative and Executive Calendar [Final Edition]* (Washington, D.C.: GPO, 1968), 233.

104. Laurence Speiser to James O. Eastland, chairman, Senate Judiciary Committee, July 7, 1967, NA, RG 46, 90th Congress, Committee on the Judiciary, box 35, folder S. 2007.

105. Chief Judge Quinn's summary of the evidence in *United States v. Keenan,* 18 U.S.C.M.A. 108, at 112, 114–16.

106. Gary D. Solis, *Marines and Military Law in Vietnam: Trial by Fire* (Washington, D.C.: Department of the Navy, Headquarters United States Marine Corps, n.d. [c. 1988]), 4-35; Slack to Clifford, June 14, 1968, cited in ibid., 4-53n80. See 18 U.S.C.M.A. 108, 39 C.M.R. 108 (1969).

107. Gary D. Solis, *Son Thang: An American War Crime* (New York: Bantam Books, 1997), 201.

108. Bernd Greiner, *War without Fronts: The USA in Vietnam* (London: Bodley Head, 2009), 332.

109. Solis, *Marines and Military Law,* 4-53n80. The corporal who instigated the unjustified killings by shooting the victims and ordering his squad to shoot them was acquitted of

murder by reason of insanity. James B. Insco, "Defense of Superior Orders before Military Commissions," *Duke Journal of Comparative and International Law* 13 (2003): 406n105.

110. *Miranda v. Arizona,* 384 U.S. 436 (1966); Campbell, *Senator Sam Ervin, Last of the Founding Fathers,* 214. It was frequently pointed out that suspects in the armed services had enjoyed the right to preinterrogation warnings against self-incriminatory evidence before the Supreme Court had recognized the equivalent constitutional right for civilian suspects, meaning that in this instance civilian law had to catch up with military law rather than vice versa.

111. Bennett to Ervin, September 20, 1968. Bennett may have intended to say "other much-needed reforms."

112. H.R. 4225, Mr. Bennett, Jan 23, 1969. "To amend title 10, United States Code, to confer jurisdiction on United States district courts to try certain civilians who are or have been connected with the armed services." Jan 27, 1969: Referred to Department of Defense and Department of Justice for Reports. *United States House of Representatives Committee on Armed Services, Legislative Calendar, 91st Congress, Final Calendar 1969–1970* (Washington, D.C.: GPO, 1971), 41.

113. Bennett to Rivers, February 12, 1969.

114. Rivers to Bennett, February 13, 1969, H.R. 4225 bill file.

115. The Constitutional Rights Subcommittee held hearings on privacy issues—one of Ervin's abiding interests—and the census in the spring of 1969. In the same period, Ervin opposed a proposal to end the electoral college system in presidential elections. Ervin was also preoccupied with the renewal of the Voting Rights Act. In the autumn of 1969 the Separation of Powers Subcommittee considered the Nixon administration's "Philadelphia Plan" to promote economic opportunities for African Americans, and Ervin, in hearings of the Senate Judiciary Committee, opposed Nixon administration proposals for "no-knock" searches of homes and preventive detention. Campbell, *Senator Sam Ervin, Last of the Founding Fathers,* 224, 227, 23; Paul R. Clancy, *Just a Country Lawyer: A Biography of Senator Sam Ervin* (Bloomington: Indiana University Press, 1974), 220–21, 237; Ervin, *Preserving the Constitution,* 275, 309.

4. "Uncharted Legal Waters"

1. *Americal* is a contraction of *American* and *New Caledonia,* the Pacific island where the 23rd Infantry Division was formed during the Second World War. The division was reactivated in Vietnam in 1967 and was generally referred to by the name Americal rather than by its number. The divisional commander in March 1968 was Maj. Gen. Samuel W. Koster.

2. William Eckhardt, the chief prosecutor in the My Lai cases, has questioned the accuracy of two of the sources on which this chapter relies, Seymour Hersh, *My Lai 4: A Report on the Massacre and Its Aftermath* (New York: Vintage Books, 1970), and Richard Hammer, *One Morning in the War* (London: Rupert Hart-Davis, 1970), because the statements soldiers and veterans made to the investigative reporters differ from those made later to "prosecutorial officials" and from testimony given under oath. William G. Eckhardt, "Command Responsibility: A Plea for a Workable Standard," *Military Law Review* 97 (1982): 13n21. As Eckhardt acknowledges elsewhere, though, the witnesses "progressively remembered less and less" under the advice of lawyers as they tried to avoid being caught up in a legal process. Some rejected the legal immunity offered by prosecutors in return for their testimony because of fears of prosecution by an international tribunal. William G. Eckhardt, "My Lai: An American Tragedy," *University of Missouri Kansas City Law Review* 68 (1999–2000): 682.

Veteran witnesses, including those required for reinterview, became difficult to locate as they moved around the country attempting to avoid investigators. Department of the Army, "Information for Members of Congress: Alleged Murder of Noncombatant Civilians in the Hamlet of My Lai (4), Republic of Vietnam," n.d. [c. November 1969], 4, NA, RG 319, ODC-SPER, VWCWG, MLM, box 7, folder: Congressional Correspondence—My Lai: Hebert Subcommittee Investigation. Hodson, who was judge advocate general of the army at the time of the prosecutions, observed the deterioration of the witnesses' ability to remember and their refusal to cooperate because of fear of self-incrimination. Kenneth Hodson, Transcript of On-Camera Interview 263, November 10, 1988, 4, LHC 2/5. Some witnesses invoked the Fifth Amendment protection against self-incrimination and declined to answer questions by investigators after they had previously made public statements or spoken to investigators and the media. See, e.g., Paul Meadlo, TPI, Book 25, 6; David Mitchell, TPI, Book 25, 6. In the trial of Ernest Medina the prosecution witnesses repeatedly surprised Eckhardt by testifying differently from the statements they had made to investigators, indicating that the deterioration in their recollections and lack of cooperation was progressive. Mary McCarthy, *Medina* (London: Wildwood House, 1972), 14. For these reasons there are no grounds for regarding the statements witnesses and suspects made to reporters as inferior to later investigative interviews and witness testimony: quite the opposite. Although Mark Taylor has identified inaccuracies, largely in the details of local geography, in the work of Hammer, there are no substantial disagreements about many of the basic facts of the events of March 16, 1968. Mark J. Taylor, "The Massacre at My Khe 4: A Different Story" (Ph.D. diss., University of Hull, England, 2010), 9–10.

3. They were Alpha Company, 3rd Battalion, 1st Infantry Brigade; Bravo Company, 4th Battalion, 3rd Infantry Brigade; and Charlie Company, 1st Battalion, 20th Infantry Brigade.

4. *Report of the Department of the Army Review of the Preliminary Investigations into the My Lai Incident,* "The Report of the Investigation" (Washington, D.C.: United States Department of the Army, March 14, 1970) [hereafter Peers Inquiry Report], 1:8-2. A declassified copy of this document was sent to the author from OSD, in the author's possession; see also Eugene Kotouc, S-2 (intelligence officer) and an aide to Colonel Barker at the time of the My Lai massacre, TPI, Book 16, 2, 11–12. The designation of the hamlet where the majority of killings took place as My Lai is incorrect: the central target of the attack was a subhamlet, Xom Lang (also known as Thuan Yen), in the hamlet Tu Cung, labeled My Lai (4) on American maps. Tu Cung was one of four hamlets that comprised part of Son My village. Hammer, *One Morning in the War,* 32–33. The misnomer was acknowledged by the army. W. R. Peers, Memorandum for the Secretary of the Army and Chief of Staff of the Army, January 21, 1970, NA, RG 319, PI–CI box 5, folder: LTG Peers Notes # 3 House Invest[igating] Subcomm[ittee] [5]. See "Village, Hamlet, and Sub-Hamlet Organization," attached to this memorandum. The subhamlet marked on American maps as My Khe (4) was known to the Vietnamese as My Hoi. In keeping with conventional usage in the United States, including the discussions held at the time, I refer to the massacre sites as My Lai (4) and My Khe (4) and to the incident as the My Lai massacre.

5. Peers Inquiry Report, 1:8-2.

6. Inspector General Witness Interviews with Pham Dai, December 28, 1969; Phom Dat, December 24, 1969; Nguyen Thi Em, December 30, 1969; LHC 6/1.

7. Hammer, *One Morning in the War,* 118–19.

8. Peers Inquiry Report, 1:2-2.

9. W. R. Peers, *The My Lai Inquiry* (New York: Norton, 1979), 175.

10. Hammer, *One Morning in the War,* 120. For corroboration of this description of the

landscape, see the aerial photographs in NA, RG 153, OCC, box 11, folder: Calley Court-Martial Exhibits, Prosecution Exhibits 1–6.

11. Hammer, *One Morning in the War,* 124.

12. Hersh, *My Lai 4,* 48; Hammer, *One Morning in the War,* 123; Peers, *The My Lai Inquiry,* 175.

13. Dennis I. Conti, TPI, Book 24, 32; James J. Dursi, TPI, Book 24, 11; Hersh, *My Lai 4,* 50; Hammer, *One Morning in the War,* 134; Peers Inquiry Report, 1:2-2. Joseph Goldstein, Burke Marshall, and Jack Schwartz, *The My Lai Massacre and Its Cover-Up: Beyond the Reach of Law? The Peers Commission Report with a Supplement and Introductory Essay on the Limits of Law* (New York: Free Press, 1976), 499, 514; Michael Bilton and Kevin Sim, *Four Hours in My Lai: A War Crime and Its Aftermath* (New York: Penguin, 1992), 119; Richard Hammer, *The Court-Martial of Lt. Calley* (New York: Coward, McCann, and Geoghagen, 1971), 225.

14. Hammer, *One Morning in the War,* 124; Phom Dat, Inspector General Witness Interview, December 24, 1969, LHC 6/1.

15. Bilton and Sim, *Four Hours in My Lai,* 372.

16. Hammer, *One Morning in the War,* 136.

17. Ibid., 122–23; Bilton and Sim, *Four Hours in My Lai,* 7; Varnado Simpson, Army CID Investigation Interview, November 9, 1969, NA, RG 319, VWCWG, MLM, box 7, folder: Public Correspondence—My Lai [Part 2].

18. Hersh, *My Lai 4,* 52.

19. Hammer, *Court-Martial of Lt. Calley,* 33.

20. Seymour Hersh, *Cover-Up: The Army's Secret Investigation of the Massacre at My Lai 4* (New York: Vintage Books, 1973), 7–8.

21. Bilton and Sim, *Four Hours in My Lai,* 124.

22. Peers, *The My Lai Inquiry,* 188.

23. Peers, *The My Lai Inquiry,* 190; Goldstein et al., *The My Lai Massacre and Its Cover-Up,* 174.

24. Hammer, *One Morning in the War,* 145–46; Hersh, *Cover-Up,* 13–17.

25. Hersh, *Cover-Up,* 19.

26. Goldstein et al., *The My Lai Massacre and Its Cover-Up,* 180.

27. Peers, *The My Lai Inquiry,* 198.

28. "Lt. Col. Barker's Combat Action Report (March 28, 1968)," in Peers, *The My Lai Inquiry,* 268–71.

29. Michal Belknap, *The Vietnam War on Trial: The My Lai Massacre and the Court-Martial of Lieutenant Calley* (Lawrence: University Press of Kansas, 2002), 83; Bilton and Sim, *Four Hours in My Lai,* 300–302.

30. Hersh, *Cover-Up,* 133–38, 162–69, 176–78, 204–5, 218; Bilton and Sim, *Four Hours in My Lai,* 300–304; U.S. Congress, House, 91st Cong., 2nd Sess., *Investigation of the My Lai Incident: Report of the Armed Services Investigating Subcommittee of the House of Representatives Committee on Armed Services,* July 15, 1970 (Washington, D.C.: GPO, 1970) [hereafter *My Lai Investigating Subcommittee Report*], 26, 34.

31. Oran K. Henderson, "Report of Investigation," April 24, 1968, in James Olson and Randy Roberts, *My Lai: A Brief History with Documents* (New York: Palgrave Macmillan, 1998), 127–28.

32. Westmoreland was aware of the imbalance between the enemy killed in action (128) and the number of weapons captured, six by the time the report reached him, in Task Force Barker's activities on March 16, 1968. COMUSMACV [Commander, U.S. Military Assistance Command, Vietnam, i.e., Westmoreland] to NMCC [National Military Command

Center] and CINCPAC [Commander in Chief, Pacific Forces], March 16, 1968, NA, RG 319, PI–OI, box 5, folder: MACV Reports [10].

33. Westmoreland to CG [Commanding General] Americal Division, Subject: Congratulatory Message, March 16, 1968, NA, RG 319, PI–AC, box 38, folder: Son My Chron # 19 [1 of 2].

34. Peers, *The My Lai Inquiry,* 208; Olson and Roberts, *My Lai: A Brief History,* 113–32.

35. Philip Caputo, *A Rumor of War* (New York: Ballantine, 1977), 217; Robert Jay Lifton, "Beyond Atrocity," in *Crimes of War,* ed. Richard A. Falk, Gabriel Kolko, and Robert Jay Lifton (New York: Vintage Books, 1971), 25; Nick Turse, *Kill Anything That Moves* (New York: Henry Holt, 2013), 47, 50. As one officer remarked about Americal Division procedures, "I think that the general feeling over there was that anything that was shot was VC [Viet Cong]." Hersh, *Cover-Up,* 48.

36. Goldstein et al., *The My Lai Massacre and Its Cover-Up,* 299.

37. *The My Lai Inquiry,* 208.

38. Ronald Ridenhour, "Letter to Military and Political Leaders," March 29, 1969, in Olson and Roberts, *My Lai: A Brief History,* 147–52.

39. Bilton and Sim, *Four Hours in My Lai,* 220.

40. Belknap, *Vietnam War on Trial,* 104.

41. "List of Witnesses (Pinkville Case)," July 23, 1969; "IG Investigation into the My Lai (4) Incident," December 1, 1969; "Talking Paper: CID Phase of the My Lai (4) Investigation," December 3, 1969. NA, NPM, NSCF, Alexander M. Haig Special File, box 1004, folder 8: My Lai Incident (2 of 2) (copies of these two chronologies are also in OSD); "Chronology of Key Events and Congressional Notification: Son My Incident," NA, RG 319, PI–AC, box 12, folder: Index. For the records of the investigative interviews, see the extensive holdings in the NA, RG 319, ODCSPER, VWCWG, MLM; a substantial sample of the interviews is also available in the LHC, series 5.

42. Hersh, *My Lai 4: A Report on the Massacre,* 128–29.

43. *My Lai Investigating Subcommittee Report,* 1; "Chronology of Key Events and Congressional Notification."

44. David Packard, Memorandum for the President, Subject: The My Lai Atrocity, September 4, 1969, NA, NPM, NSCF, Alexander M. Haig Special File, box 1004, folder 9: Possible My Lai Commission.

45. "The Assistant Secretary of Defense (Public Affairs) will be in touch with his counterpart on your staff to work out an appropriate press plan." Packard, Memorandum for the President.

46. William M. Hammond, *Reporting Vietnam: Media and Military at War* (Lawrence: University Press of Kansas, 1998), 189.

47. Hersh, *My Lai 4,* 128–29.

48. Hammond, *Reporting Vietnam,* 189.

49. H. D. Quigg, "Editors Ask: Why Were We So Slow in Uncovering Songmy 'Massacre'?" *Editor and Publisher,* December 13, 1969, 11. "Songmy" and "Song My" are misspellings of Son My, the village of which My Lai (4) was a subhamlet.

50. Hammond, *Reporting Vietnam,* 190.

51. As Haeberle admitted some forty years later, "I had actual photos of actual guys who were doing the shooting and stuff like that. . . . I never showed those. No, no, no. . . . I mean, I was there in the operation, but I'm not gonna point a finger at some soldier out there and have him, you know, put up. No. We were all guilty. So I'm just as guilty as anyone else in the cover-up. I'll admit to that." Evelyn Theiss, "My Lai Photographer Ron Haeberle Admits He

Destroyed Pictures of Soldiers in the Act of Killing," *Cleveland Plain Dealer,* November 20, 2009, http://blog.cleveland.com/pdextra/2009/11/post_25.html.

52. Bilton and Sim, *Four Hours in My Lai,* 260.

53. Henry Kissinger, Telecon, Secretary Laird, November 21, 1969, 3:50 p.m., National Security Archive, www.gwu.edu/~nsarchiv/NSAEBB/NSAEBB123/Box%203,%20File%203,%20Secretary%20Laird,%2011-21-69%20083-084.pdf.

54. "Fact Sheet: Court-Martial of First Lieutenant William Calley," attached to Robert E. Miller, Department of the Army, Office of the Judge Advocate General, to Sam J. Ervin, May 5, 1971, SJE, folder 10064, Correspondence Files 1971, ASC, Calley Incident; Hersh, *My Lai 4,* 139; Belknap, *Vietnam War on Trial,* 133; Quigg, "Editors Ask: Why Were We So Slow?" 11.

55. "Investigation of Son My Incident," Approved by Brig. Gen. R. G. Gard, Jr., January 17, 1972, NA, RG 319, ODCSPER, VWCWG, MLM, box 6, folder: Congressional Backup Sheets—My Lai Case 1970–1972.

56. E. W. Kenworthy, "Resor Called to Testify about Alleged Massacre," *NYT,* November 26, 1969.

57. Kendrick Oliver, *The My Lai Massacre in American History and Memory* (Manchester: Manchester University Press, 2006), 50.

58. Fred P. Graham, "Army Lawyers Seek Way to Bring Ex-G.I.'s to Trial," *NYT,* November 26, 1969.

59. "Network Coverage of My Lai Case," NA, RG 153, OCC, box 15.

60. Robert M. Smith, "26 Are Investigated in Vietnam Deaths," *NYT,* November 22, 1969; Bilton and Sim, *Four Hours in My Lai,* 256–58.

61. "Chronology of Key Events and Congressional Notification."

62. Ibid.; Statement of General W. C. Westmoreland, Chief of Staff, U.S. Army, before the Special Subcommittee—Son My, Committee on Armed Services, House of Representatives, n.d., 3, RG 319, PI–AC, box 38, folder: Son My Chron # 19 [1 of 2]. For the list of twenty-two civilian suspects, see "Son My Investigation—Civilian Suspects," NA, RG 319, PI–AC, box 12, folder: Index.

63. E. W. Kenworthy, "Songmy 1: Questions for the Conscience of a Nation," *NYT,* November 30, 1969; Mark D. Carson, "F. Edward Hébert and the Congressional Investigation of the My Lai Massacre," *Louisiana History: The Journal of the Louisiana Historical Association* 37 (Winter 1996): 67.

64. "Statements by Ziegler, Resor and Stennis," *NYT,* November 27, 1969. For Resor's identical statement to the House subcommittee, see Statement by Stanley R. Resor, U.S. Congress, House, 91st Cong., 1st Sess., Committee on Armed Services, Special Subcommittee on Armed Services Investigations, November 26, 1969, NA, NPM, NSCF, Alexander M. Haig Special File, box 1004, folder 8: My Lai Incident (2 of 2).

65. Kenworthy, "Songmy 1."

66. Robert M. Smith, "White House Says U.S. Policy Bars Any Mass Slaying," *NYT,* November 27, 1969.

67. "Chronology of Key Events and Congressional Notification."

68. John P. Mackenzie, "Special War Crimes Panel Weighed to Try Ex-GIs," *Washington Post,* November 27, 1969.

69. Silliman and Everett contend that the president might have that inherent authority. Robinson O. Everett and Scott L. Silliman, "Forums for Punishing Offenses against the Law of Nations," *Wake Forest Law Review* 29 (1994): 515. Fisher holds that the president lacks the inherent power to convene a military commission and that *Hamdan v. Rumsfeld,* 548 U.S. 557 (2006) settles this question. Louis Fisher, personal communication, January 31, 2012.

Hamdan does not lay the matter to rest, as the court found that, whether the president may "constitutionally convene military commissions 'without the sanction of Congress' in cases of 'controlling necessity' is a question this Court has not answered definitively, and need not answer today." 548 U.S., part 4. A plurality found that, in the absence of congressional authorization, the president may not convene a military commission to prosecute a defendant except under circumstances of military government or martial law or in a case of a defendant suspected of violating the law of war. 548 U.S., part 5. The first two conditions did not apply, and Salim Ahmed Hamdan was therefore prosecutable by a presidentially convened military commission solely for a breach of the law of war. The charges against him involved conspiracy for his alleged role in the September 11, 2001, attacks on targets in the United States—not a violation of the law of war and hence not, in the absence of congressional authorization, a crime prosecutable by a military commission. Following the court's ruling, Congress stepped in to provide the authorization that had been lacking. Stephen L. Vladeck, "The Laws of War as a Constitutional Limit on Military Jurisdiction," *Journal of National Security Policy* 4 (2010): 296. A federal appeals court later threw out Hamdan's conviction because the crime of which he was convicted was not a war crime at the time of his conviction. Charlie Savage, "Military Panel's Conviction of bin Laden Driver Voided," *IHT,* October 12, 2012.

70. The Military Commissions Act of 2006, Pub. L. No. 109-366, October 17, 2006, 120 Stat. 2600.

71. S. 3188 was intended "to provide for compliance with constitutional requirements in the trials of persons who are charged with having committed certain offenses while subject to trial by court-martial, who have not been tried for such offenses, and who are no longer subject to trial by court-martial."

72. Ervin to Laird, December 1, 1969, RG 319, ODCSPER, VWCWG, MLM, box 7, folder: Congressional Correspondence—My Lai: Hebert Subcommittee Investigation.

73. *Congressional Record—Senate,* December 1, 1969, 36154.

74. Ibid.

75. John P. McKenzie, "Jurisdiction Sought for Ex-Military," *Washington Post,* December 2, 1969.

76. Ibid.

77. *Congressional Record—Senate,* December 1, 1969, 36155.

78. In an archival copy of the press release someone has inserted handwritten brackets around the sentence "I have omitted the limitation which made the legislation effective only as to offenses committed after the enactment of the bills." A one-word manuscript annotation reads, "Omit." Senate Subcommittee on Constitutional Rights, "Ervin Introduces Bill to Permit Federal District Court Trials of Former Servicemen," December 1, 1969, RG 319, ODCSPER, VWCWG, MLM, box 7, folder: Congressional Correspondence—My Lai: Hebert Subcommittee Investigation.

79. *Congressional Record—Senate,* December 1, 1969, 36154.

80. Article I, § 9, cl. 3 of the Constitution states, "No Bill of Attainder or ex post facto Law shall be passed."

81. Mackenzie, "Special War Crimes Panel Weighed to Try Ex-GIs"; Graham, "Army Lawyers."

82. James Rosen, *The Strong Man: John Mitchell and the Secrets of Watergate* (New York: Doubleday, 2008), 71.

83. Ibid., 76.

84. Deborah Nelson, *The War Behind Me: Vietnam Veterans Confront the Truth about U.S. War Crimes* (New York: Basic Books, 2008), 152. Notebooks 10 and 11, William H. Rehnquist Papers, Hoover Institution Archives, Stanford, CA, box 332. The meeting of December 19, 1969, was attended by George Aldrich, deputy legal adviser for the State Department, and Benjamin Forman, assistant general counsel of the Defense Department. I appreciate the research assistance of Sarah Pines, and the advice of Carol Leadenham.

85. Richard Reeves, *President Nixon: Alone in the White House* (New York: Simon and Schuster, 2001), 151; Richard Nixon, *RN: The Memoirs of Richard Nixon* (London: Book Club Associates, 1978), 424. Another of Rehnquist's high-ranking White House admirers was John Ehrlichman, counsel to the president, who had been in law school at Stanford University with Rehnquist. John Ehrlichman, *Witness to Power: The Nixon Years* (New York: Simon and Schuster, 1982), 136.

86. John Dean, *Blind Ambition: The White House Years* (New York: Simon and Schuster, 1976), 51.

87. Fred P. Graham, "Government Lawyers Who Seek a War Crimes Tribunal Tread Softly on Constitutional Ground," *NYT,* November 30, 1969.

88. Lyle Denniston, "Army Assesses Ways to Try Former GIs," *Washington Star,* December 3, 1969.

89. See, e.g., Charles W. Corddry, "Army Studies How to Try My Lai Ex-GIs," *Baltimore Sun,* November 29, 1969.

90. Robert E. Jordan III, Memorandum for the Assistant Attorney General (Office of Legal Counsel) on Trial of Discharged Servicemen for Violation of the Law of War, December 2, 1969 [hereafter Jordan Memorandum], 1, citing *United States v. Schuering,* 16 U.S.C.M.A. 324, 36 C.M.R. 480 (1966), EA.

91. Jordan Memorandum, citing *United States v. Hudson and Goodwin,* 11 U.S. 32 (1812).

92. Article I, § 8, cl. 10 of the Constitution.

93. *Trial of the Major War Criminals Before the International Military Tribunal* [the Nuremberg Tribunal] (1947), 1:221, quoted in W. Michael Reisman and Chris T. Antoniou, *The Laws of War: A Comprehensive Collection of Primary Documents on International Laws Governing Armed Conflict* (New York: Vintage Books, 1997); Jordan Memorandum, 5.

94. Edward F. Sherman, "Songmy 2: Some Knotty Legal Questions," *NYT,* December 7, 1969.

95. Jordan Memorandum, 5–6.

96. Jordan Memorandum, 2. Military tribunals or commissions had been created in the past, during the Mexican-American War, the Civil War era, and the Second World War II. Since their origination in nineteenth-century America, military commissions had been used for a number of purposes, one of which was to prosecute offenses against the laws and usages of war. Jordan Memorandum, 3. See also the historical review of the use of military tribunals in Michal R. Belknap, "A Putrid Pedigree: The Bush Administration's Military Tribunals in Historical Perspective," *California Western Law Review* 38 (2001–2): 443–79. The principal authorities on which Jordan relies here are *Ex parte Quirin,* 317 U.S. 1 (1942), and *Madsen v. Kinsella.* For relevant discussions, see Louis Fisher, *Constitutional Conflicts between Congress and the President,* 5th ed., rev. (Lawrence: University Press of Kansas, 2007), 249; Brian C. Baldrate, "The Supreme Court's Role in Defining the Jurisdiction of Military Tribunals: A Study, Critique, and Proposal for *Hamdan v. Rumsfeld,*" *Military Law Review* 186 (Winter 2005): 3n11; Louis Fisher, *Military Tribunals and Presidential Power* (Lawrence: University Press of Kansas, 2005), 117, 121–24.

97. Article 18 of the UCMJ allows general courts-martial jurisdiction to "try any person who by the law of war is subject to trial by a military tribunal and may adjudge any punishment permitted by the law of war." Article 21 of the UCMJ states, "The provisions of this chapter conferring jurisdiction upon courts-martial do not deprive military commissions, provost courts, or other military tribunals of concurrent jurisdiction with respect to offenders or offenses that by statute or by the law of war may be tried by military commissions, provost courts, or other military tribunals."

98. Jordan Memorandum, 2, 7. A leading contemporary authority on the historical role of military commissions and tribunals regards the terms *commission* and *tribunal* as interchangeable in this context. Fisher, *Military Tribunals and Presidential Power,* xiii. See also Eugene R. Fidell, Dwight H. Sullivan, and Detlev F. Vagts, "Military Commission Law," *Army Lawyer* (December 2005), 49n22; L. K. Underhill, "Jurisdiction of Military Tribunals in the United States Over Civilians," *California Law Review* 12 (January 1924).

99. Article I, § 8, cl. 10, 14, 16. Gibson argues to the contrary: "Constitutionally, tribunals do not have the same legitimacy as courts-martial. Tribunals are formed under the President's authority as Commander-in-Chief. Courts-martial are formed under Congress's express Article I power to regulate the military *and* conducted pursuant to rules promulgated by the President under his authority as Commander-in-Chief. Because the President and Congress act together to form courts-martial, courts-martial have greater constitutional validity than tribunals." Susan S. Gibson, "Lack of Extraterritorial Jurisdiction Over Civilians: A New Look at an Old Problem," *Military Law Review* 148 (1995): 140n168. The distinction is invalid if one accepts Jordan's point that Congress authorized the convening of military tribunals and commissions by enacting Article 21 of the UCMJ.

100. As well as the constitutional barriers to the prosecution of civilians, there might conceivably have been objections that a military commission would have deprived the former servicemen of procedural protections afforded by the UCMJ and the Manual for Courts-Martial; however, consistent with the uniformity requirements set out in Article 36 of the UCMJ, the commissions could have been set up, so far as was practicable, in conformity with court-martial procedures. See Everett and Silliman, "Forums for Punishing Offenses against the Law of Nations," 518.

101. Jordan Memorandum, 7.

102. Ibid. Paust expresses doubts on this point, as he says that the Supreme Court restricted the attempted application of the UCMJ to civilians "only in connection with laws based upon the congressional power to regulate the armed forces [Article I, § 8, cl. 14 of the Constitution] and on the general jurisdictional sections of the U.C.M.J." The restriction, according to this theory, did not apply to the constitutional authority to define and punish offenses against the law of nations. Jordan J. Paust, "After My Lai: The Case for War Crime Jurisdiction over Civilians in Federal District Courts," *Texas Law Review* 50 (1971–72): 13–14.

103. Graham, "Government Lawyers."

104. Graham, "Army Lawyers." Jordan had argued this point in his memorandum, which lends weight to the theory that he or an associate acting in concert with him was briefing the press. Jordan Memorandum, 2. Jordan J. Paust, in an article published after the government's announcement of its abandonment of the plan to prosecute the My Lai veteran suspects, recommends initiating a trial against the veteran suspects in federal district court. Paust, "After My Lai," 13.

105. *O'Callahan v. Parker,* 395 U.S. 258 (1969).

106. 395 U.S., at 267.

107. Gibson, "Lack of Extraterritorial Jurisdiction Over Civilians," 177–78. See also Robinson O. Everett, "*O'Callahan v. Parker*—Milestone or Millstone in Military Justice?" *Duke Law Journal* 18 (October 1969): 867.

108. Although Jordan did not address this point, in *O'Callahan,* the court departed from the *Covert* line of cases in which the test for jurisdiction had been the military or nonmilitary status of the accused. Albert N. Cavagnaro, "Notes: *Solorio v. United States:* A Return to the Unrestrained Subject Matter Jurisdiction of Military Courts," *North Carolina Law Review* 66 (1987–88): 1026. Paust, however, places *O'Callahan* in the line of cases starting with *Toth,* in which the Supreme Court had imposed restrictions on court-martial jurisdiction. Paust, "After My Lai," 14.

109. Jordan Memorandum, 7. It is a matter of curiosity that in oral arguments before the court, the appellant's advocate, Victor Rabinowitz, had in places used a concept of "interest" close to the one on which Jordan relies. Oral Argument of Victor F. Rabinowitz, Esq., on Behalf of Petitioner, Supreme Court of the United States, October Term, 1968, Docket No. 646, In the Matter of James F. O'Callahan, Petitioner, vs. J. J. Parker, Respondent, 11, 12–13, EW, box 134, folder: Supreme Court File, Argument Transcripts, No. 646, O'Callahan v. Parker.

110. *O'Callahan v. Parker,* 395 U.S., at 267, and n. 14. In these passages "military interest" clearly signifies some discernable relationship between the crime and military activities.

111. Jordan Memorandum, 7.

112. The view that in *O'Callahan* "military interest" means service-connectedness is uncontroversial and has been ever since the court handed down its ruling. See, for example, "Military Law—Military Jurisdiction over Crimes Committed by Military Personnel Outside the United States: The Effect of *O'Callahan v. Parker,*" *Michigan Law Review* 68 (1969–70): 1021. The precise boundaries around the concept have needed specification, though. The Supreme Court attempted to clarify and define *service-connected* in *Relford v. Commandant,* 401 U.S. 355 (1971). The United States Court of Appeals for the Fifth Circuit cites a number of cases that, following *O'Callahan,* turned on the concept of service-connectedness. *Cole v. Laird,* 468 F.2d 829 (1972), n. 4. As Vladeck argues, the boundaries of the service connection test proved quite difficult to locate precisely, leading to difficulties in judging marginal cases. Vladeck, "The Laws of War as a Constitutional Limit on Military Jurisdiction": 309–10. The armed services took a restricted view of *O'Callahan,* holding a wide range of crimes to be service-connected and finding that *O'Callahan* had no extraterritorial effect. Everett, "*O'Callahan v. Parker*—Milestone or Millstone?," 875–76. The Supreme Court overturned *O'Callahan* in *Solorio v. United States,* 483 U.S. 435 (1987), abandoning the service connection test.

113. A MACV directive defined a war crime as any violation of the law of war, and "grave breaches" as "the most serious type of war crime," such as "willful killing": "Examples of grave breaches are: willful killing; torture, or inhumane treatment, including biological experiments; willfully causing great suffering or serious injury to body or health; taking of hostages; and compelling a prisoner of war to serve in the forces of the hostile power." Headquarters, United States Military Assistance Command, Vietnam, "Directive Number 20-4," "Inspections and Investigations–War Crimes," July 10, 1970, RG 319, VWCWG, MLM, box 6, folder: Hebert Subcommittee Investigation of My Lai Incident 1970. The My Lai massacre certainly fits the definition of willful killing. For the prohibition of war crimes and investigative procedures, see also "An Analysis of the Evolution of MACV Rules of Engagement Pertaining to Ground Operations, 1965–69," 20–23, RG 319, PI–CI, box 7, folder: Conduct of the War in Vietnam Chron File # 4 [2 of 2].

114. Paust reaches a very different conclusion, arguing that "it would be unforgivable to intentionally initiate prosecution likely to be overturned on appeal and thus shift to the Court any guilt resulting from failure of the United States to carry out its international obligations." Paust, "After My Lai," 33–34.

115. Jordan Memorandum, 8; Graham, "Government Lawyers."

116. Nelson, *War Behind Me,* 152.

117. For example, Sherman, "Songmy 2," and Graham, "Government Lawyers."

118. Hersh, *My Lai 4,* 162.

119. Arman Derfner to Office of the Provost Marshall General, Department of the Army, January 16, 1970; Col. John S. Holeman, Jr., chief, Security and Investigation Division, to Derfner, February 19, 1970. NA, RG 319, ODCSPER, VWCWG, MLM, box 7, folder: Public Correspondence—My Lai [Part 2].

120. "Civilian Prosecution/My Lai," a question-and-answer sheet adjacent to Buchanan, Memorandum for the President, RE: My Lai Incident, December 5, 1969, NA, NPM, NSCF, Alexander M. Haig Special File, box 1004, folder: 7 My Lai Incident (1 of 2). An annotation, "(Justice)," may indicate the department assigned to take the lead in the matter. The president underlined and annotated the proposed responses about his own knowledge of the atrocity and the call for a civilian commission. See the copy of the memorandum in NA, NPM, WHSF, SMOF, President's Office Files, President's Handwriting, box 4, folder 1, President's Handwriting December 1 thru 15, 1969.

121. "Army Submits Plan for Massacre Trials," *Baltimore Sun,* December 8, 1969.

122. "Slayers of Civilians Will Be Tried: Laird," *Columbus Enquirer,* December 15, 1969.

123. Lt. Col. [Matthew B.] O'Donnell, Office of the Judge Advocate General, Talking Paper, Subject: Military Justice Matters—Developments in Case of Alleged Murders of Vietnamese Civilians at My Lai, Vietnam, Since Talking Paper of 9 January 1970, January 16, 1970, § 6, "Status of Study of Jurisdiction over Former Servicemen," 2, NA, RG 319, ODCSPER, VWCWG, MLM, box 1, folder: TJAG Talking Papers, Jan 1970–June 1971.

124. "Son My (My Lai) Incident," January 14, 1972, approved by Maj. Gen. George S. Prugh, Action Officer Capt. G. R. Campbell, 3, NA, RG 319, ODCSPER, VWCWG, MLM, box 6, folder: Congressional Backup Sheets—My Lai Case 1970–1972, 1. Prugh had succeeded Hodson as the judge advocate general of the army on July 1, 1971.

125. O'Donnell, Talking Paper, January 16, 1970, 2.

126. "Son My (My Lai) Incident," January 14, 1972, 3.

127. "Discussion of Jurisdiction over Former Army Members Who May Have Committed Offenses at My Lai," n.d., NA, RG 319, ODCSPER, VWCWG, MLM, box 7, folder: Congressional Correspondence—My Lai: Hebert Subcommittee Investigation. It is difficult to pin down the date of this document, although the content suggests it followed the discussion between the judge advocate general and Jordan. The date of creation of documents in the same folder ranged from December 1969 to February 1971, the date of the adjacent letter.

128. In addition to previously cited news articles, see also "26 Are Probed on Massacre," *Atlanta Constitution,* November 22, 1969; "The Legal Dilemmas," *Time,* December 5, 1969, 32; "Biased 'Juries,'" *Wall Street Journal,* December 8, 1969; "The Killings at Son My," *Newsweek,* December 8, 1969, 36.

129. Rose M. D'Apolito, "My Lai: Jurisdiction over the Guilty Civilians," *New England Law Review* 6 (1970): 105.

130. Testimony of Gen. William C. Westmoreland, U.S. Congress, House, 91st Cong., 2nd Sess., Committee on Armed Services, Hearings of the Armed Services Investigating Subcommittee, June 10, 1970: "Investigation of the My Lai Incident," 851–52.

5. A "Tragedy of Major Proportions"

1. See, e.g., Raymond T. Reid, Office of the Secretary of the Army, to Ervin, November 12, 1969; Reid to Ervin, November 21, 1969; with attachments. SJE, folder 7918, My Lai, Vietnam, Lt. Wm L. Calley.

2. Ervin to Sen. Abraham Ribicoff, December 5, 1969, SJE, folder 8554: J[udiciary] C[ommittee], Constitutional Rights Subcommittee, Correspondence Files 1969.

3. Despite the nominal date of Westmoreland's and Resor's memorandum to Peers, Resor announced the creation of the Peers Inquiry on November 24, the same day Rivers announced the launch of the House subcommittee investigation. Richard Homan, "Trial Set in Viet Killings," *Washington Post,* November 25, 1969.

4. The Peers Inquiry was independent of the CID investigation, but they operated cooperatively, whereas both were often at cross-purposes with the House Armed Services Subcommittee.

5. Mark D. Carson, "F. Edward Hébert and the Congressional Investigation of the My Lai Massacre," *Louisiana History: The Journal of the Louisiana Historical Association* 37 (Winter 1996): 67.

6. Michal R. Belknap, *The Vietnam War on Trial: The My Lai Massacre and the Court-Martial of Lieutenant Calley* (Lawrence: University Press of Kansas, 2002), 138.

7. Michael Bilton and Kevin Sim, *Four Hours in My Lai: A War Crime and Its Aftermath* (New York: Penguin, 1992), 292.

8. "Rivers Differs with Nixon on Songmy," *NYT,* December 10, 1969.

9. Bryce N. Harlow, White House Congressional Liaison, Memorandum for the President, Thru Dr. Henry Kissinger, Subject: My Lai Atrocities, December 3, 1969, NA, NPM, NSCF, Alexander M. Haig Special File, box 1004, folder 8: My Lai Incident (2 of 2); "Senator Wants 'Outside' Probe," *Columbus Enquirer,* December 8, 1969.

10. See, for example, "Former Diplomats Call for War-Conduct Probe," *Seattle Times,* December 4, 1969; Al Haig, Memorandum for Henry A. Kissinger, Subject: My Lai Atrocities, December 4, 1969, NA, NPM, NSCF, Alexander M. Haig Special File, box 1004, folder 8: My Lai Incident (2 of 2); Patrick J. Buchanan, Memorandum for the President, RE: My Lai Incident, December 5, 1969, 2: NA, NPM, NSCF, Alexander M. Haig Special File, box 1004, folder 7: My Lai Incident (1 of 2); Dr. Carl Kaysen et al., Telegram to the President, Attn. Henry Kissinger, December 6, 1969, and the draft response, Henry A. Kissinger, Memorandum for the President, Subject: Telegram on the My Lai Incident, December 15, 1969, NA, NPM, NSCF, Alexander M. Haig Special File, box 1004, folder 9, Possible My Lai Commission; and the question by Hearst newspapers' J. William Theis, Richard Nixon, "The President's News Conference," December 8, 1969, APP, www.presidency.ucsb.edu/ws/?pid=2365.

11. Manuscript annotation in Nixon's hand, "News Summary, December 1, 1969," "News Summary, December 3, 1969," NA, NPM, WHSF, SMOF, President's Office Files, Annotated News Summaries, box 31, folder: December 1969.

12. Kendrick Oliver, *The My Lai Massacre in American History and Memory* (Manchester: Manchester University Press, 2006), 221.

13. Peers, Memorandum for the Secretary of the Army and Chief of Staff of the Army, January 21, 1970; Richard Hammer, *One Morning in the War* (London: Rupert Hart-Davis, 1970), 6, 193.

14. Al Haig, Memorandum for Henry A. Kissinger, Subject: Vietnam Atrocity Stories, December 4, 1969. See also the same query from the president in John R. Brown, Memorandum for Dr. Kissinger, December 2, 1969, NA, NPM, NSCF, Alexander M. Haig Special File, box 1004, folder 9: Possible My Lai Commission; and Nixon's manuscript annotation, "Does

Defense expect more of these exposés?" "Digest of Recent News Reports," November 29, 1969, NA, NPM, WHSF, SMOF, President's Office Files, Annotated News Summaries, box 31, folder: November 1969.

15. Kissinger, manuscript annotation to Haig to Kissinger, December 4, 1969.

16. Henry A. Kissinger, Memorandum for the President, December 4, 1969, NA, NPM, NSCF, Alexander M. Haig Special File, box 1004, folder 8: My Lai Incident (2 of 2).

17. Melvin Laird, Memorandum for Henry A. Kissinger, Subject: Vietnam Atrocity Stories, December 11, 1969, NA, NPM, NSCF, Vietnam Subject Files, box 118, folder: Lt. Calley Case (1 of 2).

18. W. C. Westmoreland and Stanley Resor, Memorandum for Lt. Gen. William R. Peers, Subject: Addendum to Directive for Investigation, n.d. [January 1970]; W. R. Peers, Memorandum for Secretary of the Army [Resor], Chief of Staff U.S. Army [Westmoreland], Subject: Scope of Investigation, January 21, 1970. NA, RG 319, PI–CI, box 5, folder: LTG Peers Notes # 5, House Invest Subcomm [5]. Bernd Greiner, *War without Fronts: The USA in Vietnam* (London: Bodley Head, 2009), 312.

19. W. C. Westmoreland and Stanley R. Resor, Memorandum for Lieutenant General William R. Peers, n.d. [December 10, 1969], NA, RG 319, PI–CI box 5, folder: LTG Peers Notes # 3 House Invest[igating] Subcommittee [5]; Bilton and Sim, *Four Hours in My Lai,* 290; "Chronology of Key Events and Congressional Notification: Son My Incident," NA, RG 319, PI–AC, box 12, folder: Index.

20. Fred P. Graham, "Government Lawyers Who Seek a War Crimes Tribunal Tread Softly on Constitutional Ground," *NYT,* November 30, 1969. See also "Vietnam Probe Widens: 26 Implicated in Massacre Investigation," *Washington Post,* November 22, 1969; Bill Neikirk, "Probe of 'Massacre' Touches Additional 24," *Columbus [Georgia] Ledger,* November 22, 1969. Calley was charged with murder and other offenses just before the date of his discharge, after which he remained in the army before and during his trial by court-martial. Richard Hammer, *The Court-Martial of Lt. Calley* (New York: Coward, McCann, and Geoghagen, 1971), 30–34.

21. Graham, "Government Lawyers."

22. Greiner, *War without Fronts,* 310.

23. "Chronology of Key Events and Congressional Notification."

24. Article 43, UCMJ. There is no statute of limitations for murder in the UCMJ.

25. Stanley R. Resor, Memorandum to the Secretary of Defense, March 5, 1970, OSD; W. R. Peers, *The My Lai Inquiry* (New York: Norton, 1979), 214, 217; Belknap, *Vietnam War on Trial,* 127.

26. The words were spoken by the commanding officer of a marine corporal who was not charged following an incident in Fallujah in which he killed an unarmed insurgent. The Iraqi man had been lying for an entire day on the floor of a mosque with other wounded and dying fighters. "Secret Iraq," BBC2 (UK television broadcast), October 12, 2010.

27. See the description of the sections published on March 17, 1970, in Seymour Hersh, *Cover-Up: The Army's Secret Investigation of the Massacre at My Lai 4* (New York: Vintage Books, 1973), 247. The sections correspond to chapters 3, 4, and 9 in United States, Department of the Army, *Report of the Department of the Army Review of the Preliminary Investigations into the My Lai Incident,* vol. 1, *The Report of the Investigation* (Washington, D.C.: Department of the Army, March 14, 1970). The White House spokesman Ron Ziegler, the secretary of defense, the secretary of state, the secretary of the army, and the president all stated that the massacre was "an isolated case" in violation of American policy and contrary to military orders. Maj. Gen. Edward Bautz, MACV Assistant Chief of Staff for Opera-

tions, Confidential Message, For PSYOP [Psychological Operations] Single Managers and Advisory Elements, Subject: Song My/My Lai Incident, December 19, 1969, NA, RG 319, PI–OI, box 3, folder: MACV Directives [4]. For Resor's view that the massacre at My Lai was "almost certainly a unique and isolated event," see, e.g., Resor to Max Singer, President, Hudson Institute, January 9, 1970, NA, RG 319, ODCSPER, VWCWG, MLM, box 1, folder: My Lai Army Staff Monitor Summaries, January 1970. In this letter Resor repeated the encomium to U.S. troops' "decency, consideration, and restraint" which he had made in his statements to the Senate and the House in November 1969.

28. Greiner, *War without Fronts,* 320–23; Hersh, *Cover-Up,* 6.

29. William Beecher, "Army Inquiry Charges Fourteen Officers in Suppression of Songmy Facts; West Point Head, Accused, Quits," *NYT,* March 18, 1970; Hersh, *Cover-Up,* 6.

30. Beecher, "Army Inquiry Charges Fourteen Officers."

31. Belknap, *Vietnam War on Trial,* 67–68; Statement of PFC Pendleton, TPI, Book 26, 14.

32. Solis states that, unusually for prosecutions of American defendants, Willingham and Kotouc were initially charged with violations of the law of war, although the specifications of the charges were otherwise worded as ordinary UCMJ offenses. Gary D. Solis, "Military Justice, Civilian Clemency: The Sentences of Marine Corps War Crimes in South Vietnam," *Transnational Law and Contemporary Problems* 10 (2000): 65n33.

33. Resor, Memorandum for the Secretary of Defense, March 5, 1970, 3. As Peers discloses, some of the investigations were conducted by staff judge advocates, not independent Article 32 investigating officers. Peers, *The My Lai Inquiry,* 222.

34. "Telcon, Nixon/Kissinger," March 17, 1970, 8:07 p.m., National Security Archive, www.gwu.edu/~nsarchiv/NSAEBB/NSAEBB123/telcon-19700317.pdf.

35. For the dates of the charges, see William Thomas Allison, *My Lai: An American Atrocity in the Vietnam War* (Baltimore: Johns Hopkins University Press, 2012), 91.

36. George C. Wilson and Richard Homan, "Pilot's Story Leaves Rivers Uncertain on Viet Massacre," *Washington Post,* December 11, 1969; Muriel Dobbin, "Rivers Denies My Lai Talk," *Baltimore Sun,* December 12, 1969. For an example of Rivers's leaks from the closed hearings, see "Prejudging My Lai," *Chicago Tribune,* December 12, 1969.

37. "Rivers Names Panel to Investigate My Lai," *Washington Post,* December 13, 1969; Muriel Dobbin, "Rivers Seeks 'Whole Truth' from Panel Probing My Lai," *Baltimore Sun,* December 20, 1969; "Rivers Differs with Nixon on Songmy"; Carson, "F. Edward Hébert and the Congressional Investigation of the My Lai Massacre," 67–68; Allison, *My Lai,* 89. For the circumstances leading to the "face saving" solution of the select panel, see Hersh, *My Lai 4,* 168–69.

38. "Rivers Opens Study of Vietnam Policy," *NYT,* August 2, 1967. The hearings ran parallel to the better-publicized ones in the Senate called by Stennis, another Southern Democrat, which also criticized the Johnson administration for its failure to take decisive military action in Vietnam. U. S. G. Sharp, *Strategy for Defeat: Vietnam in Retrospect* (Novato, Calif.: Presidio Press, 1998), 190–98.

39. Walter Rugaber, "Defender of the Military," *NYT,* December 20, 1969.

40. Rugaber, "Defender of the Military."

41. King, "Creed of a Congressman"; Rugaber, "Defender of the Military"; Richard Halloran, "Advocate of the Military: Felix Edward Hébert," *NYT,* October 17, 1970.

42. "F. Edward Hébert, Ex-Lawmaker, Dies," *NYT,* December 30, 1979.

43. Carson, "F. Edward Hébert and the Congressional Investigation of the My Lai Massacre," 63.

44. Larry L. King, "Creed of a Congressman," *NYT,* February 21, 1971.

45. Carson, "F. Edward Hébert and the Congressional Investigation of the My Lai Massacre," 64.

46. King, "Creed of a Congressman."

47. Rugaber, "Defender of the Military."

48. Carson, "F. Edward Hébert and the Congressional Investigation of the My Lai Massacre," 68.

49. Hersh, *Cover-Up,* 7.

50. Actually, the effort had begun with S. 2791 in 1956, but the staff of the Constitutional Rights Subcommittee had lost track of that starting date. The same mistake, identifying 1957 as the year the relevant legislation was first introduced, appears in the subcommittee's press release announcing the introduction of S. 3188. "Ervin Introduces Bill to Permit Federal District Court Trials of Former Servicemen," December 1, 1969.

51. Muriel Dobbin, "My Lai Revives Legal Issue," *Baltimore Sun,* April 26, 1970. Brooke had tended to vote with Senate doves from 1967 onward. "Vietnam Voting Record of Senator Edward W. Brooke," EB, box 497, folder: Vietnam EWB Position, and Statements, Undated. For Nixon's contrasting attitudes to conservative Democrats and to liberal Republicans like Brooke, see John Ehrlichman, *Witness to Power: The Nixon Years* (New York: Simon and Schuster, 1982), 202.

52. U.S. Congress, House, 92nd Cong., 2nd Sess., Committee on Armed Services, *Investigation of the My Lai Incident: Report of the Armed Services Investigating Subcommittee of the Committee on Armed Services,* July 15, 1970 (Washington, D.C.: GPO, 1970) [hereafter *My Lai Investigating Subcommittee Report*], 4.

53. "Discussion of Jurisdiction over Former Army Members Who May Have Committed Offenses at My Lai," NA, RG 319, ODCSPER, VWCWG, MLM, box 7, folder: Congressional Correspondence—My Lai: Hebert Subcommittee Investigation.

54. *My Lai Investigating Subcommittee Report,* 7.

55. L. Mendel Rivers to Melvin Laird, July 16, 1970, NA, RG 319, VWCWG, MLM box 6, folder: Hebert Subcommittee Investigation of My Lai Incident 1970. According to a Department of the Army memorandum, Rivers wrote an identical letter the same day to Secretary of the Army Resor. Roy H. Steele, chief, Investigations Division, Office of the Secretary of the Army, Memorandum for Deputy Secretary of the General Staff Coordination and Reports, August 4, 1970, NA, RG 319, VWCWG, MLM box 6, folder: Hebert Subcommittee Investigation of My Lai Incident 1970.

56. "Discussion of Recommendations Contained in the Report of the My Lai Incident Subcommittee of the House Armed Services Committee Dated July 15, 1970," and responses of service secretaries to Department of Defense requests for comments, OSD.

57. For Hébert's account of the army's attempt to pressure him, see Carson, "F. Edward Hébert and the Congressional Investigation of the My Lai Massacre," 70.

58. Ibid., 78.

59. Ibid., 71.

60. *My Lai Investigating Subcommittee Report,* 47–48.

61. Laird to Rivers, July 17, 1970, RG 319, VWCWG, MLM, box 6, folder: Hebert Subcommittee Investigation of My Lai Incident 1970.

62. L. Niederlehner, Acting General Counsel, Department of Defense, to L. Mendel Rivers, July 17, 1970, H.R. 4225 bill file; Niederlehner to James O. Eastland, Chairman, Senate Judiciary Committee, July 24, 1970, in NA, RG 46, 91st Congress, Senate Judiciary Committee, box 40, folder S. 3188 [hereafter S. 3188 bill file].

63. Acting Department of Defense General Counsel Niederlehner provided the draft bills

in enclosures accompanying the Department of Defense reports on H.R. 4225 and S. 3188. H.R. 4225 and S. 3188 bill files.

64. H.R. 18857, Mr. Bennett, August 10, 1970. "To amend title 18, United States Code, to subject certain nationals or citizens of the United States to the jurisdiction of the United States district courts for their crimes committed outside the United States." The bill replaced H.R. 18548, which had been introduced at the same time as H.R. 18547.

65. H.R. 18547, Mr. Bennett, July 21, 1970. "To amend title 10, United States Code, to provide for the apprehension, restraint, removal, and delivery of certain persons serving with, employed by, or accompanying the armed forces outside the United States, and for other purposes."

66. J. Fred Buzhardt, general counsel, Department of Defense, to Emanuel Celler, Chairman, House Committee on the Judiciary, September 11, 1970, H.R. 4225 bill file. See also the narrative of the Defense Department's involvement with the legislation in U.S. Congress, House, 95th Cong., 1st Sess., Committee on the Judiciary, Hearing before the Subcommittee on Immigration, Citizenship, and International Law on H.R. 763, H.R. 6148, and H.R. 7842, "Extraterritorial Criminal Jurisdiction," July 21, 1977, 52.

67. Buzhardt to Celler, September 11, 1970.

68. U.S. House of Representatives, Committee on Armed Services, 91st Congress, *Executive Calendar; Final Calendar* (Washington, D.C.: GPO, 1971), 41, 123. See also the correspondence between Rivers and Bennett in NA, RG 233, Committee on the Armed Services, 91st Congress, Legislative Files, House Bills H.R. 18037 to H.R. 19051, folder H.R. 18547.

69. H. G. Torbert, Jr., Acting Assistant Secretary of State for Congressional Relations, to James O. Eastland, December 16, 1969, S. 3188 bill file; U.S. Congress, *Committee on the Judiciary, United States Senate, Legislative and Executive Calendar, 91st Congress, [Final Edition]*, 267.

70. *CIS Five-Year Cumulative Index, 1970–1974* (Washington, D.C.: Congressional Information Service, 1975).

71. Lawrence P. Rockwood, *Walking Away from Nuremberg* (Amherst: University of Massachusetts Press, 2007), 117.

72. NA, RG 319, ODCSPER, VWCWG, War Crimes Allegations Case Summaries, box 1, [hereafter Vietnam War Crimes Case Summaries], folder: War Crimes Allegations, Part 2 of 3, Case 112. "Cases Monitored by the Office of the Judge Advocate General Relating to War Crimes Allegations Other than Son My (As of 20 May 1971)," document attached to Maj. General Kenneth J. Hodson, Judge Advocate General of the Army, to John W. Dean III, May 21, 1971, NA, RG 319, ODCSPER, VWCWG, MLM, box 6, folder: Correspondence—Office of the Judge Advocate General: War Crimes Allegations, 1971–72. The "Cases Monitored" list also summarizes cases 39, 147, and 150 (see below) as well as case 112.

73. Vietnam War Crimes Case Summaries, folder: War Crimes Allegations, Part 2 of 3, Case 124.

74. Vietnam War Crimes Case Summaries, folder: War Crimes Allegations, Part 2 of 3, Case 147.

75. Vietnam War Crimes Case Summaries, folder: War Crimes Allegations, Part 2 of 3, Case 150.

76. War Crimes Allegations Case Summaries, folder: War Crimes Allegations, Part 1 of 3, Case 39.

77. Hersh, *Cover-up*, 239.

78. Solis, "Military Justice, Civilian Clemency," 64, 75–77, 79, 81. For further instances of leniency, see Greiner, *War without Fronts*, 324.

79. As noted in chapter 4, note 62, by February 1970 the army counted twenty-two suspects who were no longer in uniform, and that number is reflected in a draft of Westmoreland's statement to the House subcommittee. By the time Westmoreland appeared before the subcommittee, the count of veteran suspects he cited, according to the published record, had crept up to twenty-five. His statement had been updated to reflect recent developments, such as the dropping of charges against one officer shortly before his appearance. The number of suspects he cited may reflect such new developments but is not supported by other near-contemporaneous documents. Testimony of Gen. William C. Westmoreland, U.S. Congress, House, 91st Cong., 2nd Sess., Committee on Armed Services, Hearings of the Armed Services Investigating Subcommittee, June 10, 1970: "Investigation of the My Lai Incident," 833, 851. By July 1970 the number of veterans listed as being investigated by the CID was said to be twenty-one. This was the number of cases in which the evidence was regarded as sufficiently strong for prosecution by a military commission. "Son My Investigation," July 17, 1970, OSD.

6. "Inexcusable and Terrible"

1. Memorandum for the President, November 10, 1969, NA, NPM, WHSF, SMOF, President's Office Files, President's Handwriting, box 3, President's Handwriting November 1 thru 15, 1969.

2. Raymond K. Price, Jr., Memorandum for the President RE: The Election and After, November 13, 1970, 2, 6. NA, NPM, WHSF, SMOF, President's Office Files, President's Handwriting, box 8, folder 1 [November 1970].

3. William Safire, Memorandum for the President RE: Approaches to 1972, November 11, 1970, 2. NA, NPM, WHSF, SMOF, President's Office Files, President's Handwriting, box 8, folder 1 [November 1970].

4. Robert Dallek, *Nixon and Kissinger: Partners in Power* (London: Penguin Books, 2008), 185.

5. Ibid., 186; William M. Hammond, *Reporting Vietnam: Media and Military at War* (Lawrence: University Press of Kansas, 1998), 191; Henry A. Kissinger, Memorandum for the President, Subject: My Lai Incident, December 4, 1969, NA, NPM, NSCF, Alexander M. Haig Special File, box 1004, folder 8: My Lai Incident (2 of 2).

6. "Dan" [Captain Dan Murphy], Office of the Secretary of Defense, Memorandum for General Haig Regarding "Points Made by Our General Counsel," December 4[, 1969], NA, NPM, NSCF, Alexander M. Haig Special File, box 1004, folder 8: My Lai Incident (2 of 2).

7. Richard Nixon, "The President's News Conference," December 8, 1969, APP, www.presidency.ucsb.edu/ws/?pid=2365. The answer had been prepared in a set of Q. and A.'s by Pat Buchanan. Pat Buchanan, Memorandum for Dr. Kissinger, December 5, 1969, NA, NPM, NSCF, Alexander M. Haig Special File, box 1004, folder 7: My Lai Incident (1 of 2).

8. James Keogh, Memorandum for the Staff Secretary, December 24, 1969, NA, NPM, WHSF, SMOF, President's Office Files, President's Handwriting, box 4, folder 2: President's Handwriting December 16, 1969–December 31, 1969; "Nixon's Rating with Public Reaches New High," *Sindlinger's Wednesday Report* 842-W46, December 3, 1969; Richard Reeves, *President Nixon: Alone in the White House* (New York: Simon and Schuster, 2001), 154.

9. Kendrick Oliver, *The My Lai Massacre in American History and Memory* (Manchester: Manchester University Press, 2006), 105.

10. "Subject: Discreet Interview of Ronald Lee Ridenhour on December 4, 1969 at Cla-

remont College, California," NA, NPM, WHSF, SMOF, President's Office Files, President's Handwriting, box 4, folder 2: President's Handwriting December 16, 1969–December 31, 1969.

11. John R. Brown III, Memorandum for Alex Butterfield, December 19, 1969, NA, NPM, WHSF, WHCF, Subject Files: Confidential Files, 1969–1974, box 41, folder: ND 8-5 Military Courts/Courts Martial [1969–70]. Butterfield, the aide who saw Nixon more frequently than any other save Haldeman, later disclosed the existence of the White House tape-recording system. James Rosen, *The Strong Man: John Mitchell and the Secrets of Watergate* (New York: Doubleday, 2008), 349.

12. Robert E. Jordan III, Memorandum for the Record, Subject: Meeting with Mr. Ronald Ridenhour, February 2, 1970, OSD.

13. Seymour Hersh, "My Lai 4: A Report on the Massacre and Its Aftermath," *Harper's* (May 1970).

14. The Random House edition appeared first and the Vintage Books edition appeared in September 1970.

15. Maj. Gen. Winant Sidle, Army General Staff Chief of Information, Memorandum for Chief of Staff [Westmoreland], Subject: Followup Actions on the Peers Report, July 16, 1971; Wesley G. Pippert, UPI [United Press International news agency], teletype article describing the first of two planned articles by Seymour Hersh in the *New Yorker*, n.d.; Sidle, Memorandum for Secretary of the General Staff, Subject: Follow-Up Actions on the Peers Report, August 2, 1971. NA, RG 319, PI–AC, box 39, folder: Son My Chron File # 20 [2 of 2]. SGS [Secretary of the General Staff], Office Memorandum for General Westmoreland, Subject: Seymour Hersh's Comments on Son My, February 7, 1972, with attached transcripts of Hersh's appearances on *CBS Morning News*, January 19, 1972, and NBC's *Today Show*, January 31, 1972, NA, RG 319, PI–AC, box 39, folder: My Lai Chron File # 22 [1 of 3].

16. Lt. Col. Jared B. Schopper, Department of the Army, Office of the Chief of Staff, Memorandum for the Record, Subject: Followup Actions on the Peers Report, July 8, 1971. RG 319, PI–AC, box 38, folder: Son My Chron File # 19 [2 of 2].

17. Schopper, Memorandum for the Record, Subject: Followup Actions on the Peers Report, July 8, 1971.

18. Sidle, Memorandum for Chief of Staff, July 16, 1971.

19. Maj. Gen. Warren K. Bennett, Acting Secretary of the Army General Staff, Memorandum for Chief of Military History, April 27, 1970, NA, RG 319, PI–AC, box 38, folder: Son My Chron # 19 [1 of 2].

20. Office of the Chief of Military History, Summary Sheet for Deputy Chief of Staff for Operations, Chief of Staff, and Secretary of the Army, Subject: Harper's Magazine Article "My Lai 4," May 1, 1970, NA, RG 319, PI–AC, box 38, folder: Son My Chron # 19 [1 of 2].

21. "Status of Cases as of 28 February 1971," NA, RG 319, VWCWG, MLM, box 1, folder: TJAG My Lai Talking Papers, Jan 1970–June 1971; "My Lai Chronology," in *The My Lai Massacre and Its Cover-Up: Beyond the Reach of Law? The Peers Commission Report with a Supplement and Introductory Essay on the Limits of Law,* ed. Joseph Goldstein, Burke Marshall, and Jack Schwartz (New York: Free Press, 1976), ix.

22. SGS, Office Memorandum to General Westmoreland Thru General Palmer, July 26, 1971.

23. Michal Belknap, *The Vietnam War on Trial: The My Lai Massacre and the Court-Martial of Lieutenant Calley* (Lawrence: University Press of Kansas, 2002), 227.

24. "The Army Position," n.d., NA, RG 319, ODCSPER, VWCWG, MLM, box 6, folder: Congressional Back up Sheets – My Lai Case 1970–1972.

25. "Army's Position," n.d., NA, RG 319, ODCSPER, VWCWG, MLM, box 1, folder: TJAG Talking Papers, July 1971–July 1972.

26. "Chronology of Key Events and Congressional Notification." The target dates for delivering volumes 2 and 3 of the report of the investigation to the printer were April 30, 1970, and April 10, 1970, respectively. Lt. Col. Charles J. Bauer, executive officer, Peers Inquiry, Memorandum for Secretary of the General Staff, attn. Lt. Col. Schopper, subject: Status of Operations, Peers Inquiry, April 1, 1970, 1, LHC 8/16.

27. Stanley R. Resor, Memorandum to the Secretary of Defense, March 5, 1970, 3, OSD.

28. Goldstein et al., *The My Lai Massacre and Its Cover-Up,* 167.

29. "Status of Congressional Actions" in Lt. Col. Andrew Mansinne, Army Staff Monitor Section, "Son My Army Staff Monitor Summary of Activities—Week Ending 17 April 1970," April 18, 1970, NA, RG 319, ODCSPER, VWCWG, MLM, box 1, folder: My Lai Army Staff Monitor Summaries Feb–May 1970.

30. Ken Cole, Memorandum for General Hughes, August 27, 1970, NA, NPM, WHCF, Subject Files, National Security—Defense (ND), box 70, folder: Gen ND 8-5, Military Courts and Courts Martial, Begin 12/31/72. Brig. Gen. James D. Hughes was a military aide to Nixon.

31. The Jencks Act, Pub. L. No. 85-269 (September 2, 1957); 18 U.S.C. 3500. Section (b) of the statute requires the United States, on the motion of the defendant, to produce any statement that the witness in a trial has given which is in its possession and that pertains to the subject matter of the witness's trial testimony. Section (d) provides that, if the United States fails to produce such a statement, the court may strike the witness testimony or declare a mistrial. The army was aware of this possibility when the Hébert subcommittee asked it to allow witnesses on active duty to testify at its hearings and deferred furnishing them until the court-martial proceedings in which they might be witnesses were concluded. Stanley R. Resor, Secretary of the Army, to F. Edward Hébert, January 6, 1970, NA, RG 319, ODCSPER, VWCWG, MLM, folder: My Lai Army Staff Monitor Summaries, January 1970.

32. Belknap, *Vietnam War on Trial,* 224.

33. Richard Hammer, *The Court-Martial of Lt. Calley* (New York: Coward, McCann, and Geoghagen, 1971), 41.

34. Ibid., 42.

35. Ibid.

36. Michael Bilton and Kevin Sim, *Four Hours in My Lai: A War Crime and Its Aftermath* (New York: Penguin, 1992), 330; "Status of Cases as of 30 May 1971," 8, NA, RG 319, ODCSPER, VWCWG, MLM, box 1, folder: TJAG My Lai Talking Papers, Jan 1970–June 1971.

37. See, for example, Mario Fernandez, TPI, Book 18 [hereafter Fernandez, Peers Inquiry Testimony].

38. SGS [Secretary of the General Staff], Office Memorandum to General Westmoreland Thru General Palmer, Subject: Followup Actions on the Peers Report, July 26, 1971, NA, RG 319, PI–AC, box 39, folder: Son My Chron File # 20 [2 of 2].

39. Goldstein et al., *The My Lai Massacre and Its Cover-Up,* 174.

40. Robert D. Holmes, CID Witness Statement, February 11, 1970, RG 319, PI–AC, box 46, folder: Son My—Suspects [2 of 3].

41. Mario Jesus Fernandez, CID Witness Statement, April 8, 1970, NA, RG 319, PI–AC, box 46, folder: Son My—Suspects [2 of 3].

42. Maj. Gen. Kenneth J. Hodson, Summary Sheet, Subject: Administrative Review of Son My Cases, April 26, 1971, NA, RG 319, ODCSPER, VWCWG, MLM, box 1, folder: Administrative Review—My Lai Cases [Part 1 of 4].

43. Raymond E. Miller and Roland W. Thompson, Criminal Investigators, CID Report of Investigation, April 23, 1971, NA, RG 319, PI–AC, box 46, folder: Son My—Suspects [2 of 3]. As early as April 1970 the army had established that a charge of murder against the veteran was "founded." CIDA [Army Criminal Investigation Division], "Son My Village: Status of Investigation," October 2, 1970, entry regarding Donald Hooton, ROI 70-00049, completed April 23, 1970, 8/33, LHC. For a discussion of the actions of 1st Platoon's point team, see Mark J. Taylor, "The Massacre at My Khe 4: A Different Story" (Ph.D. diss., University of Hull, England, 2010), 33, 43–44.

44. Kenneth J. Hodson, Summary Sheet, Subject: Administrative Review of Son My Cases, April 26, 1971.

45. W. R. Peers, *The My Lai Inquiry* (New York: Norton, 1979), 222.

46. Taylor, "The Massacre at My Khe 4," 12.

47. For a description of the Bravo Company platoons' actions, see Peers, *The My Lai Inquiry,* 186–92. The only platoon in Task Force Barker that came into close contact with civilians and did not massacre them was Bravo Company's 3rd Platoon. Ibid., 188.

48. "Summary of the New Yorker Article by Seymour Hersh," January 26, 1970, NA, RG 319, ODCSPER, VWCWG, MLM, box 6, folder: Congressional Back Up Sheets—My Lai Case 1970–1972.

49. "Status of Cases as of 28 February 1971."

50. Hammer, *Court Martial of Lt. Calley,* 42–43.

51. Belknap, *Vietnam War on Trial,* 233.

52. Maj. Gen. Franklin M. Davis, Director of Military Personnel Policies, "Request for Flagging Action," February 4, 1971; William Anderson, "'Flag' Army Files of Mylai Figures," *Chicago Tribune,* February 11, 1971, article transcribed via teletype, stamped "From CINFO" [Department of the Army, Chief of Information]. NA, RG 319, ODCSPER, VWCWG, MLM, box 1, folder: Flagging Actions—Personnel Involved in My Lai Incident; Lt. Col. King M. Goffman, Memorandum for the Record, Subject: Administrative Review of Son My Cases, June 2, 1971, NA, RG 319, ODCSPER, VWCWG, MLM, box 1, folder: Administrative Actions—My Lai Cases. No administrative action was taken against Captain Willingham or Staff Sergeant Mitchell, and their cases were closed.

53. "Son My (My Lai) Incident," January 14, 1972, 3; "Son My," July 12, 1972, 3.

54. "Charge: Violation of the Uniform Code of Military Justice, Article 118, Specifications 1–4, Additional Charge, Specifications 1–2," charge sheet attached to Department of the Army, Office of the Secretary of the Army, Information for Members of Congress, November 24, 1969, SJE, box 179, folder 7918, My Lai, Vietnam, Lt. Wm. L. Calley; Hersh, *My Lai 4,* 180.

55. "Status of Cases as of 28 February 1971," 1–3; "Status of Cases as of 21 March 1971," 2, NA, NPM, WHSF, SMOF, John W. Dean III Subject File, box 15, folder: My Lai Cases—General (Calley).

56. "Status of Cases as of 28 February 1971," 4.

57. Reeves, *President Nixon,* 307.

58. Jeffrey Kimball, *Nixon's Vietnam War* (Lawrence: University Press of Kansas, 1998), 251.

59. Lawrence R. Jacobs and Robert Y. Shapiro, "The Rise of Presidential Polling: The Nixon White House in Historical Perspective," *Public Opinion Quarterly* 59 (Summer 1995): 166–67.

60. Questions R4 and R5, Opinion Research Corporation, telephone survey of national adult samples conducted April 1, 1971. Data provided by RC.

61. H. R. Haldeman, *The Haldeman Diaries: Inside the Nixon White House* (New York: Berkley Books, 1995), 321–22; "April 2, 1971, Telephone Conversation with Sec. Laird" (transcript); "April 2, 1971[,] Telephone Conversation with Sec. Rogers" (transcript). NA, NPM, WHSF, SMOF, John D. Ehrlichman, box 16, folder: Calley.

62. "Calley Prosecutor Asserts Nixon Undermines Justice," *NYT,* April 7, 1971; Belknap, *Vietnam War on Trial,* 203–6.

63. Reeves, *President Nixon,* 307.

64. Eric J. Fygi, Memorandum for the Honorable John W. Dean III, Counsel to the President, RE: Presidential Actions in the General Court-Martial Case of United States v. Calley, April 6, 1971, NA, NPM, NSCF, Vietnam Subject Files, box 118, folder: Lt. Calley Case (1 of 2); John Dean, *Blind Ambition: The White House Years* (New York: Simon and Schuster, 1976), 44.

65. Questions R8, R9, and R10, Opinion Research Corporation, telephone survey of national adult sample conducted April 5–6, 1971. Data provided by RC.

66. Dick Cook, Memorandum to John Ehrlichman, Subject: Calley Report, April 7, 1971, NA, NPM, NSCF, Vietnam Subject Files, box 118, folder: Lt. Calley Case (1 of 2).

67. Bilton and Sim, *Four Hours in My Lai,* 340. By mid-May 1971 the number had settled at about sixty to one against the verdict and sentence. "Calley Mail," n.d., NA, NPM, WHSF, SMOF, John W. Dean III Subject File, folder: Calley Correspondence. The date can be inferred from the surrounding correspondence and from the number of items received, a total of just over 312,000 letters and telegrams, of which close to 4,900 approved the verdict and sentence, the remainder disapproving. Other tallies of the correspondence establish that this number was reached around the second week of May.

68. Kennedy to Nixon, March 31, 1971, NA, NPM, WHCF, Subject Files, 1969–74, National Security—Defense (ND), Gen ND 8/Calley, 5/1/71–5/3/71, box 13, folder 2: Gen ND8/Calley 5/4/71.

69. Small to Nixon, received April 7, 1971, NA, NPM, WHCF, Subject Files, 1969–74, National Security—Defense (ND), Gen ND 8/B, box 11, folder 7: Ex ND8/Calley, Begin 4/20/71.

70. Breidenstein to Nixon, received April 29, 1971, NA, NPM, WHCF, Subject Files, 1969–74, National Security—Defense (ND), Gen ND 8/Calley, 5/1/71–5/3/71, box 13, folder 2: Gen ND 8/Calley 5/4/71.

71. "Court Martial Echoes," *Oklahoma City Times,* April 2, 1971.

72. "Calley Correspondence as of 7th May 1971," NA, RG 319, PI–AC, box 38, folder: Son My Chron File # 18 [1 of 2].

73. Editorial, *Providence Journal,* April 6, 1971, *Editorials on File* 2, January 1–15, 1971, 411.

74. Brig. Gen. DeWitt C. Smith, Acting Chief of Information, "The Issue of Civilian Casualties in Southeast Asia: Initial Thoughts," April 13, 1971, RG 319, PI–AC, box 6, folder: Conduct of the War in Vietnam, Chron File # 2 [2 of 2].

75. Louis Harris and Associates survey of a national adult sample conducted April 1971. Data provided by RC.

76. Haldeman, *The Haldeman Diaries,* 324.

77. Rick Perlstein, *Nixonland: The Rise of a President and the Fracturing of America* (New York: Scribner, 2008), 556.

78. Richard Nixon, *RN: The Memoirs of Richard Nixon* (London: Book Club Associates, 1978), 513.

79. John Dean, Memorandum for John Ehrlichman, Bud Krogh, Al Haig, April 15, 1971, with attachment "Game Plan—My Lai Cases," NA, NPM, NSCF, Vietnam Subject Files, box

118, folder: Lt. Calley Case (1 of 2). The working group consisted of John Ehrlichman, Alexander Haig, John Dean, and Egil "Bud" Krogh. John D. Ehrlichman, Memorandum for Dr. Kissinger, April 15, 1971, NA, NPM, NSCF, Vietnam Subject Files, box 118, folder: Lt. Calley Case (1 of 2).

80. John Dean, Memorandum for White House Staff, Subject: White House Comments on Calley and Related Cases, April 9, 1971, NA, NPM, WHCF, Subject Files, 1969–74, National Security—Defense (ND), Gen ND 8/B, box 10, folder 10: Ex ND8/Calley, 4/1/71–4/25/71.

81. Bud Krogh, Memorandum for John Dean, August 16, 1971, NA, NPM, WHCF, Subject Files, 1969–74, National Security—Defense (ND), Gen ND 8/B, box 10, folder 14: Ex ND8/Calley, 6/1/71–12/31/72.

82. Peers, *The My Lai Inquiry,* 253–54.

83. Dana Adams Schmidt, "U.S. Drops Efforts to Try Ex-G.I.'s Over My Lai," *NYT,* April 9, 1971; William Chapman, "Pentagon Can't Find Way to Prosecute Former Servicemen," *Washington Post,* April 9, 1971. There is no explanation for the discrepancy between the number of veterans the announcement said were immune from prosecution and the twenty-one against whom the secretary of defense had been told there were prosecutable cases in July 1970.

84. Chapman, "Pentagon Can't Find a Way to Prosecute Former Servicemen."

85. "Status of Cases as of 30 May 1971," § 6, "Jurisdiction over Former Servicemen," 10.

86. "Son My (My Lai) Incident," January 14, 1972, Approved by Maj. Gen. George S. Prugh, Action Officer Capt. G. R. Campbell, 3, NA, RG 319, ODCSPER, VWCWG, MLM, box 6, folder: Congressional Backup Sheets—My Lai Case 1970–1972, 1.

87. Deborah Nelson, *The War Behind Me: Vietnam Veterans Confront the Truth about U.S. War Crimes* (New York: Basic Books, 2008), 152. In an e-mail message to me of April 27, 2011, R. Kenly Webster, the Department of Defense deputy general counsel at the time, confirmed that Jordan was the one handling the matter: "The General Counsel at the time, Robert E. Jordan, handled the matter involving the possible trial of discharged or retired military personnel, and I do not recall being significantly involved. I do recall that correspondence was directed on this matter to the Office of Legal Counsel, Department of Justice, then headed by to-be Chief Justice Rehnquist."

88. The disposition of the relevant documents makes it difficult to establish how much additional paper traffic there was on the matter. Jordan's documents from the period were supposedly accidentally destroyed when he submitted them for declassification. Nelson, *War Behind Me,* 151. I was unable to locate the relevant papers of Attorney General Mitchell and those of Assistant Attorney General Rehnquist in the National Archives. They appear not to have been deposited there or in the Richard Nixon Presidential Library. The seemingly promising series of boxes in NA, RG 46 described as "Senate Committee on Constitutional Rights Correspondence Relating to Military Justice, 1957–1972" yielded nothing related to the jurisdictional matters covered in this book, even though Ervin's well-organized collection in North Carolina demonstrates that he and his staff were meticulous record keepers, and the dates closely match the efforts by Ervin and Hennings to close the jurisdictional gap. The army records in the National Archives are insufficiently well described to allow a systematic search for relevant materials from the army general counsel's office. The efforts of Glen R. Asner, senior historian in the Historical Office, Office of the Secretary of Defense, and the staff involved in the declassification of the materials yielded a number of useful documents from that office.

89. Chapman, "Pentagon Can't Find Way to Prosecute Former Servicemen."

90. Peers, *The My Lai Inquiry,* 190; Fernandez, Peers Inquiry Testimony, 22. Taylor's examination of the CID records indicates that Peers undercounts 1st Platoon, which consisted of twenty-seven men. Taylor, "The Massacre at My Khe 4," 32n94.

91. Peers, *The My Lai Inquiry,* 192.

92. Only Donald Hooton, one of the four members of the point element, identifiable from the Peers Inquiry testimony of other members of Bravo Company, is named in "Son My Investigation—Civilian Suspects," with the notation that the charge was "founded." Another member of Bravo Company is listed but is not included among the twenty-two civilian suspects, as the evidence against him was said to be inconclusive.

93. Peers, *The My Lai Inquiry,* 185. Peers does not name them, but, for example, one former soldier who had limited recall was Peter Bretenstein, a forward observer for Bravo Company's weapons platoon who was attached to 1st Platoon when it entered My Khe (4). He reported seeing three or four bodies there, although, given the substantially larger number that Willingham reported were killed, the Peers Inquiry interrogators were understandably skeptical about that claim. Peter Bretenstein, TPI, Book 18, 25; Henry Cardines, a squad leader in the weapons squad of Bravo Company's 1st Platoon, remembered even less, to the extent that his interrogator asked if he was trying to protect someone. Henry Cardines, TPI, Book 18, 23.

94. SGS, Office Memorandum to General Westmoreland Thru General Palmer, July 26, 1971, 2.

95. Col. Jared B. Schopper, Memorandum for the Record, Subject: Followup Actions on the Peers Report, July 3, 1971, NA, RG 319, PI–AC, box 38, folder: Son My Chron File # 19 [2 of 2]. The memorandum records the discussion at a conference Westmoreland held on July 2, 1971, with Lt. Gen. Walter T. Kerwin, deputy chief of staff for personnel, Maj. Gen. Harold E. Parker, deputy judge advocate general, and Brig. Gen. DeWitt C. Smith, deputy chief of information.

96. Manuscript check mark at the end of the July 26, 1971, General Staff memorandum, alongside the typed entry "VCSA [Vice Chief of Staff of the Army]: Concur in SS [Summary Sheet] Approval: With Annotation"; see also Lt. Col. Tenho R. Hukkala, Asst. Secretary of the General Staff, document headed, "Approved—COFS [Chief of Staff] US Army (As Revised)," July 28, 1971; George S. Prugh, Summary Sheet JAGJ 1969/8751, Subject: Followup Action on the Peers Report, July 23, 1971. NA, RG 319, PI–AC, box 39, folder: Son My Chron File # 20 [2 of 2].

97. Manuscript check mark at the end of the July 26, 1971, General Staff memorandum. The manuscript word "shortened" was inserted to make the wording of the approval "With *Shortened* Annotation." A line was drawn through the typed page just above the quoted passage, with the manuscript annotation, "CSA [Chief of Staff, Army]—Recomm[end] ending annotation at this point."

98. Winant Sidle, Memorandum for the Secretary of the General Staff, Subject: Follow-Up Actions on the Peers Report, August 2, 1971, 2, NA, RG 319, PI–AC, box 39, folder: Son My Chron File # 20 [2 of 2].

99. Col. Robert C. Kingston, Deputy General Secretary of the General Staff (Coordination and Reports), Referral Slip, Subject: Seymour Hersh's Article (*New Yorker* Magazine, 22 Jan 1972), January 20, 1972; Memorandum for ADCSPER [Assistant Deputy Chief of Staff for Personnel], Subject: Seymour Hersh Article in the *New Yorker,* Purpose: To Obtain ODCSPER [Office of the Deputy Chief of Staff for Personnel] Coordination on a DAJA Talking Paper on Subject, n.d. [approved January 21, 1972]; Col. Clausen, "Talking Paper," Subject: "Coverup–1," the Seymour Hersh Article in *The New Yorker,* 22 January, 1972, Con-

cerning Son My, January 22, 1972; Col. Clausen, "Talking Paper," Subject: "Coverup," the Seymour Hersh Articles in *The New Yorker,* Concerning Son My, January 29, 1972, stamped "Noted: Maj. Gen. S. Prugh"; "Army's Position," n.d., with manuscript corrections and annotations; "Army's Position [incorporating corrections]," n.d. NA, RG 319, ODCSPER, VWCWG, MLM, box 1, folder: TJAG Talking Papers, July 1971–July 1972.

100. Telford Taylor, "The Course of Military Justice," *NYT,* February 2, 1972.

101. Taylor, "The Course of Military Justice." The clipping is preserved in NA, NPM, WHSF, SMOF, John W. Dean III Subject File, box 14, folder: Calley—Later Developments.

102. SGS, Memorandum for General [Bruce] Palmer, Army Vice Chief of Staff, February 4, 1972, Subject: *New York Times* Article, "The Course of Military Justice" by Telford Taylor (2 Feb 72), February 2, 1972; [Jared B.] Schopper, Message to Col. Kingston, Subject: Telford Taylor's Article "The Course of Military Justice," February 5, 1972. NA, RG 319, PI–AC, box 39, folder: Son My Chron File # 22 [1 of 3].

103. Maj. Gen. Harold E. Parker, Acting the Judge Advocate General, "Consideration of DCSOPS Comments and Tab C," February 7, 1972, NA, RG 319, PI–AC, box 39, folder: Son My Chron File # 22 [1 of 3].

104. John Dean, Memorandum, Subject: Analysis of and Recommendations Regarding War Crimes Cases, Discussion Draft, May 14, 1971, 24. NA, NPM, NSCF, Vietnam Subject Files, box 118, folder: Lt. Calley Case (1 of 2). The document is also preserved in NA, NPM, WHSF, SMOF, John D. Ehrlichman, box 16, folder: Calley.

105. Dean, *Blind Ambition,* 40.

106. Richard Nixon, Memorandum for the Secretary of the Army, Subject: General Court-Martial Case, United States vs. Calley, May 3, 1974; J. Fred Buzhardt, Memorandum for the President, Subject: Review of United States vs. Calley, May 3, 1974. NA, NPM, WHCF, Subject Files, 1969–74, National Security—Defense (ND), Gen ND 8/B, folder 15: EX ND8/C, 1/1/73–8/9/74.

107. Belknap, *Vietnam War on Trial,* 251.

108. Rep. Samuel S. Stratton to Robert F. Froehlke, Secretary of the Army, February 8, 1972, NA, RG 319, ODCSPER, VWCWG, MLM, box 7, folder: Congressional Correspondence—My Lai: Correspondence with Rep. Samuel S. Stratton.

109. Aspin filed his suit under the Freedom of Information Act on April 3, 1972. "Son My," July 12, 1972, 3, NA, RG 319, ODCSPER, VWCWG, MLM, box 1, folder: TJAG My Lai Talking Papers July 1971–July 1972, 3. Volumes 1 and 3 of the Peers Inquiry report, the main body and documentation, were eventually released in November 1974; Volumes 2 and 4, the testimony and CID statements, were released the following March. Peers, *The My Lai Inquiry,* 244.

110. Hersh writes that two teams reviewed the report when it was first released: lawyers from the army's general counsel's office and "another group of officers," whose role and affiliation he does not disclose. Seymour Hersh, *Cover-Up: The Army's Secret Investigation of the Massacre at My Lai 4* (New York: Vintage Books, 1973), 247.

111. In contrast, several constituents had written to Ervin when he was in the midst of proposing the bill that would become the Military Justice Act of 1968, demonstrating that what was lacking in 1971 was not knowledge of the subcommittee's role but interest in the legislative issue. For the relevant correspondence, see SJE, folder 6689, JC, Constitutional Rights Subcommittee, Correspondence Files 1967.

112. "ABC News Special: The Calley Case: A Nation's Agony," May 23, 1971, transcript, 2, 12. Transcript in SJE, folder 10064, Correspondence Files 1971, ASC, Calley Incident.

113. "Status of Cases as of 30 May 1971," 2.

114. Robinson O. Everett says that Senator Ervin "repeatedly proposed legislation to fill some of [the] jurisdictional voids." Prepared Statement of Hon. Robinson O. Everett, Professor of Law, Duke University School of Law, and Senior Judge, U.S. Court of Appeals for the Armed Forces, U.S. Congress, House, 104th Cong., 2nd Sess., Committee on the Judiciary, *Hearing before the Subcommittee on Immigration and Claims of the Committee on the Judiciary on H.R. 2587, War Crimes Act of 1995,* June 12, 1995, 22.

115. Ervin to Mr. and Mrs. Elliott I. Petterson, March 31, 1971, SJE, folder 10065, Correspondence Files 1971, ASC, Calley Incident.

116. Ervin to Collins Wyatt, Fletcher, North Carolina, April 9, 1971, SJE, folder 10065, Correspondence Files 1971, ASC, Calley Incident.

117. Edgar Abernethy, Stanley, North Carolina, to Ervin, April 13, 1971, SJE, folder 10065, Correspondence Files 1971, ASC, Calley Incident. See also Joseph A. Morris to Ervin, April 16, 1971; and Walter R. Guild to Ervin, April 15, 1971. SHE, SJE, folder 10064, Correspondence Files 1971, ASC, Calley Incident.

118. Natalie Hevener Kaufman, *Human Rights Treaties and the Senate: A History of Opposition* (Chapel Hill: University of North Carolina Press, 1990), 183–85, 190; Karl E. Campbell, *Senator Sam Ervin, Last of the Founding Fathers* (Chapel Hill: University of North Carolina Press, 2007), 296.

119. S. 1744, "To provide for compliance with constitutional requirements in the trials of persons who are charged with having committed certain offenses while subject to trial by court-martial, who have not been tried for such offenses, and who are not longer subject to trial by court-martial." S. 1745, "To provide for compliance with constitutional requirements in the trials of persons who, while serving as employees of the United States or while accompanying the Armed Forces, commit certain offenses outside the United States." *Congressional Record—Senate,* May 3, 1971, S 6040–41.

120. For a brief account of the problem of fraud, theft, black marketeering, and customs evasion in the military exchange system, crimes which led to the loss of millions of dollars, see George S. Prugh, *Vietnam Studies: Law at War, Vietnam 1964–1973* (Washington, D.C.: Department of the Army, 1975), 93–94.

121. *Congressional Record—Senate,* May 3, 1971, S 6041. "PX" is an abbreviation for post exchange, a type of military exchange store.

122. Ervin refers to *Calder v. Bull,* 3 Dall. 386, 390 (1798).

123. Ervin refers to *Cook v. United States* 139 U.S. 157 (1891); that unanimous decision in turn relies on *Gut v. The State,* 76 U.S. (9 Wall) 35, 38 (1869).

124. *Congressional Record—Senate,* May 3, 1971, S 6041. See also the discussion in Charles W. Corddry, "Jurisdiction to Try Discharged Servicemen for Violations of the Laws of War," *JAG Journal* 26 (Fall 1971): 72–75.

125. *United States Senate, Committee on the Judiciary, Legislative and Executive Calendar, 92nd Congress,* June 30, 1972, 121; RG 46, 92nd Congress, Judiciary Committee, box 16, Judiciary Committee Bill Files, folders 794 and 795: S. 1744 and S. 1745.

126. Judge José A. Cabranes stated in his opinion for the United States Court of Appeals for the Second Circuit that year after year "a Subcommittee of the Senate Armed Services Committee conducted annual hearings on the operation of Article VII of the NATO Status of Forces Treaty." He cited testimony at hearings in 1966 and 1972. "In almost every one of these hearings, the Subcommittee discussed the jurisdictional gap." *United States v. Gatlin,* 216 F.3d 207 (2nd Cir. 2000), nn. 17, 22.

127. Arthur John Keeffe, "Practicing Lawyers' Guide to the Current Law Magazines," *American Bar Association Journal* 53 (October 1967): 961–62, in CEB, box 14, 1967, folder 1

of 2. Following these judgments, in any particular prosecution it still had to be determined whether a civilian suspect had a sufficiently close relationship with the armed forces to justify the judgment that he or she was "accompanying" them "in the field," as set out in the provisions of the UCMJ's Article 2(a)(10).

128. Waldemar A. Solf, Department of the Army, Military Justice Division, Memorandum for the Judge Advocate General, November 2, 1966, reproduced in U.S. Congress, House, 90th Cong., 1st Sess., Committee on the Judiciary, *Report of Special Subcommittee on Application of the Uniform Code of Military Justice to American Civilians in the Republic of Vietnam,* June 1967, 3. The Supreme Court decisions of 1957 and 1960 had established that the UCMJ did not apply to civilians accompanying the armed forces *in time of peace* and therefore demanded a decision whether the conflict in Vietnam counted as a war within the meaning of the UCMJ.

129. *United States v. Anderson,* 17 U.S.C.M.A. 588, 38 C.M.R. 386 (1968). Mary L. Dudziak, "Law, War, and the History of Time," University of Southern California Legal Studies Working Paper 27 (2009): 1686n77. See also Dudziak, *War Time: An Idea, Its History, Its Consequences* (New York: Oxford University Press, 2012), 37. The issue was that under Article 43 of the UCMJ there was no statute of limitations for desertion "in time of war." In *Broussard v. Patton,* 466 F.2d 816 (1972), which also dealt with the issue of the statute of limitations in a desertion case, the United States Court of Appeals for the Ninth Circuit followed the Court of Military Appeals in *Anderson* and the Air Force Court of Military Review in *United States v. Broussard,* 41 C.M.R. 1004 (1970) in determining that "time of war" applied to the Vietnam War following the Tonkin Gulf Resolution.

130. Robert E. Jordan III, Memorandum for the Assistant Attorney General (Office of Legal Counsel) on Trial of Discharged Servicemen for Violation of the Law of War, December 2, 1969, 5, EA.

131. *United States v. Averette,* 19 U.S.C.M.A. 363, 41 C.M.R. 363 (1970). The Court of Military Appeals ruled that the designation "in time of war" did not apply to the situation of a civilian contractor stationed at Long Binh, Vietnam, who had attempted to steal thousands of batteries owned by the U.S. government and that charges against the defendant had to be dismissed. See also Comptroller General of the United States, *Report to Congress: Some Criminal Offenses Committed Overseas by DoD Civilians Are Not Being Prosecuted: Legislation Is Needed,* September 11, 1979, 17, http://archive.gao.gov/f0302/110369.pdf, which refers to S. 1437, 95th Cong., a bill designed to close the jurisdictional gap opened up by *Covert* and *Averette.*

132. The last congressional declaration of war was against Romania on June 5, 1942. Jennifer K. Elsea and Richard F. Grimmett, *Declarations of War and Authorizations of the Use of Military Force: Historical Background and Legal Implications,* CRS Report, March 17, 2011, 1, 2n 3, www.fas.org/sgp/crs/natsec/RL31133.pdf.

133. "With the sentences of courts martial which have been convened regularly and have proceeded legally, and by which punishments are directed, not forbidden by law, or which are according to the laws and customs of the sea civil courts have nothing to do, nor are they in any way alterable by them." *Dynes v. Hoover,* 61 U.S. 65 (1857), at 82. See also the discussion of Chief Justice Vinson's opinion in *Burns v. Wilson,* 346 U.S. 137 (1953), at 140–42, in chapter 1, above; testimony of Eugene R. Fidell, U.S. Congress, Senate, 110th Cong., 2nd Sess., Committee on Foreign Relations, Subcommittee on International Operations and Organizations, Democracy and Human Rights, Hearing on "Closing Legal Loopholes: Prosecuting Sexual Assaults and Other Violent Crimes Committed Overseas by American Civilians in a Combat Environment," April 9, 2008, 26–31; and James J. Slattery Jr., "Federal

Court Review of Decisions of Military Tribunals," *University of Cincinnati Law Review* 40 (1971): 569–91.

134. Congress gave the Supreme Court the power to grant a writ of certiorari over decisions of the Court of Appeals for the Armed Forces through the Military Justice Act of 1983, Pub. L. No. 98-209, § 10, 97 Stat. 1393. Brian C. Baldrate, "The Supreme Court's Role in Defining the Jurisdiction of Military Tribunals: A Study, Critique, and Proposal for *Hamdan v. Rumsfeld*," *Military Law Review* 186 (Winter 2005): 17.

135. A month after *Averette,* and applying the same principle, in *Zamora v. Woodson* 19 U.S.C.M.A. 403, 42 C.M.R. 5 (1970) the Court of Military Appeals reversed the conviction of another civilian tried pursuant to Article 2(a)(10) of the UCMJ, which provided for the prosecution of civilians accompanying the armed forces in time of war. On the same grounds, the Court of Military Review overturned the conviction of a civilian who had murdered three soldiers in *United States v. Grossman,* 42 C.M.R. 529 (A.C.M.R. 1970). A federal court confirmed that "time of war" did not apply to the Vietnam War in *Robb v. United States,* 456 F.2d 768 (Ct. Cl. 1972). "Report of the U.S. Court of Military Appeals," *AR January 1, 1970 to December 31, 1971,* 7.

136. Prugh, *Law at War: Vietnam,* 110.

137. Lawrence J. Schwarz, "The Case for Court-Martial Jurisdiction over Civilians under Article 2 of the Uniform Code of Military Justice," *Army Lawyer* (October–November 2002): 34; Charles W. Boohar Jr., "Military Law—Persons Subject to the Uniform Code of Military Justice," *William and Mary Law Review* 12 (1970): 450n20.

138. See Susan S. Gibson, "Lack of Extraterritorial Jurisdiction Over Civilians: A New Look at an Old Problem," *Military Law Review* 148 (1995): 132, for the line of cases the *Averette* court invoked, including *Covert, O'Callahan,* and *Latney v. Ignatius,* 416 F. 2d 821 (1969).

139. The *Averette* precedent stood until 2006, when the National Defense Authorization Act for Fiscal Year 2007 authorized courts-martial to prosecute civilians serving with or accompanying the armed forces during contingency operations as well as conflicts following a declaration of war (see chapter 7, below).

7. "Why Can't We Just Shoot Them All?"

1. U.S.C. Title 10, Chapter 47, § 802, Article 2 "Persons Subject to this Chapter," 2(10), "In time of declared war or a contingency operation, persons serving with or accompanying an armed force in the field."

2. There is also an argument to be made that, while the United States was the occupying power in Iraq, courts-martial could prosecute civilians under the holding in *Madsen v. Kinsella,* 343 U.S. 341 (1952). This concept was not put to the test. Jennifer K. Elsea, Moshe Schwartz, and Kennon K. Nakamura, *Private Security Contractors in Iraq: Background, Legal Status, and Other Issues,* CRS Report, August 25, 2008, 28, www.fas.org/sgp/crs/natsec/RL32419.pdf.

3. Matthew Dahl, "'Runaway Train': Controlling Crimes Committed by Private Contractors through Application of the Uniform Code of Military Justice," *Barry Law Review* 14 (2010): 64; Katherin J. Chapman, "Notes: The Untouchables: Private Military Contractors' Criminal Accountability under the UCMJ," *Vanderbilt Law Review* 63 (2010): 1065.

4. John F. O'Connor, "Contractors and Courts-Martial," *Tennessee Law Review* 77 (2009–10): 796; Dahl, "Runaway Train," 69.

5. Among the relevant legislative proposals are H.R. 103, 93rd Cong., 1st Sess. (1973); S. 1, 94th Cong., 1st Sess. (1975); H.R. 763, 95th Cong., 1st Sess. (1977); H.R. 255, 99th Cong., 1st

Sess. (1985); S. 147, 101st Cong., 1st Sess. (1989); H.R. 5808, 102nd Cong., 2nd Sess. (1992), and S. 2083, 104th Cong., 2nd Sess. (1996). Over a dozen other legislative proposals to fill the gap affecting nonveteran civilians are cited in *United States v. Gatlin,* 216 F.3d 207 (2nd Cir. 2000), n. 23. See also Susan S. Gibson, "Lack of Extraterritorial Jurisdiction Over Civilians: A New Look at an Old Problem," *Military Law Review* 148 (1995): 115n2.

6. H.R. 763, "To subject certain nationals or citizens of the United States to the jurisdiction of the United States district courts for their crimes committed outside the United States and to provide for the apprehension, restraint, removal, and delivery of such persons," introduced by Bennett on January 4, 1977, and referred to the House Judiciary Committee's Subcommittee on Immigration, Citizenship, and International Law.

7. Bennett testified that the Departments of Defense, State, and Justice and the administrative office of the U.S. courts submitted favorable reports to H.R. 107 introduced in the 93rd Congress, which was similar to the proposal that came from the Defense Department in 1970. The bill failed to pass, and no reports were received in response to identical legislation in the 94th Congress. The Departments of Defense, State, and Justice all testified in favor of identical successor legislation, H.R. 763, in the 95th Congress. U.S. Congress, House, 95th Cong., 1st Sess., Committee on the Judiciary, Hearing before the Subcommittee on Immigration, Citizenship, and International Law on H.R. 763, H.R. 6148, and H.R. 7842, "Extraterritorial Criminal Jurisdiction," July 21, 1977 [hereafter 1977 Hearing on Extraterritorial Criminal Jurisdiction], 27–28, 33–34, 43–44, 52, 64–65; Eugene R. Fidell, "Criminal Prosecution of Civilian Contractors by Military Courts," *South Texas Law Review* 50 (2008–9): 850.

8. 1977 Hearing on Extraterritorial Criminal Jurisdiction, 50.

9. "Memorandum on Legislation (H.R. 763 and H.R. 6148) Relating to Extraterritorial Criminal Jurisdiction," n.d., 1; Benjamin Forman, Department of Defense, Office of General Counsel, to Joshua Eilberg, chairman, House Subcommittee on Immigration, Citizenship, and International Law, May 26, 1978. NA, RG 233, 95th Cong., Judiciary Committee, Legislative Files, box 11, H.R. 733–H.R. 896 [hereafter H.R. 763 bill file].

10. James E. Macklin Jr., chief, Criminal Justice Division, to Arthur P. Enders Jr., Subcommittee on Immigration, Citizenship, and International Law, August 1, 1977, H.R. 763 bill file.

11. Comptroller General of the United States, *Report to the Congress of the United States: Some Criminal Offenses Committed Overseas by DoD Civilians Are Not Being Prosecuted: Legislation Is Needed,* Report No. FPCD 79-45, September 11, 1979, 1, 4, http://archive.gao.gov/f0302/110369.pdf.

12. George S. Prugh, *Vietnam Studies: Law at War, Vietnam 1964–1973* (Washington, D.C.: Department of the Army, 1975), 110.

13. Comptroller General of the United States, *Report to Congress: Some Criminal Offenses Committed Overseas by DoD Civilians Are Not Being Prosecuted,* 19.

14. E. A. Gates and Gary V. Casida, "Report to the Judge Advocate General by the Wartime Legislation Team," *Military Law Review* 104 (1984): 147–49; Gibson, "Lack of Extraterritorial Jurisdiction Over Civilians," 137.

15. Gates and Casida, "Report to the Judge Advocate General," 148.

16. Dahl, "Runaway Train," 60.

17. U.S. Congress, Senate, 98th Cong., 1st Sess., Committee on Armed Services, Report No. 98-53 to Accompany S. 974, "The Military Justice Act of 1983," April 5, 1983; U.S. Congress, House, 98th Cong., 1st Sess., Committee on Armed Services, Report No. 98-549, to Accompany S. 974, "The Military Justice Act of 1983," November 15, 1983.

18. Fidell, "Criminal Prosecution of Civilian Contractors," 849. Fidell has also pointed out, however, that those convicted by a court-martial still have only a limited right to review

by the Supreme Court. "Separate Statement of Board Member Eugene Fidell," Defense Legal Policy Board, *Report of the Subcommittee on Military Justice in Combat Zones: Final Report,* May 30, 2013, www.caaflog.com/wp-content/uploads/20130531-Subcommittee-Report-REPORT-OF-THE-SUBCOMMITTEE-ON-MILITARY-JUSTICE-IN-COMBAT-ZONES-31-May-13-2.pdf, Appendix 6, 184. See also ibid., 132.

19. R. Peter Masterson, "Court-Martial Jurisdiction over Civilians in Contingency Operations: A New Twist," *New England Journal on Criminal and Civil Confinement* 35 (2009): 108.

20. O'Connor, "Contractors and Courts-Martial," 782.

21. "Military Justice Amendments of 1986," Pub. L. No. 99–661, November 14, 1986, 100 Stat. 3905, Title VIII, Uniform Code of Military Justice, § 804 "Court-Martial Jurisdiction over Reserve Members." I am grateful to J. T. Parker for drawing my attention to this statute.

22. S. 147, "To amend title 10, United States Code[,] to provide for jurisdiction, apprehension, and detention of members of the Armed Forces and certain civilians accompanying the Armed Forces, and for other purposes," introduced by Sen. Inouye and referred to the Committee on Armed Services, *Congressional Record—Senate,* January 25, 1989, S. 494.

23. S. 129, 103rd Cong., "To amend title 10, United States Code, to provide for jurisdiction, apprehension, and detention of members of the Armed Forces and certain civilians accompanying the Armed Forces outside the United States, and for other purposes," introduced by Sen. Inouye on January 21, 1993, and referred to the Committee on Armed Services; H.R. 4531, 103rd Cong., "To amend title 10, United States Code, to provide for jurisdiction, apprehension, and detention of certain civilians accompanying the Armed Forces outside the United States, and for other purposes," introduced by Rep. Thomas on May 26, 1994, and referred to the Committee on Armed Services.

24. Gibson, "Lack of Extraterritorial Jurisdiction Over Civilians," 137. The bills were S. 74, 104th Cong., 1st Sess. (1995), introduced by Sen. Inouye; S. 288, 104th Cong., 1st Sess. (1995), introduced by Sen. John McCain; H.R. 808, 104th Cong., 1st Sess. (1995), introduced by Rep. William M. Thomas.

25. H.R. 3680, introduced June 19, 1996, "To amend title 18, United States Code, to carry out the international obligations of the United States under the Geneva Conventions to provide criminal penalties for certain war crimes." Signed into law on August 21, 1996, enacted as Pub. L. No. 104-192, 110 Stat. 2104; 18 U.S.C. 2441 et seq. Title 18 of the U.S.C. was amended, with the addition of chapter 118—War Crimes. § 2401 defined the offense as follows: "Whoever, whether inside or outside the United States, commits a grave breach of the Geneva Conventions, in any of the circumstances described in subsection (b), shall be fined under this title or imprisoned for life or any term of years, or both, and if death results to the victim, shall also be subject to the penalty of death." The specified circumstances were that the person committing the breach or the victim of the breach must be a member of the U.S. armed forces or a national of the United States. In the original legislation, H.R. 2587, the statute would have applied only to crimes in which the victim, but not the perpetrator, was a member of the armed forces or a citizen of the United States.

26. U.S. Congress, House, 104th Cong., 2nd Sess., Report 104-698, "War Crimes Act of 1996," 7.

27. As of 2006 no one had been charged with an offense under the War Crimes Act. Michael John Garcia, *The War Crimes Act: Current Issues,* CRS Report, October 2, 2006, www.dtic.mil/dtic/tr/fulltext/u2/a458725.pdf; and John Sifton, "United States Military and Central Intelligence Agency Personnel Abroad: Plugging the Prosecutorial Gaps," *Harvard Journal on Legislation* 43 (2006): 501. Scheffer too records that the War Crimes Act was not

used to prosecute violations of Common Article 3 of the Geneva Conventions between 1997, when it was amended to cover such crimes, and 2006; and that as of 2009 there had been no prosecution under the statute as amended by the Military Commissions Act. David Scheffer, "Closing the Impunity Gap in U.S. Law," *Northwestern Journal of International Human Rights* 8 (Fall 2009): 46, 49. As far as I have been able to establish, this appears still to be true at the time of writing. The author's queries to the Defense, State, and Justice Departments as to whether any such prosecutions had taken place or were in their preliminary stages went unanswered. Examples include Hagopian, e-mail message to State Department Office of Global Criminal Justice, July 27, 2012; Hagopian, e-mail messages to Department of Justice, September 6, 2011, and July 27, 2012; Hagopian, e-mail message to Department of Defense Office of Public Communication, September 6, 2011. The authority on military law Eugene Fidell, in his e-mail response to my query on July 28, 2012, wrote that he was not aware of any such prosecutions under the War Crimes Act. E-mail messages in my possession. A search of relevant congressional testimony and other such documents has not disclosed any such prosecutions.

28. The 1956 Army Field Manual says, "The United States normally punishes war crimes as such only if they are committed by enemy nationals or by persons serving the interests of the enemy State. Violations of the law of war committed by persons subject to the military law of the United States will usually constitute violations of the Uniform Code of Military Justice and, if so, will be prosecuted under that Code." Article 507 (b), FM 27-10 Department of the Army Field Manual, "The Law of Land Warfare" (18 July 1956), 182, www.loc.gov/rr/frd/Military_Law/pdf/law_warfare-1956.pdf; see also Joseph Goldstein, Burke Marshall, and Jack Schwartz, *The My Lai Massacre and Its Cover-Up: Beyond the Reach of Law? The Peers Commission Report with a Supplement and Introductory Essay on the Limits of Law* (New York: Free Press, 1976), 457. The field manual is not a binding legal document, but this description of prosecutorial practices matches the politically determined policy regarding offenses by American personnel.

29. Robinson O. Everett, "American Servicemembers and the ICC," in *The United States and the International Criminal Court,* ed. Sarah B. Sewell and Carl Kaysen (Lanham, Md.: Rowman and Littlefield, 2000), 143–44. Pub. L. No. 105-118, 111 Stat. 2436, November 26, 1997.

30. U.S. Congress, House, 106th Cong., 2nd Sess., Judiciary Committee, H. Rept. 106-778, "Military Extraterritorial Jurisdiction Act of 2000," July 20, 2000, 5, 7.

31. Sifton, "United States Military and Central Intelligence Agency Personnel Abroad," 491, 502.

32. Comptroller General of the United States, *Report to the Congress of the United States: Some Criminal Offenses Committed Overseas by DoD Civilians Are Not Being Prosecuted: Legislation Is Needed,*, cited in Glenn R. Schmitt, "Closing the Gap in Criminal Jurisdiction Over Civilians Accompanying the Armed Forces Abroad—A First Person Account of the Creation of the Military Extraterritorial Jurisdiction Act of 2000," *Catholic Law Review* 55 (2001), 74n137; Rep. Saxby Chambliss, Remarks on Introducing the Military Extraterritorial Jurisdiction Act, *Extensions of Remarks—Congressional Record,* November 17, 1999, E2419.

33. Garcia, "The War Crimes Act: Current Issues," 5–8.

34. Laura A. Dickinson, *Outsourcing War and Peace: Preserving Public Values in a World of Privatized Foreign Affairs* (New Haven: Yale University Press, 2011), 32.

35. GAO, *DOD Force Mix Issues: Greater Reliance on Civilians in Support Roles Could Provide Significant Benefits* (Chapter Report, 10/19/94, GAO/NSIAD-95-5).

36. Dickinson, *Outsourcing War and Peace,* 34.

37. Matthew Dahl, "Soldiers of Fortune—Holding Private Security Contractors Accountable: The Alien Tort Claims Act and Its Potential Application to Abtan v. Blackwater USA" (June 2008), http://works.bepress.com/matthew_dahl/1, 2.

38. Chapman, "The Untouchables," 1055.

39. Dahl, "Runaway Train," 60; K. Elizabeth Waits, "Avoiding the 'Legal Bermuda Triangle': The Military Extraterritorial Jurisdiction Act's Unprecedented Expansion of U.S. Criminal Jurisdiction over Foreign Nationals," *Arizona Journal of International and Comparative Law* 23 (2005–6): 498. The GAO reports that over fourteen thousand civilians were deployed during the Persian Gulf War, although that number includes contractors as well as civilian employees. GAO, *DOD Force Mix Issues,* 3.1.

40. Gibson, "Lack of Extraterritorial Jurisdiction Over Civilians," 148.

41. H. Rept. 106-778, 6.

42. Dahl, "Runaway Train," 60.

43. Robert E. Reed, Associate Deputy General Counsel, Department of Defense, Prepared Statement, U.S. Congress, House, 106th Cong., 2nd Sess., Committee on the Judiciary, Hearing on H.R. 3380 before the Subcommittee on Crime, "Military Extraterritorial Jurisdiction Act of 1999," March 30, 2000 [hereafter MEJA Hearing], 13–14. The advisory committee was established according to the terms of Pub. L. No. 104-106, February 10, 1996, 110 Stat. 186, the National Defense Authorization Act for FY 1996, § 1151.

44. Dahl, "Runaway Train," 61.

45. H. Rept. 106-778, 9; Overseas Jurisdiction Advisory Committee, Report to the Secretary of Defense, the Attorney General, the Congress of the United States (1997), iv–vi, www.fas.org/irp/doddir/dod/ojac.pdf.

46. Office of the Inspector General, Department of Defense, *Criminal Investigative Policy & Oversight; Evaluation of Military Criminal Investigative Organizations' Investigative Effectiveness Regarding U.S. Forces Civilians Stationed Overseas,* Report No. 9950009I, September 7, 1999, www.dodig.mil/inspections/ipo/reports/9950009I.pdf.

47. In 1997 the Omnibus Crime Control Bill contained a provision that would have allowed the prosecution by federal courts of those serving with, employed by, or accompanying the armed forces outside the United States. S. 3, 105th Cong., 1st Sess., "Omnibus Crime Control Act of 1997," introduced by Sen. Orrin Hatch, January 21, 1997. Counterpart legislation was passed in the House. H.R. 4651, 105th Cong., 2nd Sess., "To make minor and technical amendments relating to Federal criminal law and procedure," introduced by Rep. Ira McCollum, September 28, 1998. S. 172, proposed in the same Congress, would have plugged the gap opened up by *Covert* and *Averette.* S. 172, 105th Cong., 1st Sess., introduced by Sen. Jim DeMint, January 21, 1997. A provision of S. 899, proposed in 1999, would have had the same effect as the one proposed in the Omnibus Crime Control Bill of two years earlier. S. 899, 106th Cong., 1st Sess., introduced by Sen. Orrin Hatch on April 28, 1999.

48. S. 768, 106th Cong., 1st Sess., The Military and Extraterritorial Jurisdiction Act of 1999, "To establish court-martial jurisdiction over civilians serving with the Armed Forces during contingency operations, and to establish Federal jurisdiction over crimes committed outside the United States by former members of the Armed Forces and civilians accompanying the Armed Forces outside the United States," introduced by Sen. Jeff Sessions on April 13, 1999.

49. U.S. Congress, House, 106th Cong., 2nd Sess., Committee on the Judiciary, Report 106-778, pt. 1, Military Extraterritorial Jurisdiction Act of 2000, to Accompany H.R. 3380, 9n18. The explanation of the Department of Defense for its opposition to S. 768's extension of UCMJ jurisdiction over civilian employees and contractors and for its preference for the

extension of Title 18 jurisdiction over them is provided in Reed, Prepared Statement, MEJA Hearing, 15. See also Remarks of Sen. Patrick Leahy, Senate Floor Debate on S. 768, *Congressional Record—Senate,* October 26, 2000, 24897; Douglas A. Dworkin, acting general counsel, Department of Defense, to Rep. Floyd D. Spence, Chairman, House Committee on Armed Services, February 28, 2000, in H. Rept. 106-778, 22.

50. Olivia Zimmerman Miller, "Murder or Authorized Combat Action: Who Decides? Why Civilian Court Is the Improper Forum to Prosecute Former Military Service Members Accused of Combat Crimes," *Loyola Law Review* 56 (2010): 459, 461; Schmitt, "Closing the Gap in Criminal Jurisdiction Over Civilians Accompanying the Armed Forces Abroad," 84, 87–91, 111; e-mail message from Glenn R. Schmitt, May 23, 2012, in my possession.

51. *United States v. Gatlin,* 216 F.3d 207 (2nd Cir. 2000).

52. *United States v. Gatlin,* para. 40.

53. *United States v. Gatlin,* para. 39.

54. H. Rept. 106-778, 9; "Jurisdiction over Criminal Offenses by American Civilians in Iraq and Afghanistan," Testimony of Eugene R. Fidell, President, National Institute of Military Justice, Hearing before the Subcommittee on Human Rights, International Operations and Organizations, Senate Committee on Foreign Relations, April 9, 2008, www.foreign.senate.gov/imo/media/doc/FidellTestimony080409a.pdf.

55. H.R. 3380, 106th Cong., 2nd Sess., The Military Extraterritorial Jurisdiction Act of 2000, "To amend title 18, United States Code, to establish Federal jurisdiction over offenses committed outside the United States by persons employed by or accompanying the Armed Forces, or by members of the Armed Forces who are released or separated from active duty prior to being identified and prosecuted for the commission of such offenses, and for other purposes," introduced by Rep. Saxby Chambliss on November 16, 1999, amended July 20, 2000. The law was enacted as Pub. L. No. 106-523, November 22, 2000, 114 Stat. 2488; 18 U.S.C. § 3261.

56. 18 U.S.C. Chapter 212, Military Extraterritorial Jurisdiction, § 3261 (a). The special maritime and territorial jurisdiction (SMTJ) of the United States consists generally of consular, diplomatic, and military buildings and their land and appurtenances. Jennifer K. Elsea, Moshe Schwartz, and Kennon K. Nakamura, *Private Security Contractors in Iraq: Background, Legal Status, and Other Issues,* CRS Report, August 25, 2008, 21, www.fas.org/sgp/crs/natsec/RL32419.pdf. For interpretations of the SMTJ, see Sifton, "United States Military and Central Intelligence Agency Personnel Abroad," 505–6.

57. H. Rept. 106-778, 15. The legislative report on the bill states that it "would amend Federal law to establish Federal criminal jurisdiction over offenses committed outside the United States by persons employed by or accompanying the United States Armed Forces. It would also establish Federal criminal jurisdiction over offenses committed outside the United States by . . . persons who commit crimes abroad while members of the Armed Forces but who are not tried for those crimes by military authorities and later cease to be subject to military control." U.S. Congress, House, 106th Cong., 2nd Sess., Committee on the Judiciary, *Report to Accompany H.R. 3380, Military Extraterritorial Jurisdiction Act of 2000,* July 20, 2000, 4.

58. Dahl, "Runaway Train," 56.

59. Rep. Henry Waxman, Opening Statement, and Rep. John F. Tierney, remarks, U.S. Congress, House, 110th Cong., 1st Sess., Hearing before the Committee on Oversight and Government Reform, "Blackwater USA," October 2, 2007 [hereafter, House Blackwater Hearing], 2, 17.

60. Dickinson, *Outsourcing War and Peace,* 39.

61. Elsea, Schwartz, and Nakamura, *Private Security Contractors in Iraq;* Chapman, "The Untouchables," 1050; Dahl, "Soldiers of Fortune," 4–5.

62. Dahl, "Soldiers of Fortune," 23–24.

63. Elsea, Schwartz, and Nakamura, *Private Security Contractors in Iraq,* 12.

64. Philip Alston, "Promotion and Protection of All Human Rights, Civil, Political, Economic, Social and Cultural Rights, Including the Right to Development: Report of the Special Rapporteur on Extrajudicial, Summary or Arbitrary Executions," United Nations General Assembly Human Rights Council, Report no. A/HRC/11/2/Add.5, 28 May 2009, 23.

65. Moshe Schwartz, *The Department of Defense's Use of Private Security Contractors in Afghanistan and Iraq: Background, Analysis, and Options for Congress,* CRS Report, May 13, 2011, www.fas.org/sgp/crs/natsec/R40835.pdf, 14–16.

66. Elsea, Schwartz, and Nakamura, *Private Security Contractors in Iraq,* 12.

67. Fidell, "Jurisdiction over Criminal Offenses by American Civilians in Afghanistan and Iraq," 6.

68. The procedures are set out in Department of Defense instruction 5525.11, issued March 3, 2005.

69. H. Rept. 106-778, 21, 26.

70. Victor Hansen, "Military Justice Over Civilians: Opening a Can of Worms?," *The Jurist,* April 9, 2008, http://jurist.org/forum/2008/04/.

71. Dahl, "Runaway Train," 64–65.

72. Dickinson, *Outsourcing War and Peace,* 42.

73. Miller, "Murder or Authorized Combat Action?," 462–63.

74. John C. Yoo, "Memorandum for Alberto R. Gonzales, Counsel to the President, August 1, 2002," in *The Torture Papers: The Road to Abu Ghraib,* ed. Karen J. Greenberg and Joshua L. Dratel (Cambridge: Cambridge University Press, 2005), 218; Jay S. Bybee, assistant attorney general, Department of Justice, "Memorandum for Alberto R. Gonzales, Counsel to the President, August 1, 2002," in ibid., 172, 213–14. For a fuller discussion of the prisoner abuse scandal, see Patrick Hagopian, "The Abu Ghraib Photographs and the State of America: Defining Images," in *Contested Spaces: Representation and the Histories of Conflict,* ed. Graham Dawson, Louise Purbrick, and Jim Aulich (New York: Palgrave Macmillan, 2007), 23–27, 35–37.

75. Alston, "Promotion and Protection of All Human Rights," 23.

76. H.R. 4390, 108th Cong., 2nd Sess., "To extend the Military Extraterritorial Jurisdiction Act (MEJA) to provide for the arrest and commitment of contractor personnel who commit Federal offenses or war crimes while supporting the mission of the Department of Defense overseas," introduced by Rep. David E. Price of North Carolina, May 19, 2004.

77. H.R. 4200, 108th Cong., 2nd Sess., "Ronald W. Reagan National Defense Authorization Act for Fiscal Year 2005," introduced by Rep. Duncan Hunter, April 22, 2004, Military Extraterritorial Jurisdiction Over Contractors Supporting Defense Missions Overseas; enacted as Pub. L. No. 108-375, October 28, 2004, § 1088, 118 Stat. 1811, 2066–67.

78. For a discussion of the jurisdictional problems, see Glenn R. Schmitt, "Amending the Military Extraterritorial Jurisdiction Act of 2000: Rushing to Close an Unforeseen Loophole," *The Army Lawyer* (June 2005): 42–44.

79. Department of Defense, "MEJA (18 U.S.C. § 3261 et seq.), Federal Prosecutions, and Alternative Article 2, UCMJ Dispositions, as of June 30, 2010," www.dod.gov/dodgc/images/meja_statistics.pdf.

80. Alissa J. Rubin and Paul von Zielbauer, "News Analysis; The Judgment Gap. In a Case

Like the Blackwater Shootings, There Are Many Laws But More Obstacles," *NYT,* October 11, 2007.

81. Senator Bill Nelson, Opening Remarks, U.S. Congress, Senate, 110th Cong., 2nd Sess., Committee on Foreign Relations, Hearing before the Subcommittee on International Operations and Organization, Democracy and Human Rights, "Closing Legal Loopholes: Prosecuting Sexual Assaults and Other Violent Crimes Committed Overseas by American Civilians in a Combat Environment," April 9, 2008, 1–3.

82. Scott Horton, a professor at Columbia University who specializes in the law of armed conflict, quoted in Rubin and Zielbauer, "News Analysis; The Judgment Gap."

83. Eugene Fidell, Testimony, U.S. Congress, Senate, 110th Cong., 2nd Sess., Committee on Foreign Relations, Hearing before the Subcommittee on International Operations and Organizations, Democracy and Human Rights, "Closing Legal Loopholes: Prosecuting Sexual Assaults and Other Violent Crimes Committed Overseas by American Civilians in a Combat Environment," April 9, 2008, 28.

84. Lanny A. Breuer, Assistant Attorney General, Criminal Division, Department of Justice, Statement before the U.S. Senate Judiciary Committee, hearing on "Holding Criminals Accountable: Extending Criminal Jurisdiction for Government Contractors and Employees Abroad," May 25, 2011, 3, www.judiciary.senate.gov/pdf/11-5-25%20Breuer%20Testimony.pdf.

85. "The General Counsel of the Department of Defense (GC, DoD) shall provide initial coordination and liaison with the [Department of Justice] and the Department of State (DoS), on behalf of the Military Departments and the Office of the Inspector General of the Department of Defense, regarding a case for which Federal criminal prosecution under the Act is contemplated." Department of Defense instruction 5525.11, March 3, 2005, para. 5.1, 4. This is the first of several paragraphs that describe the respective responsibilities and sequence of coordination of these and additional agencies and officials, including the Office of the Inspector General of the Department of Defense and the Assistant Attorney General, Criminal Division, Department of Justice.

86. Dahl, "Runaway Train," 64.

87. Steven Paul Cullen, "Out of Reach: Improving the System to Deter and Address Criminal Acts Committed by Contractor Employees Accompanying Armed Forces Overseas," *Public Contract Law Journal* 38 (2009): 533.

88. Chapman, "The Untouchables," 1065; Gibson, "Lack of Extraterritorial Jurisdiction Over Civilians," 137, 166. Difficulties in the organization, conduct, and resourcing of overseas criminal investigations have been recognized even for military investigation teams enforcing the UCMJ, despite their years of experience of such responsibilities. Defense Legal Policy Board, *Report of the Subcommittee on Military Justice in Combat Zones: Final Report,* 80–82. This underlines the even more complex problems confronting those responsible for investigating and prosecuting MEJA violations.

89. Dahl, "Runaway Train," 64.

90. Cullen, "Out of Reach," 535.

91. P. W. Singer, "The Law Catches Up to Private Militaries, Embeds," *DefenseTech,* January 3, 2007, http://defensetech.org/2007/01/03/.

92. Hansen, "Military Justice Over Civilians: Opening a Can of Worms?"; "Five Blackwater Employees Indicted on Manslaughter and Weapons Charges for Fatal Nisur Square Shooting in Iraq," Department of Justice Press Release, December 8, 2008, www.justice.gov/opa/pr/2008/December/08-nsd-1068.html.

93. James Glanz and Alissa J. Rubin, "From Errand to Fatal Shot to Hail of Fire to Seventeen Deaths," *NYT,* October 3, 2007; Chapman, "The Untouchables," 1050–51.

94. Dahl, "Runaway Train," 56.

95. Statement by Henry Waxman, House Blackwater Hearing, 3; Rep. Tom Davis, Prepared Statement, ibid., 14.

96. Charlie Savage, "Judge Drops Charges from Blackwater Deaths in Iraq," *NYT,* January 1, 2010. The arrangement was subsequently changed to provide for Iraq's primary jurisdiction over contractors. Cullen, "Out of Reach," 518.

97. Testimony of Erik Prince, chairman of Blackwater USA, House Blackwater Hearing, 57.

98. Chapman, "The Untouchables," 1066.

99. Rubin and Zielbauer, "News Analysis; The Judgment Gap."

100. Chapman, "The Untouchables," 1066; *Memorandum Opinion of Judge Ricardo M. Urbina,* December 31, 2009, *United States of America vs. Paul A. Slough et al.*, Criminal Action No. 08-0360 (RMU), United States District Court for the District of Columbia, http://documents.nytimes.com/memorandum-of-dismissal-of-charges-against-blackwater-guards, 5.

101. Savage, "Judge Drops Charges"; David Johnston, "Immunity Deals Offered to Blackwater Guards," *NYT,* October 30, 2007; *Memorandum Opinion of Judge Ricardo M. Urbina,* 1–3, 15–19, 20–24, 50–56.

102. The appeals court vacated the ruling and found that the district court had erred not only in treating all the tainted testimony as single "lumps" and throwing them out in their entirety rather than distinguishing the tainted from the untainted parts, but also in assuming that the government had developed certain lines of enquiry from tainted evidence when they may have been developed from untainted evidence. *U.S.A. v. Paul Alvin Slough et al.,* United States Court of Appeals for the District of Columbia Circuit, 641 F.3d 544 (D.C. Cir. 2011), decided April 22, 2011, http://docs.justia.com/cases/federal/appellate-courts/cadc/10-3006/10-3006-1304592-2011-04-22.pdf. The case was remanded to the lower court for a decision, in the case of each defendant, about what tainted evidence against him the government presented and what effect it had. The government filed memoranda in the district court setting out its account of the process of filtering the evidence and other issues. See, e.g., "Government's Status Report and Memorandum Regarding *Kastigar* Issues," *U.S.A. v. Paul Slough et al.,* United States District Court for the District of Columbia, October 31, 2012, Case 1:08-cr-00360-RCL Document 259. "Government's Memorandum Regarding Defendant Slatten's Status as a Party," *U.S.A. v. Paul Slough et al.,* United States District Court for the District of Columbia, December 5, 2012, Case 1:08-cr-00360-RCL Document 264.

103. Masterson, "Court-Martial Jurisdiction over Civilians in Contingency Operations," 66n5.

104. *Congressional Record—House,* October 3, 2007, H. 11178.

105. H.R. 2740, 110th Cong.; Chapman, "The Untouchables," 1064–65.

106. John Warner National Defense Authorization Act for Fiscal Year 2007, 109 Pub. L. No. 364; 120 Stat. 2083 (2006), § 552. Clarification of Application of Uniform Code of Military Justice during a Time of War: "Paragraph (10) of section 802(a) of title 10, United States Code (article 2 (a) of the Uniform Code of Military Justice), is amended by striking 'war' and inserting 'declared war or a contingency operation.'" This change in the law meant that Article 2(a)(10) of the UCMJ now applied to civilians accompanying the armed forces during contingency operations as well as during wars declared by Congress. The definition of "contingency operations" (10 U.S.C. § 101[a] [13]) includes any military operation that

"is designated by the Secretary of Defense as an operation in which members of the armed forces are or may become involved in military actions, operations, or hostilities against an enemy of the United States or against an opposing military force."

107. Dahl, "Runaway Train," 65.

108. Deputy Assistant Attorney General Sigal P. Mandelker, Testimony, U.S. Congress, Senate, 110th Cong., 2nd Sess., Committee on Foreign Relations, Subcommittee on International Operations and Organizations, Democracy and Human Rights, Hearing on "Closing Legal Loopholes: Prosecuting Sexual Assaults and Other Violent Crimes Committed Overseas by American Civilians in a Combat Environment," April 9, 2008, 43; Dahl, "Runaway Train," 65. The Defense Department guidelines are set out in Robert Gates, Memorandum for Secretaries of the Military Departments et al., RE: UCMJ Jurisdiction over DoD Civilian Employees, DoD Contractor Personnel, and Other Persons Serving with or Accompanying the Armed Forces Overseas During Declared War and in Contingency Operations, March 10, 2008, www.justice.gov/criminal/hrsp/docs/03-10-08dod-ucmj.pdf.

109. Gates, Memorandum for Secretaries of the Military Departments et al., Attachment 3. Masterson, "Court-Martial Jurisdiction over Civilians in Contingency Operations," 73.

110. Chapman, "The Untouchables," 1050, 1076. The Defense Legal Policy Board finds that commanders lack sufficient authority adequately to handle alleged contractor misconduct relating to civilian casualties and recommends that Article 2 of the UCMJ should be amended to allow for jurisdiction over all U.S. government contractors on the battlefield, regardless of U.S. government departmental affiliation. Defense Legal Policy Board, *Report of the Subcommittee on Military Justice in Combat Zones: Final Report,* 36–37.

111. Dahl, "Runaway Train," 67.

112. Ibid., 66.

113. Ibid., 68; Masterson, "Court-Martial Jurisdiction over Civilians in Contingency Operations," 92, 111.

114. Fidell, "Criminal Prosecution of Civilian Contractors by Military Courts," 851; O'Connor, "Contractors and Courts-Martial," 757, 763; Kara M. Sacilotto, "Jumping the (Un)Constitutional Gun?: Constitutional Questions in the Application of the UCMJ to Contractors," *Public Contract Law Journal* 37 (2007–8): 193. For a discussion of the meaning of "serving with or accompanying an armed force" and "in the field," see *United States v. Burney,* 6 C.M.A. 776, 788, 21 C.M.R. 98, 110 (1956). These definitional issues were raised in a challenge to the amended UCMJ. *United States vs. Ali,* U.S. Court of Appeals for the Armed Forces, decided July 12, 2012, 15, 18, www.armfor.uscourts.gov/newcaaf/opinions/2011SepTerm/12-0008.pdf.

115. Masterson, "Court-Martial Jurisdiction over Civilians in Contingency Operations," 74–84.

116. Ibid., 86, 88, 103. See also Robinson O. Everett, "Military Law Is to Law as . . . ," *U.S.A.F. Judge Advocate General Law Review* 12 (1970): 202–14.

117. Stephen L. Vladeck, "The Laws of War as a Constitutional Limit on Military Jurisdiction," *Journal of National Security Policy* 4 (2010): 308n76.

118. O'Connor, "Contractors and Courts-Martial," 754, 785.

119. "Limitations on Jurisdiction over Civilians," para. 4 of discussion following RCM [Rules for Courts-Martial] 202(a), *Manual for Courts-Martial,* 2012 edition, II-14, www.loc.gov/rr/frd/Military_Law/pdf/MCM-2012.pdf; Executive Order 13552, 2010 Amendments to the Manual for Courts-Martial, United States, August 31, 2010.

120. Eugene R. Fidell, "Ten Years On: Military Justice and Civil Liberties in the Post-9/11 Era," *New York Law School Law Review* 56 (2011–12): 106–7.

121. Gibson, "Lack of Extraterritorial Jurisdiction Over Civilians," 168.

122. Dahl, "Runaway Train," 69. See also O'Connor, "Contractors and Courts-Martial," 790, 796.

123. Lexis-Nexis Congressional, 2007 Bill Tracking H.R. 2740, https://lapa.princeton.edu/conferences/military07/restricted/Lexis_110HR2740_Bill_Track.pdf; U.S. Congress, House, 110th Cong., 1st Sess., Committee on the Judiciary, H. Rept. 110-352, MEJA Expansion and Enforcement Act of 2007, September 27, 2007. The bill would not have provided for any additional funds for MEJA enforcement but assumed that the Congressional Budget Office's modest estimate of $23 million in total over a period of five years would be appropriated near the start of each fiscal year.

124. U.S. Department of Justice, Human Rights and Special Prosecutions Section, www.justice.gov/criminal/hrsp/about/. The section was created as a result of passage of S. 1472, enacted as the Human Rights Enforcement Act of 2009, Pub. L. No. 111-222, 123 Stat. 2480, December 22, 2009; 28 U.S.C. Chapter 31, § 509B.

125. Gibson, "Lack of Extraterritorial Jurisdiction Over Civilians," 164.

126. Michael R. Gordon, "U.S. Charges Contractor at Iraq Post Stabbing," *NYT,* April 5, 2008; Michael Doyle, "Alaa Ali Case Questions Whether Civilians Should Be Court-Martialed," *McClatchy,* April 6, 2012, www.mcclatchydc.com. For the measures used to impose contractor accountability, see Charles T. Kirchmaier, "Command Authority over Contractors Serving with or Accompanying the Force," *The Army Lawyer* (December 2009): 38–39.

127. Judge Erdmann, Opinion of the Court, *United States v. Ali,* 6, 8, 17, U.S. C.A.A.F., No. 12-0008/AR, Crim. App. No. 20080559, July 18, 2012, www.armfor.uscourts.gov/newcaaf/opinions/2011SepTerm/12-0008.pdf.

128. Fidell, "Ten Years On," 106.

129. Fidell, "Criminal Prosecution of Civilian Contractors by Military Courts," 853; *United States v. Ali,* 70 M.J. 514 (A. Ct. Crim. App. 2011).

130. *United States v. Ali,* 26, citing *United States v. Curtiss-Wright Export Corp,* 299 U.S. 304 (1936) and *Johnson v. Eisentrager,* 339 U.S. 763 (1950); but compare *Boumediene v. Bush,* 553 U.S. 723 (2008), in which the court determined that extraterritoriality questions turn on objective factors and practical concerns, not on formalism. Chief Judge Baker, Concurrent Opinion, *United States v. Ali,* U.S. C.A.A.F., 2, www.armfor.uscourts.gov/newcaaf/opinions/2011SepTerm/12-0008.pdf. Baker points out that factual matters were important to the justices who judged *Covert.* See also Steve Vladeck, "Brehm: Fourth Circuit Creates Split in Contractor-Contacts Analysis," August 12, 2012, www.lawfareblog.com/author/steve/; and the careful parsing of the judges' opinions in Brittany Warren, "The Case of the Murdering Wives: *Reid v. Covert* and the Complicated Question of Civilians and Courts-Martial," *Military Law Review* 212 (2012): 191.

131. Baker, Concurrent Opinion, 13.

132. Judge Andrew S. Effron refers to the case of a foreign (that is, not a citizen of the host country) military contractor who stabbed another foreign national and was convicted in a federal court under MEJA. *U.S. v. Brehm* (E.D. Va. March 30, 2011); *U.S. v. Brehm* (4th Cir. 2012), www.ca4.uscourts.gov/Opinions/Published/114755.P.pdf; Judge Effron, Concurrent Opinion, *U.S. v. Ali* (U.S. C.A.A.F.), 3, www.armfor.uscourts.gov/newcaaf/opinions/2011SepTerm/12-0008.pdf.

133. *United States v. Ali,* U.S. C.A.A.F, 1, 29–30, 33–34. The immunity from prosecution of host country nationals is established in U.S.C. §§ 3267(1)(C), 3267(2)(C). The House Report on MEJA states that the category of persons subject to the law "does not include persons who are nationals of the country in which the crime is believed to have been committed

or persons ordinarily resident there. This limitation recognizes that the host nation has the predominant interest in exercising criminal jurisdiction over its citizens and other persons who make that country their home." U.S. Congress, House, 106th Cong., 2nd Sess., Judiciary Committee, H. Rept. 106-778, "Military Extraterritorial Jurisdiction Act of 2000," July 20, 2000, 21.

134. Supreme Court docket 12-805, www.supremecourt.gov/Search.aspx?FileName=/docketfiles/12-805.htm. I am grateful to Eugene Fidell for alerting me to the court's imminent decision whether to accept the case. Eugene R. Fidell, personal communication, December 27, 2012 (in my possession).

135. David Bellavia, with John R. Bruning, *House to House* (London: Pocket Books, 2008), 48.

136. Miller, "Murder or Authorized Combat Action?," 447.

137. Bellavia, *House to House*, 192.

138. Miller, "Murder or Authorized Combat Action?," 465.

139. Tony Perry, "Iraq: Marine Set for Court-Martial on Charge of Killing Prisoner in Fallouja," *Los Angeles Times Blog*, February 19, 2009, http://latimesblogs.latimes.com/babylonbeyond/2009/02.

140. Steve Liewer, "Federal Trial Begins for Ex-Marine in Fallujah Case," *San Diego Union-Tribune*, August 21, 2008.

141. Nathaniel R. Helms, "Not Guilty On All Counts! 'Marine Dream Team,' and Justice, Prevails in Nazario Trial," *Defend Our Marines*, August 28, 2008, http://warchronicle.com (no longer available); Jason W. Armstrong, "Lawyers Offer No Defense in Marine's Trial: Lack of Eyewitnesses Prompted Unusual Move, Attorney Says," *Los Angeles Daily Journal*, August 28, 2008, www.gaplegal.com/news-publications.php.

142. Johnny Dwyer, "Former Marine Jose Nazario Acquitted of All Charges in Fallujah Killings: Would Have Been First American Serviceman Convicted in Civilian Court for Battlefield Crimes," *LA Weekly*, December 30, 2008.

143. Tony Perry, "Marine Is Acquitted in Killings of 4 Iraqis," *Los Angeles Times*, August 29, 2008.

144. Helms, "Not Guilty on All Counts!"

145. Pepper Hamilton LLP, "Acquittal of Former Marine in Landmark Case Expected to Cause Change in Legislation" (press release), September 9, 2008, www.labarberalaw.com/html/ExMarine.html.

146. Chelsea J. Carter, "Ex-Marine Decries Prosecution in Civilian Court," Associated Press, www.sddt.com/News/article.cfm?SourceCode=20080818le.

147. Helms, "Not Guilty on All Counts!"

148. Miller, "Murder or Authorized Combat Action?," 469.

149. Two years after the operation in which the alleged crimes occurred, fewer than half of the marines surveyed by researchers in Iraq said they would report a team member for injuring or killing an innocent noncombatant. *Mental Health Advisory Team MHAT IV Operation Iraqi Freedom 05-07 Final Report*, Office of the Surgeon Multinational Task Force Iraq and Office of the Surgeon General United States Army Medical Command, November 17, 2006, 37, http://i.a.cnn.net/cnn/2007/images/05/04/mhat.iv.report.pdf.

150. Pepper Hamilton LLP, "Acquittal."

151. Ibid.

152. Helms, "Not Guilty on All Counts!"

153. Steve Liewer, "Civilians to Try Iraq War Case against Ex-Marine," *San Diego Union-Tribune*, August 20, 2008.

154. Pepper Hamilton LLP, "Acquittal"; Brig. Gen. Joseph R. Barnes, assistant judge advocate general, United States Army, concentrated exclusively on the question of jurisdiction over civilians accompanying U.S. forces in his congressional testimony; Brig. Gen. James B. Smith, commander of Kadena Air Force Base, Japan, did the same in his testimony. MEJA Hearing, 18–20, 20–22.

155. Carter, "Ex-Marine Decries Prosecution." Everett, for example, had wanted to preserve concurrent jurisdiction by courts-martial and military commissions over offenses against the War Crimes Act. War Crimes Act Hearing, 21, 40.

156. Helms, "Not Guilty on All Counts!" See also "Iraq: For Jose Nazario, the Trial and the War Are Over," *Los Angeles Times Blogs,* http://latimesblogs.latimes.com/babylonbeyond/2008/08/.

157. Joe Mozingo and Tony Perry, "Former Marine Charged in Killings of 8 Iraqi Prisoners," *Los Angeles Times,* August 16, 2007.

158. Pepper Hamilton LLP, "Acquittal."

159. See also the discussion in J. Mackey Ives and Michael J. Davidson, "Court-Martial Jurisdiction over Retirees under Articles 2(4) and 2(6): Time to Lighten Up and Tighten Up?" *Military Law Review* 175 (2003): 84–85.

160. Miller, "Murder or Authorized Combat Action?," 469–71, 476.

161. "Iraq: For Jose Nazario, the Trial and the War Are Over."

162. Miller, "Murder or Authorized Combat Action?," 468, 468n145.

163. Tony Perry, "Marine Is Acquitted in Killings of 4 Iraqis," *Los Angeles Times,* August 29, 2008.

164. Helms, "Not Guilty on All Counts!"

165. Mark Walker, "Military: Nelson Gets Reduction in Rank for Fallujah Killing," *North County Times* (North San Diego and Southwest Riverside counties, California), September 30, 2009, www.utsandiego.com/news/2009/sep/30/.

166. Eliot Spagat, "Marine Apologises for Killing Iraqi Detainee," *guardian.co.uk,* September 30, 2009, www.guardian.co.uk/world/feedarticle/8733048.

167. Miller, "Murder or Authorized Combat Action?," 447. Miller suggests that the reference to an "absurd" prosecution is to Nazario's, but the quotation refers to a court-martial, not a civilian court, prosecution.

168. Associated Press, "Marine Acquitted of Murder in Iraq Slaying," April 9, 2009, www.msnbc.msn.com/id/30138885.

169. Mary McCarthy, *Medina* (London: Wildwood House, 1972), 74–75.

170. Mark Walker, "Military: Marine Acquitted on All Counts," *North County Times* (North San Diego and Southwest Riverside counties, California), April 9, 2009, www.utsandiego.com/news/2009/apr/9/. At the time Solis made this statement, one prosecution in the Haditha case was still outstanding.

171. Mark Walker, "Military: Court Upholds Dismissal of Haditha Prosecution," *North County Times* (North San Diego and Southwest Riverside counties, California), March 17, 2009, www.utsandiego.com/news/2009/mar/17/; Associated Press, "Marine Acquitted of Murder in Iraq Slaying." See also "Selected Testimony from the Haditha Investigation," www.nytimes.com/interactive/2011/12/15/world/middleeast/haditha-selected-documents.html. For a well-argued comparison of commanders' actions after the killings at Haditha and at My Lai, see Amy J. Sepinwall, "Failures to Punish: Command Responsibility in Domestic and International Law," *Michigan Journal of International Law* 30 (2008–9): 275–86. For further discussion of the shortcomings in commanders' investigations of the

killings at Haditha, see Defense Legal Policy Board, *Report of the Subcommittee on Military Justice in Combat Zones: Final Report,* 154–65.

172. "Discuss, Marine Acquitted of Murder in Iraq Slaying" (public comments after publication by the Associated Press of the article "Marine Acquitted of Murder in Iraq Slaying").

173. Ibid. For the Vietnam War–era draft board reactions to the Calley verdict, see, e.g., Chairman, Secretary and three members of Local Board 182, Pittsfield, Illinois, to Nixon, April 1, 1971; and the records of the resignations of local selective service board members in Georgia, Indiana, Kansas, Massachusetts, New York, and Texas. NA, NPM, WHCF, Subject Files, 1969–74, National Security—Defense (ND), Gen ND 8/B, box 10, folder 10: Ex ND8/Calley, 4/1/71–4/25/71.

174. Jim Frederick, *Black Hearts: One Platoon's Descent into Madness in Iraq's Triangle of Death* (London: Macmillan, 2010); "Green Admitted Crime, Ex-Sergeant Says," April 30, 2009, http://gorillasguides.com/2009/04/30/; Defense Legal Policy Board, *Report of the Subcommittee on Military Justice in Combat Zones: Final Report,* 171–74; John Tirman, *The Deaths of Others: The Fate of Civilians in America's Wars* (New York: Oxford University Press, 2011), 252.

175. Jim Frederick, "The Threat from Within," *Time,* February 22, 2010, 32–33.

176. James Dao, "Ex-Soldier Gets Life Sentence for Iraq Murders," *NYT,* May 21, 2009.

177. Frederick, *Black Hearts,* 358.

178. Associated Press, "Ex-GI Found Guilty of Raping, Killing Iraqi Girl," May 7, 2009, MSNBC.com, www.msnbc.msn.com/id/30628635/. Defense Legal Policy Board, *Report of the Subcommittee on Military Justice in Combat Zones: Final Report,* 182–83.

179. Miller, "Murder or Authorized Combat Action?," 464n118; Frederick, *Black Hearts,* 360. The death sentence in 1961 followed a conviction for the rape of an Austrian child. Gary D. Solis, *Marines and Military Law in Vietnam: Trial by Fire* (Washington, D.C.: Department of the Navy, Headquarters United States Marine Corps, n.d. [c. 1988]), 1-17. According to Solis, it has been two hundred years since a marine has been executed following a court-martial. Thomas Watkins, "Lawyers: Threats Used Against Marines," *Washington Post,* June 16, 2006. The leniency shown in subsequent capital cases faced a significant test in the trial of S.Sgt. Robert Bales, accused of killing sixteen civilians in Afghanistan in 2012. In pretrial Article 32 hearings the prosecution treated the murder charges as capital offenses. Having determined that a plea of insanity or diminished capacity was unlikely to succeed, Bales's defense team announced that he would plead guilty in order to avoid the death penalty. The announcement of the possibility of a plea bargain outraged members of the victims' families, one of whom said that they would be satisfied with nothing less than Bales's execution. In June 2013 the military judge accepted Bales's guilty plea on charges of murder and other crimes; in exchange for the plea, Bales will avoid the death penalty. "Afghan Attacks Soldier Robert Bales to Plead Guilty," BBC News US and Canada, May 30, 2013, www.bbc.co.uk/news/world-us-canada-22712004; Peter Finn, "Staff Sgt. Robert Bales Admits to Killing 16 Afghans," *Washington Post,* June 6, 2013.

180. Frederick, *Black Hearts,* 360.

181. Miller, "Murder or Authorized Combat Action?," 464n118.

182. The sentence must have disappointed, but not surprised, the relatives of the murdered Iraqi family. After the verdict was rendered but before sentencing, Karim Janabi, the uncle of the murdered children, said, "By all measures, this was a very criminal act. We are just waiting for the court to sentence him so he gets justice and the court can change the image of Americans." Yusuf Mohammed Janabi, another relative, said, "So they decided

this criminal was guilty, but we don't expect he'll be executed. Only if he's executed, will it mean American courts are just." Reuters Alertnet, "Iraqi Relatives Urge Death for US Rape Soldier," May 8, 2009, http://gorillasguides.com/2009/05/08/.

183. Justin Watt, "I Was a Whistleblower," *Guardian Weekend,* March 23, 2013, 16; for the death threats against Thompson, see Patrick Hagopian, *The Vietnam War in American Memory* (Amherst: University of Massachusetts Press, 2009), 418, 524n87.

Conclusion: "The One Significant Holdout"

1. In 1994, in an article largely concerned with the prosecution of foreign nationals, Everett and Scott L. Silliman advocated the use of military commissions and tribunals to prosecute offenses against the law of war, reminding their readers of the existence of the jurisdictional gap and positing Article I, § 8 of the Constitution as the basis for statutes allowing prosecution of offenses against the law of nations. Robinson O. Everett and Scott L. Silliman, "Forums for Punishing Offenses against the Law of Nations," *Wake Forest Law Review* 29 (1994): 512–13.

2. Scott L. Silliman, "Robinson O. Everett and National Security," *Duke Law Journal* 59 (2009–10): 1449.

3. Everett, U.S. Congress, House, 104th Cong., 2nd Sess., Committee on the Judiciary, *Hearing before the Subcommittee on Immigration and Claims of the Committee on the Judiciary on H.R. 2587, War Crimes Act of 1995,* June 12, 1995 [hereafter Hearing on War Crimes Act], 40.

4. Everett, Prepared Statement, Hearing on War Crimes Act, 23 (emphasis added).

5. Statement of Michael J. Matheson, Hearing on War Crimes Act, 9.

6. Ibid.

7. The UN Security Council adopted a resolution establishing the International Criminal Tribunal for the Former Yugoslavia on May 25, 1993; the Security Council adopted a resolution establishing the International Criminal Tribunal for Rwanda on November 8, 1994. Adam Roberts and Richard Guelff, *Documents of the Law of War,* 3rd ed. (Oxford: Oxford University Press, 2000), 566, 616.

8. Susan S. Gibson, "Lack of Extraterritorial Jurisdiction Over Civilians: A New Look at an Old Problem," *Military Law Review* 148 (1995): 118, 143, 147.

9. John H. McNeill, senior deputy general counsel (International Affairs and Intelligence), Office of General Counsel, Department of Defense, Hearing on War Crimes Act, 18.

10. William J. Clinton, "Remarks at the University of Connecticut in Storrs," October 15, 1995. APP, www.presidency.ucsb.edu/ws/?pid=50655; Editorial, "Endgame for the International Court," *NYT,* November 3, 1995.

11. Thomas W. Lippman, "A Good Idea, but Not for Americans," *IHT,* July 28, 1998.

12. U.S. Congress, Senate, 105th Cong., 2nd Sess., Committee on Foreign Relations, Subcommittee on International Operations, Hearing: "Is a U.N. International Criminal Court in the U.S. National Interest?," July 23, 1998 [hereafter, Senate ICC Hearing], 12–13; David Scheffer, *All the Missing Souls: A Personal History of the War Crimes Tribunals* (Princeton: Princeton University Press, 2012), 218–22.

13. Sen. John Ashcroft, Testimony and Prepared Statement, Senate ICC Hearing, 9.

14. U.S. Congress, Senate, 106th Cong., 2nd Sess., Hearing before the Committee on Foreign Relations, "The International Criminal Court: Protecting American Servicemen and Officials from the Threat of International Prosecution," June 14, 2000, 5.

15. Scheffer, *All the Missing Souls,* 192. This preoccupation recurs throughout his account

of the views of the Pentagon, the Joint Chiefs of Staff, Clinton administration officials, and U.S. senators. Ibid., 212, 217, 228, 232–33, 236, 420.

16. Lawrence Weschler, "Exceptional Cases in Rome: The United States and the Struggle for an ICC," in *The United States and the International Criminal Court,* ed. Sarah B. Sewell and Carl Kaysen (Lanham, Md.: Rowman and Littlefield, 2000), 91–92; Scheffer, *All the Missing Souls,* 184; David Scheffer, interview, Channel Four News (UK), June 19, 1998.

17. Robinson O. Everett, "American Servicemembers and the ICC," in *The United States and the International Criminal Court,* ed. Sewell and Kaysen, 146.

18. Articles 17, 18, 19, Rome Statute of the International Criminal Court, July 17, 1998, http://untreaty.un.org/cod/icc/statute/romefra.htm [hereafter, Rome Statute].

19. David Scheffer, "Closing the Impunity Gap in U.S. Law," *Northwestern Journal of International Human Rights* 8 (Fall 2009): 38. Scheffer states that government employees and contractors might not be covered because of gaps in U.S. extraterritorial jurisdiction; Blackwater and DynCorps, another private security firm, serve as examples. Ibid., 32–33.

20. Everett, "American Servicemembers and the ICC," 142.

21. *The Responsibility to Protect: Report of the International Commission on Intervention and State Sovereignty* (Ottawa: International Development Research Centre, 2001), 14; Austen L. Parrish, "Reclaiming International Law from Extraterritoriality," *Minnesota Law Review* 93 (2008–9): 850. By 2012 eighteen countries had statutes giving their courts universal jurisdiction over offenses against international law, including violations of treaties and customary law. Michael P. Scharf, "Universal Jurisdiction and the Crime of Aggression," *Harvard International Law Journal* 53 (2012): 359.

22. Scharf, "Universal Jurisdiction and the Crime of Aggression," 368.

23. Anita C. Johnson, "The Extradition Proceedings against General Augusto Pinochet: Is Justice Being Met under International Law?," *Georgia Journal of International and Comparative Law* 29 (2000–2001): 206–7, 221; David Sugarman, "The Pinochet Precedent and the 'Garzón Effect,'" *Amicus Curiae* 42 (2002): 9–15.

24. Wolfgang Kaleck, "From Pinochet to Rumsfeld: Universal Jurisdiction in Europe, 1998–2008," *Michigan Journal of International Law* 30 (2008–9): 929.

25. Wechsler, "Exceptional Cases in Rome," 97–101.

26. Reed, Prepared Statement, U.S. Congress, House, 106th Cong., 2nd Sess., Committee on the Judiciary, Hearing on H.R. 3380 before the Subcommittee on Crime, "Military Extraterritorial Jurisdiction Act of 1999," March 30, 2000 [hereafter MEJA Hearing], 17.

27. Rep. Robert Scott, Statement, MEJA Hearing, 7.

28. Robert E. Reed, Testimony, MEJA Hearing, 13.

29. Brig. Gen. Joseph R. Barnes, Testimony, MEJA Hearing, 41.

30. "Jurisdiction over Criminal Offenses by American Civilians in Iraq and Afghanistan," Testimony of Eugene R. Fidell, Hearing before the Subcommittee on Human Rights, International Operations and Organizations, Senate Committee on Foreign Relations, April 9, 2008, 5, www.foreign.senate.gov/imo/media/doc/FidellTestimony080409a.pdf.

31. Eugene Fidell, e-mail message to the author, July 28, 2012 (in my possession).

32. *United States v. Corey,* 232 F.3rd 1166, 1172n3 (9th Cir. 2000), cited in Glenn R. Schmitt, "Closing the Gap in Criminal Jurisdiction Over Civilians Accompanying the Armed Forces Abroad—A First Person Account of the Creation of the Military Extraterritorial Jurisdiction Act of 2000," *Catholic Law Review* 55 (2001): 102n252.

33. Ibid., 83, 101n252. Schmitt accepts that *Gatlin* "helped to prompt Congress to pass MEJA." Glenn R. Schmitt, "Amending the Military Extraterritorial Jurisdiction Act of 2000: Rushing to Close an Unforeseen Loophole," *The Army Lawyer* (June 2005): 41n4. Schmitt

was the chief counsel to the House Judiciary Committee's Subcommittee on Crime, which held a hearing on MEJA on March 30, 2000.

34. K. Elizabeth Waits, "Avoiding the 'Legal Bermuda Triangle': The Military Extraterritorial Jurisdiction Act's Unprecedented Expansion of U.S. Criminal Jurisdiction over Foreign Nationals," *Arizona Journal of International and Comparative Law* 23 (2005–6): 513; U.S. Congress, House, 106th Cong., 2nd Sess., Committee on the Judiciary, Report 106-778, pt. 1, Military Extraterritorial Jurisdiction Act of 2000, to Accompany H.R. 3380, 12. The House report on H.R. 3380 summarizes Cabranes's admonition to Congress in less than a page, and the argument the report sets out in favor of the bill stands with or without *Gatlin*. Ibid., 9.

35. Gibson, "Lack of Extraterritorial Jurisdiction Over Civilians," 153.

36. William J. Clinton, "Statement on the Rome Treaty on the International Criminal Court," December 31, 2000. APP, www.presidency.ucsb.edu/ws/?pid=64170.

37. H.R. 4654, 106th Cong., 2nd Sess., "To protect United States military personnel and other elected and appointed officials of the United States Government against criminal prosecution by an international criminal court to which the United States is not a party," introduced by Rep. Tom DeLay on June 14, 2000; S. 2726, 106th Cong., 2nd Sess., introduced by Sen. Helms on June 14, 2000.

38. H.R. 4775, 107th Cong., 2nd Sess., Title II, American Servicemembers' Protection Act, Pub. L. No. 107-206, title II, Aug. 2, 2002, 116 Stat. 899; 22 U.S.C. 7401 et seq. By the end of 2008 all of ASPA's punitive sanctions had been repealed, after both diplomats and military officers came to see it as a hindrance to relations between the United States and its allies. Scheffer, *All the Missing Souls,* 198; "International Criminal Court: Let the Child Live," *The Economist,* January 25, 2007; Testimony of Gen. Bantz J. Craddock, Commander, U.S. Southern Command, U.S. Congress, House, 109th Cong., 2nd Sess., Committee on Armed Services, Hearing on the National Defense Authorization Act for Fiscal Year 2007, March 16, 2006, 4–5.

39. H.R. 4775, Title II, § 2002, paras. 7, 8.

40. H.R. 4775, Title II, § 2002, para. 11. The statute exaggerates the effect of the decision by the United States to reject the ICC. A refusal to sign the Rome Treaty does not immunize U.S. citizens, troops, and nationals from prosecution by the ICC any more than it authorizes a U.S. citizen to go to Canada, murder someone in that country, and then claim immunity from prosecution by that nation's courts. Wechsler, "Exceptional Cases in Rome," 101.

41. H.R. 4775, Title II, § 2005.

42. Patrick Hagopian, *The Vietnam War in American Memory: Veterans, Memorials, and the Politics of Healing* (Amherst: University of Massachusetts Press, 2009), 427.

43. The Nethercutt Amendment was passed as a section of the Consolidated Appropriations Act for FY 2005 and was renewed in the equivalent act covering FY 2006. Jennifer K. Elsea, *U.S. Policy Regarding the International Criminal Court,* CRS Report, June 14, 2006, 17, www.au.af.mil/au/awc/awcgate/crs/rl31495.pdf.

44. Article 98 of the Rome Statute refers to issues of diplomatic or state immunity.

45. Sen. Norm Coleman, Opening Statement, U.S. Congress, Senate, 109th Cong., 2nd Sess., Committee on Foreign Relations, Hearing before the Subcommittee on Western Hemisphere, Narcotics, and Peace Corps Affairs, "The Impact on Latin American of the American Servicemembers' Protection Act," March 8, 2006 [hereafter 2006 Senate ASPA Hearing], 2; Statements by Latin American and Caribbean leaders, quoted in Adam Isacson, Prepared Statement, 2006 Senate ASPA Hearing, 14; Ruth Wedgwood, Prepared Statement, 2006 Senate ASPA Hearing, 24; Clare M. Ribando, *Article 98 Agreements and Sanctions on U.S. Foreign Aid to Latin America,* CRS Report, April 10, 2006, 2, www.policyarchive.org

/handle/10207/bitstreams/2788.pdf; European Parliament Resolution on the International Criminal Court, P5 TA-PROV (2002) 0449, www.amicc.org/docs/EPres9_26_02.pdf.

46. Fatou Bensouda, "International Justice and Diplomacy," *IHT,* March 20, 2013.

47. Howard LaFranchi, "U.S. Opposes ICC Bid to Make 'Aggression' a Crime under International Law," *Christian Science Monitor,* June 15, 2010.

48. Article 51 of the Charter of the United Nations allows the use of force only in self-defense. *Charter of the United Nations and Statute of the International Court of Justice,* http://treaties.un.org/doc/Publication/CTC/uncharter-all-lang.pdf. Harry Truman declared preventive war to be a "weapon of dictators." Steven W. Hook, *U.S. Foreign Policy: The Paradox of World Power* (Washington, D.C.: CQ Press, 2005), 311. See also the discussion in Jeffrey Record, "The Bush Doctrine and War with Iraq," *Parameters* (Spring 2003): 7.

49. "The International Criminal Court," U.S. State Department, Office of Global Criminal Justice, www.state.gov/j/gcj/icc/index.htm.

50. Ibid.

51. Stephen J. Rapp, "Where Can the Victims of Atrocities Find Justice?" Remarks at a forum in the Philippines, May 10, 2011, http://manila.usembassy.gov/stephen_rapp.html.

52. Wechsler, "Exceptional Cases in Rome," 103.

53. Parrish, "Reclaiming International Law from Extraterritoriality," 862.

54. Chicago Council on Global Affairs, *Worldviews 2002: American Public Opinion and Foreign Policy,* 33–34, 48. This survey and its successors can be accessed at www.thechicagocouncil.org/files/Studies_Publications/POS/Survey2012/USForeignPolicy.aspx.

55. Chicago Council on Global Affairs, *Global Views 2006: The United States and the Rise of China and India. Results of a 2006 Multination Survey of Public Opinion,* 20.

56. Chicago Council on Global Affairs, *Foreign Policy in the New Millennium: Results of the 2012 Chicago Council Survey of American Public Opinion and U.S. Foreign Policy,* 23.

57. Editorial, " Time for a Global Criminal Court," *NYT*, November 21, 1994.

INDEX